Witch-hunting in Seventeenth-Century New England

WITCH-HUNTING

in Seventeenth-Century New England

A Documentary History, 1638–1692

▲

Edited and with an Introduction

by David D. Hall

Northeastern University Press

BOSTON

Northeastern University Press

Library of Congress Cataloging-in-Publication Data

Witch-hunting in seventeenth-century New England : a documentary
history, 1638–1692 / edited and with an introduction by
David D. Hall.
p.   cm.
Includes bibliographical references and index.
ISBN 1-55553-084-2 (alk. paper)
ISBN 1-55553-085-0 (pbk. : alk. paper)
1. Witchcraft—New England—History. 2. Persecution—New England—
History. 3. New England—Social life and customs—Colonial period,
ca. 1600–1775. I. Hall, David D. II. Title: Witch-hunting in 17th-
century New England.
BF1575.W62   1991
133.4′3′097409032—dc20   90-40803

Designed by Virginia Evans

Composed in Walbaum by Coghill Composition, Richmond, Virginia.
Printed and bound by Hamilton Printing Co., Rensselaer, New York. The
paper is Sebago Antique, an acid-free sheet.

MANUFACTURED IN THE UNITED STATES OF AMERICA
96   5   4

Contents

▲

Witch-hunting in Seventeenth-Century New England

Introduction

▲

The purpose of this book is to tell the history of witchcraft and witch-hunting in seventeenth-century New England—a history that, as related here, emerges through the original documents. Many of these documents appear here in print for the first time. Others were published long ago by antiquarians, or in editions of colony and court records. The story that these texts narrate begins in 1638 and extends to the Salem trials of 1692.

This story has many dimensions. Some of the documents reveal with compelling immediacy the emotions of parents as they struggle to understand why a child has fallen ill or died. We learn of quarrels between neighbors and of long-lasting fears that one party to a quarrel wants to gain revenge. Other texts describe the psychological disturbance that people in the seventeenth century thought of as "diabolical possession." Still others show the civil state intent on suppressing deviant behavior. Or it may be neighbors who want to punish someone they dislike. In most cases someone describes "preternatural" events—an apparition, a shape-changing animal, a magical pudding. There is much about religion, as when scriptural texts are used to repel the devil. We learn of countermagic, which is always controversial. In telling us about witchcraft and witch-hunting, the documents illuminate the social history of New England. They capture deep-rooted attitudes and expectations; they reveal the tensions that underlay communal life and family relationships.

The Incidence of Witch-hunting in Early New England

These documents are full of surprises. For many readers, the first of these surprises may be that people were being punished for the crime of witchcraft long before the celebrated trials at Salem. Everyone knows *something* about Salem. But how many of us know that witch-hunting figured in the social history of seventeenth-century New England almost from its founding? The early cases are slimly documented. But once we get to the 1650s, a wealth of court records, diaries, and letters opens up a world different from our own—a world in which the natural and the "preternatural" were strangely intermingled, and where powerful feelings of anger, grief, and revenge led neighbors to accuse one another of committing witchcraft.

According to a careful count, at least a hundred persons were complained of or indicted for witchcraft *before* the Salem trials of 1692. When the hysteria at Salem came to an end, almost another two hundred persons had been named as witches in that massive outpouring of suspicion and self-doubt.[1] Behind these numbers lie significant variations in the institutional response to particular accusations. Many times, the cry (or whisper) of "witch" did not result in formal charges. Instead, the outcome could be a suit for defamation by the person so accused. When there was a court hearing, or examination, it could fail to yield persuasive evidence; and in certain cases higher judicial authority threw out or suspended the verdict of a jury. Despite these many exceptions, in the years between 1648 and 1663 the courts in Massachusetts, Connecticut, and New Haven (then a separate colony) ordered the execution of some fifteen persons. Another nineteen died as a consequence of the Salem trials.[2] Witch-hunting was an ever-present reality in seventeenth-century New England.[3]

The Lore of Witchcraft

Everyone in the seventeenth century seems to have known something of the lore of witchcraft—that female witches had a distinctive "teat" (or tit) on their bodies; that imps or animal "familiars" came at night to suck this tit; that shape-changing animals (cats, birds, dogs, and snakes) embodied the devil or his agents and that witches covenanted with the devil. So too, people knew the lore of countermagic— that a horseshoe nailed up over a front door would prevent a witch from entering, and that witches were revealed ("discovered") by burning an enchanted object. This lore of magic and countermagic must not be confused with the actual practice of witchcraft. True, these documents reveal that some women, and possibly a few men, may have spoken of themselves as witches. The idea of calling on the devil's powers (as though he were a kind of genie), together with the fantasy of being tempted by the devil, occurs in these documents. Mary Johnson, a servant in Wethersfield, Connecticut, imagined that the devil had agreed to perform a chore she disliked; and a sixteen-year-old girl, Elizabeth Knapp, believed that the devil had offered her a covenant to sign. But the history of witchcraft in New England is not one of persons who dressed up in black hats and long capes (as in the Hallowe'en tradition) and muttered spells over steaming cauldrons.[4]

A few of the women and men who were accused of committing witchcraft may have been fortune-tellers, and several others had reputations as healers. These "cunning" persons, as they were often called,[5] played a role in the village community that most of their neighbors tolerated—and may have welcomed. But the ability to heal or tell fortunes was morally ambiguous: the power to heal was also the power to do harm. Moreover, the art of healing did not rely on confession of sin, the remedy that the Reverend Samuel Willard pursued in attempting to relieve the "possession" of Elizabeth Knapp. For this and other reasons the people who were healers in seventeenth-century New England seem to have been especially vulnerable to the accusation of witchcraft.[6]

Witch-hunting and Social Relationships

It may be no surprise to learn from reading these documents that, in case after case, village people were accusing neighbors of doing them harm—making them or their children sick, causing cattle and chickens to die, inducing the symptoms of "possession." Or perhaps the evidence was strange events, or the peculiarities of someone's character. The depositions in the case of Hugh Parsons of Springfield, who was accused of being a witch in 1651, reveal what I would like to call the "ordinariness" of witch-hunting. A pudding had slipped from a kettle and split open, a trowel was missing, a minister's two children had died—people felt Hugh Parsons was to blame. Why did he not mourn the death of one of his children? Why did he mutter in his sleep and quarrel with the neighbors for whom he made bricks? In many other cases, as in this, the evidence added up to little more.[7]

Hence the history of witchcraft and witch-hunting in seventeenth-century New England is essentially a history of face-to-face interaction within communities where relationships became charged with suspicion, anger, and revenge. Historians such as John P. Demos and Carol F. Karlsen have reconstructed in rich detail the circumstances and relationships—familial, spatial, gendered, economic—that lie behind certain cases. Some of these circumstances are immediately visible in the depositions. Others emerge when we look for patterns that run through all the evidence. Still others come to light only after thorough study of other kinds of records. But a general rule for understanding the structure of witch-hunting is to expect that social tensions (in all likelihood a quarrel), intersecting with episodes of personal or familial misfortune, lie at the core of these cases. No one has grasped this rule better than a man who actually observed the Salem witch-hunt, the Reverend John Hale of Beverly. As Hale remarked in his posthumous *A Modest Enquiry Into the Nature of Witchcraft,* "If after anger between neighbors mischief followed, this oft bred suspicion of witchcraft in the matter."[8]

Another historian, David Konig, had complemented this interpretation through an analysis of the role of the judicial system in Essex County, Massachusetts. The function of the county court was, he argues, to maintain social control. Many of the colonists accepted the authority of the court and attempted to resolve their disputes within the framework of the legal system. Another group, however, showed little respect for the courts and turned to extralegal means of resisting authority. Some of these people threatened their neighbors by calling on the devil. We may broaden the connection between witch-hunting and social control by observing, as Konig does, that anyone who threatened established authority—that is, who threatened social order—could be perceived as engaged in witchcraft. Witch-hunting can thus be understood as a process of reaction against disruptively "extralegal" outsiders.[9]

This is why the term "witch-hunting" is preferable to "witchcraft," for it directs our attention to the crucial fact that the term "witch" in seventeenth-century New England functioned as a label people used to control or punish someone.[10] In general, village people applied the term to quarrelsome or "difficult" people, or to those who somehow trespassed on the mores of community—say, the Quakers. The minister George Burroughs, who was executed at Salem in 1692, had attracted attention because he failed to have one of his children baptized. And in certain cases it was the authorities who intervened, as happened with Jane Hawkins, the Bayleys in New Haven, and the Jenningses in Connecticut.

Gender and Witch-hunting

The cry of "witch" was raised against women far more often than against men. The raw numbers work out to a ratio of better than 4:1. When historians have compared the penalties imposed on women and men, further differences emerge; the men were less likely to be tried and convicted, and their sentences were less severe. Moreover, a good many of the men were husbands or sons of women who were deemed witches. These patterns are evident in the documents that follow, though the fullest account of them is Carol Karlsen's *The Devil in the Shape of a Woman.*

Why were women (and especially women over the age of forty) singled out and punished so disproportionately? The prosecution of women as witches occurred in a society in which men exercised substantial authority—legal, political, ideological, and economic—over women. It is possible to interpret witch-hunting as a means of reaffirming this authority at a time when some women (like the charismatic spiritual leader Anne Hutchinson) were testing these constraints, and when others were experiencing a degree of independence, as when women without husbands or male siblings inherited property.[11]

The gender politics of witch-hunting is strikingly evident in a case that occurred in Connecticut in 1669. Sarah Dibble of Stamford accused her husband, Zachary, of physical abuse. He denied the charge and attributed the bruises on her body to "witchcraft." "She was a witch," he declared. The court rejected this accusation. But Dibble's statement indicates that the accusation of witchcraft was a commonly recognized instrument for dealing with the conflicts produced by the relationship between men and women.[12]

The vulnerability of women stemmed in part from attitudes about women's sexuality and their role as mothers. In the documents that follow, the references to a sexual relationship between women witches and the devil are relatively scant in comparison to those in some of the European witch-hunts. Yet the idea (or image) of women as especially licentious lingers on the edge of these documents. From the vantage of psychoanalytical theory, John P. Demos has proposed that tensions in the mother-child relationship were played out in witch-hunting.[13]

Even so, witch-hunting in New England was gender-related, not gender specific. Whatever the relevant factors, the response of the colonists in seventeenth-century New England, like the response of Europeans in general, was to assume that women were peculiarly drawn to witchcraft and the devil.[14] Lest we suppose, however, that women were defenseless, these cases include several in which women actively resisted being named a witch—as did Elizabeth Godman, Mary Staples, and Mary Parsons of Northampton, to cite three examples.

Religion and Witch-hunting

Accusations of witchcraft grew out of beliefs that we no longer share. Accordingly, the depositions reprinted in this book are full of statements that seem irrational and bizarre, as when someone testified to seeing another person in the form of a cat, or as a ghost. Why did such statements make sense to people in the seventeenth century? The answer in general is that, for the colonists as for their European contemporaries, the natural forces at work in the everyday world were overlain by and interwoven with moral, spiritual, and supernatural forces. The most powerful force of all was the supernatural, which is to say, God. God's "providence" accounted for everything that happened in everyday life. Events that we consider merely natural, like a thunderstorm, were charged with meaning as expressions of providence, and were open to interpretation as signs of God's judgment or of his protecting mercy. The moral and the physical (sin and sickness) were interrelated. Hence, when four of John Goodwin's children became the victims of "possession," the father interpreted their illness as possibly resulting from his own inadequacies as a sinner. This intertwining of the moral and the physical also explains why at Salem in early 1692, as in Boston with the Goodwin children, the ministers turned to penitential prayer and fasting to overcome "possession."

But there was another cluster of assumptions involved, a set of meanings packed into a single word, the *wonder*. The wonder was any unexpected event, be it someone's sudden death, a comet passing overhead, or sounds that had no obvious source. At some deeper level the wonder was any event that reminded people of the radical contingency of their existence—how insecure they were, and how vulnerable to judgment. At a deeper level still, the wonder drew on pre-Christian notions of nature as animate, or as charged with spirits. What seem to us to be physical impossibilities, like someone's being in two different places at the same time (as people said of John Godfrey) or appearing as a ghost (as was reported time and again in the witchcraft cases), or uttering words that caused bodily harm, were easily credible to people who thought of the relationship between the physical and the spiritual as plastic and open-ended. Witchcraft, which was but one of many forms of wonders, drew on all these meanings.[15]

Popular and Learned Understandings of Witchcraft and the Devil

Witchcraft is about doing evil. That is how people in the seventeenth century thought about it: a witch was someone who harmed others, or tried to do so. But for the magistrates and ministers (and for many of the colonists) a witch was also someone who allied himself or herself with that great figure of evil, Satan. The witch repudiated true religion. None of the documents in this collection lays out a systematic theory of the devil. To find such a theory we have to turn to the sermons of the ministers and a European literature on which they depended.[16] Nonetheless, these texts contain striking images of the devil and evoke scenes in which he was actor, as in the "possession" of Elizabeth Knapp. The most important of these scenes was the signing of the devil's compact, or covenanting with the devil, in exchange for receiving the power to work harm. The idea of the devil's compact turns up in some of the earliest cases, though it played its most dramatic role at Salem in 1692.

Historians have asked the question, did the people's (or "popular") understanding of witchcraft differ from the clergy's?[17] The answer is a qualified yes. Usually the witnesses who testified against their neighbors did not refer to the devil. We may surmise that, for most people, witchcraft was doing someone harm by occult means—a curse, an evil eye (as in "overlooking" someone). Not until we reach Cotton Mather's summaries of the Salem trials of 1692 do we encounter the fearful vision of Satan as grand conspirator laboring to overthrow the kingdom of Christ. But even at Salem most of the testimony had to do with quarrels, misfortune, and "preternatural" events, which is to say, the very kinds of testimony that villagers had been giving for half a century. Yet at Salem, as at other moments in the history of witch-hunting in New England, certain persons also confessed to having entered into compact with the devil. It would seem, therefore, that the possibility of the devil's compact was generally acknowledged among the colonists.

The Role of the Legal System

These different kinds of testimony complicated the judicial process of deciding whether someone was a witch. As the historian Richard

Godbeer has emphasized, the courts were looking for reliable evidence that the devil was involved in acts of apparent witchcraft.[18] According to the legal system, witchcraft was defined as a crime on the basis of the devil's compact.[19] But what if the witnesses described occult acts of harm in which the devil did not seem to figure? Could this testimony be regarded as sufficient to convict someone of the crime? A more basic problem was differentiating reliable evidence from mere fantasies or delusions.

Time and again in the cases that follow, the magistrates, clergy, and townspeople wrestled with these questions. The clergy knew that certain sceptics in England and on the Continent had challenged the very concept of witchcraft. George Burroughs cited one of these critics at his trial in 1692, but to no avail. Of more immediate importance, the clergy and the magistrates disapproved of certain kinds of evidence — for example, the "swimming test" that was used in the Hartford witch-hunt of 1662–63. Cotton Mather's summaries of the Salem witch trials reveal a hesitancy on his part to endorse some of the testimony, and a similar uneasiness was expressed by the Connecticut ministers in the case of Katherine Harrison. The documents contain other expression of elite or learned distance from what the common people took as signs of witchcraft.[20] The people went their own way, as I noted in remarking on the absence of references to the devil in most of the depositions. Yet they were also confused or in conflict with each other. Goodwife Staples questioned the presence of witch marks on the body of an executed witch, and in other cases witnesses offered sharply conflicting testimony about the reasons for the sickness of children and animals.

Witch-hunting was thus a process of interpretation that began at the village level before moving to the courts. Throughout the seventeenth century magistrates, juries, and the common people were able to interpret some attempts at magic as mere "lies" (see the case of John Bradstreet), and to recognize what we would term mental illness (see the response to Mrs. Stearns in the case of Winifred and Mary Holman). Someone who was called a witch could riposte by filing suit for defamation, and thus leave it to the court to figure out the truth. A particular problem for the courts was the two-witness rule in capital crimes.[21] In sorting out these possibilities, the courts (and the clergy) came to regard confession as the most reliable form of evidence. Early on, Mary Johnson seems to have confessed, as did Mary Parsons of Springfield (though more ambiguously) and Rebecca Greensmith. Since those who confessed were asked to name confederates and sometimes did so, confession could become an explosive means of widening the search for suspects. This is what happened in the Salem witch-hunt.

The laws on witchcraft in New England took their cue from the 1604 English statute (1 James I. ch. 12) and defined it as a felony, with the penalty of death.[22] It is important to note that witchcraft was not formally considered heresy, or a crime against religion. In New England, as in old, trials for witchcraft took place in a civil court. The means of execution was death by hanging, and *never* that of being burned at the stake.

Three levels of courts existed in the colony of Massachusetts and, with slight variations, in Connecticut and New Haven. The lowest level was the local magistrate or "commissioner," someone empowered by the colonial government to hear and decide certain kinds of cases. Thus William Pynchon, a magistrate in Springfield, was the person who initially conducted a pretrial "examination" of Hugh and Mary Parsons. The second level were county or "particular" courts, where several magistrates conducted trials and decided verdicts. Cases of defamation invariably came before a county court; and it was often in such courts that people accused someone of being a witch. If the evidence seemed credible, a county court referred a case of witchcraft to the highest court, named in Massachusetts the Court of Assistants. A grand jury was summoned to issue an indictment, and trial by jury followed. The Assistants (or "magistrates") could accept or overturn the jury verdict. To understand the workings of the legal system, it helps to keep in mind the difference between an "examination" and a trial. The scenes at Salem that Deodat Lawson described in *A Brief and True Narrative* fall into the former category. However, the testimony at an examination could be forwarded to another court, as happened in the case of Mary and Hugh Parsons. In general (with occasional exceptions), the people who were being examined or tried were not represented by attorneys.[23]

The workings of the courts, together with the issue of reliable evidence, alert us to three crucial aspects of witch-hunting in New England. First, the legal system handled the scores of accusations of witchcraft in ways that, *more often than not,* resulted in acquittals. Second, magistrates and juries (though especially magistrates—and sometimes a governor) were *increasingly* rejecting popular accusations of witchcraft as the seventeenth century advanced. The trend is clear: there were no executions for witchcraft for twenty-five years after 1663. This trend was brutally interrupted by the Salem witch-hunt. Third, the trials in 1692 were brought to an abrupt end when certain ministers and influential laymen raised anew the question of evidence. Thereafter, confusion was so great that no court in New England was able to sentence anyone for the crime.

But though the Salem witch trials were a turning point, village people continued to accuse their neighbors of witchcraft until early in the eighteenth century. And the lore of witches lingered on well after the civil state had ceased to regard witchcraft as a crime.[24]

The documents in this collection unfold the complexity of culture and society in the seventeenth century. The process of witch-hunting involved a multilayered worldview that was less consistent than we commonly suppose. It fed on many kinds of social relationships—between husbands and wives, parents and children, men and women, the young and the old, the clergy and the people, outsiders and the more secure. We can read the documents in this collection narrowly, for what they tell us about witchcraft and witch-hunting. And we can read them broadly, to learn about different ways of knowing and behaving in the long-vanished world of early New England.

Editorial Principles

Most of the texts in this collection are literal transcriptions of seventeenth-century manuscript originals, modified as follows: I have changed capitalizations and spellings to conform to modern practice and expanded all abbreviations and contractions. I have introduced paragraphing in two documents: John Gibson's statement and Samuel Willard's report of Elizabeth Knapp's possession. The punctuation remains as it appears in the originals, with these exceptions: I have removed commas before or within parentheses and placed them outside the closing parenthesis; and I have uniformly ended each paragraph or other division with a period. Most of the dates have been rearranged into the sequence month/day/year. Brackets indicate (1) additions to words or the insertion of words and punctuation, to clarify the sense of a word or a sentence; (2) an uncertain reading, when followed by a question mark; (3) a blank space, possibly a tear, in the manuscript; or (4) a word or words that could not be deciphered. In a few instances the brackets are those of a previous editor. Ellipses within brackets indicate deletions by this editor; to my knowledge, there are no other deletions. I have usually not reprinted the notations on the back of a court deposition (for instance, the name of the witness) or the names of magistrates and jurors, and have not reprinted most affidavits indicating the service of a summons. My goal has been to keep as close as possible to the diction people used in these statements. No doubt a few errors have resulted from the process of interpreting the sense behind an unusual spelling.

The documents that are taken from seventeenth- and eighteenth-century printed sources (for example, Cotton Mather's *Memorable Providences*) are reprinted without change except for the modernizing of italicizations, abbreviations, and capitalizations. The spelling of proper names varies greatly within the manuscripts, as it also does in the citations of historians and antiquarians. I have regularized the spelling of proper names but indicate in the index some of the alternative spellings, which are many.

Some of the documents in this collection are reprinted from editions of the records of courts and civil governments. In every instance I have relied on these editions for my texts. For a number of other cases the records have been published, but the originals remain easily accessible. I have edited these texts from the manuscripts, though I have occasionally relied on the printed version in deciphering difficult passages. In general, previous editors introduced extensive punctuation that is not in the originals. Anyone who has worked with the originals knows that their punctuation is elusive—and very different from our own. My versions of the manuscripts and those printed or quoted elsewhere vary in a great many particulars; in my judgment, however, none of these differences affects matters of substance.

The documents that are printed here for the first time in full, verbatim versions include: depositions relating to William Graves, Katherine Harrison and the Hartford witch-hunt of 1662–65, from the Wyllys Papers; records relating to Elizabeth Seager, from the Connecticut Court of Assistants records; the depositions relating to Mary Parsons of Northampton; the documents from the Massachusetts Archives and the Suffolk County Court Records concerning Eunice Cole; John Gibson's lengthy statement regarding Winifred and Mary Holman, and related depositions; documents concerning John Godfrey; and documents from several archives that detail the problems besetting William and Elizabeth Morse.

How to read these documents

These documents can be confusing to read. One source of confusion is their dating. The calendar in seventeenth-century New England began with March; thus the "first" month of the year was not January but March. The colonists often used numbers instead of names. In doing so they wrote the date in the sequence day/month/year, not as we would do, month/day/year. Thus a deposition dated February, 1650 was actually made in February, 1651; and the citation 16 (8) 1650 stands for October 16, 1650. In no instance has a date been modernized where I have had access to the manuscripts. All dates (excepting those that may have been altered by other editors) are as they appear in the original documents.

Cases not included

This collection is selective, not inclusive, of the cases of witchcraft and defamation that occurred in New England before the Salem witchhunt of 1692. Every case resulting in an execution is included, as is every case for which there is extensive documentation. The exceptions to this statement are the case of Elizabeth Garlick of Southampton, L.I., the possessions of Mercy Short and Margaret Rule, and two examples of disturbed houses, one in Salmon Falls, New Hampshire, that belonged to Antonio Hortado, the other in Portsmouth, New Hampshire, that belonged to George Walton. The most important of the hitherto unpublished records omitted from this collection are those concerning Mercy Disborough of Fairfield, Connecticut, who with several other women was accused of witchcraft in 1692. Anne S. Brown and I hope to publish these records separately. The cases that have been omitted may be identified by consulting the bibliographical references in footnote 1 in the Introduction.

Acknowledgments

At every stage of the process of assembling and transcribing these documents I have enjoyed the collaboration of Anne S. Brown. Her skills as a historian have been indispensable to the making of this book. Jessica Marshall has helped with certain details. Elizabeth Clark gave the entire manuscript a careful reading. The Trustees of Houghton Library, Harvard University, the Trustees of the Boston Public Library, and the State Archivist of Massachusetts have kindly granted permission to publish the documents in their possession; I am grateful to them, and to the other libraries cited in the notes, for generously facilitating access to the texts in their possession. My father has reminded me from time to time that an ancestress was executed at Salem. My debt to the painstaking scholarship of John P. Demos and Carol Karlsen is substantial; in particular, I have depended on their work in locating unpublished documents.

1. A "List of Known Witchcraft Cases in Seventeenth-Century New England" (exclusive of the Salem trials) is included in John P. Demos, *Entertaining Satan: Witchcraft and the Culture of Early New England* (New York, 1982), pp. 401–10. See also Carol Karlsen, *The Devil in the Shape of a Woman: Witchcraft in Colonial New England* (New York, 1987), chap. 2; and "Appendix 5: Witches Accused in New England, 1620–99," in Lyle Koehler, *A Search for Power: The "Weaker Sex" in Seventeenth-Century New England* (Urbana, Ill., 1980). Richard Godbeer has a slightly higher figure for the pre-Salem cases; Godbeer, "The Devil's Dominion: Magic and Religion in Early New England" (Ph.D. thesis, Brandeis University, 1989).

2. As is indicated in the headnotes, the records do not always make it clear if or when a convicted witch was executed.

3. No one in the colony of Rhode Island was convicted of witchcraft. Witch-hunting occurred in New York, Pennsylvania, and Virginia, though not with the frequency that it did in New England. It was also occurring in most regions of Europe, where the rate (in relation to the population) varied from the high of certain parts of Germany to the low of Italy and the Netherlands. John P. Demos suggests that the incidence of witch-hunting in New England was "intermediate" between the European extremes: *Entertaining Satan*, pp. 11–13.

4. Contrary to the position I take here, Chadwick Hansen has argued that some of the persons accused and executed in the Salem trials of 1692 were practicing witches. See his *Witchcraft at Salem* (New York, 1969).

5. Keith Thomas has described the role of "cunning people" in sixteenth- and seventeenth-century England in *Religion and the Decline of Magic* (New York, 1971), chaps. 7–8.

6. The method of healing by confession of sin is described in David D. Hall, *Worlds of Wonder, Days of Judgment: Popular Religious Belief in Early New England* (New York, 1989), chap. 4.

7. See, for example, the long statement of the Gibson family against the Widow Mary Holman and her daughter, and William Morse's refutation of evidence presented against his wife, Elizabeth.

8. John Hale, *A Modest Enquiry Into the Nature of Witchcraft* (Boston, 1702), p. 21.

9. David Thomas Konig, *Law and Society in Puritan Massachusetts: Essex County, 1629–1692* (Chapel Hill, N.C., 1979), esp. chaps. 6 and 7.

10. As Christina Larner argued in *Enemies of God: The Witch-hunt in Scotland* (London, 1981).

11. Karlsen, *Devil in the Shape of a Woman*, chap. 3.

12. Crimes and Misdemeanors 1662–1789, First Series, *3*, pp. 211–13, Connecticut State Archives (CSL).

13. See, in general, Karlsen, *Devil in the Shape of a Woman*, chap. 4; Demos, *Entertaining Satan*, pt. 2, and Laurel Ulrich, *Good Wives: Image and Reality in the Lives of Women in Northern New England 1650–1750* (New York, 1982), pp. 158–59. The problem of women's sexuality is emphasized in a recent study of European witch-hunting: Joseph Klaits, *Servants of Satan: The Age of the Witch Hunts* (Bloomington, Ind., 1985), chap. 3.

14. The figure for European trials is cited in Klaits, *Servants of Satan*, p. 58.

15. The fullest explication of these meanings is Hall, *Worlds of Wonder*, chap. 2. The heritage of older beliefs is described in George Lyman Kittredge, *Witchcraft in Old and New England* (Cambridge, Mass., 1929).

16. See, e.g., the Reverend Thomas Hooker to John Winthrop, *Coll. CHS., 1* (Hartford, 1860), p. 3; Samuel Willard, *The Christians Exercise by Satans Temptations* (Boston, 1701); Deodat Lawson, *Christ's Fidelity* (Boston, 1693); and Increase Mather, *An Essay for the Recording of Illustrious Providences* (Boston, 1684).

17. See, in particular, Thomas, *Religion and the Decline of Magic;* Richard Weisman, *Witchcraft, Magic, and Religion in Seventeenth-Century Massachusetts* (Amherst, Mass., 1984).

18. Godbeer, "The Devil's Dominion."

19. The relevant statutes are printed in an appendix.

20. For example, William Hubbard's report of the case of Anne Hibbins.

21. The Massachusetts *Body of Liberties* of 1641 included the rule, "No man shall be put to death without the testimony of two or three witnesses." William Whitmore, ed., *The Colonial Laws of Massachusetts* (Boston, 1889), p. 43. Hugh Parsons invoked this rule. But see also the deliberations of the ministers in the case of Elizabeth Morse.

22. N. E. H. Hull, *Female Felons: Women and Serious Crime in Colonial Massachusetts* (Urbana, Ill., 1987), chap. 2. Some scholars have argued that the colonists relied on the Bible in defining capital crimes, and point to the citations of Leviticus 20:27, Deuteronomy 18:11, and Exodus 22:18 in the statutes (see the appendix).

23. The workings of the court system are explained in Konig, *Law and Society;* John M. Murrin, "Magistrates, Sinners, and a Precarious Liberty: Trial by Jury in Seventeenth-Century New England," in *Saints and Revolutionaries: Essays on Early American History,* ed. David D. Hall et al. (New York, 1984); and in several of the essays gathered in *Law in Colonial Massachusetts 1630–1800,* Colonial Society of Massachusetts, *Publications 62* (Boston, 1984).

24. Herbert Leventhal, *In the Shadow of the Enlightenment: Occultism and Renaissance Science in Eighteenth-Century America* (New York, 1976), chap. 3; Karlsen, *Devil in the Shape of a Woman,* pp. 43–45.

Guide to Sources and Abbreviations

▲

The primary sources for this documentary history are as follows:

The Massachusetts State Archives (MA) contain the Middlesex and Suffolk County Court Records, and volume 135 of the Massachusetts Archives (MA *135*).

The Connecticut State Archives, in the Connecticut State Library (CSL), contain the records of the Court of Assistants, the Samuel Wyllys Papers, and the Matthew Grant Diary.

The Essex Institute (EI), Salem, is the depository for the Essex County and Norfolk County Court Records and File Papers.

Houghton Library, Harvard University (HLH), owns a collection of depositions and related documents, "Trials for Witchcraft in New England."

The Department of Rare Books and Manuscripts, New York Public Library (NYPL), owns the John Pynchon Notebook, a collection of depositions relating to Hugh and Mary Parsons.

The Annmary Brown Memorial Library (AMBL), Brown University, owns the Wyllys Papers.

The Boston Public Library (BPL) is the repository for the Prince Collection, which includes the Mather Papers.

The printed sources from which other documents are taken are as follows:

Coll. CHS: Collections of the Connecticut Historical Society.
Coll. MHS: Collections of the Massachusetts Historical Society.
Conn. Col. Recs.: The Public Records of the Colony of Connecticut..., vol. 1, ed. J. Hammond Trumbull (Hartford, Conn., 1850).
Dow, *Hist. of Hampton:* Joseph Dow, *History of the Town of Hampton, New Hampshire,* 2 vols. (Salem, Mass., 1893).
Drake, *Annals of Witchcraft:* Samuel G. Drake, *Annals of Witchcraft in New England* (Boston, 1869).
Essex Ct. Recs.: Records and Files of the Quarterly Courts of Essex County, 9 vols., ed. George F. Dow (Salem, Mass, 1914–75).
Mass. Bay Recs.: Records of the Governor and Company of the Massa-

chusetts Bay in New England, 5 vols., ed. N. B. Shurtleff (Boston, 1853–54).

NEHGR: New England Historical and Genealogical Register.

New Haven Col. Recs.: Records of the Colony and Plantation of New Haven, ed. Charles J. Hoadly (New Haven, Conn., 1857).

New Haven Town Recs.: Ancient Town Records I: New Haven Town Records 1649–1662, ed. Franklin B. Dexter (New Haven, Conn., 1917).

N.H. Ct. Recs.: New Hampshire Court Records 1640–1692: State Papers Series 40, ed. Otis G. Hammond (Concord, N.H., 1943).

N.H. Prov. Ct. Papers: Documents and Records Relating to the Province of New Hampshire: Provincial Papers, 1, ed. Nathaniel Bouton (Concord, N.H., 1867).

OED: Oxford English Dictionary.

Recs. Ct. Assistants: Records of the Court of Assistants of the Colony of Massachusetts Bay 1630–1692, 3 vols., ed. John Noble and John F. Cronin (Boston, 1901–28).

Winthrop's Journal: John Winthrop's History of New England, 2 vols., ed. James K. Hosmer (New York, 1910).

1. The Early Cases
(1638–1651)
▲

Jane Hawkins

Jane Hawkins of Boston was never formally accused of witchcraft. Banished from Massachusetts in the aftermath of the Antinomian controversy (1636–37),[1] Mrs. Hawkins had been the midwife when Mary Dyer gave birth in October 1637 to a deformed fetus—termed a "monster" by those in power, who cited it as a sign of God's displeasure with the Antinomians. Hawkins and Dyer were friends and supporters of Anne Hutchinson, a woman of remarkable spiritual and intellectual qualities and the lay leader of the Antinomians. Hutchinson was also banished in 1638. Mary Dyer, who left the colony as well, returned in 1659 to witness her faith as a Quaker. She was executed by the government in 1660. Mrs. Hawkins was banished a second time in 1641, possibly because she had returned from Rhode Island, where she had gone to live in 1638. John Winthrop, the first governor of Massachusetts, kept a journal-history in which he described the "monster" birth and its discovery.[2] His journal entry about Mrs. Hawkins connects religious heresy to women's sexuality and witchcraft. These connections, which were traditional in European culture, influenced the response of the Massachusetts authorities to Quaker women missionaries in the 1650s; two such women, Mary Fisher and Ann Austin, were stripped and searched for witch marks.[3]

1. The Antinomian controversy was a theological dispute about the relationship between "justification" and "sanctification" that turned into a major political struggle and ended with the exiling of the leading "Antinomians."

2. The uses that were made of this "monster birth" and another of Anne Hutchinson's are described in David D. Hall, *Worlds of Wonder, Days of Judgment: Popular Religious Belief in Early New England* (New York, 1989), pp. 100, 102.

3. [Humphrey Norton and others], *New-England's Ensigne* (London, 1659), p. 7. The role of religious heresy in the Salem witch-hunt of 1692 is explored in Christine L. Heyrman, "Spectres of Subversion, Societies of Friends: Dissent and the Devil in Provincial Essex County," in *Saints and Revolutionaries: Essays on Early American History*, ed. David D. Hall et al. (New York, 1984).

The magistrates restrict and then expel Jane Hawkins

Jane Hawkins, the wife of Richard Hawkins, had liberty till the beginning of the third month, called May, and the magistrates (if she did not depart before) to dispose of her; and in the meantime she is not to meddle in surgery, or physic, drinks, plasters, or oils, nor to question matters of religion, except with the elders[1] for satisfaction. March 12, 1638.

Jane Hawkins is enjoined to depart away tomorrow morning, and not to return again hither, upon pain of severe whipping and such other punishment as the court shall think meet; and her sons bound in £ 20 to carry her away, according to order. June 2, 1641.

1. The ministers.
Source: *Mass. Bay Recs., 1*, pp. 224, 329.

John Winthrop on Jane Hawkins as healer and midwife

The midwife, presently after this discovery [of the deformed fetus], went out of the jurisdiction; and indeed it was time for her to be gone, for it was known, that she used to give young women oil of mandrakes and other stuff to cause conception; and she grew into great suspicion to be a witch, for it was credibly reported, that, when she gave any medicines (for she practised physic), she would ask the party, if she did believe, she could help her, etc. [April 1638].

... these, and the other the like before, when she[1] dwelled in Boston, gave cause of suspicion of witchcraft, for it was certainly known, that Hawkins's wife (who continued with her, and was her bosom friend) had much familiarity with the devil in England, where she dwelt at St. Ives, where divers ministers and others resorted to her and found it true. [summer 1640].

1. Anne Hutchinson.
Source: *Winthrop's Journal, 1*, p. 268; *2*, p. 8.

Alice Young (EXECUTED)

Other than the brief entries that follow, nothing is known for certain of the first person in New England to be executed as a witch. Alice Young was possibly the wife of John Young of Windsor, Connecticut, who may have been a carpenter. She may also have been the mother of Alice Young Beamon, who lived in Springfield, Massachusetts. A son of this Alice Young sued a man for slander in 1677 for saying "his mother was a witch, and he looked like one."[1]

1. John P. Demos, *Entertaining Satan: Witchcraft and the Culture of Early New England* (New York, 1982), p. 505 n. 29.

The execution of Alice Young

[1647]. One —— of Windsor arraigned and executed at Hartford for a witch.

Source: *Winthrop's Journal*, 2, p. 323.

May 26, [16]47 Alse Young was hanged.

Source: Matthew Grant, "Diary, 1637–1654," CSL.

Margaret Jones (EXECUTED)

Margaret Jones of Charlestown, Massachusetts, was a healer with the reputation (if we can believe John Winthrop) of being able to foretell the future. Margaret may have been a "cunning" woman, someone who performed a variety of services—including possibly, in her case, midwifery—on the margins of the religious and social system.[1] *Margaret was married to Thomas Jones. He, too, was suspected of committing witchcraft but was never prosecuted. Margaret was tried in May and executed on June 15, 1648. A friend, Alice Stratton, declared that she had "died wrongfully . . . and her blood would be required at the magistrates' hands." These words got Alice in trouble with the authorities.*[2]

1. The role of "cunning" people is described above, in the Introduction, and more fully in Keith Thomas, *Religion and the Decline of Magic* (New York, 1971), chap. 8.
2. Demos, *Entertaining Satan*, p. 92.

John Winthrop describes Margaret Jones as healer

At this court one Margaret Jones of Charlestown was indicted and found guilty of witchcraft, and hanged for it. The evidence against her was, 1. that she was found to have such a malignant touch, as many persons (men, women, and children), whom she stroked or touched with any affection or displeasure, or, etc., were taken with deafness, or vomiting, or other violent pains or sickness, 2. she practising physic, and her medicines being such things as (by her own confession) were harmless, as aniseed, liquors, etc., yet had extraordinary violent effects, 3. she would use to tell such as would not make use of her physic, that they would never be healed, and accordingly their diseases and hurts continued, with relapse against the ordinary course, and beyond the apprehension of all physicians and surgeons, 4. some things which she foretold came to pass accordingly; other things she could tell of (as secret speeches, etc.) which she had no ordinary means to come to the knowledge of, 5. she had (upon search) an apparent teat in her secret parts as fresh as if it had been newly sucked, and after it had been scanned, upon a forced search, that was withered, and another began on the opposite side, 6. in the prison, in the clear daylight, there was seen in her arms, she sitting on the floor, and her clothes up, etc., a little child, which ran from her into another room, and the officer following it, it was vanished. The like child was seen in two other places, to which she had relation; and one maid that saw it, fell sick upon it, and was cured by the said Margaret, who used means to be employed to that end. Her behavior at her trial was very intemperate, lying notoriously and railing upon the jury and witnesses, etc., and in the like distemper she died. The same day and hour she was executed, there was a very great tempest at Connecticut, which blew down many trees, etc. [June 1648].

Source: *Winthrop's Journal*, 2, pp. 344–45. Winthrop went on to describe the strange behavior of the ship on which Thomas Jones wished to travel to Barbados; ibid., p. 346.

The court orders that she be watched

The court desire the course which hath been taken in England for discovery of witches, by watching them a certain time. It is ordered, that the best and surest way may forthwith be put in practice, to begin this night if it may be, being the 18th of the 3rd month, and that the husband may be confined to a private room, and be also then watched. May 10, 1648.

Source: *Mass. Bay Recs.*, 2, p. 242.

John Hale visits Margaret Jones in prison

The first[1] was a woman of Charlestown, anno 1647 or 48. She was suspected partly because that after some angry words passing between her and her neighbors, some mischief befell such neighbors in their creatures, or the like: partly because some things supposed to be bewitched, or have a charm upon them, being burned, she came to the fire and seemed concerned.

The day of her execution, I went in company of some neighbors, who took great pains to bring her to confession and repentance. But she constantly professed herself innocent of that crime: Then one prayed her to consider if God did not bring this punishment upon her for some other crime, and asked, if she had not been guilty of stealing many years ago; she answered, she had stolen something, but it was long since, and she had repented of it, and there was grace enough in Christ to pardon that long ago; but as for witchcraft she was wholly free from it, and so she said unto her death.

1. Hale counted her as the first convicted witch in New England.
Source: John Hale, *A Modest Enquiry Into the Nature of Witchcraft* (Boston, 1702), p. 17.

Mary Johnson (EXECUTED)

A resident of Wethersfield, Connecticut, where she apparently was a servant, Mary Johnson had been convicted of thievery in 1646 and punished by a public whipping.[1] In 1648 she confessed to the act of entering into compact with the devil and was executed. Hers was the first such confession in New England.

1. *Coll. CHS, 22* (1928), p. 43.

Mary Johnson is indicted

The jury finds the bill of indictment against Mary Johnson, that by her own confession she is guilty of familiarity with the devil. December 7, 1648.

Source: *Conn. Col. Recs., 1,* p. 171.

Cotton Mather on Mary Johnson

Section I. There was one Mary Johnson tried at Hartford, in this country, upon an indictment of *familiarity with the devil*. She was found guilty of the same, chiefly upon her own confession, and condemned.

Sect. II. Many years are past since her execution; and the records of the court are but short; yet there are several memorables that are found credibly related and attested concerning her.

Sect. III. She said, that a devil was wont to do her many services. Her master once blamed her for not carrying out the ashes, and a devil did clear the hearth for her afterwards. Her master sending her into the field, to drive out the hogs that used to break into it, a devil would scour them out, and make her laugh to see how he feazed[1] 'em about.

Sect. IV. Her first familiarity with the devils came by discontent; and wishing the devil to take that and t'other thing; and, the devil to do this and that: whereupon a devil appeared unto her, tendering her the best service he could do for her.

Sect. V. She confessed that she was guilty of the murder of a child, and that she had been guilty of uncleanness with men and devils.

Sect. VI. In the time of her imprisonment, the famous Mr. Samuel Stone[2] was at great pains to promote her conversion unto God, and represent unto her both her misery and remedy; the success of which, was very desirable, and considerable.

Sect. VII. She was by most observers judged very penitent, both before and at her execution; and she went out of the world with many hopes of mercy through the merit of Jesus Christ. Being asked, what she built her hopes upon; she answered, on those words, *Come to me all ye that labor and are heavy laden, and I will give you rest* [Matthew 11:28]; and those, *There is a fountain open for sin and for uncleanness* [Zechariah 13:1]. And she died in a frame extremely to the satisfaction of them that were spectators of it.

1. Variant of *feeze*, "to drive or drive away": *OED*.
2. Minister in Hartford, Connecticut.
Source: Cotton Mather, *Memorable Providences, Relating to Witchcrafts and Possessions* (Boston, 1689), pp. 62–63.

Elizabeth Kendall (EXECUTED)

The only report of this case is John Hale's in A Modest Enquiry *(1702). No one has yet been able to identify Elizabeth Kendall or to date her execution, which took place sometime between 1647 and 1651.*

A woman is wrongfully blamed for a child's death

Another suffering in this kind was a woman of Cambridge, against whom a principal evidence was a Watertown nurse, who testified, that the said Kendall (so was the accused called) did bewitch to death a child of Goodman Genings[1] of Watertown; for the said Kendall did make much of the child, and then the child was well, but quickly changed its color and died in a few hours after. The court took this evidence among others, the said Genings not knowing of it. But after Kendall was executed (who also[2] denied her guilt to the death), Mr. Richard Brown[3] knowing and hoping better things of Kendall, asked said Genings if they suspected her to bewitch their child, they answered no. But they judged the true cause of the child's death to be thus, viz. the nurse had the night before carried out the child and kept it abroad in the cold a long time, when the red gum was come out upon it, and the cold had struck in the red gum, and this they judged the cause of the child's death. And that said Kendall did come in that day and make much of the child, but they apprehended no wrong to come to the child by her. After this the said nurse was put into prison for adultery, and there delivered of her base child, and Mr. Brown went to her and told her, *It was just with God to leave her to this wickedness, as a punishment for her murdering Goody Kendall by her false witness bearing.* But the nurse died in prison, and so the matter was not farther inquired into.

1. Or Jennings.
2. John Hale's "also" refers to Mrs. Lake and Mary Johnson.
3. A deputy to the General Court from Watertown, Massachusetts.
Source: Hale, *A Modest Enquiry,* pp. 18–19.

Widow Marshfield

Cases of defamation and slander are a major source of evidence for accusations of witchcraft. People went to court to complain of someone's calling them "witch" as well as going to enter charges of witchcraft. An early case of this kind concerned the Widow Marshfield, who lived in Windsor, Connecticut, before moving upriver to Springfield, Massachusetts. There in 1649 she brought suit for defamation against Mary Parsons. William Pynchon, the magistrate in Springfield, heard the case without a jury and decided for the plaintiff. Two years later the circumstances of this case figured in the

charge of witchcraft brought against Mary and her husband Hugh.[1]
Widow Marshfield appeared as a witness.

1. See chapter 2.

Witnesses describe Mary Parsons's act of defamation

The Widow Marshfield complained against Mary the wife of Hugh
Parsons of Springfield for reporting her to be suspected for a witch
and she produced John Mathews and his wife for her witnesses: who
were examined upon oath.

John Mathews said that Mary Parsons told him how she was taught
to try a witch by a widow woman that now lived in Springfield and
that she had lived in Windsor and that she had 3 children and that one
of them was married and at last she said it was the Widow Marshfield.

The said John Mathews answered her that he believed no such
thing of her: but thereupon said he Mary Parsons replied you need not
speak so much for Goody Marshfield for I am sure (said she) she hath
envied every woman's child in the end till her own daughter had a
child and then said she their child died and their cow died: and I am
persuaded said she they were bewitched: and she said moreover it
was reported to her by one in town that she was suspected to be a
witch when she lived in Windsor and that it was publicly known that
the devil followed her house in Windsor and for aught I know said she
follows her here.

Goodwife Mathews saith upon oath that when Goody Parsons came
to her house she said to her I wonder what is become of the half
pound of wool. Goody Parsons said that she could not tell except the
witch had witched it away: I wonder said I that you talk so much of a
witch do you think there is any witch in town: then said she, and she
came into my house while the wool was a-carding: who is it said I[?]
She said that Ann Stebbins had told her in Mr. Smith's chamber[1] that
she was suspected to be a witch in Windsor and that there were divers
strong lights seen of late in the meadow that were never seen before
the Widow Marshfield came to town and that she did grudge at other
women that had children because her daughter had none and about
that time (namely of her grudging) the child died and the cow died.

Goody Parsons did stiffly deny the truth of their testimonies: but as
the said witnesses had delivered their testimony upon oath and finding that she had defamed the good name of the Widow Marshfield I
sentenced her to be well whipped on the morrow after lecture with 20
lashes by the constable unless she could procure the payment of £3 to

the Widow Marshfield for and towards the reparation of her good name. May 29 and 30, 1649.

1. Henry Smith, a magistrate in Springfield and prominent landowner.
Source: Joseph Smith, ed., *Colonial Justice in Western Massachusetts (1639–1702): The Pynchon Court Record* (Cambridge, Mass., 1961), pp. 219–20.

Joan and John Carrington (EXECUTED)

John Carrington arrived in New England in 1635 at the age of thirty-three. He practiced the trade of carpentry in Wethersfield, Connecticut. He and Joan, his second wife, had children. The value of John's estate at death was a very modest £23 11s.[1] Nothing is known of the circumstances that led to their executions, which occurred in 1651.

1. Charles W. Manwaring, comp., *A Digest of the Early Connecticut Probate Records* (Hartford, Conn., 1904), *1*, p. 104; Demos, *Entertaining Satan*, p. 349.

The indictment and conviction of the Carringtons

A Particular Court in Hartford upon the trial of John Carrington and his wife 20th February 1650.

Magistrates[:] Edward Hopkins Esq., Governor John Haynes Esq., Deputy Mr. Wells, Mr. Wolcott, Mr Webster, Mr. Cullick, Mr Clarke.

[*omitted: names of jury*]

John Carrington thou art indicted by the name of John Carrington of Wethersfield carpenter, that not having the fear of God before thine eyes thou hast entertained familiarity with Satan the great enemy of God and mankind and by his help hast done works above the course of nature for which both according to the law of God and of the established law of this commonwealth thou deservest to die.

The jury finds this indictment against John Carrington March 6, 1650/51.

Joan Carrington thou art indicted by the name of Joan Carrington the wif[e] of John Carrington that not having the fear of God before thine eyes thou hast entertained familiarity with Satan the great enemy of God and mankind and by his help hast done works above the course of nature for which both according to the laws of God, and the established law of this commonwealth thou deservest to die.

The jury finds this indictment against Joan Carrington March 6, 1650/51.

Source: *Coll. CHS*, 22 (1928), pp. 92–93.

Alice Lake (EXECUTED)

Alice Lake, wife of Henry and resident of Dorchester, Massachusetts, was convicted of witchcraft and executed about 1650. She had four young children. As the historian Carol Karlsen has pointed out, her case involved two recurrent themes in the prosecution of female witches, "illicit sexual behavior" and infanticide.

1. Carol Karlsen, *The Devil in the Shape of a Woman: Witchcraft in Colonial New England* (New York, 1987), p. 141.

Alice Lake is called a harlot

Another that suffered on that account some time after, was a Dorchester woman. And upon the day of her execution Mr. Thompson minister at Braintree, and J. P. her former master took pains with her to bring her to repentance[.] And she utterly denied her guilt of witchcraft; yet justified God for bringing her to that punishment: for she had when a single woman played the harlot, and being with child used means to destroy the fruit of her body to conceal her sin and shame, and although she did not effect it, yet she was a murderer in the sight of God for her endeavors, and showed great penitency for that sin; but owned nothing of the crime laid to her charge.

Source: Hale, *Modest Enquiry,* pp. 17–18.

Alice Lake and her grief for a dead child

Dear Brother. . . . I have also received by way of London one of your books of the *Remarkable Providences.*[1] . . . Why did you not put in the story of Mrs. Hibbins's witchcrafts, and the discovery thereof, as also of H. Lake's wife of Dorchester whom as I have heard the devil drew in by appearing to her in the likeness and acting the part of a child of hers then lately dead on whom her heart was much set . . . ?

1. Increase Mather's recently published *An Essay for the Recording of Illustrious Providences* (Boston, 1684).
Source: Nathaniel Mather to Increase Mather, December 31, 1684. Mather Papers, Prince Collection, BPL. Printed in *Coll. MHS* 4th ser., *8* (1868), p. 58.

2. The Parsons of Springfield: A Family at Odds (1651–1652)

▲

Mary Parsons (EXECUTED?) and Hugh Parsons

Hugh Parsons earned his living as a brickmaker and wood sawyer in Springfield, Massachusetts. His wife, the former Mary Lewis, whom he married in 1645, accused the Widow Marshfield, a newcomer to Springfield, of witchcraft in 1649. Mrs. Parsons was convicted of defamation and whipped.[1] Not long thereafter she turned on her husband and accused him of practicing witchcraft. He in turn suspected her. Hugh and the town minister, George Moxon (who returned to England in 1652), had disagreed about his work as a brickmaker. When two of Moxon's children died, the townspeople reasoned that Hugh was being vengeful. Thirty-five neighbors made depositions before the magistrates. From their statements a picture emerges of Hugh Parsons as a testy workman who often quarreled with his employers.

The Parsons had two children of their own; one died in 1650, and a second, born in October 1650, died on March 1, 1651. Mrs. Parsons blamed these deaths on her husband, who was "attached upon suspicion of witchcraft" on or about March 1, 1651, and who underwent two examinations in Springfield. A week or so before her husband, Mary was also accused of witchcraft. The sequence of events is not entirely clear, but on May 13 the Massachusetts General Court, which heard capital cases, indicted her for witchcraft. She pleaded not guilty, and the court concurred. Indicted a second time for the murder of one of her children, she confessed and was sentenced to death by hanging. She may have died in jail; the evidence for her execution is indirect.[2] It seems clear from the statements she made during the examination of her husband that Mrs. Parsons imagined being a witch; thus she told of speaking with the devil and of being persuaded to participate in a witches' meeting "in Goodman Stebbins his lot," where her fellow celebrants included Hugh and two women of the town.

Hugh Parsons had been examined before the Springfield magistrate, William Pynchon, on March 1 and 18, 1651. The documents allow us to imagine the scene: Pynchon presiding, the neighbors speaking in their turn, and Hugh Parsons answering or remaining silent. His wife was there as well to testify against him. Pynchon forwarded these depositions to the General Court, which also collected others (or repeat versions). In 1652 a jury found Hugh guilty, but the General Court refused to accept the verdict. He never returned to Springfield. The historian Stephen Innes has analyzed the townspeople's reaction to Hugh Parsons in Labor in a New Land: Economy and Society in Seventeenth-Century Springfield *(Princeton, N.J., 1983). The case is also analyzed in John P. Demos,* Entertaining Satan: Witchcraft and the Culture of Early New England *(New York, 1982), pp. 280–90.*

1. See chapter 1.
2. The evidence is summarized in Joseph Smith, ed., *Colonial Justice in Western Massachusetts (1639–1702): The Pynchon Court Record* (1961), p. 22 n. 56.

Mary Parsons is acquitted of witchcraft and convicted of infanticide

Mary Parsons, wife to Hugh Parsons, of Springfield, being committed to prison for suspicion of witchcraft, as also for murdering her own child, was this day called forth and indicted for witchcraft: By the name of Mary Parsons, you are here, before the General Court, charged, in the name of this commonwealth, that, not having the fear of God before your eyes nor in your heart, being seduced by the devil, and yielding to his malicious motion, about the end of February last, at Springfield, to have familiarity, or consulted with a familiar spirit, making a covenant with him, and have used diverse devilish practices by witchcraft, to the hurt of the persons of Martha and Rebecca Moxon, against the word of God, and the laws of this jurisdiction, long since made and published. To which indictment she pleaded not guilty: all evidences brought in against her being heard and examined, the court found the evidences were not sufficient to prove her a witch, and therefore she was cleared in that respect.

The court, understanding that Mary Parsons, now in prison accused for a witch, is likely, through weakness, to die before trial if it be deferred, do order, that on the morrow, by eight of the clock in the morning, she be brought before, and tried by, the General Court, the rather that Mr. Pynchon may be present to give his testimony in the case.

At the same time she was indicted for murdering her child, by the name of Mary Parsons: you are here before the General Court, charged, in the name of this commonwealth, that, not having the fear of God before your eyes nor in your heart, being seduced by the devil, and yielding to his instigations and the wickedness of your own heart, about the beginning of March last, in Springfield, in or near your own house, did willfully and most wickedly murder your own child, against the word of God, and the laws of this jurisdiction, long since made and published. To which she acknowledged herself guilty.

The court, finding her guilty of murder by her own confession, etc., proceeded to judgment: You shall be carried from this place to the place from whence you came, and from thence to the place of execution, and there hang till you be dead. May 13, 1651. [*Marginal note:*] Sentence against Mary Parsons: she was reprieved to 29 of May.

Source: *Mass. Bay Recs., 4,* pt. 1, pp. 47–48. Another form of the indictment and condemnation appear in *Mass. Bay Recs., 3,* p. 229.

Order to hear witnesses

It is ordered, that on the second Tuesday in the 3d month next, there shall be a Court of Assistants held at Boston, for the trial of those[1] in prison accused for witchcraft, and that the most material witnesses at Springfield be summoned to the Court of Assistants, to give in their evidence against them accordingly. Oct. 24, 1651.

1. The plural pronoun is puzzling; some accounts, however, e.g., John Hale's, allude to other persons besides Hugh and Mary Parsons as being accused and possibly tried.
Source: *Mass. Bay Recs., 4,* pt. 1, p. 73.

John Hale on witchcraft in Springfield

And two or three of Springfield, one of which confessed; and said the occasion of her familiarity with Satan was this: She had lost a child and was exceedingly discontented at it, and longed; Oh that she might see her child again! And at last the devil in likeness of her child came to her bedside and talked with her, and asked to come into the bed to her, and she received it into the bed to her that night and several nights after, and so entered into covenant with Satan and became a witch. This was the only confessor in these times in this government.

Source: John Hale, *A Modest Enquiry Into the Nature of Witchcraft* (Boston, 1702), p. 19. Hale may have confused Mary Parsons with Alice Lake; see above, chapter 1.

The examination of Hugh Parsons

Examination of Hugh Parsons, of Springfield, on a charge of witchcraft, and the testimonies given against him, before Mr. William Pynchon, at Springfield, 1651.

Hugh Parsons's examinations. All these testimonies now taken upon oath before me, William Pynchon.

The examination of Hugh Parsons. 1st day of [March?] and his second examination the [*obliterated*].

Hugh Parsons you are attached upon suspicion of witchcraft:

The magical pudding

George Lancton and Hannah his wife do jointly testify upon oath: that on Friday last being the 21 February, they had a pudding in the same bag and that as soon as it was slipped out of the bag it was cut lengthwise like the former pudding, and like another on the 23 [of] February as smooth as any knife could cut it namely one slice all along wanting but very little from end to end.

Also Hannah the wife of George Lancton saith upon oath that a neighbor came in and she showed it to him, and that neighbor took a piece of it and threw [it] into the fire: and she saith that about an hour after perhaps a little more, she heard one mutter and mumble at the door, then she asked Goody Sewell who was then at her house (and near the door) who it was, she said it was Hugh Parsons and that he asked whether Goodman Lancton were at home or no[.] I said no and so he went away, but left not his errand neither did he ever since come to signify his errand.

Deposed in court by Hannah [Lancton].

Hugh Parsons being asked what his errand was: he spake to other things and not to the question, being asked the second time what his errand was, he spake again of other by matters and not to the question: being asked the third time what his errand was and charged to make a direct answer then he said it was to get some hay of him: Being asked again whether he had propounded his errand since to Goodman Lancton: he said he never saw him since.

Then one or two that were present testified that they see him meet

Goodman Lancton next day below. Simon Beamon and Rice Bedortha say upon oath that the next day but one they saw Hugh Parsons meet Goodman Lancton accompanied with Thomas Sewell in the street and that they saw him speak to Goodman Lancton.

George Lancton saith on oath that he never to this day asked him for any hay.

When Hugh Parsons saw himself taken tardy in this put of[f?], then he said that he did not ask him because John Lombard had told him that Goodman Lancton had sold more hay to Goodman Herman than he could spare: But after inquiry John Lombard saith upon oath March 17, 1650 that the Wednesday before that Hugh Parsons came to Goodman Lancton's house for hay that he had spoken to buy some hay of Goodman Lancton namely as he passed by where he and Hugh Parsons were at work together, and had a denial: and then he told Hugh Parsons that Goodman Lancton could not spare him any hay because he had already sold more to Goodman Herman than he could spare and said he should now want himself.

John Lombard also saith on oath that the Friday after when the said pudding was so strangely cut he told Hugh Parsons again that Lancton had no hay to sell.

Hugh Parsons not being able to reply any further it is evident that his coming to the door of Goodman Lancton's presently after the burning of the pudding, which was the next day after John Lombard had told him that he had no hay to spare, that his errand to get hay was no true cause of his coming thither but rather that the spirit that bewitched the pudding brought him thither.

Mary Parsons and her husband's bargains

Mary Parsons being present at the second examination saith: one reason why I have suspected my husband to be a witch is because almost all that he sells to anybody doth not prosper: I am sorry said she for that poor man Thomas Miller for two days after my husband and he had bargained for a piece of ground Thomas Miller had that mischance of that cut in his leg.

Thomas Miller being present saith upon oath that he being in company with several other workmen about timber trees in the woods, as we were at dinner and merry together: Hugh Parsons sat on a bough somewhat higher than the rest[.] Then one of the company started this question: I wonder why he sits there: Thomas Miller saith he answered: to see what we have: and then I began to speak of the cutting of the pudding in town.

Thomas Cooper being present with the said workmen saith that he was much troubled in his mind because Thomas Miller spake so plainly to Hugh Parsons lest some ill event should follow.

And both Thomas Cooper and Thomas Miller say upon oath that Hugh Parsons was as merry and as pleasant before this speech about the pudding as any in the company but after this he was wholly silent and spake not a word in reply about the pudding: but sat dumb: and Thomas Miller saith that about half a quarter of an hour after at his first setting to work his leg was cut.

Thomas Burnham is puzzled by Hugh Parsons's silence

April 3, 1651. Thomas Burnham saith upon oath that he said to Hugh Parsons a little before his apprehension: here is strange doings in town about cutting of pudding and whetting of saws in the nighttime: Hugh Parsons heard these things much agitated among divers then present and was wholly silent but at last he said I never heard of this thing before this night: Thomas Burnham saith he said to him, that is strange, that you should not hear of these things: and I being but a stranger in town do hear of it in all places wherever I come: At this Hugh Parsons held down his head and was wholly silent, but he took occasion to speak of other by matters as pleasantly as anybody else but to the matter of the pudding he would say nothing[:] and yet saith Thomas Burnham I spake to him of it several times and of the whetting of saws on purpose to see what Hugh Parsons would say to it but still he continued silent and would not speak any thing about these things. Then Goodman Munn being present said I would that those that whet saws in the nighttime on the Lord's days were found out: Then saith Thomas Burnham I said you sawyers you had need to look to it: Hugh Parsons being also a sawyer never returned any answer but still continued silent: This matter about the pudding and whetting of saws was often tossed up and down between several persons, and many said they never heard the like: and Hugh Parsons was often spoken to in particular and asked if he ever heard the like but still he continued wholly silent.

Joan Warrinar and Abigail Munn corroborate the same

Joan, the wife of William Warrinar and Abigail the wife of Goodman Munn being present when the said speeches were used do acknowledge that they remember all things that have been related by Thomas

Burnham and that Hugh Parsons was wholly silent and do testify the same upon oath the day and year above said.

Blanche and Rice Bedortha recall threatening speeches

Secondly, Blanche Bedortha saith on oath February 27 and March 1st. and March 18, 1649. That about two years since Hugh Parsons being at our house we had some speeches about a bargain with my husband about some bricks: and then Blanche Bedortha saith that she spake something about the said bricks that did much displease Hugh Parsons: Thereupon he said unto me Gammer, you needed not have said anything, I spake not to you but I shall remember you when you little think on it.

Also Rice Bedortha saith upon oath that he took notice of the said threatening and was much offended at it, and told Hugh Parsons that it was no good speech: but I have often heard him use such threatening both against myself and others when he hath been displeased.

Blanche Bedortha took oath in court to all she witnesseth.

Samuel Marshfield being also present at the same time testifies upon oath that he heard Hugh Parsons use the said threatening speech to Blanche Bedortha.

At this Hugh Parsons was wholly silent and answered not.

Then I told him of some evil events that did follow not long after this threatening.

Samuel Marshfield testifieth in court.

Blanche Bedortha tells of strange lights

Blanche Bedortha doth testify upon oath: that soon after this threatening speech as she was going to bed and had put of[f] her waistcoat made of red shag cotton and as she was going to hang it up on a pin, she held it up between her hands, and then she saw a light as [if] it had been the light of a candle crossing the back of her waistcoat on the inside 3 times one after another, at which she was amazed: and therefore she saith that after she had laid it down she took it up again to try if the firelight might not be the cause of it, but she saith that the firelight being all one as it was before she could not perceive any such light by it, and besides she saith it could not be the firelight, because there was a double Indian mat compassing the bed and the place where she was, so that it could not be the firelight; for this double mat was betwixt her and the fire: and she saith moreover that because this light was so strange to her, she took her waistcoat several other nights to try if the firelight would not give such a light as she saw at first and held it up the same way that she did at first but she saith she could not perceive any such light afterward.

Blanche Bedortha on afflictions in her body

Secondly. About a month after this, she saith that when she was in childbed: and as well as most women use to be, and better than she used to be: yet at the week's end being desirous to sleep she lay still that she might sleep and she did sleep: and yet about an hour or more after she awaked and felt a soreness about her heart and this soreness increased more and more in three places, namely under her left breast and on her left shoulder and in her neck: and in these three places the pain was so tedious, that it was like the pricking of knives so that I durst not lie down but was fain to be shored up with a bag of cotton wool, and with other things: and this extremity continued from Friday in the forenoon till Monday about noon, and then the extremity of the pain began a little to abate and by Tuesday it was pretty well gone: and suddenly after my thoughts were that this evil might come upon me from the said threatening speech of Hugh Parsons.

I do not apprehend that I was sick in any other part of my body but in the said three places only and by the extremity of these pricking[s] only.

The Widow Marshfield testifies upon oath March 22, 1650 that when she kept in Rice Bedortha's wife she was not there in the night but in the daytime only: when I went home at night I left her well as could be expected of a woman in child bed, but in the morning when I came she was in lamentable torment[;] she grew worse and worse for 2 or 3 days and she cried out as if she had been pricked with knives in such a lamentable manner that I did much fear her life: I never saw a woman in such a condition in child bed for she could not lie down in her bed: neither do I apprehend that she had any other kind of sickness but that pricking pains only in her side and shoulder.

An imaginary dog

Thirdly. Blanche Bedortha saith upon oath that my child being about two years old, as he was standing near to his father did hastily run to him and strived to get up upon his knees and cried I am afraid of the dog, and yet there was no dog there: his father asked him where the dog was: he said it was gone under the bed: his father asked him whose dog it was: he said it was Lombard's dog: his father said that

Lombard had no dog: then he said again it was Parsons's dog: but the child's meaning was at first that it was Parsons's dog: I know it by this, because when Parsons did often use to come to our house he did often call him Lombard: and ever and anon he is much affrighted with this dog and doth often speak of it: and yet Parsons hath no dog neither was there any dog in the house: But the earnestness of the child both then and since doth make me conceive it might be some evil thing from Hugh Parsons.

Hugh Parsons having heard all these testimonies alleged stood still at his second examination as at the first and made no answer.

Rice Bedortha saith upon oath that ever since the first time the child was afraid of this dog he will often speak of it and point at it with such earnestness that he hath often made me afraid with his earnest pointing at it[;] sometimes he saith it is there under the stool and sometimes it is there under the cradle and so under other places.

A dispute over bricks, threatening words, and Mr. Moxon's children

Thirdly. Your wife saith that she suspects you may be the cause of all the evil that is befallen to Mr. Moxon's children because when she hath spoken to you about the bargain of bricks that you undertook to make for Mr. Moxon's chimneys and that she thought Mr. Moxon would expect the performance of the said bargain: thereupon you said if Mr. Moxon do force me to make bricks according to bargain I will be even with him or he shall get nothing by it, for she saith that these two speeches are very usual with you when you are displeased with anybody.

Answer. Hugh Parsons saith I said not that I would be even with him, but this I said if he would hold me to my bargain, I could puzzle him in the bargain.

John Mathews being present saith upon oath that when he went with Hugh Parsons to fetch some of his samel bricks,[1] he said to Hugh Parsons do not you make more bricks for Mr. Moxon's chimneys, he will stay with us now, and then I believe he will have up his chimneys: Hugh Parsons said no that I know of, then said I Mr. Moxon will hold you to your bargain about the said bricks, then said he if he do I will be even with him: And when Hugh Parsons made my chimneys he did often use the same speech: and when he is displeased with anybody it is his usual speech.

At the testimony of John Mathews Hugh Parsons was silent and made no reply.

Mr. Moxon being present saith the same week that I spake to Hugh Parsons about the bricks and to his wife about another business my daughter Martha was taken ill with her fits[.] I confess also that when I spake to him of the said bargain that Hugh said I could not in strictness hold him to the bargain[:] But this last answer doth not take of[f] the ill purpose of his former threatening.

Sarah Edwards describes a request for milk and its consequences

Fourth. Sarah the wife of Alexander Edwards testifies upon oath February 27, 1650 that about two years ago more or less Hugh Parsons being then at the Long Meadow came to her house to buy some milk: she said I'll give you a halfpenny worth but I cannot let you have any more at this time: This was at that time when my cow gave three quarts at a meal, but the next meal after she gave not above a quart and it was as yellow as saffron, and yet the cow ailed nothing that I could discern: the next meal it altered to another strange odd color, and so it did every meal for a week together it still altered to some odd color or other and also it grew less and less: and yet all the while the cow was as well as at any time before as far as I could discern: and about a week after she began to mend her milk again without any means used: upon this I had thoughts that Hugh Parsons might be the cause of it.

Alexander Edwards swore that George Colton saw the milk in strange colors.

Answer. Hugh Parsons saith that he did not lie one night at the Long Meadow that summer, but only in the spring of the year, either in March or in the beginning of April when he set up fencing there, and that he never had milk of her but that one time: and at that time of the year he thinks her cow could not give three quarts at a meal.

But now, at his second examination March the 18, 1650 he seeing Alexander Edwards about to testify the contrary he confesseth that he lay a night there in planting time about the end of May.

I remember that Alexander Edwards came to me to tell me of this accident and said that he was persuaded the cow was bewitched by Hugh Parsons: but I did not believe him at that time I rather conceived that the cow was falling into some dangerous sickness[;] for such a sudden abatement I told him was a sign of some dangerous sickness at hand: but seeing no sickness followed I told Hugh Parsons that such a sudden change could not come from a natural cause.

Sharing the tongue of a cow, and a missing piece of it

Fifthly. Anthony Dorchester saith upon oath February 25, 1650 the 1 day of the 1 month and the 18 day that about September was twelve months 4 men had equal shares in a cow: each had a quarter and the offal was to be divided also: and Hugh Parsons desired to have the root of the tongue: but he had it not: it fell to my share: and a certain time after I had salted it: I took the said root and another piece of meat and put it into the kettle as it was boiling over the fire at Hugh Parsons's house where I lived at that present: and there was nobody there but he and his wife and I and my wife who was sick of a consumption sitting on her bed and not able to get of[f] without help: neither were any of my children able to take such a thing out of a boiling kettle: This being the Sabbath day Hugh Parsons and his wife went to the church before me, then I made myself ready and went presently after them and came home before them: and took up my meat before they came home, but the root of the tongue which Hugh Parsons formerly desired was gone: his wife came home presently after me (but he came not with her). Then I told her and she wondered how it could be gone: and she went to the tub where it was salted to see if it might not be forgotten and it was not there: Then said I to her I am sure I put it into the boiling kettle: and she confessed that she saw me pick it and wash it: and being present did much wonder [at] the strange going of it away: and said that she feared her husband might convey it away: she told me that her husband went along with her till we came near to Goodman Merick's and was very pleasing to her more than usually he had been a great while before: but there he laid the child down and went no further with her: and she saw him no more till the meeting was almost done: (all this, Mary Parsons being present doth acknowledge). Presently after this he came home: Then I spake of it to him: and all that he said was that he thought I did not put it in: But I told him that I was sure I put it into the boiling kettle: And I have ever since believed that no hand of man did take it away: but that it was taken away by witchcraft.

Answer. Hugh Parsons confesseth that he desired the root of the tongue but withal saith he is ignorant as the child unborn which way it went.

Some by stand[er] objected it might be taken away by his wife as well as by him: But that is not so likely because Hugh Parsons went not with her to the meeting but laid down her child and went from her and she saw him no more till meeting was almost done.

Answer. Hugh Parsons saith, that he doth not remember that he went any whither unless he might go into Goodman Merick's house to take a pipe of tobacco and though his wife saw him no more till the meeting was almost done yet he saith he might be standing without the door though she saw him not[;] and at his second examination he was asked how it did appear that he came not to the meeting till it was almost done.

Abigail Munn being present doth testify upon oath that she knew by the talk about the strange going away of this root of the tongue: what Sabbath was meant and she saith that she saw him come that Sabbath to the meeting when the sermon was well onward.

Jonathan Taylor deposed in open court: saith that he heard the said Parsons say (notwithstanding the root of the tongue was desired by Anthony Dorchester for his wife being sick) yet he said I will have it.

Edward Rawson Secretary.

A tale of missing knives

Sixthly. Griffith Jones doth suspect you for witchcraft about [the] knife. Griffith Jones saith upon oath February 25, 1650 March 1 and 18th day that when he lived at his house near Hugh Parsons's house about 2 years ago: on a Lords day I went home to dinner but my wife stayed behind at a neighbor's house to dinner[.] I took up my dinner and laid it on a little table made on the cradle head: I sought for a knife but I could not find any: I cleared the table where I dined to see if any were there and I searched everywhere about the house and I could find none, yet I knew I had more than two and when I could find none I went to an old basket where I had things to mend shoes withal, and there was a rusty knife and with that I was fain to eat my dinner[.] After I had dined I took away the victuals that were left and laid it up: and then I laid the rusty knife on the corner of the table to cut a pipe of tobacco withal[.] But before I cut my tobacco I first went out of door to serve a pig that was but a very little of[f] the door and no man could come in but I must see them and as soon as I came in to cut my tobacco with the said rusty knife there lay 3 knives together on the table which made me blush: wondering how they came there seeing nobody was in the house but myself: and as I was going to cut the tobacco, Hugh Parsons came in: and said where is the man are you ready to go to the meeting: I said by and by as soon as I have taken a pipe of tobacco[.] So he stayed and took some with me.

Answer. Hugh Parsons saith he is ignorant of any such thing and in the sight of God can clear his conscience.

It was told him that such a strange thing falling out just at his coming in, did minister just occasion of suspicion of witchcraft: he replied that one witness was not sufficient.

Mary Parsons reports her husband's attitude toward witches

Seventhly. Mary Parsons his wife saith that one reason why she doth suspect you to be a witch is because you cannot abide that anything should be spoken against witches[.] She saith that you told her that you were at a neighbor's house a little before lecture when they were speaking of Carrington and his wife,[2] that were now apprehended for witches, she saith that when you came home and spake these speeches to her: she said to you I hope that God will find out all such wicked persons and purge New England of all witches ere it be long[.] To this she saith you gave her a naughty look but never a word, but presently after on a light occasion you took up a block and made as if you would throw it at her head but yet in the end you did not but threw it down on the hearth of the chimney[.] This expression of your anger was because she wished the ruin of all witches.

Mary Ashley testifies this substance, upon oath.

Answer. Hugh Parsons saith he does not remember that ever he took up a block to throw at her, but upon further debate he said at last that he took up a block but remembered not the occasion: at his second answer he saith that he took up no block on that occasion.

Reply[:] it might well be on that occasion for not long since she saith that you said to her if ever any trouble do come unto you it will be by her means and that she would be the means to hang you.

Answer. Hugh Parsons saith that he might say so because in his anger he is impatient and doth speak what he should not: At his second examination he said he might say so because she is the worst enemy that I have considering the relation that is between us: and if anybody bespeak evil of me she will speak as ill and as much as anybody else.

Mary Parsons replied I have often entreated him to confess whether he were a witch or no, I told him that if he would acknowledge it I would beg the prayers of God's people on my knees for him, and that we are not our own, we are bought with a price [1 Cor. 6:20] and that God would redeem from the power of Satan, etc.

Hugh Parsons was asked if his wife had spoken anything to him at any time to confess witchcraft.

Answer. Not anything to me about witchcraft that I remember.

The death of Hugh Parsons's child

Eighthly. Mary Parsons saith: did not I speak of it to you upon the death of my child: did not I tell you then that I had jealousies that you had bewitched your own child to death.

To this he was silent and made no answer.

Then she desired Anthony Dorchester that lived then in their house whether he could not remember that she had charged her husband with the bewitching of his child.

Anthony Dorchester said that he did not remember that ever she spake directly to him of bewitching his child but that she had jealousies that he had bewitched his child to death.

Mary Parsons said that when her last child was ill she told him that she suspected he had bewitched that [child] as he had done his other child, and said I have spoken of it to him and to other folks together above forty times.

It was alleged that he might well be suspected to have bewitched his former child to death because he expressed no kind of sorrow at the death of it.

Answer. Hugh Parsons saith that he was loath to express any sorrow before his wife, because of the weak condition that she was in at that time.

Witnesses say Hugh Parsons did not grieve his dead child

Mr. Moxon desired to ask him a question which was this: It seems he had conference with his wife about his sick child and about her grief for it, or else why should he forbear to express the affliction of sorrow before her, that he might not grieve her.

Hugh Parsons saith that his wife might wonder at it but yet that was the true reason of it.

It was asked him why he did not show more respect to his wife and child but went into the Long Meadow and lay there all night when his child lay at the point of death and when he heard of the death of it the next morning never showed any sorrow for it.

George Colton stood forth to testify on oath that coming to Hugh Parsons's house where his wife was sitting by the fire with the child in her lap, and she showed to me the strange condition of the child and I was amazed at it for the child's secrets did rot or were consuming: and she said though my child be so ill and I have much to do with it yet my husband keeps ado at me to help him about his corn: I said to her your husband had more need to get you some help than to keep ado at you to help him: and she spake very harsh things against him before his face: and if he had been innocent he would have blamed her for her speeches for she spake such things against him as are not ordinary for persons to speak one of another and yet he being present said nothing for himself in way of blaming anything that she had spoken against him.

Sworn in court.

It was also objected to Hugh Parsons that if he had been innocent about the death of his child he would have reproved her speeches.

Answer. Hugh Parsons saith that he had such speeches from her daily and therefore he made the best of it now and he also saith I set her not about business: I required none at her hands except it were to throw in some Indian corn from the door, I have often blamed her for doing work and bid her do less.

Anthony Dorchester who lived in their house stood forth to testify that he never knew him to blame her for doing too much work except (saith he) that she helped my wife at any time which work did not bring in any profit to him[.] But saith Anthony Dorchester he [Parsons] need not say that he forebore grief for his sick child before his wife for fear it should trouble her in her weak condition, for he never feared either to grieve or displease his wife any time.

Being asked whether he did ever do anything to comfort his wife in her sorrow for the death of her child he answered not.

Mary Parsons said no, he did nothing to comfort me but still when he came home he kept ado at me to throw in the corn from the door, and when I saw my husband in this frame it added more grief to my sorrow.

Anthony Dorchester saith I saw nothing he did to comfort his wife but he did often blame her that she did not throw in the corn from the door.

More testimony about his lack of grief

It was evidenced by George Colton upon oath that he [Parsons] showed no natural sorrow for the death of his child when he first heard of it in the Long Meadow.

Jonathan Burt's testimony upon oath was for the time of the morning when he brought word to Hugh Parsons of the death of his child: Jonathan saith it was as he thought about 8 or 9 a clock in the morning: and the place where he was first told of the death of it was at the great oak about 16 or 20 poles from George Colton's house.

George Colton testifies upon oath March 1 and March 18, 1650 that

Hugh Parsons came into the Long Meadow when his child lay at the point of death: and that having word of the death of it the next morning, by Jonathan Burt he was not affected with it, but he came after a light manner rushing into my house and said I hear my child is dead: but I will cut a pipe of tobacco first before I go home: and after he was gone my wife and myself did much wonder at the lightness of his carriage because he showed no affliction of sorrow for the death of his child.

Sworn in court.

Answer. Hugh Parsons saith that he was very full of sorrow for the death of it in private though not in public[;] he saith that he was much troubled for the death of it when he first heard of it before he came into Goodman Colton's house.

Other witnesses say that Hugh Parsons showed no grief

George Colton being present doth testify that Hugh Parsons came to his house he thinks about 8 a clock in the morning and therefore he is very sure of it that he heard of it but a little while before he came to his house[;] for Jonathan Burt that brought the news of it spake of it to Hugh Parsons but about 12 or 20 poles from George Colton's house and he came presently thither: and therefore if he had had any sorrow for the death of his child he could not but have showed some sign of it when he came to his house but he saith that both he and his wife discerned no sign of sorrow at all.

Sworn in court.

Hugh Parsons desired that Goodman Cooley would testify whether he was not affected with the death of his child when he came to speak to him to go to the burial of it, he saith he could not speak to him for weeping.

Benjamin Cooley saith that when he spake to him to go to the burial of his child he cannot remember any sorrow that he showed, for he came to him taking a pipe of tobacco.

Anthony Dorchester testifies upon oath March 1 and 18, 1650, that when Hugh Parsons's child was dead which was last Indian harvest was 12 months, he then living at the house of Hugh Parsons did much wonder that when the said Hugh Parsons came home from the Long Meadow, he expressed no kind of sorrow for his child after he came home: but carried himself as at other times without any regard of it that either I or my wife could discover.

Also Blanche Bedortha saith on oath that she was at Hugh Parsons's house when he came from the Long Meadow and he showed no kind of sorrow for the death of his child.

Hugh Parsons saith that when his child was sick and like to die, he run barefoot and barelegged, and with tears to desire Goody Cooley to come to his wife because his child was so ill.

Mary Parsons saith that this was out of a sudden fear at the very first time that the child was taken, for it was suddenly and strangely taken, with a trembling beginning at the toes and coming upwards and so it stopped the child's breath.

Goody Cooley also testifies, that this was at the first time that the child was taken.

There was some speeches used that it might be bewitched for these that are now bewitched have oftentimes something rise up into their throats that doth stop their breath: and it seems by George Colton's testimony that the child was strangely taken.

Mary Ashley and Sara Leonard stood up to give testimony that they saw the child in the time of its sickness and that they apprehended the secrets of the child to consume and waste away.

Mary Parsons says why she suspects her husband

Mary Parsons being asked what reasons she had to suspect her husband for a witch, gave these reasons[:]

1. Because when I say anything to anybody never so secretly to such friends as I am sure would not speak of it, yet he would come to know it by what means I cannot tell: I have spoken some things to [Mrs.] Smith that goes little abroad and I am sure would not speak of it yet he hath known it and would speak of it to me as soon as I came home.

Secondly. Because he useth to be out a nights till midnight (till of late), and about half an hour before he comes home I shall hear some noise or other about the door or about the house.

Thirdly. Because he useth to come home in a distempered frame so that I could not tell how to please him[;] sometimes he hath pulled off the bed clothes and left me naked a bed and hath quenched the fire[;] sometimes he hath thrown peas about the house and made me pick them up.

4. Because oftentimes in his sleep he makes a gabbling noise but I cannot understand one word that he says and when I did ask what it was that he talked [of] in his sleep he would say that he had strange dreams and one time he said that the devil and he were fighting and that the devil had almost overcome him but at last he got the master of the devil.

Being asked if ever she knew her husband do anything beyond the power of nature: she said on[e] a time her husband sent her to Jonathan Taylor to get him to work on the morrow: and as I returned home in the twilight I saw a thing like a great nasty dog by the path side[.] I suspected it was done by witchcraft from my husband he sent me out [*worn from the margin*] because usually he doth such things himself.

Witnesses confirm that Mary Parsons suspected her husband

February 27, 1650. Benjamin Cooley saith upon oath that Mary Parsons told him above a year since that she feared her husband was a witch and that she so far suspected him that she hath searched him when he hath been asleep in bed and could not find anything about him unless it be in his secret parts.

February 27, 1650. Anthony Dorchester saith upon oath, that about a year and a quarter since I and my wife lived for a time at Hugh Parsons's house and then I have several times heard Mary Parsons say that she suspected and greatly suspected her husband to be a witch, and that her husband once in 24 hours would be from home, if not in the day time then in the night time whatever weather it was: and that in his absence she hath heard a rumbling noise in the house, sometimes in one place and sometimes in another: and that she did much suspect him to be a witch because if she had any private talk with any he would come to know it, by what means she could not tell being confident that those she revealed herself unto would never tell it.

Benjamin Cooley and Anthony Dorchester say upon oath that being charged by the constable to watch Mary Parsons this last night she told them that if her husband had fallen out with anybody he would say that he would be even with them and then she found he did bewitch his own child that she might be at liberty to help him in his Indian harvest, for he expected help from her, and because her time was taken up about her child, he being eager after the world seemed to be troubled at it, and she suspected that he was a means to make an end of his child quickly that she might be at liberty to help him: another thing she said made her to suspect her husband to be a witch was because most things he sold to others did not prosper[:] another ground of suspicion was, because he was so backward to go to the ordinances either to the lecture or to any other meeting, and she hath been faint to threaten him that she would complain to the magistrate or else she thought he would not let her go once in the year[:] another thing made her suspect him to be a witch was because of the great noise that she should hear in the house when he was abroad and she said that last Tuesday at night when he was abroad she heard a noise in the house as if 40 horses had been there, and after he was come to bed he kept a noise and a gabbling in his sleep but she could not understand one word and so he hath done many times formerly and when she asked him what he ailed he would say he had strange dreams and one time he said that the devil and he were a fighting and once he had almost overcome him but at last he overcome the devil.

Francis Pepper and Mary Ashley report Mary's suspicions

Francis Pepper saith upon oath when I came to see Mary Parsons that Sabbath that she kept at Robert Ashley's house, as soon as she saw me she said unto me the heifer was bewitched, I asked her how she could tell she said her husband had bewitched it, and now he had bewitched me, and he knows now what I say and he now terrifies me in this place[,] striking her hand upon her thigh.

February 27, 1650. Mary the wife of Robert Ashley saith upon oath that Mary Parsons was at her house last lecture day was sen'night, before meeting and among other speeches she said as for the death of Mr. Smith's children[5] it lay very sad upon her, I asked her why she said because my husband would have had me to have nursed his children: but said she doth any one think me a fit nurse for them: I asked her why he would have her to nurse them: she said for lucre and gain, one may well know his reason: after this she fetched a great sigh and said little doth any one think how the death of those children lies upon me, and she said it was her near relation but said she it is better for others to bring him out than for me but I can speak a great deal of him if others bring him out.

Mary Parsons was asked what ground she had to think that her husband bewitched Mr. Smith's children: because, my husband would often say that he would be even with Mr. Smith if he denied to let him have any peas or to plow his ground or to do any other thing for him that he desired[:] he would often say I would be even with him.

John Lombard on a missing trowel

John Lombard saith upon oath March 17, 1650 that one day the last summer he set a trowel and a stick which he used to hold to his clay when he daubed: on the ground just without his door: after this two Indians came in and also presently went away again, then I also went out to look for my trowel: and there was my said stick but my trowel was gone: I and my wife sought for it very narrowly both in that place and also within the house and could not find it: But about two days after as Hugh Parsons was at the door of my house I saw the said two Indians and I called them to ask them for my trowel: said Hugh Parsons what do you want I said they have stolen my trowel: said Hugh Parsons look here it is and there it was in the very place where I laid it[.] I did not see him lay it there but I do really think it came there by witchcraft.

Hugh Parsons answered that he cannot remember that he laid it there. John Lombard saith that the reason why he did not ask him how it came there, was because he had been at Hugh Parsons's but the day before to borrow a trowel: to make an end of his daubing for that trowel he had left was Goodman Lancton's. Hugh Parsons at this stood dumb and answered no more.

John Mathews testifies about Mrs. Parsons's suspicions

John Mathews saith upon oath February 27, 1650 that a little before the trial with the Widow Marshfield, which was about May 1649 being in talk with Mary Parsons about witches she said to me that her husband was a witch: I asked her how she knew it, she said the devil came to him in the night at the bed and sucked him one night and made him cry out one time, she could not tell what it should be else but the devil[.] She said also that her husband was often tormented in his bowels and cried out as though he were pricked with pins and daggers and I know not what else it should be unless it were the devil that should torment him so.

March 3, 1650. Thomas Merick the constable saith upon oath that this last night towards morning Hugh Parsons lying by the fireside said to him two several times Good[man] now come and lance my belly for I am in lamentable pain or torment[.] I said to him if you will go forth to ease yourself I'll take off the chains and let you go: he said, no I have no need that way.

Hugh Parsons answer[ed] March 18 that he had a pain in his belly but did not speak of lancing it.

Sarah, the wife of Thomas Merick stood forth and testified that all that her husband had testified was true.

Mary Parsons on the devil, and her fantasies of witch meetings

April 3d, 1651. Thomas Cooper saith upon oath that being appointed to watch Mary Parsons about mid-March last among other things she told me that she was now hampered for relating so much as she had done against her husband at Mr. Pynchon's[.] But said she if that dumb dog could but have spoken it would have been better with me than it is: but said she if I might but speak with him before Mr. Pynchon face to face I would make that dumb dog to speak. I said to her why do you speak so of your husband me thinks if he were a witch there would some apparent sign or mark of it appear upon his body for they say witches have teats upon some part or other of their body, but as far as I hear there is not any such apparent thing upon his body. She answered it is not always so: but said she why do I say so, I have no skill in witchery: but said she why may it not be with him as it was with me that night that I was at Goodman Ashley's: the devil may come into his body only like a wind and so go forth again, for so the devil told me that night (for I think I should have been a witch afore now but that I was afraid to see the devil lest he should fright me)[.] But the devil told me that I should not fear that, I will not come in any apparition, but only come into the body like a wind and trouble thee a little while, and presently go forth again: and so I consented and that night I was with my husband and Goodwife Merick and Besse Sewell in Goodman Stebbins his lot and we were sometimes like cats and sometimes in our own shape, and we were applauding for some good cheer and they made me to go barefoot and make the fires because I had declared so much at Mr. Pynchon's.

Hugh Parsons is told that his wife is his chief accuser

April 7, 1651. Jonathan Taylor saith upon oath that in the day that Mary Parsons was first examined Hugh Parsons came to me to Merick's barn and desired to ask me a question and to tell him who were his accusers: I said I cannot tell: said he why do you say so you can tell I know you can tell[.] Was it ever known said he that a man should be accused and not know his accusers: tell me who they are, for whatever you tell me shall be as in your own breast, I said I wonder you are so earnest with me to tell you, you will know soon enough, I will not tell you anything, but said I I believe your wife will be your biggest accuser: at this speech he saw his wife go by to be examined, then said he it is like I shall be examined now.

Jonathan Taylor describes an enchanted beer tap

At night when I was ready to go home I asked Goody Merick for some beer, she said go down into the cellar and draw it so I did, but could not wring out the tap with all the strength I had, then I took a piece of an inch board and knocked the tap on each side to loosen it and then I tried to wring it out again with my hand till the blood started in my hand with wringing at it and yet I could not get it out: I came up and told Goody Merick and she laughed at me and said, I am persuaded I will fetch it out with my little finger: I told her it was impossible, then she said light a candle and go see: so I lighted a candle and she and Hugh Parsons went with me, and as soon as ever she touched it the tap came out[.] I said to her what are you a witch (though I did not think so) but I do verily believe it could not have been so except it were bewitched. After we were come up she said let me see your hand, then said she I confess your hand is very tender, and she said to Hugh Parsons the blood stands in his hand: But I would not have you think it was by witchery, for I think the least child in the house might have got it out.

Attacked by snakes

After I came home and when I was a bed there was a light in the room as if it had been daylight: I was amazed to see such a light: I thought it could not be day: I sat up in the bed to see if it were day or no: and as I looked over the bed I saw three snakes on the floor, and I was in a maze to see them: I [thought it] strange that snakes should be abroad at this time of the year: two of them were great ones the other was a little one with blackish and yellow streaks: and the little one came to the bed side and got up upon the bed[;] with that I struck it down with my hand: it came up again and I struck it down again: then I began to fear that if my wife should see them, being then very near her time, it would half undo her with fear: therefore I did not wake her, but lay down again: and then I thought thus let God do what he will: and as soon as I was laid down the said snake ran up a third time and hit me on the forehead which pricked like a needle[;] then I heard a voice that said, death, and that voice was like Hugh Parsons's voice to my best apprehension[;] and now I was a little revived in spirit and I said death: that is a lie it was never known that such a snake killed a man: then it was dark again: and I was taken with such a strange shaking as if every limb had been pulled in pieces: then my wife awaked and she said husband what ail you that you shake so, are you cold: no said I, I am hot enough, but I am very ill, she said shall I rise and warm you some clothes, I said no: but this extremity continued all night as if one limb had been rent from another, and in the morning she arose and called in some neighbors: this was on Friday night and I was held so till Tuesday morning, as if I had been rent in pieces[;] one fit began at my forehead where the snake bit me and ended at my knees, and then the next time it began at my knees and ended at my forehead and in this order it continued all the foresaid time.

Tuesday being a day of humiliation[4] I said to my wife though I be ill yet I will go thither[;] I am persuaded I shall be better and so I was, but yet I have been troubled with gripping pains ever since, and am not after my former usual manner.

Mary Parsons explains the snakes and the voice

April 7, 1651. Jonathan Taylor saith upon oath that two nights before Mary Parsons was carried into the Bay[5] I watched her: she said I have two things to say to you: one is I forgive you the wrong you have done me: the other is about the three snakes that you saw: they were three witches said she: I asked who they were, she said one was my husband[.] I asked her who were the other[s], she said I have pointed at them already: but you will not believe me, I am counted but as a dreamer: but when this dreamer is hanged, then remember what I said to you: the town will not be clear yet: then said she if you had believed the voice that spake to you, you had died: but seeing you spake to it and resisted it, it had not power to kill you: for you do not know how my husband hath threatened you.

All sworn in court May 13.

Additional testimony about the pudding

February 25, 1650. George Lancton saith on oath that his wife made a pudding in a bag and because my wife had the child I took it and put it out of the bag at dinner this day fortnight (which was the 11 of February) and as it slipped out of the bag it fell into two pieces lengthwise and in appearance it was cut straight along as smooth as if it had been cut with a knife: It was cut straight along almost the whole length, it lacked but a very little.

Hannah the wife of George Lancton doth upon oath concur with her husband in the said testimony.

February 21, 1650. George Lancton and Hannah his wife do jointly testify upon oath, that they had another pudding in the same bag that was cut lengthwise like unto the former, as smooth in appearance as any could cut it with a knife, namely one slice all along the side of the pudding wanting but a very little from end to end.

Also Hannah the wife of George Lancton saith on oath a neighbor came in and she showed to him how the pudding was cut: and that neighbor took a piece of it and threw it into the fire: and she saith that about an hour after perhaps a little more she heard one mutter and mumble at the door, then she asked Goody Sewell, who was then at her house (and nearer the door) who it was, she said it was Hugh Parsons, and that he asked whether Goodman Lancton were at home or no, I said no, and so he went away but left not his errand, neither did he ever since come to signify his errand.

Hannah Lancton sworn in court May 13.

February 23, 1650. George Lancton and Hannah his wife jointly testify upon oath that they had another pudding in the former bag that was cut lengthwise and as it was slipped out of the bag it fell into three parts: one piece being cut all along on the one side and two pieces all along on the other side: then they sent for some neighbors to see it: Roger Pritchard testified upon oath that he saw the said pudding and it seemed to him to be cut all the three pieces as evident and as plain to him as that which George Lancton cut with his knife.

These testimonies were all taken upon oath before me

William Pynchon.

Samuel Marshfield on Hugh's challenging the judgment against his wife

March 12, [*inserted above:* 18, 22] 1650. Samuel Marshfield saith upon oath that when Hugh Parsons came to pay the 24 bushels of Indian [corn] to my mother for the discharge of the action of slander against Mary Parsons that he desired my mother to abate 20s, but my mother said she would not abate because she heard that he had said the witnesses gave in a false testimony[.] Hugh Parsons replied well if you will not it had been as good you had it will be but as wild fire in this house and as a moth in your garment and it will do you no good I'll warrant it, and make account it is but lent you: this corn was paid in winter was 12 months and the spring after my sister Sara was taken with strange fits at times but never so bad as when Mr. Moxon's children were taken.

Sworn in court.

March 22, 1650. The Widow Marshfield testifies upon oath that when Hugh came to tender the said corn he said I hear that you will abate 20s of the money[.] I told him I would not abate anything because I heard that his wife had said the witnesses had taken a false oath: then said he if you will not abate, it shall be but as lent it shall do you no good, it shall be but as wild fire in your house and as a moth in your clothes, and these threatening speeches he uttered with much anger: and shortly after in the spring about May my daughter began to be taken with her fits of witchcraft.

John Lombard saith upon oath March 17 and 22, 1650 that I have heard Hugh Parsons and his wife also say that the corn which they paid to the Widow Marshfield for the slander would do her no good, and that it had been better she had never taken it[.] I have heard both her and him say so several times and I have often heard him say when he hath been displeased with anybody that he would be even with them for it.

Hugh Parsons being present answered not, but at last he asked when did I give such threatening words[?] It was told him when his corn was paid in.

Hugh Parsons said he did not remember that he gave such threatening word[s]: he said that in justice the corn was due to her: but because we apprehended my wife was falsely accused that was the reason of my speeches.

Mary Parsons also said that when her husband came home he told her what speeches he had used to the Widow Marshfield namely according to the testimonies she said it might well be so for she was falsely accused.

Thomas Miller on his wife's fits and accusing Hugh Parsons

March 18, 1650. Thomas Miller testifies upon oath (Hugh Parsons being present) that my wife being in one of her fits March 17, 1650 she said thus[:] get thee gone Hugh Parsons get thee gone, if thou wilt not go I will go to Mr. Pynchon and he shall have thee away.

Miles Morgan and Prudence his wife and Griffith Jones being all present do testify [to] the said speech: upon their oaths.

Then all the aforesaid persons: and Frances Pepper do testify upon oath that it is an usual thing with Goody Miller in her fits to use the word Sirra and thou witch.

More about Sara Miller's fits

Prudence Morgan saith upon oath that the 27 of March 1651 Sara Miller was at her house, and then between her fits she said, look you there is a man, at Goodman Cooper's barn, I said no there is no man there that I can see, she said you might see him if you would[.] But now he is gone said she: then she fell into a fit: and after she came to herself she said look you there he is, I said to her who is it, she said it is one in a red waistcoat and a lined cap[.] It is like Hugh Parsons[;] then said she he points his finger at me he would have me come to him: But Hugh Parsons was gone into the Bay the Monday before: but he used to wear a red waistcoat and a lined cap.

Samuel Marshfield saith upon oath that he came into Goody Morgan's house the day aforesaid: and as soon as Sara Miller came to herself out of her fit she said look you there he is: Goody Morgan asked her who it was, she said one in a red waistcoat and a lined cap: It is like Hugh Parsons: and said she he pointed his finger at me, he would have me come to him[.] I said to her there is nobody there that I can see: she said yes there he is 2 or 3 times over but there was nobody there that we could discover, though she did often affirm it.

Sworn in court.

Ann Stebbins in her fits accuses Hugh Parsons

March 18, 1650. John Stebbins testifies upon oath (Hugh Parsons being present): that as my wife was entering into one of her fits she looked up the chimney[.] I asked her what she looked at, and observing her eye fixed on something, asked her again (for she did not answer at first) what she looked on, and she said with a gesture of strange wonderment O[h] dear there hangs Hugh Parsons upon the pole (for there stood a small pole upright in the chimney corner), and then she gave a start backward and said Oh he will fall upon me: and at that instant she fell down into her fit.

Rowland Stebbins being present doth also testify the same upon oath.

William Brooks testifies upon oath March 18, 1650 that the same day that Hugh Parsons was apprehended and about the same time of the day that the constable brought him along by the door of Goody Stebbins's she was first taken with her fits and cried Ah Witch Ah Witch just as he was passing by the gate.

Hugh Parsons is asked whether his wife is a witch

Hugh Parsons at his examination March 1, 1650 being asked whether he thought there was not some witchcraft in the distemper of Mr. Moxon's children said I question not but there is witchcraft in it: but I wish the saddle may be set upon the right horse. Being demanded who was the right horse, and whether he knew of anybody else, he said no, I am clear for myself neither do I suspect any other. Being asked whether he had any grounds to suspect his wife: he answered no, I do not know that ever I had any such thought of her.

March 22, 1650. Jonathan Taylor saith upon oath that the same day that Mary Parsons went to be examined to Mr. Pynchon's: Hugh Parsons came to me to Merick's barn and said that he had often been afraid that his wife was a witch: and her examination was the day before his. Jonathan Taylor also saith upon oath that Hugh Parsons told him that he hath so far suspected his wife to be a witch, that he would have searched her, and she resisted for she told him it was an immodest thing.

Threatening speeches by Hugh Parsons

March 13, 1650. William Branch saith upon oath that he hath often heard Hugh Parsons say when he is displeased with anybody I do not question but I shall be even with him at one time or other: I remember he said so of Goodman Bridgman upon the difference that was between them about a tree: and I heard him say he would fit John Mathews speaking about the bargain of bricks.

Jonathan Taylor saith upon oath March 21, 1650. That when I was at the house of Hugh Parsons this winter and he told me that he had been at Mr. Pynchon's to get as much whiteleather as to make a cap for a flail and he was willing. But Simon would not let him have any: it had been as good said he he had, he shall get nothing by it. I will be even with him. Mary Parsons said husband why do you threaten the fellow so, it is like he was busy: he answered again if Goodman Cooley or anyone else that he had liked had come he should have had it: But I'll remember him.

Deposed before the court 17: 4 month 1651.

Edward Rawson Secretary.

All the testimonies thus far taken upon oath before me.

William Pynchon.

Simon Beamon describes strange events

May 20, 1651. The deposition of Simon Beamon on oath: This deponent saith that about February last Hugh Parsons came to him in his master's name for a piece of whiteleather, to make a cap for a flail, and that he having his horses then in the cart, and going out with them into the woods, told him he could not now stay to give it him, but another time he would. Now the same day after, he being loaden with a piece of timber under the cart and coming home, the horses set a running suddenly as if they were scared, and yet he saw nothing that should scare them. And as he held back the thillhorse[6] to stay them, he was beaten down with the cart, and if in his fall he had not put off the thillhorse with a kick of his foot, the cart wheel had run over him, it went over part of his jacket and close to his body. And one of the wheels ran over a great stub of pine 2 foot and half high at least, and yet the cart did not overturn. I thought there was some mischief in it from Hugh Parsons, for my horses had often gone that road, and never did the like before nor ever since.

Deposed before the court 17 4 month 1651.

Edward Rawson Secretary.

This deponent also saith upon oath, that about the end of last summer he being at the mill to fetch home meal: Hugh Parsons being there desired him to carry home a bag of meal for him. But he refusing to do it, Hugh Parsons was offended at his refusal: And when he was gone about 6 rod[s] from the mill, his horse being a gentle quiet horse, he fell down from the horse and the meal upon him. He laid his meal on the horse again, got up and was well settled and being gone about 2 or 3 rod[s] further he fell down again and the meal upon him, and yet the horse never started to occasion it. He laid up his sack again the third time and got up, and when he was well settled and gone a rod or two further, he fell down again and the sack upon him and yet the horse stood quietly in his place and the fourth time he laid it up and came away.

Testified upon oath before me Henry Smith.

Deposed before the court, 17 4 month 1651.

Edward Rawson Secretary.

William Branch sees an apparition and hears a voice

William Branch saith upon oath March 13, 1650 that about 2 years since when I lived in town, and when I went to bed about two hours within night and before I was asleep there was a light all over the chamber like [a] fire, and there came a thing upon me like a little boy, with a face as red as fire and put his hand under my chin as I apprehended: and I felt something like scalding water on my back and then I heard a voice saying It is done, It is done, then I waked my wife and told her of it and I have been ill ever since[.] I have thought Hugh Parsons to be naught and have been troubled that he hath made so many [ ] errands to my house for several things: and yet I could not tell how to deny him what he desired.

William Branch saith upon oath that at summer was twelve months,

I went to the Long Meadow, and as I was going before Hugh Parsons's door I was taken with such a strange stiffness in my two thighs, as if two stakes had been bound to my two thighs: so that I was faint to thrust myself forward with great difficulty: and this stiffness continued all that day[:] after this I fell into such a distemper of burning heat in the bottoms of my feet, that I never had the like before, and this heat in the bottoms of my feet continued near 12 months ere I was well[.] I thought then it was some work of witchcraft (from him) and so I think to this day.

These last two testimonies were taken upon oath before me

William Pynchon.

Testimonies about Sara Miller and Ann Stebbins, against Hugh Parsons. Taken upon oath before me

William Pynchon.

Jonathan Taylor describes a quarrel, and a missing boy

Jonathan Taylor on oath saith sometime this winter on a night a pair of good Mr. Mathews's pails fell down with a noise and going out presently to see the occasion thereof could not perceive anything[;] but going into his house again it being very dark Hugh Parsons was at his back his hand on his door as soon as his was of[f] he bidding him sit down which he did[.] Parsons saying Goodman Cooley's boy Nothing but beat my calf. His master will take no order with him but I will: anon after Goody Cooley came and inquired after her boy whether this deponent had seen him he telling her no: she replied I sent him to Goodman Mathew a good whiles since and cannot tell what is become of him and desired him this deponent to help her look [for] him which he did in all the hay mows and outhouses with hooping and halloing for him but could not find him nor hear of him: at last they gave over looking [for] him, and this deponent inquired of the said Goody Cooley whether Hugh Parsons had not met him and took order with him as he threatened him for beating his calf: and after they were parted a while the boy came home, and his dame asking him where he had been he said in a great cellar and was carried headlong into it, Hugh Parsons going before him and fell down [with] me there and afterward he [*torn*] into it.

1. Samel bricks are "half-burnt" (*OED*) and therefore possibly defective.
2. A striking illustration of oral lore; the reference is to John and Joan Carrington, who were executed in 1651.
3. Henry Smith, a Springfield justice of the peace, lost two daughters in June 1648.
4. A fast day.

5. "The Bay," or Massachusetts-Bay, the name used for the area of original settlement around Boston.
6. The shaft or wheel horse (*OED*).
Source: Pynchon Notebook, Rare Books and Manuscripts, NYPL. Printed in Samuel G. Drake, *Annals of Witchcraft in New England* (1869; repr. New York, 1972), pp. 219–58, with useful identifications of the witnesses. The notebook was probably put together for the trial of Hugh Parsons in Boston in 1652.

The missing trowel

The testimony of Joanna the wife of John Lombard taken on oath May 22, 1651. This deponent saith that her husband the last summer being daubing his house laid down his trowel at the door of his house on the sill and going to fetch more mortar, afterward came to fetch his trowel where he laid it, and it was gone. Both she and her husband sought it all over their house but could not find it. The third day after Hugh Parsons came to our house, and he and her husband were standing at the door at which time an Indian passed by that had been in the house the day that the trowel was lost, who called to the Indian to come to him, intending to ask him if he had not stole the trowel. Hugh Parsons said why do you call him—her husband said, to inquire of him if he had not stole my trowel. Said Hugh Parsons, here is the trowel, and there it was on the door sill where her husband had laid it, but it was not to be seen there formerly.

Henry Smith.

Source: Stanley Waters, "Witchcraft in Springfield, Mass.," *NEHGR 35* (1881), pp. 152–53.

A quarrel, and a cow's milk changes color

The testimony of Alexander Edwards taken on oath May 26, 1651. This deponent saith that he took good notice that his cow lessened her milk on a sudden, and from 3 quarts she gave not above one quart at most: also that her milk was of a very odd color in all her teats, yellowish and somewhat bloody as if it were festered and it continued so about a week. This fell out to the cow the next meal after that his wife had denied Hugh Parsons milk, and that the cow ailed nothing to any of their apprehensions and grew well again and came to her milk without any means used.

Henry Smith.

The testimony of Richard Exell taken on oath May 20th 1651.

Richard Exell affirmeth that he heard Hugh Parsons ask Sarah Edwards for milk, and she told him she could spare him no more milk, she would pay him what else she owed him some other way. He replied he had rather have what was due to him in milk. The next meal Richard Exell saw the milk the cow gave, and it was far differing from the usual color of milk it was very yellow and unfit for any to eat, and it was not above a quart that the cow gave if it were so much. All testified on oath before me Henry Smith.

Source: Stanley Waters, "Witchcraft in Springfield, Mass.," *NEHGR 35* (1881), p. 153.

The indictment and jury verdict

The grand jury for this commonwealth present Hugh Parsons of Springfield not having the fear of God before his eyes in or about March last and divers times before and since at Springfield aforesaid (as they conceived) had familiar and wicked converse with the devil and did use divers devilish practices and witchcraft to the hurt of divers persons as by several witnesses and circumstances doth appear and do leave him to the court for his further trial for his life.

The jury of life and death finds against Hugh Parsons by the testimony of such as appeared in court, so much as gives them ground not to clear him, but considered with the testimonies of divers that are at Springfield, whose testimonies were only sent in writing as also the confession of Mary Parsons and the impeachment of some of the bewitched persons of the said Hugh Parsons which if the General Court make the confession of Mary Parsons and the impeachment of the bewitched persons or other of them and the testimonies that are in writing but appeared not in person authentic testimonies according to law then the jury finds the said Hugh Parsons guilty of the sin of witchcraft. [May 12, 1652.]

Source: Pynchon Notebook, Rare Books and Manuscripts, NYPL. Printed in Drake, *Annals of Witchcraft*, pp. 68–69.

The magistrates review the case and acquit Hugh Parsons

The magistrates not consenting to the verdict of the jury in [the] Parsons case, the case coming legally to the General Court for issue, the court on perusal of the evidences brought in against him for witchcraft, do judge that he is not legally guilty of witchcraft, and so not to die by our law. May 27, 1652.

Source: *Mass. Bay Recs., 3*, p. 273.

Whereas Hugh Parsons, of Springfield, was arraigned and tried at a Court of Assistants, held at Boston, May 12, 1652, for not having the fear of God before his eyes, but being seduced by the instigation of the devil, in March, 1651, and divers times before and since, at Springfield, as was conceived, had familiar and wicked converse with the devil, and hath used diverse devilish practices, or witchcrafts, to the hurt of diverse persons, as by several witnesses and circumstances appeared, was left by the grand jury for further trial for his life.

The jury of trials found him guilty. The magistrates not consenting to the verdict of the jury, the case came legally to the General Court. The General Court, after the prisoner was called to the bar for trial of his life, perusing and considering the evidences brought in against the said Hugh Parsons, accused for witchcraft, they judged he was not legally guilty of witchcraft, and so not to die by law. June 1, 1652.

Source: *Mass. Bay Recs., 4,* pt. 1, p. 96.

3. Suspicion:
A Widow's Resistance
(1653–1655)

▲

Elizabeth Godman

Elizabeth Godman, a widow, lived in New Haven, Connecticut, in the house of Stephen Goodyear. He was deputy governor of New Haven Colony, a political jurisdiction that encompassed several of the early settlements along the Connecticut coastline. Elizabeth was not a member of the church. She left an estate of £200 when she died in 1660. In 1653, and again in 1655, she was brought before the court on suspicion of witchcraft; initially she had charged that she was being defamed. The court records are unusual in preserving so explicitly someone's resistance to the suspicions of her neighbors; we have encountered similar resistance in Hugh Parsons, and will again in William Morse's defense of his wife. The suspicions leveled against her were the classic ones of causing the death or sickness of animals and people, and of having magical abilities, such as knowing what others had said. Some of Mrs. Godman's accusers had refused to aid her, and their response when misfortune struck is also classic.

At one point in the proceedings Goodyear complained that Mrs. Godman had sufficient property, a statement that contrasts oddly with her apparent practice of going from house to house to buy or sell or beg.[1] The court records are full of references to the lore of witches and witchcraft; Elizabeth seems to have talked about witches and their situation. Religion is also present; one witness, Goodwife Larrimore, quoted a sermon by the leading minister of

New Haven Colony, John Davenport, and in other testimony Eliza-
beth Godman is quoted as saying she had "spiritual armor."

1. Carol Karlsen offers a thoughtful evaluation of her economic status in *The*
Devil in the Shape of a Woman: Witchcraft in Colonial New England (New
York, 1987), p. 297 n. 6. Stephen Goodyear died in 1658 in a shipwreck returning to England. His debts, which far exceeded the value of his estate,
included the sum of £152 owed to Mrs. Godman. *New Haven Col. Recs.*, p. 306.

The court hears Mrs. Godman's complaint, and others express their suspicions

At a Court of Magistrates held at New Haven
for the jurisdiction, August 4, 1653.

Mrs. Elizabeth Godman accused Goodwife Larrimore that one time
when she saw her come in at Goodman Whitnell's she said so soon as
as she saw her she thought of a witch. Goodwife Larrimore said that
one time she had spoken to that purpose at Mr. Hooke's,[1] and her
ground was because Mr. Davenport about that time had occasion in
his ministry to speak of witches, and showed that a froward discontented frame of spirit was a subject fit for the devil to work upon in
that way, and she looked upon Mrs. Godman to be of such a frame of
spirit, but for saying so at Goodman Whitnell's she denies it. Mrs. Godman said, Goodman Whitnell's maid can testify it. The maid was sent,
and when she came she said she heard Mrs. Godman and Goodwife
Larrimore a talking, and she thinks she heard Goodwife Larrimore
say she thought of a witch in the Bay[2] when she see[s] Mrs. Godman.
Goodwife Larrimore further said that Mrs. Godman had her before
the Governor for this, and the Governor asked her if she thought Mrs.
Godman was a witch, and she answered no.

Mrs. Godman was told she hath warned to the court divers persons,
viz.: Mr. Goodyear, Mrs. Goodyear, Mr. Hooke, Mrs. Hooke, Mrs. Atwater, Hannah and Elizabeth Lamberton, Goodwife Larrimore, Goodwife Thorpe, etc., and was asked what she hath to charge them with,
she said they had given out speeches that made folks think she was a
witch, and first she charged Mrs. Atwater to be the cause of all, and to
clear things desired a writing might be read which was taken in way
of examination before the magistrate (and is hereafter entered),
wherein sundry things concerning Mrs. Atwater is specified which
were now more fully spoken to, and she further said that Mrs. Atwater
had said that she thought she was a witch and that Hobbamocke[3] was
her husband, but could prove nothing, though she was told that she
was beforehand warned to prepare her witnesses ready, which she
hath not done, if she have any. After sundry of the passages in the

writing were read, she was asked if these things did not give just ground of suspicion to all that heard them that she was a witch. She confessed they did, but said if she spake such things as is in Mr. Hooke's relation she was not herself. She was told she need not say, if she spake them, for she did at at the Governor's before many witnesses confess them all as her words, though she made the same excuse that she was not in a right mind; but Mrs. Hooke now testified she was in a sober frame and spake in a deliberate way, as ordinarily she is at other times.

Mrs. Godman reacts to hearing a chapter of the Bible read

Beside what is in the paper, Mrs. Godman was remembered of a passage spoken of at the Governor's about Mr. Goodyear's falling into a swonding[4] fit after he had spoken something one night in the exposition of a chapter, which she (being present) liked not but said it was against her, and as soon as Mr. Goodyear had done duties she flung out of the room in a discontented way and cast a fierce look upon Mr. Goodyear as she went out, and immediately Mr. Goodyear (though well before) fell into a swond, and beside her notorious lying in this business, for being asked how she came to know this, she said she was present, yet Mr. Goodyear, Mrs. Goodyear, Hannah and Elizabeth Lamberton all affirm she was not in the room but gone up into the chamber.

After the agitation of these things the court declared to Mrs. Godman, as their judgment and sentence in this case, that she hath unjustly called hither the several persons before named, being she can prove nothing against them, and that her carriage doth justly render her suspicious of witchcraft, which she herself in so many words confesseth, therefore the court wisheth her to look to her carriage hereafter, for if further proof come, these passages will not be forgotten, and therefore gave her charge not to go in an offensive way to folks' houses in a railing manner as it seems she hath done, but that she keep her place and meddle with her own business.

Mrs. Godman is described as malicious, and being fascinated with witches

The examination of Elizabeth Godman, May 21, 1653.

Elizabeth Godman made complaint of Mr. Goodyear, Mrs. Goodyear, Mr. Hooke, Mrs. Hooke, Mrs. Bishop, Mrs. Atwater, Hannah and Elizabeth Lamberton, and Mary Miles, Mrs. Atwater's maid, that they have suspected her for a witch; she was now asked what she had against Mr. Hooke and Mrs. Hooke; she said she heard they had something against her about their son. Mr. Hooke said he was not without fears, and he had reasons for it; first he said it wrought suspicion in his mind because she was shut out at Mr. Atwater's upon suspicion, and he was troubled in his sleep about witches when his boy was sick, which was in a very strange manner, and he looked upon her as a malicious one, and prepared to that mischief, and she would be often speaking about witches and rather justify them than condemn them; she said why do they provoke them, why do they not let them come into the church. Another time she was speaking of witches without any occasion given her, and said if they accused her for a witch she would have them to the Governor, she would trounce them. Another time she was saying she had some thoughts, what if the devil should come to suck her, and she resolved he should not suck her.

Preternatural knowledge of events and speeches

Mr. Hooke said another thing which strengthened his fears was, that whatever was done in the church meetings she would know it presently, and his son John was vexed at it, and she being then questioned about it said some of the members told her, she was asked who, and she instanced Brother Whitnell, concerning the agreement for catechizing, and some sisters she said told her something, but named none nor what they told her. Jane Hooke said Mrs. Elizabeth could tell sundry things that was done at the church meeting before meeting was done, as about Delaware Bay, about Mr. Cheever,[5] and about Goodman Lamson and some other things. Time, Mr. Hooke's Indian, said in church meeting time she would go out and come in again and tell them what was done at meeting. Time asking her who told, she answered plainly she would not tell, then Time said did not the devil tell you. She was also accused for talking and muttering to herself; testified by Henry Boutle and some others. Time said she heard her one time talking to herself, and she said to her, who talk you to, she said, to you; Time said you talk to the devil, but she made nothing of it.

Mr. Hooke associates his son's sickness with Elizabeth Godman

Mr. Hooke further said, that he hath heard that they that are addicted that way would hardly be kept away from the houses where they do mischief, and so it was with her when his boy was sick, she would not be kept away from him, nor got away when she was there, and one time Mrs. Hooke bid her go away, and thrust her from the boy, but she turned again and said she would look on him. Mrs. Goodyear said that one time she questioned with Elizabeth Godman about the boy's sickness, and said what think you of him, is he not strangely handled, she replied, what, do you think he is bewitched; Mrs. Goodyear said nay I will keep my thoughts to myself, but in time God will discover.

It was also said that it is suspicious that she hath put the boy's sickness upon some other cause, as that he had turned his brains with sliding, and said the boy would be well again, though he was handled in such a strange manner as the doctor said he had not met with the like. Mr. Goodyear asked her if she was not the cause of his disease, she denied it, but in such a way as if she could scarce deny it.

Other illnesses she may have caused

Mr. Hooke further said, that when Mr. Bishop was married, Mrs. Godman came to his house much troubled, so as he thought it might be from some affection to him, and he asked her, she said yes; now it is suspicious that so soon as they were contracted Mrs. Bishop fell into very strange fits which hath continued at times ever since, and much suspicion there is that she hath been the cause of the loss of Mrs. Bishop's children, for she could tell when Mrs. Bishop was to be brought to bed, and hath given out that she kills her children with longing, because she longs for everything she sees, which Mrs. Bishop denies; and being required to give an instance, she said Mrs. Hooke said Mrs. Bishop longed for some pease, but that made against her when Mrs. Hooke was spoken with, and Jane Hooke said that Mrs. Godman said to her Mrs. Bishop was much given to longing, and that was the reason she lost her children.

More strange actions and illnesses

Another thing suspicious is, that she could tell Mrs. Atwater had figs in her pocket when she saw none of them; to that she answered she smelt them, and could smell figs if she came in the room, near them that had them; yet at this time Mrs. Atwater had figs in her pocket and came near her, yet she smelled them not; also Mrs. Atwater said that Mrs. Godman could tell that they one time had pease porridge, when they could none of them tell how she came to know, and being asked she saith she see them on the table, and another time she saith she was there in the morning when the maid set them on. Further Mrs.

Atwater saith, that that night the figs was spoken of they had strangers to supper, and Mrs. Godman was at their house, she cut a sop and put [it?] in [the] pan; Betty Brewster called the maid to tell her and said she was about her works of darkness, and was suspicious of Mrs. Godman, and spake to her of it, and that night Betty Brewster was in a most miserable case, hearing a most dreadful noise which put her in great fear and trembling, which put her into such a sweat as she was all on a water when Mary Miles came to go to bed, who had fallen into a sleep by the fire which she used not to do, and in the morning she looked as one that had been almost dead. Mrs. Atwater said she told Mrs. Godman of sundry things which render[ed] her suspicious, and forwarned her of her house; she said she would have her to the court, Mrs. Atwater said very willingly; yet the next night she came thither again for beer.

Elizabeth Godman responds to the charges

Mrs. Godman accused Mr. Goodyear for calling her down when Mrs. Bishop was in a sore fit, to look upon her, and said he doubted all was not well with her, and that he feared she was a witch, but Mr. Goodyear denied that; upon this Mrs. Godman was exceeding angry and would have the servants called to witness, and bid George the Scotsman go ask his master who bewitched her for she was not well, and upon this presently Hannah Lamberton (being in the room) fell into a very sore fit in a very strange manner.

Mrs. Godman and Mrs. Goodyear share witch lore

Mrs. Godman said the reason of her saying as before was because Mrs. Goodyear a little before said they was bewitched. Mrs. Goodyear said she said not so, but she and her daughter went to Mrs. Godman and said some thought they were bewitched, and said here is a poor weak woman (meaning Mrs. Bishop), what think you of her, some have thought she is bewitched; she laughed and said alas who should bewitch her, she had a cousin [who] was so; Mrs. Goodyear said, if there be any such persons, she was persuaded God would find them out and discover them, for, said she, I never knew a witch die in their bed; Mrs. Godman answered you mistake, for a great many die and go to the grave in an orderly way.

Another time Mrs. Goodyear said to her, Mrs. Elizabeth what think you of my daughter's case; she replied what, do you think I have bewitched her; Mrs. Goodyear said if you be the party look to it, for they intend to have such as is suspected before the magistrate.

Elizabeth Godman denies that the devil sucked her

Mrs. Godman charged Hannah Lamberton that she said she lay for somewhat to suck her, when she came in hot one day and put off some clothes and lay upon the bed in her chamber. Hannah said she and her sister Elizabeth went up into the garret above her room, and looked down and said, look how she lies, she lies as if somebody was sucking her, and upon that she arose and said, yes, yes, so there is; after said Hannah, she hath something there, for there seemed as if something was under the clothes; Elizabeth said what have you there, she said nothing but the clothes, and both Hannah and Elizabeth say that Mrs. Godman threatened Hannah, and said let her look to it for God will bring it upon her own head, and about two days after, Hannah's fits began, and one night especially [she] had a dreadful fit, and was pinched, and heard a hideous noise, and was in a strange manner sweating and burning, and some time[s] cold and full of pain that she shrieked out.

Elizabeth Godman speaks to someone

Elizabeth Lamberton saith that one time the children came down and said Mrs. Godman was talking to herself and they were afraid, then she went up softly and heard her talk, what, will you fetch me some beer, will you go, will you go, and the like, and one morning about break of day Henry Boutle said he heard her talk to herself, as if somebody had lain with her.

The examination of Elizabeth Godman

May 24, 1653. Mrs. Godman being examined (Mr. Davenport being present), she was asked why she said Mrs. Bishop longed almost for everything she see[s], and when she could not have it, that was the cause of her fainting fits and the loss of her children; she said she heard something of Mrs. Hooke to that purpose, that she longed for pease, but Mrs. Hooke being sent for denied that ever she told her so, and Jane Hooke being present said Mrs. Godman told her that Mrs. Bishop was much given to longing and that was the reason she lost her children, and Hannah Lamberton said Mrs. Godman told her so also, and Mrs. Bishop said another woman in the town told her that she had heard Mrs. Godman say as much, so that she could not deny it; she was told she hath much inquired after the time of Mrs. Bishop's delivery of her children, and would speak of it so as Mrs. Goodyear and her daughters marveled how she could know, and Hannah Lamberton one time told her mother that Mrs. Godman kept her sister's count; she was asked the reason of this and of her saying Mrs. Bishop was so given to longing as it was a means to lose her children when it was not so; she said she could give no reason, then she was told it was a high slander upon Mrs. Bishop, she said she can say nothing but must lie under it.

Mrs. Godman is accused of predicting fainting fits

Mrs. Goodyear said when Mr. Atwater's kinswoman was married Mrs. Bishop was there, and the room being hot she was something faint, upon that Mrs. Godman said she would have many of these fainting fits after she was married, but she saith she remembers it not; she was told she hath also said that Mrs. Bishop hath had such fits of a child and Hannah Lamberton said she told her so, which thing is not; Mrs. Godman says she denies it not but she remembers it not; she was asked the reason why she should report these things if it were not to hide some other things which she would not have discovered, and to hide these fits, therefore give a reason; she said she cannot tell the reason.

A refusal to sell chickens, and the chickens die

June 16, 1653. Goodwife Thorpe complained that Mrs. Godman came to her house and asked to buy some chickens, she said she had none to sell, Mrs. Godman said will you give them all, so she went away, and she thought then that if this woman was naught as folks suspect, maybe she will smite my chickens, and quickly after one chicken died, and she remembered she had heard if they were bewitched they would consume within, and she opened it and it was consumed in the gizzard to water and worms, and divers others of them dropped, and now they are missing and it is likely dead, and she never saw either hen or chicken that was so consumed within with worms. Mrs. Godman said Goodwife Tichnor had a whole brood so, and Mrs. Hooke had some so, but for Mrs. Hooke's it was contradicted presently. This Goodwife Thorpe thought good to declare that it may be considered with other things.

1. William Hooke, minister in New Haven.
2. Massachusetts; the official name of the colony was Massachusetts-Bay.
3. Hobbammock, a manitou (spirit or "god") among the Native Americans of southern New England. In other cases (e.g., the depositions in the Hartford witch-

hunt of 1662) the colonists made the same associations between witchcraft, the devil, and the Native Americans. That the devil "resembles an Indian" was a motif of the Salem witch trials of 1692.
4. An archaic variation of *swound*, "a fainting fit."
5. Ezekiel Cheever, schoolmaster of New Haven; he was involved in a disciplinary hearing before the New Haven church in 1649.
Source: *New Haven Col. Recs., 2,* pp. 29–36.

Elizabeth Godman returns to court two years later

At a court held at New Haven August 7, 1655.

. . . Elizabeth Godman was called before the court, and told that she lies under suspicion for witchcraft, as she knows, the grounds of which were examined in a former court, and by herself confessed to be just grounds of suspicion, which passages were now read, and to these some more are since added, which are now to be declared.

Mr. Goodyear said that the last winter, upon occasion of God's afflicting hand upon the plantation by sickness, the private meeting where of he is had appointed to set a day apart to seek God: Elizabeth Godman desired she might be there; he told her she was under suspicion, and it would be offensive; she said she had great need of it, for she was exercised with many temptations, and saw strange apparitions, and lights about her bed, and strange sights which affrighted her: some of his family said if she was afraid they would work with her in the day and lie with her in the night, but she refused and was angry and said she would have none to be with her for she had her spiritual armor about her. She was asked the reason of this: she answered, she said so to Mr. Goodyear, but it was her fancy troubled her, and she would have none lie with her because her bed was weak: she was told that might have been mended: then she said she was not willing to have any of them with her, for if anything had fallen ill with them they would have said that she had been the cause.

Mrs. Godman is accused of harming cows

Goodwife Thorpe informed the court that concerning something about chickens she had formerly declared, which was now read, after which she one time had some speech with Mrs. Evance about this woman, and through the weakness of her faith she began to doubt that may be she would hurt her cows, and that day one of her cows fell sick in the herd, so as the keeper said he thought she would have died, but at night when she came into the yard was well and continued so, but would never give milk nor bring calf after that; therefore they bought another cow, that they might have some breed, but that cast calf also; after that they got another, and she continued well about a fortnight, but then began to pine away and would give no milk and would sweat so as she would be all of a water wherever she lay, without or within; then she thought there was something more than ordinary in it, and could not but think that she was bewitched; God helped her to examine herself, and to be humbled for her unbelief, and to seek him twice or thrice to deliver the beast, but upon the day that John Knight was executed[1] (having more freedom than ordinary) she sought God earnestly to resist the evil spirit, and if the beast was ill by that means he would deliver it, and presently the Lord answered and the beast was well and continues so. About a week after, she went by Mr. Goodyear's, and there was Elizabeth Godman pulling cherries in the street; she said, how doth Goody Thorpe? I am beholden to Goody Thorpe above all the women in the town: she would have had me to the gallows for a few chickens; and gnashed and grinned with her teeth in a strange manner, which she confesseth was true, but owned nothing about the cows.

Other passages there were about Goodwife Hodgkins churning and at Mr. Samuel Eaton's also, who after some discontent with her or something spoke of her have met with many hindrances in their way, and Goodwife Hodgkins said many times, but saith she cannot charge her with it.

Mr. Goodyear's daughter frightened in the night

Mr. Goodyear further declared that about three weeks ago he had a very great disturbance in his family in the night (Elizabeth Godman having been the day before much discontented because Mr. Goodyear warned her to provide her another place to live in) his daughter Sellevant, Hannah Goodyear, and Desire Lamberton lying together in the chamber under Elizabeth Godman; after they were in bed they heard her walk up and down and talk aloud, but could not tell what she said; then they heard her go down the stairs and come up again; they fell asleep, but were after awakened with a great fumbling at the chamber door, and something came into the chamber which fumbled at the other end of the room and about the trunk and among their shoes and at the beds head; it came nearer the bed and Hannah was afraid and called father, but he heard not, which made her more afraid: their clothes were pulled of[f] their bed by something two or three times; they held and something pulled, which frighted them so that Hannah Goodyear called her father so loud as was thought might be heard to the meetinghouse, but the noise was heard to Mr. Samuel Eaton's by them that watched with her:[2] so after a while Mr. Goodyear came and found them in a great fright: they lighted a candle and he went to Elizabeth Godman's chamber and asked her why she disturbed the family; she said, no, she was scared also and thought the house had been on fire, yet the next day she said in the family that she knew nothing till Mr. Goodyear came up, which she saith is true she heard the noise but knew not the cause till Mr. Goodyear came; and being asked why she went downstairs after she was gone up to bed, she said to light a candle to look for two grapes she had lost in the floor and feared the mice would play with them in the night and disturb the family, which reason [in] the court's apprehension renders her more suspicious.

Mrs. Godman is refused a drink of buttermilk, and animals die

Allen Ball informed the court that one time Elizabeth Godman came to his house and asked his wife for some buttermilk; she refused, and bid her be gone, she cared not for her company: she replied, what, you will save it for your pigs, but it will do them no good; and after this his pigs all but one died, one after another, but the cause he knows not. Another time she came into his yard: his wife asked what she came for; she said to see her calf: now they had a sucking calf, which they tied in the lot to a great post that lay on the ground, and the calf ran away with that post as if it had been a feather and ran among Indian corn and pulled up two hills and stood still: after[wards] he tied the calf to a long heavy rail, as much as he could well lift, and one time she came into the yard and looked on the calf and it set a running and drew the rail after it till it came to a fence and gave a great cry in a lowing way and stood still; and in the winter the calf died, do what he could, yet eat its meat well enough.

A quarrel is followed by strange events

Some other passages were spoken of about Mrs. Yale, that one time there being some words betwixt them, with which Elizabeth Godman was unsatisfied, the night following Mrs. Yale's things were thrown about the house in a strange manner; and one time being at Goodman Thorpe's, about weaving some cloth, in which something discontented her, and that night they had a great noise in their house, which much affrighted them, but they know not what it was.

These things being declared, the court told Elizabeth Godman that they have considered them, with her former miscarriages, and see cause to order that she be committed to prison, there to abide the court's pleasure, but because the matter is of weight, and the crime whereof she is suspected capital, therefore she is to answer it at the Court of Magistrates in October next.

1. See *New Haven Col. Recs., 2,* p. 138.
2. Mrs. Eaton, wife of Samuel Eaton, a magistrate in New Haven, was dying.
Source: *New Haven Town Recs., 1,* pp. 249–52.

The court releases her from prison

At a Court of Magistrates
. . . Elizabeth Godman was called and told that the court have considered her case according as things have been presented, and find the suspicion of her lewd miscarriages exceeding strong, for which she hath now been a prisoner since the last court, but considering her weakness and with respect to her health, they do now release her from the prison, but do order that she without any further warning and at her peril attend the Court of Magistrates the third Wednesday in October next to answer such things as shall be laid to her charge, and seeing Thomas Johnson is willing to receive her into his family, she hath liberty to remain there, but must not go up and down among neighbors to give offence, nor come to the contribution[1] as she hath formerly done, and that she pay the marshall for the charge and trouble he hath been at with her, during the time of her imprisonment. September 4, 1655.

1. The offering or collection in the church.
Source: *New Haven Town Recs., 1,* pp. 256–57.

She is still suspected of witchcraft

At a General Court held at New Haven for the jurisdiction, October 17, 1655.
. . . Elizabeth Godman was called before the court and told that upon grounds formerly declared, which stand upon record, she by her own confession remains under suspicion for witchcraft, and one more is now added, and that is, that one time this last summer, coming to Mr. Hooke's to beg some beer, was at first denied, but after, she was offered some by his daughter which stood ready drawn, but she refused it and would have some newly drawn, which she had, yet went away

in a muttering discontented manner, and after this, that night, though the beer was good and fresh, yet the next morning was hot, sour and ill tasted, yea so hot as the barrel was warm without side, and when they opened the bung it steamed forth; they brewed again and it was so also, and so continued four or five times, one after another.

She brought divers persons to the court that they might say something to clear her, and much time was spent in hearing them, but to little purpose, the grounds of suspicion remaining full as strong as before and she found full of lying, wherefore the court declared unto her that though the evidence is not sufficient as yet to take away her life, yet the suspicions are clear and many, which she cannot by all the means she hath used, free herself from, therefore she must forebear from going from house to house to give offence, and carry it orderly in the family where she is, which if she do not, she will cause the court to commit her to prison again, and that she do now presently upon her freedom give security for her good behavior; and she did now before the court engage fifty pound of her estate that is in Mr. Goodyear's hand, for her good behavior, which is further to be cleared next court, when Mr. Goodyear is at home.

Source: *New Haven Col. Recs., 2,* pp. 151-52.

Bond for good behavior

January 1, 1655/56: Mr. Goodyear did now engage for, and promise to secure to the jurisdiction fifty pound[s] which he hath in his hand of Elizabeth Godman's estate, which she engaged as security for her good behavior the last Court of Magistrates.

Source: *New Haven Town Recs., 1,* p. 264.

4. The High Price of Silence (1654)

▲

Goodwives Bassett (EXECUTED), Knapp (EXECUTED), and Mary Staples

A quarrel between Mary Staples of Fairfield, Connecticut, and a neighbor, Roger Ludlow, intensified when Ludlow told others that Mary "made a trade of lying" and was probably a witch.[1] Thomas Staples, Mary's husband, filed suit for defamation. The magistrates of New Haven Colony, of which Fairfield was part, took up the case in May 1654. At this trial, witnesses recalled the execution of Goodwife Knapp of Fairfield for witchcraft in 1653.[2] The depositions also include a passing reference to a third woman, Goodwife Bassett, who had been executed as a witch in 1651.

Roger Ludlow attempted to prove that Goodwife Knapp "came down from the" scaffold just before her execution and told him Mary Staples was a witch. He tried to make it seem suspicious that Mary had questioned whether Goody Knapp were properly convicted. Several women examined the dead woman once her body was brought down from the scaffold; the depositions show them disputing among themselves the presence of "witches teats." Mary Staples insisted that "here are no more teats than I myself have, or any other women." Apparently she changed her mind when a midwife pointed out certain marks. Nonetheless, Mary voiced a cogent scepticism. The scenes of women visiting Goody Knapp in jail and plead-

ing with her to confess are remarkably revealing of the pressure to name confederates—pressure that in the Salem witch-hunt of 1692 had disastrous consequences. The weight of the evidence suggests that Goodwife Knapp remained silent even though she knew of the rumor that Goodwife Bassett of Stratford, executed for witchcraft in 1651, had "said there was another witch in Fairfield." Her self-searching and her final resolution to be silent were notably religious.

Mary Staples had the support of the Reverend John Davenport, the leading minister in New Haven Colony, who testified on her behalf. The magistrates decided in favor of her husband's suit and fined Roger Ludlow £15. Yet a reputation for witchcraft lingered about Mrs. Staples, for in 1692 she was indicted for the crime, together with a daughter and granddaughter. These cases ended in acquittal.[3]

1. Ludlow had filed suit against Staples for slander and defamation in 1651, a suit he won. *Coll. CHS,* 22 (1928), pp. 86–87. He filed suit again in June 1654 for "false imprisonment" but failed to show up and was fined the costs; ibid., p. 127.
2. Goodwife Knapp has not otherwise been identified, and no other evidence seems to have survived.
3. John P. Demos, *Entertaining Satan: Witchcraft and the Culture of Early New England* (New York, 1982), p. 70.

The Trial of Goody Bassett

The Governor, Mr. Cullick and Mr. Clark are desired to go down to Stratford to keep court upon the trial of Goody Bassett for her life, and if the Governor cannot go, then Mr. Wells is to go in his room, May 15, 1651.

Source: *Col. Recs. Conn., 1,* p. 220.

A suit of defamation is heard

At a Court of Magistrates held at New Haven
for the Jurisdiction, May 29, 1654.
Thomas Staples of Fairfield, plaintiff.
Mr. Roger Ludlow late of Fairfield, defendant.

John Banks, attorney for Thomas Staples, declared, that Mr. Ludlow had defamed Thomas Staples's wife, in reporting to Mr. Davenport and Mrs. Davenport that she had laid herself under a new suspicion of being a witch, that she had caused Knapp's wife to be new searched after she was hanged, and when she saw the teats, said if they were the marks of a witch, then she was one, or she had such marks; secondly, Mr. Ludlow said Knapp's wife told him that Goodwife Staples was a witch; thirdly, that Mr. Ludlow hath slandered Goodwife Staples in saying that she made a trade of lying, or went on in a tract of lying, etc.

Ensign Bryan, attorney for Mr. Ludlow, desired the charge might be proved, which accordingly the plaintiff did, and first an attestation under Master Davenport's hand, containing the testimony of Master and Mistress Davenport, was presented and read; but the defendant desired what was testified and accepted for proof might be upon oath, upon which Mr. Davenport gave in as followeth, that he hoped the former attestation he wrote and sent to the court, being compared with Mr. Ludlow's letter, and Mr. Davenport's answer, would have satisfied concerning the truth of the particulars without his oath, but seeing Mr. Ludlow's attorney will not be so satisfied, and therefore the court requires his oath, and that he looks at an oath, in a case of necessity, for confirmation of truth, to end strife among men, as an ordinance of God, according to Hebrews 6:16, he thereupon declares as followeth,

The two Davenports testify

That Mr. Ludlow, sitting with him and his wife alone, and discoursing of the passages concerning Knapp's wife the witch, and her execution, said that she came down from the ladder (as he understood it), and desired to speak with him alone, and told him who was the witch spoken of; and so far as he remembers, he or his wife asked him who it was; he said she named Goodwife Staples; Mr. Davenport replied that he believed it was utterly untrue and spoken out of malice, or to that purpose; Mr. Ludlow answered that he hoped better of her, but said she was a foolish woman, and then told them a further story, how she tumbled the corpse of the witch up and down after her death, before sundry women, and spake to this effect, if these be the marks of a witch I am one, or I have such marks. Mr. Davenport utterly disliked the speech, not having heard anything from others in that particular, either for her or against her, and supposing Mr. Ludlow spake it upon such intelligence as satisfied him; and whereas Mr. Ludlow saith he required and they promised secrecy, he doth not remember that either he required or they promised it, and he doth rather believe the contrary, both because he told them that some did overhear what the witch said to him, and either had or would spread it abroad, and because he is careful not to make unlawful promises, and when he hath made a lawful promise he is, through the help of Christ, careful to keep it.

Mrs. Davenport saith, that Mr. Ludlow being at their house, and speaking about the execution of Knapp's wife (he being free in his speech), was telling several passages of her, and to the best of her remembrance said that Knapp's wife came down from the ladder to speak with him, and told him that Goodwife Staples was a witch, and that Mr. Davenport replied something on behalf of Goodwife Staples, but the words she remembers not; and something Mr. Ludlow spake, as some did or might overhear what she said to him, or words to that effect, and that she tumbled the dead body of Knapp's wife up and down and spake words to this purpose, that if these be the marks of a witch she was one, or had such marks; and concerning any promise of secrecy she remembers not.

Mr. Davenport and Mrs. Davenport affirmed upon oath, that the testimonies before written, as they properly belong to each, is the truth, according to their best knowledge and memory.

Mr. Davenport desired that in taking his oath to be thus understood, that as he takes his oath to give satisfaction to the court and Mr. Ludlow's attorney, in the matters attested betwixt Mr. Ludlow and Thomas Staples, so he limits his oath only to that part and not to the preface or conclusion, they being no part of the attestation and so his oath not required in them.

To the latter part of the declaration, the plaintiff produced the proof following.

Other witnesses say that Ludlow accused Staples of lying

Goodwife Sherwood of Fairfield affirmeth upon oath, that upon some debate betwixt Mr. Ludlow and Goodwife Staples, she heard Mr. Ludlow charge Goodwife Staples with a tract of lying, and that in discourse she had heard him so charge her several times.

John Tompson of Fairfield testifieth upon oath, that in discourse he hath heard Mr. Ludlow express himself more than once that Goodwife Staples went on in a tract of lying, and when Goodwife Staples hath desired Mr. Ludlow to convince her of telling one lie, he said she need not say so, for she went on in a tract of lying.

Goodwife Gould of Fairfield testifieth upon oath, that in a debate in the church with Mr. Ludlow, Goodwife Staples desired him to show her wherein she had told one lie, but Mr. Ludlow said she need not mention particulars, for she had gone on in a tract of lying.

The defense responds

Ensign Bryan was told, he sees how the plaintiff hath proved his charge, to which he might now answer; whereupon he presented several testimonies in writing upon oath, taken before Mr. Wells and Mr. Ludlow. The plaintiff objected that the writing presented was not that which was written from the witnesses by Mr. Ludlow himself, which he thought was not so fair proceeding as if another who was not interested had writt[en] them, but these are copies, yet not attested by the hand of any public officer to be true copies, yet the court caused them to be read that they might make such use of them as they should see cause, which testimonies are as followeth.

Hester Ward describes Indian gods

May 13, 1654. Hester Ward, wife of Andrew Ward, being sworn deposeth, that about a day after that Goodwife Knapp was condemned for a witch, she going to the prison house where the said Knapp was kept, she, the said Knapp, voluntarily, without any occasion given her, said that Goodwife Staples told her, the said Knapp, that an Indian brought unto her, the said Staples, two little things brighter than the light of the day, and told the said Goodwife Staples they were Indian gods, as the Indian called them; and the Indian withal told her, the said Staples, if she would keep them, she should be so big [and] rich, all one god, and that the said Staples told the said Knapp, she gave them again to the said Indian, but she could not tell whether she did so or no.

Lucy Pell on witches naming other witches

Lucy Pell, the wife of Thomas Pell, being sworn deposeth as followeth, that about a day after Goodwife Knapp was condemned for a witch, Mrs. Jones earnestly entreated her to go to the said Knapp, who had sent for her, and then this deponent called the said Hester Ward, and they went together; then the said Knapp voluntarily, of her own accord, spake as the said Hester Ward hath testified, word by word; and the said Mrs. Pell further saith, that she being one of the women that was required by the court to search the said Knapp before she was condemned, and then Mrs. Jones pressed her, the said Knapp, to confess whether there were any other that were witches, because Goodwife Bassett, when she was condemned, said there was another witch in Fairfield that held her head full high, and then the said Goodwife Knapp stepped a little aside, and told her, this deponent, Goodwife

Bassett meant not her; she asked her whom she meant, and she named Goodwife Staples, and then uttered the same speeches as formerly concerning the Indian gods, and that Goodwife Staples her sister Martha told the said Goodwife Knapp, that her sister Staples stood by her, by the fire in their house, and she called to her, sister, sister, and she would not answer, but she, the said Martha, struck at her and then she went away, and the next day she asked her sister, and she said she was not there; and Mrs. Ward doth also testify with Mrs. Pell, that the said Knapp said the same to her; and the said Mrs. Pell saith, that about two days after the search aforesaid, she went to the said Knapp in [the] prison house, and the said Knapp said to her, I told you a thing the other day, and Goodman Staples had been with her and threatened her, that she had told something of his wife that would bring his wife's name in[to] question, and this deponent she told nobody of it but her husband, and she was much moved at it.

Elizabeth and Mary Brewster on the search for teats

Elizabeth Brewster being sworn, deposeth and saith, that after Goodwife Knapp was executed, as soon as she was cut down, she, the said Knapp, being carried to the graveside, Goodwife Staples with some other women went to search the said Knapp, concerning finding out teats, and Goodwife Staples handled her very much, and called to Goodwife Lockwood, and said, these were no witch's teats, but such as she herself had, and other women might have the same, wringing her hands and taking the Lord's name in her mouth, and said, will you say these were witch's teats, they were not, and called upon Goodwife Lockwood to come and see them; then this deponent desired Goodwife Odell to come and see, for she had been upon her oath when she found the teats, and she, this deponent, desired the said Odell to come and clear it to Goodwife Staples; Goodwife Odell would not come; then the said Staples still called upon Goodwife Lockwood to come, will you say these are witch's teats, I, says the said Staples, have such myself, and so have you if you search yourself; Goodwife Lockwood replied, if I had such, she would be hanged; would you, says Staples, yes, saith Lockwood, and deserve it; and the said Staples handled the said teats very much, and pulled them with her fingers, and then Goodwife Odell came near, and she, the said Staples, still questioning, the said Odell told her no honest women had such, and then all the women rebuking her and said they were witches teats, then the said Staples yielded it.

Mary Brewster being sworn and deposed, saith as followeth, that she was present after the execution of the said Knapp, and she being brought to the graveside, she saw Goodwife Staples pull the teats that were found about Goodwife Knapp, and was very earnest to know whether those were witch's teats which were found about her, the said Knapp, when the women searched her, and the said Staples pulled them as though she would have pulled them off, and presently she, this deponent, went away, as having no desire to look upon them.

Susan Lockwood on the disputed teats

Susan Lockwood, wife of Robert Lockwood, being sworn and examined saith as followeth, that she was at the execution of Goodwife Knapp that was hanged for a witch, and after the said Knapp was cut down and brought to the grave, Goodwife Staples, with other women, looked after the teats that the women spake of appointed by the magistrates, and the said Goodwife Staples was handling of her where the teats were, and the said Staples stood up and called three or four times and bid me come look of them, and asked her whether she would say they were teats, and she made this answer, no matter whether there were teats or no, she had teats and confessed she was a witch, that was sufficient; if these be teats, here are no more teats than I myself have, or any other women, or you either if you would search your body; this deponent saith she said, I know not what you have, but for herself, if any find any such things about me, I deserved to be hanged as she was, and yet afterward she, the said Staples, stooped down again and handled her, the said Knapp, very much, about the place where the teats were, and several of the women cried her down, and said they were teats, and then she, the said Staples, yielded, and said very like they might be teats.

Pressure on Goody Knapp to confess

Thomas Shervington and Christopher Comstock and Goodwife Baldwin were all together at the prison house where Goodwife Knapp was, and the said Goodwife Baldwin asked her whether she, the said Knapp, knew of any other, and she said there were some, or one, that had received Indian gods that were very bright; the said Baldwin asked her how she could tell, if she were not a witch herself, and she said the party told her so, and her husband was witness to it; and to this they were all sworn and do depose.

Rebecca Hull, wife of Cornelius Hull, being sworn and examined, deposeth and saith as followeth, that when Goodwife Knapp was going to execution, Mr. Ludlow, and her father Mr. Jones, pressing the said Knapp to confess that she was a witch, upon which Goodwife Staples said, why should she, the said Knapp, confess that which she was not, and after she, the said Goodwife Staples, had said so, one that stood by, [asked] why should she say so, she the said Staples replied, she made no doubt if she the said Knapp were one, she would confess it.

Deborah Lockwood, of the age of 17 or thereabout, sworn and examined, saith as followeth, that she being present when Goodwife Knapp was going to execution, between Tryes and the mill, she heard Goodwife Staples say to Goodwife Gould, she was persuaded Goodwife Knapp was no witch; Goodwife Gould said, Sister Staples, she is a witch, and hath confessed [she] had had familiarity with the devil. Staples replied, I was with her yesterday, or last night, and she said no such thing as she heard.

April 26, 1654. Bethia Brundish, of the age of sixteen or thereabouts, maketh oath, as they were going to execution of Goodwife Knapp, who was condemned for a witch by the court and jury at Fairfield, there being present herself and Deborah Lockwood and Sarah Cable, she heard Goodwife Staples say, that she thought the said Goodwife Knapp was no witch, and Goodwife Gould presently reproved her for it.

Witness Andrew Ward. Jurat' die and anno pr[e]dicto,

Coram me,   Roger Ludlow

Witnesses for the plaintiff

The plaintiff replied that he had several other witnesses which he thought would clear the matters in question, if the court please to hear them, which being granted, he first presented a testimony of Goodwife Whitlocke of Fairfield, upon oath taken before Mr. Fowler at Milford, the 27th of May, 1654, wherein she saith, that concerning Goodwife Staples's speeches at the execution of Goodwife Knapp, she being present and next to Goody Staples when they were going to put the dead corpse of Goodwife Knapp into the grave, several women were looking for the marks of a witch upon the dead body, and several of the women said they could find none, and this deponent said, nor I; and she heard Goodwife Staples say, nor I; then came one that had searched the said witch, and showed them the marks that were upon her, and said what are these; and then this deponent heard Goodwife Staples say she never saw such in all her life, and that she was persuaded that no honest woman had such things as those were; and the dead corpse being then presently put into the grave, Goodwife Staples and myself came immediately away together unto the town, from the place of execution.

Goodwife Barlow of Fairfield before the court did now testify upon oath, that when Knapp's wife was hanged and ready to be buried, she desired to see the marks of a witch and spake to one of her neighbors to go with her, and they looked but found them not; then Goodwife Staples came to them, and one or two more, Goodwife Staples kneeled down by them, and they all looked but found them not, and said they saw nothing but what is common to other women, but after they found them they all wondered, and Goodwife Staples in particular, and said they never saw such things in their life before, so they went away.

The wife of John Tompson of Fairfield testifieth upon oath, that Goodwife Whitlocke, Goodwife Staples and herself, were at the grave and desired to see the marks of the witch that was hanged, they looked but found them not at first, then the midwife came and showed them, Goodwife Staples said she never saw such, and she believed no honest woman had such.

The wife of Richard Lyon, and Goodwife Squire of Fairfield affirm to the same purpose, as appears by a writing presented, but not upon oath.

Goody Knapp refuses to name others

Goodwife Sherwood of Fairfield testifieth upon oath, that that day Knapp's wife was condemned for a witch, she was there to see her, all being gone forth but Goodwife Odell and herself, then there came in Mrs. Pell and her two daughters, Elizabeth and Mary, Goody Lockwood and Goodwife Purdy; Mrs. Pell told Knapp's wife she was sent to speak to her, to have her confess that for which she was condemned, and if she knew any other to be a witch to discover them, and told her, before she was condemned she might think it would be a means to take away her life, but now she must die, and therefore she should discover all, for though she and her family by the providence of God had brought in nothing against her, yet there was many witnesses came in against her, and she was cast by the jury and godly magistrates having found her guilty, and that the last evidence cast the cause. So the next day she went in again to see the witch with other neighbors, there was Mr. Jones, Mrs. Pell and her two daughters, Mrs. Ward and Goodwife Lockwood, where she heard Mrs. Pell desire Knapp's wife to lay open herself, and make way for the minister to do her good; her daughter Elizabeth bid her do as the witch at the other town did, that is, discover all she knew to be witches. Goodwife Knapp said she must not say anything which is not true, she must not wrong anybody, and what had been said to her in private, before she went out of the world, when she was upon the ladder, she would reveal to Mr. Ludlow or the minister. Elizabeth Brewster said, if you keep it a little longer till you come to the ladder, the devil will have you quick, if you reveal it not till then. Goodwife Knapp replied, take heed the devil have not you, for she could not tell how soon she might be her companion, and added, the truth is you would have me say that Goodwife Staples is a witch, but I have sins enough to answer for already, and I hope I shall not add to my condemnation; I know nothing by Goodwife Staples, and I hope she is an honest woman. Then Goodwife Lockwood said, Goodwife Knapp what ail you; Goodman Lyon, I pray speak, did you hear us name Goodwife Staples's name since we came here; Lyon wished her to have a care what she said and not breed difference betwixt neighbors after she was gone; Knapp replied, Goodman Lyon hold your tongue, you know not what I know, I have ground for what I say, I have been fished [*sic*] withal in private more than you are aware of; I apprehend Goodwife Staples hath done me some wrong in her testimony, but I must not render evil for evil. Then this deponent spake to Goody Knapp, wishing her to speak with the jury, for she apprehended Goodwife Staples witnessed nothing contrary to other witnesses, and she supposed they would inform her that the last evidence did not cast the cause; she replied that she had been told so within this half hour, and desired Mr. Jones and herself to stay and the rest to depart, that she might speak with us in private, and desired me to declare to Mr. Jones what they said against Goodwife Staples the day before, but she told her she heard not Goodwife Staples named, but she knew nothing of that nature; she desired her to declare her mind fully to Mr. Jones, so she went away.

Goody Knapp denies she suspects anyone

Further this deponent saith, that coming into the house where the witch was kept, she found only the wardsman and Goodwife Baldwin there, Goodwife Baldwin whispered [to] her in the ear and said to her that Goodwife Knapp told her that a woman in the town was a witch and would be hanged within a twelve month, and would confess herself a witch and clear her that she was none, and that she asked her how she knew she was a witch, and she told her she had received Indian gods of an Indian, which are shining things, which shine lighter than the day. Then this deponent asked Goodwife Knapp if she had said so, and she denied it; Goodwife Baldwin affirmed she did, but Knapp's wife again denied it and said she knows no woman in the town that is a witch, nor any woman that hath received Indian gods, but she said there was an Indian at a woman's house and offered her a couple of shining things, but the woman never told her she took them, but was afraid and ran away, and she knows not that the woman ever took them. Goodwife [Knapp?] desired this deponent to go out and speak with the wardsmen; Thomas Shervington, who was one of them, said he remembered not that Knapp's wife said a woman in the town was a witch and would be hanged, but spake something of shining things, but Kester, Mr. Pell's man, being by said, but I remember; and as they were going to the grave, Goodwife Staples said, it was long before she could believe this poor woman was a witch, or that there were any witches, till the word of God convinced her, which saith, thou shalt not suffer a witch to live [Exodus 22:18].

Goody Knapp explains her silence

Thomas Lyon of Fairfield testifieth upon oath, taken before Mr. Fowler, the 27th May, 1654, that he being set by authority to watch with Knapp's wife, there came in Mrs. Pell, Mrs. Ward, Goodwife Lockwood, and Mrs. Pell's two daughters; the[y] fell into some discourse, that Goodwife Knapp should say to them in private which Goodwife Knapp would not own, but did seem to be much troubled at them and said, the truth is you would have me to say that Goodwife Staples is a witch; I have sins enough already, I will not add this to my condemnation, I know no such thing by her, I hope she is an honest woman; then Goodwife Lockwood called to me and asked whether they had named Goodwife Staples, so I spake to Goodwife Knapp to have a care what she said, that she did not make difference amongst her neighbors when she was gone, and I told her that I hoped they were her friends and desired her soul's good, and not to accuse any out of envy, or to that effect; Knapp's wife said, Goodman Lyon hold your tongue, you know not so much as I do, you know not what hath been said to me in private; and after they was gone, of her own accord, between she and I, Goody Knapp said she knew nothing against Goodwife Staples of being a witch.

Richard Lyon of Fairfield affirmeth to the same purpose as Thomas Lyon doth, as appears by a writing under his hand, but not upon oath.

Goodwife Gould of Fairfield testifieth upon oath, that Goodwife Sherwood and herself came in to see the witch, there was one before had been speaking about some suspicious words of one in the town, this deponent wished her if she knew anything upon good ground she would declare it, if not, that she would take heed that the devil persuaded her not to sow malicious seed to do hurt when she was dead, yet wished her to speak the truth if she knew anything by any person; she said she knew nothing but upon suspicion by the rumors she hears; this deponent told her she was now to die, and therefore she should deal truly; she burst forth into weeping and desired me to pray for her, and said I knew not how she was tempted; never, never poor creature was tempted as I am tempted, pray, pray for me. Further this deponent saith, as they were going to the grave, Mr. Buckley, Goodwife Sherwood, Goodwife Staples and myself, Goodwife Staples was next me, she said it was a good while before she could believe this woman was a witch, and that she could not believe a good while that there were any witches, till she went to the word of God, and then she was convinced, and as she remembers, Goodwife Staples went along with her all the way till they came at the gallows. Further this deponent saith, that Mr. Jones some time since that Knapp's wife was condemned, did tell her, and that with a very cheerful countenance and blessing God for it, that Knapp's wife had cleared one in the town, and said you know who I mean Sister Staples, blessed be God for it.

Ensign Bryan informed the court that one particular in the charge he heard not of before, and therefore is not prepared to answer, but desires further time for that part, and he will be bound to answer Thomas Staples in it when the court shall appoint, which the court told him they would consider of.

The decision of the court

The plaintiff and defendant having spoken what they pleased in the case, the court considered of what hath been alleged and proved on both sides, and though they are not satisfied in the evidences presented by Ensign Bryan, yet they have considered what the several witnesses speak therein, and find not that they take of the testimony given in on the other side, nor do they justify Mr. Ludlow in the defaming expressions of Goodwife Staples, yet withal they consider that he said he thought them not true, yet they tend to defamation, the court in their sentence shall incline to more favor than possibly they should do if Mr. Ludlow was here, but the third part of the charge being left till another time, upon Ensign Bryan's engagement to answer it at the next Court of Magistrates here, or sooner if called to it[.] For the former parts of the charge, they see no cause to lay any blemish of a witch upon Goodwife Staples, but must judge that Mr. Ludlow hath done her wrong, and therefore is by this court ordered to pay to Thomas Staples, by way of fine for reparation of his wife's name, ten pounds, and for his trouble and charge in following the suit, five pounds more, the latter part of the charge being left as before expressed.

Source: *New Haven Town Recs.*, *1*, pp. 77–89.

5. A Handful
of Troublemakers
(1652–1661)

▲

John Bradstreet

*John Bradstreet was brought before the Essex County Quarter Court
in 1652 on suspicion of witchcraft; he was convicted and punished
for lying. His father, Humphrey Bradstreet, had settled in Newbury
in the 1630s and became a moderately prosperous farmer. John was
one of several children. The court records suggest that he and other
young men were restless with the established order; he was
"whipped for lying" in 1650, and in 1651 it was ordered that he "sit
in the stocks for one hour for offending the court with words." These
disturbances—including the one that is documented here—may not
mean that Bradstreet was irreligious. When he died in 1660 in Mar-
blehead, his inventory included a Bible, as his father's had before
him.[1] Cursing in the name of the devil, or invoking the devil's powers, seem to have been themes of popular culture in England and
New England.[2]*

1. *Essex Ct. Recs., 1,* pp. 179, 188, 210, 234, 265; *The Probate Records of Essex
County Massachusetts 1635–1664* (Salem, Mass., 1916), *1,* pp. 318, 218.
2. Similar expressions are reported elsewhere in court records; cf. David D.
Hall, *Worlds of Wonder, Days of Judgment: Popular Religious Belief in Early
New England* (New York, 1989), pp. 74, 294 n. 111. A comparable case is John
Brown's: *New Haven Town Recs., 3,* p. 60.

John Bradstreet is presented for claiming to work magic

We present John Bradstreet of Rowley for suspicion of hav[ing] familiarity with the devil he said he read in a book of magic and that he

heard a voice asking him what work he had for him[.] He answered go make a bridge of sand over the sea go make a ladder of sand up to heaven and go to God and come down no more.

Witnesses here of Francis Parrott and his wife of Rowley.

Witness here William Bartholomew of Ipswich.

Source: Essex County Court Papers, 2:46:1 (EI).

John Bradstreet is fined

John Bradstreet upon his presentment of the last court for suspicion of having familiarity with the devil upon examination of the case they found he had told a lie which was a second being convicted once before. The court sets a fine of 20s or else to be whipped Edward Coborne is surety for the payment of the fine and fees of court. The court held at Ipswich 28th (7) 1652.

Source: Essex County Court Records, *9*, p. 31 (EI).

Lydia Gilbert (EXECUTED?)

Henry Stiles, a fifty-eight-year-old man, died in Windsor, Connecticut, on October 3, 1651, the victim of an accidental gunshot. The man who held the gun, Thomas Allyn, was indicted, tried, and convicted of "homicide by misadventure"; the penalty was a fine. Three years later, in 1654, Lydia Gilbert was indicted for causing the death of Stiles by witchcraft. She was the wife of Thomas Gilbert, who settled in Windsor in or about 1644. Henry Stiles may have boarded with the Gilberts. Except for this one possibility, nothing is known of the circumstances that resulted in the decision to charge Lydia with witchcraft. The jury found her guilty, and it is probable though not certain that she was executed.[1]

1. *Coll. CHS, 22* (1928), pp. 106–107; Homer W. Brainard et al., *The Gilbert Family: Descendants of Thomas Gilbert* (New Haven, 1953), pp. 18, 20–23; Henry R. Stiles, *The History of Ancient Windsor* (1891–92), *1*, pp. 444–50.

Lydia Gilbert is indicted and convicted

. . . Lydia Gilbert thou art here indicted by that name of Lydia Gilbert that not having the fear of God before thy eyes thou hast of late years or still dost give entertainment to Satan the great enemy of God and mankind and by his help hast killed the body of Henry Stiles besides other witchcrafts for which according to the law of God and the established law of this commonwealth thou deservest to die[.] November 28, 1654.

The party above mentioned is found guilty of witchcraft by the jury[.]

Source: *Coll. CHS, 22* (1928), p. 131.

Anne Hibbins (EXECUTED)

Anne Hibbins and her husband, William, settled in Boston in the early 1630s. A merchant, William was elected to the lower house of the Massachusetts General Court in 1641–42. In 1643 he rose to the office of Assistant, remaining one until his death in 1654. He and his wife were members of the Boston church. In 1640 the church members censured Mrs. Hibbins for continuing to accuse a carpenter of overcharging for work he had done on her house. Some members of the church felt that she was guilty of "transgressing the rule of the Apostle in usurping authority over him whom God hath made her head and husband, and in taking the power and authority which God had given to him out of his hands." Several months later, in February 1641, the church removed Mrs. Hibbins from membership by voting to excommunicate her, on the grounds that she remained unrepentant.[1] Widowed in 1654, she was tried for witchcraft in 1655. Nothing is known of the charges brought against her, or who appeared as witnesses.[2] The jury returned a verdict of guilty. The magistrates refused to accept this verdict, and a second trial occurred in 1656 before the General Court. Condemned again, Mrs. Hibbins was executed in June. The unusual circumstances of her life and the trials that brought it to an end are accentuated in two accounts of the case, both of them published much later. The one other reference, nearly contemporary, occurs in a letter from Nathaniel Mather (then living in London) to his brother Increase, remarking on stories Increase had omitted from An Essay for the Recording of Illustrious Providences *(1684), among them "Mrs. Hibbons witchcrafts, and the discovery thereof."*[3]

1. The church proceedings are printed (abridged) in *Remarkable Providences 1600–1760*, edited, with an introduction by John Demos (New York, 1972), pp. 222–39; the quotations occur on pp. 225 and 229.
2. The will that Mrs. Hibbins prepared a few weeks before her execution is printed in *NEHGR* 5 (1852), p. 283. One of the men she asked to serve as executors, Joshua Scottow, apologized to the General Court nine months later for criticizing its actions in the case. MA *135*:1.
3. *Coll. MHS* 4th Ser., *8* (1868), p. 58.

Verdict of the court on Anne Hibbins

The magistrates not receiving the verdict of the jury in Mrs. Hibbins her case, having been on trial for witchcraft, it came, and fell of course to the General Court. Mrs. Anne Hibbins was called forth, appeared at the bar; the indictment against her was read, to which she answered not guilty, and was willing to be tried by God and this court. The evidences against her was read, the parties witnessing being present, her answers considered on, and the whole court, being met together, by their vote, determined that Mrs. Anne Hibbins is guilty of witchcraft, according to the bill of indictment found against her by the jury of life and death. The Governor in open court pronounced sentence accordingly, declaring she was to go from the bar to the place from whence she came, and from thence to the place of execution, and there to hang till she was dead.

It is ordered, that warrant shall issue out from the Secretary to the Marshal General for the execution of Mrs. Hibbins on the 5th day next come fortnight, presently after the lecture at Boston, being the 19th of June next, the Marshal General taking with him a sufficient guard. May 14, 1656.

Source: *Mass. Bay Recs., 4,* pt. 1, p. 269.

William Hubbard on Anne Hibbins

One Mrs. Hibbins, in the year 1656, was arraigned for a witch after her husband's death. The [jury] found her guilty, but the magistrates consented not, so the matter came to the General Court, where she was condemned by the deputies (the first example in that kind) and executed. *Vox populi* went sore against her, and was the chiefest part of the evidence against her, as some thought. It fared with her in some sense as it did with Joan of Arc, in France, executed by the Duke of Bedford in Henry the Fifth's time; the which some counted a saint and some a witch. Many times persons of hard favor and turbulent passions are apt to be condemned by the common people for witches, upon very slight grounds. Some observed solemn remarks of providence set upon those who were very forward to condemn her, and brand others with the like infamous reproach on such grounds, about that time. Others have said that Mr. Hibbins losing £500 at once, by the carelessness of Mr. Trerice[1] the shipmaster, it so discomposed his wife's spirit that she scarce ever was well settled in her mind afterward, but grew very turbulent in her passion, and discontented, on which occasions she was cast out of the church, and then charged to be a witch, giving too much occasion by her strange carriage to common people so to judge.

1. Nicholas Trerice or Treroise, who went back and forth between Europe and New England as a shipmaster.
Source: William Hubbard, *A General History of New England*, 2d ed. (1848), p. 574. Hubbard (1621–1704), a minister in Massachusetts, wrote *A General History* in the 1670s. It remained unpublished until the nineteenth century.

Thomas Hutchinson on Anne Hibbins

The most remarkable occurrence in the colony, in the year 1655, was the trial and condemnation of Mrs. Anne Hibbins for witchcraft. Her husband, who died in the year 1654, was an agent for the colony in England, several years one of the Assistants, and a merchant of note in the town of Boston; but losses in the latter part of his life had reduced his estate, and increased the natural crabbedness of his wife's temper, which made her turbulent and quarrelsome, and brought her under church censures, and at length rendered her so odious to her neighbors as to cause some of them to accuse her of witchcraft. The jury brought her in guilty, but the magistrates refused to accept the verdict; so the cause came to the General Court, where the popular clamor prevailed against her, and the miserable old woman was condemned and executed. Search was made upon her body for teats, and in her chests and boxes, for puppets, images, etc. but there is no record of anything of that sort being found. Mr. Beach, a minister in Jamaica, in a letter to Doctor Increase Mather in the year 1684, says,

"You may remember what I have sometimes told you your famous Mr. Norton[1] once said at his own table before Mr. Wilson the pastor, elder Penn, and myself, and wife, etc. who had the honor to be his guests. That one of your magistrate's wives, as I remember, was hanged for a witch, only for having more wit than her neighbors. It was his very expression, she having, as he explained it, unhappily guessed that two of her persecutors, whom she saw talking in the street, were talking of her; which, proving true, cost her her life, notwithstanding all he could do to the contrary, as he himself told us."

It fared with her as it did with Joan of Arc in France. Some counted her a saint and some a witch, and some observed solemn marks of providence set upon those who were very forward to condemn her, and to brand others upon the like ground with the like reproach.

1. John Norton, minister of Boston First Church.
Source: Thomas Hutchinson, *The History of the Colony and Province of Massachusetts Bay* (1764), ed. Lawrence Shaw Mayo (Cambridge, Mass., 1936), *1*, p. 160–61.

Nicholas Bayley and his wife

Nicholas Bayley was a farmer in New Haven, where he first appears in the court records in 1650. He was made a freeman of Connecticut in October 1663. The complaints that were brought against his wife in 1655 and that led to their expulsion from New Haven indicate how the name of "witch," or the charge of witchcraft, was used to designate unsatisfactory social behavior. The magistrates, and probably some of her neighbors, regarded Goodwife Bayley as a troublemaker. She seems to have had a bawdy sense of humor.

The offences of Mrs. Bayley

At a court held at New Haven.

July 3, 1655. Nicholas Bayley and his wife were called before the court, and told that there are sundry things, wherein they have given offence, which they must answer for: and first, sundry passages taken in writing were read, which being duly considered doth render them both, but especially the woman, very suspicious in point of witchcraft, but for matters of that nature the court intends not to proceed at this time: but Goodwife Bayley was told there are other things wherein she hath grossly miscarried, which may be reduced to three heads; impudent and notorious lying; endeavoring to make discord among neighbors; and filthy and unclean speeches uttered by her: some instances were given in all these particulars; as, first, that she having gotten two pewter dishes of Mr. Gilbert, which he did spare her (though unwillingly) to supply her necessity, she told her neighbors Mr. Gilbert had great store of them to sell, and more than he could quickly put off, so they came to the town to Mr. Gilbert to buy some of him, but he told them he had none to sell, and that Goody Bayley knew, for he denied himself to spare her them she had.

Another time she told Thomas Barnes that if he would mow a day for Mr. Gilbert, he would pay him wool, which was not true, though he promised one pound of wool, but she saith she knew she spake not true, but she did it to get Mr. Gilbert a day's work, beside several other particulars.

For her making difference among neighbors, she one time came to Goodwife Merriman's, and said Thomas Barnes hath killed many ducks, and intimated that it was not kindly done that he gave her none: Goodwife Merriman said, she looked for none; then she went to Goodwife Barnes's, and intimated to her that Goodwife Merriman was troubled that her husband killed so many ducks and gave her none, and the like carriage she used betwixt Goodman Barnes and some other of his neighbors about some pork which Thomas Barnes had killed.

And for her filthy corrupting words, one time Nicholas Bayley had a sow went to boar, and the said Nicholas his dog beat away the boar and would act as copulating with the sow. John Moss spake to Bayley to kill his dog; he said he would, or geld him, but Bayley's wife and Goodwife Barnes speaking of this, Bayley's wife said, what would you have the poor creature do, if he had not a bitch, he must have something; and they speaking of George Larrimore, a man who had (as was heard after he was gone) miscarried with many persons in a filthy way, Bayley's wife said alas, what would you have the man do, if his own wife was weak, he must have somebody. Bayley's wife was told that in these things she hath acted as one possessed with the very devil, who is a malicious, lying, unclean spirit. She confessed the several particulars now before the court, as she had formerly done when she was examined at the Governor's in a private way, and for which carriages the court told them that they are not fit to live among such neighbors, and therefore the sentence of the court is, that betwixt this and the next court they must consider of a way how to remove themselves to some other place, or give sufficient security to the court's satisfaction for their good behavior, and pay the fine for lying, which is ten shillings; and if this be not performed, the court must then proceed to some severe, sharp correction, imprisonment or otherwise, as they shall see cause.

The Bayleys delay leaving

At a court held at New Haven.

August 7, 1655. Nicholas Bayley and his wife were called and told that the court expects to know how the sentence of the last court concerning them is fulfilled; he said, they cannot tell whether to remove, and hath endeavored to get security but cannot, but desired he might have further time to remove; they asked, how long; he said, the spring till the middle of April next; which the court granted, upon condition that he do betwixt this and the next court, or then at furthest, put in satisfying security to the value of forty pound that he will remove by that time, and that he give his own bond to the value of fifty pound for his good behavior in the meantime, and that he attend every monthly court here, that if his neighbors or others have ought against him or his wife, they may hear and consider it and proceed further with him or her, as they shall see cause.

Mrs. Bayley defends herself, but the court criticizes her

At a court held at New Haven.

September 4, 1655. Nicholas Bayley and his wife were called before the court, and she was told that she hath caused divers of her neighbors to be warned, who are now here to attend; therefore if she have ought to say and prove whereby she may clear herself of those things charged, and by herself owned before the court in July last, she hath now liberty to do it. She spake sundry things, wherein she did discover a false lying spirit, turning and winding in her answers without respect to truth, but could not clear herself in anything, but the charges remain as full and the suspicions of witchcraft as strong as before: wherefore the court demanded of them if they had attended the last court's order, in getting security for their removal the next spring; he said he could not, but he would give his own bond that he would endeavor it, but cannot tell whether he shall attain it or no; the court told him that answer cannot satisfy, and therefore if he intend to give no other, they must take some other course; which upon consideration the court declared to them that they do both without any further warning and at their peril attend the Court of Magistrates to be held at New Haven the third Wednesday in October next to answer to these miscarriages; and that they also attend the next monthly court here, the first Tuesday in October, that if anything be further informed against them they may be present to answer, and the court may also consider what they have further to do in the case, and that they do not entertain any suspicious persons at their house, which the court is informed they have done.

The court wants them to leave

At a court held at New Haven.

October 2, 1655. Nicholas Bayley appeared and was asked for his wife: he said, she is not well, nor his child, but shall attend when she is fit; he was told the court must not be put off with slight excuses, but he may now propound what he hath to say: he said he is willing to give his own bond to remove in the next spring, by the middle of April, which the court refused not to take, but perceiving that he thereby intended to be freed from attending the Court of Magistrates as he was ordered the last court, was told it will not be granted, yet if he himself be out of town then for that end, to procure himself a place to remove to, he himself shall be freed from that attendance, but his wife must appear and he also if he be in town: yet this the court granted to him, that if himself and wife do remove their habitation before then, so as the court may be no more troubled with them, they shall be freed from attending there, but not else.

Source: *New Haven Town Recs., 1,* pp. 245–46, 249, 256–58.

Jane Walford

Jane Walford of Portsmouth, New Hampshire, spent decades contending with the label of "witch." Her husband, Thomas Walford, had emigrated to New England in 1623. After living in Charlestown, Massachusetts, he left the colony in 1631 because he was not sympathetic to the Puritans and became a prosperous landowner in Portsmouth. Jane faced down one of her accusers, Elizabeth Rowe, in 1648, when the court ordered Mrs. Rowe to pay damages and publicly apologize. Nicholas Rowe, husband of Elizabeth, participated in another phase of accusations in 1656. Again, however, Jane was acquitted. In 1669 she won a suit for slander against someone who called her a witch. Yet, as Carol Karlsen has pointed out, the "stigma of witchcraft . . . was apparently passed on to all five of her daughters."[1]

1. Carol Karlsen, *The Devil in the Shape of a Woman: Witchcraft in Colonial New England* (New York, 1987), p. 62; George L. Burr, ed., *Narratives of the Witchcraft Cases, 1648–1706* (New York, 1914; repr. 1968), p. 61. A document relating to the 1669 suit is printed in *NEHGR 42* (1889), pp. 182–83.

Susannah Trimmings refuses to give Jane Walford any cotton

Complaint of Susannah Trimmings, of Little Harbor, Piscataqua.

On Lord's day 30th of March, at night, going home with Goodwife Barton, she separated from her at the freshet next her house. On her return, between Goodman Evans's and Robert Davis's she heard a rustling in the woods, which she at first thought was occasioned by swine, and presently after, there did appear to her a woman whom she apprehended to be old Goodwife Walford. She asked me where my consort was; I answered, I had none. She said, thy consort is at home by this time. Lend me a pound of cotton. I told her I had but two pounds in the house, and I would not spare any to my mother. She said I had better have done it; that my sorrow was great already, and it should be greater—for I was going a great journey but should never come there. She then left me, and I was struck *as with a clap of fire* on the back, and she vanished toward the water side, in my apprehension in the *shape of a cat.* She had on her head a white linen hood tied under her chin, and her waistcoat and petticoat were red, with an old green apron and a black hat upon her head.

Taken upon oath, April 18, 1656 before Brian Pendleton, Henry Sherburn, Renald Fernald.

Her husband says, she came home in a sad condition. She passed by me with her child in her arms, laid her child on the bed, sat down upon the chest and leaned upon her elbow. Three times I asked her how she did—She could not speak. I took her in my arms and held her up, and repeated the question. She forced breath, and something stopped in her throat as if it would have stopped her breath. I unlaced her clothes, and soon she spake and said, Lord have mercy upon me, this wicked woman will kill me. I asked her what woman. She said, Goodwife Walford. I tried to persuade her it was only her weakness. She told me no, and related as above, that her back was as a flame of fire, and her lower parts were as it were numb and without feeling. I pinched her and she felt [it] not. She continued that night and the day and night following very ill, and is still bad of her limbs and complains still daily of it.

Sworn as above.

A witness defends Jane Walford

A witness deposed, June 1656, that he was at Goodman Walford's 30th March 1656, at the time mentioned by Mrs. Trimmings, and that Goodwife Walford was at home till quite dark, as well as ever she was in her life.

An apparition of Jane Walford

Nicholas Rowe testified that Jane Walford, shortly after she was accused, came to the deponent in bed in the evening and put her hand upon his breast so that he could not speak, and [he] was in great pain till the next day. By the light of the fire in the next room it appeared to be Goody Walford, but she did not speak. She repeated her visit about a week after and did as before, but said nothing.

Elisa Barton deposed that she saw Susannah Trimmings at the time she was ill, and her face was colored and spotted with several colors. She told the deponent the story, who replied, that it was nothing but her fantasy; her eyes looked as if they had been scalded.

Jane Walford's husband calls her witch

John Puddington deposed, that three years since Goodwife Walford came to his mother's—She said that her own husband called her an old witch; and when she came to her cattle, her husband would bid her begone, for she did overlook the cattle, which is as much as to say in our country, bewitching.

Strange cats and other testimony

Agnes Puddington deposes, that on the 11th of April, 1656, the wife of W. Evans came to her house and lay there all night; and a little after sunset the deponent saw a yellowish cat; and Mrs. Evans said she was followed by a cat wherever she went. John came, and saw a cat in the garden—took down his gun to shoot her; the cat got up on a tree, and the gun would not take fire, and afterwards the cock would not stand. She afterwards saw three cats—the yellow one vanished away on the plain ground: she could not tell which way they went.

John Puddington testifies to the same effect.

Three other deponents say, they heard Elizabeth the wife of Nicholas Rowe, say, there were three men witches at Strawberry Bank,[1] one was Thomas Turpin who was drowned; another, Old Ham, and a third should be "nameless, because he should be blameless."

Action of the court

Court of Associates, June, 1656.

Jane Walford being brought to this court upon suspicion of being a witch, is to continue bound until the next court, to be responsive.

1. Strawberry Bank: the original place name for Portsmouth, New Hampshire.
Source: *Provincial Papers: Documents and Records Relating to the Province of New Hampshire 1623–86*, ed. Nathaniel Bouton (1867), pp. 217–19; reprinted in Samuel G. Drake, *Annals of Witchcraft in New England* (1869), pp. 102–107. These texts were modernized by the nineteenth-century editor and are not verbatim transcripts.

Nicholas and Margaret Jennings

A nineteenth-century antiquarian regarded the Jenningses as a "rascally pair," citing their punishment in New Haven in 1643 as runaway indentured servants who were whipped for theft and fornica-

tion. The court also ordered them to be married.[1] *There does seem to be a modest trail of troubles attached to the Jenningses and their daughter Martha. Indicted on the charge of witchcraft in 1659, when they were living in Saybrook, Connecticut, Nicholas and Margaret escaped with an ambiguous jury verdict in 1661.*

1. Charles H. Levermore, "Witchcraft in Connecticut," *New Englander and Yale Review 44* (1885), p. 806; *Coll. CHS, 22* (1928), pp. 50, 223, 225, 227.

Inquiry into witchery at Saybrook

Mr. Wyllys is requested to go down to Saybrook, to assist the Major[1] in examining the suspicions about witchery, and to act therein as may be requisite. June 15, 1659.

1. John Mason.
Source: *Conn. Col. Recs., 1,* p. 338.

The Jenningses are indicted

The indictment of Nicholas and Margaret Jennings.

Nicholas Jennings thou art here indicted by the name of Nicholas Jennings of Saybrook for not having the fear of God before thine eyes thou hast entertained familiarity with Satan the great enemy of God and mankind and by his help hast done works above the course of nature to the loss of the lives of several persons and in particular the wife of Reinold Marvin with the child of Baalshassar de Wolfe with other sorceries for which according to the law of God and the established laws of this commonwealth thou deservest to die.

What answerest thou for thy self guilty or not guilty.

The indictment being rehearsed to each person particularly the prisoners answer not guilty. September 5, 1661.

Verdict of the jury

A Particular Court at Hartford, October 9, 1661.

Respecting Nicholas Jennings the jury return that the major part find him guilty of the indictment the rest strongly suspect it that he is guilty.

Respecting Margaret Jennings the jury return that some of them find her guilty the rest strongly suspect her to be guilty of the indictment.

Source: *Coll. CHS, 22* (1928), pp. 238, 240.

6. A Long-Running Feud
(1656–1675)

▲

Mary Parsons of Northampton

*Mary (Bliss) Parsons was the wife of Joseph Parsons, a merchant
and political figure in the Connecticut River Valley who settled in
Springfield in the late 1630s.[1] The Parsonses moved upriver to
Northampton as of 1654. There the family, which included eleven
children, became members of the church. In 1656 Mary was involved
in a defamation suit initiated by her husband against a Northampton neighbor, Sarah Bridgman, for slander. Sarah and her husband,
James, blamed Mary for the death of their young son. The defamation suit produced further testimony against Mary, including de-
scriptions of conflict between wife and husband and her seeming
"fits." Still other neighbors, including the Springfield magistrate
John Pynchon, sided with the Parsonses. The Parsonses won the case.*

*In 1674 Mary Parsons became the defendant in a case of witch-
craft. Once again the Bridgmans were involved, this time following
the death of a married daughter, Mary Bartlett. The county court
held a hearing, appointed a committee of women to examine Mrs.
Parsons, and forwarded the case to the Court of Assistants in Boston.
There, in March and May 1675, Mary was indicted by a grand jury,
tried, and acquitted. One of her sons, John, was examined at the
county court in 1674 on suspicion of witchcraft; no further action
followed. At Joseph's death in 1683, he left a very substantial estate
of £2,088; his widow died in 1712. A full analysis of the defamation
case is in John P. Demos,* Entertaining Satan: Witchcraft and the
Culture of Early New England *(New York, 1982), pp. 250–74.*

1. See Gerald James Parsons, comp., *The Parsons Family: Descendants of
Cornet Joseph Parsons* (Baltimore, 1984).

Warrant for attaching Sarah Bridgman in a case of slander

To the constable of Northampton[:]

By virtue hereof you are required to attach the body of Sarah Bridg-man wife of James Bridgman of Northampton and to take bond of her to the value of an 100 pounds with sufficient surety or sureties for her personal appearance at the next County Court held at Cambridge on the 7th of October next ensuing the date thereof then and there to answer at the complaint of Joseph Parsons for slandering of his [wife Mary] Parsons and to make a true return thereof under your hand hereof [and] fail you not. Springfield, September 8, 1656. By the court Henry Burt.

Source: Middlesex County Court Records, folder 15 (MA).

A collection of testimonies on behalf of the defendant

Testimonies taken on the behalf of Sarah the wife of James Bridgman the 11th day of August, 1656.

William Hannum's wife against Mary Parsons

The wife of William Hannum of Norwottuck at Northampton sayeth that I have been warned by some of Windsor and some of Norwottuck to beware how I had to do with Mary the wife of Joseph Parsons: and she herself also told me, when she lay in of her last child, and being ill in a strange fit, that the occasion of her illness was, that her mother being lately there, had brought her news that she the said Mary was suspected to be a witch.

The said Goodwife Hannum also sayeth that this winter past I spun for the said Mary Parsons about 33 run of yarn, and this spring the said Mary desired me, to let her have one of my daughters to dwell with her, and I considering what rumors went about of her, I was loath to let her go there to dwell: but she having allured my daughter, as my daughter told me, I told my daughter she should not go thither to dwell, if she might have ten pound a year: at this time the said Mary Parsons came to me and challenged me about the yarn that I spun for her, that it wanted of the tale of the threads in the knots, upon which I went to her house and examined the yarn, and all that I examined did want almost in every knot of the yarn, sometimes there would be but 18 threads in a knot for 40 or 28 for 40: which notwithstanding when I spun it, I did my best endeavor to give a true account of and it was not found fault with till this time: and so I spun some more for her to recompence this defect: and I spun more for her besides that, and still when the yarn came to her, it would never hold out tale in the threads, though I did my best endeavor to deal truly in the thing, and I have spun for others and could have my yarn hold out. After this I spun oakum yarn for her, and sent for her weights to weigh it: and called whom I had about me to see that I made weight and so I sent it home to her: and presently she sent me word it wanted weight.

She the said Goodwife Hannum also saith that my daughter though formerly healthy, yet this summer hath been very sickly and unhelpful to me, which though I know it may be by God's own immediate hand: yet it causeth some jealousies in me against the said Mary because it fell out within 3 or 4 days after I had given her a full denial of my daughter's service. Testified on oath before me Elizur Holyoke.

William Hannum against Mary Parsons

William Hannum testifieth on oath: that I have had some jealousies against this Mary Parsons, on these grounds: first this Mary came to my house about the yarn that she missed, and then we had a falling out about it: and some discontented words passed on both sides: this was in an evening, and as I take it in March last and that evening all my cattle were well for ought I could see by them, and the next morning one cow lay in my yard, ready to die as I thought: which when I had considered I endeavored to get her up and at length got her to stand: but she languished away and died about a fortnight after, though I took great care night and day to save her: giving her samp pease wholesome drinks eggs etc. and this cow being young was lusty before this very time.

Secondly, the same week as I remember I being at work at John Webb's, I saw Joseph Parsons beating one of his little children, for losing its shoe; and to my apprehension he beat it unmercifully, and his wife coming to save it, because she had beaten it before as she said, he thrust her away: the next day I going to work again at John Webb's, there were some other neighbors there and they were talking how Joseph Parsons had in a sort beaten his wife: then I answered them that one of you being his next neighbors must ride, which manner of jesting I do not approve or allow of in myself: the same day the said Mary Parsons hearing how I had jested she dealt with me about it showing her offence: and so it fell out that the same evening, I having a sow that had 4 young pigs the sow was missing and we could not find her that night, the next morning very early I sought her a good while but found her not, but meeting a neighbor he asked me what I sought I said my sow: says he yonder in the swamp is a sow I think it is yours: I went thither and it was my sow: and there she stood with her nose to the ground looking steadily as if she had seen something in the ground: so I drove her home and before noon that day she died: she till now was a lusty swine and well fleshed.

Thirdly I having two oxen I lent them to John Bliss who is this Mary Parsons's brother and I was to have his oxen to work again for them: and so my oxen and his and Goodman Lancton's I set to break up some ground and they put John Bliss his oxen in the middle, for they were young and not very fit to go behind much less before: about which time Mary Parsons came to me and did chide with me for abusing her brother's oxen[.] I told her I did not abuse them: she said you put them in the middle where they are always under the whip, I told her they were not any way wronged by us: and she went away in anger: within 3 days after I was going to Windsor with my oxen and cart: and about 4 mile[s] from our town, as I was going thither my ox hung out his tongue or whether he went to eat for it fell out, that a rattlesnake bit him by the tongue and there he died.

These things do something run in my mind that I cannot have my mind from this woman that if she be not right this way she may be a cause of these things, though I desire to look at the overruling hand of God in all. Testified on oath before me Elizur Holyoke.

Goodwife Bridgman against Mary Parsons

Goodwife Bridgman testifies on oath that last May was a twelve month, I being brought to bed about 3 days after as I was setting up having my child in my lap, there was something that gave a great blow on the door, and at [that] very instant as I apprehended my child changed: and I thought with my self and told my girl I was afraid my child would die: and I sent out the girl to look who it was at the door, but she could see nobody about the house: presently after the girl came in, I looking towards the door through a hole by the door, I saw to my apprehension two women pass by the door with white cloths on their heads, then I concluded my child would die indeed: and I sent out the girl to see who they were but she could see nobody: this made me think there is wickedness in the place: Another time after this being the last summer my boy that is about 11 year old sayeth as he was going to look [for] our cows, in a swamp there came something and gave him a great blow on the head, that it struck off his hat and beat him almost to the ground: he thought it was a bird but could see nothing that did it: and going a little further he came to 2 logs and stumbled at one and fell on the other and put his knee out of joint: and his knee after was set as the man said that set it: but he was in grievous torture while the man staid which was 2 days to the man's admiration: For he was rather worse than before and he was in grievous torture about a month: and before he was well he cried out one night it being about break a day and with his crying out he awakened my husband: he cried out that Goody Parsons would pull off his knee, there she sits on the shelf: then I and my husband labored to quiet him and could hardly hold him in the bed: for he was very fierce: we told him there was nobody: yea says he there she sits on the shelf: and after he said there she is gone and a black mouse followed her: and both I and my husband told him in this extremity that there was nobody on the shelf: yea says he there she is do you not see her there she runs away and a black mouse follows her: and this he said many times and with great violence: and about sunrising he was like to die in our apprehension. Testified on oath before me Elizur Holyoke.

James Bridgman on his son's illness

James Bridgman testifies on oath that my child being at this time ill of his knee, he cried out and awaked me: he cried out his knee would be pulled off Goody Parsons will pull of[f] my knee: I bid him hold his peace for there was no Goody Parsons said I: yea says he there she sits on the shelf: I said there is nobody yea says he there she is and there she goes away and a black mouse follows her: and these things the child spake with much earnestness. Testified on oath before me Elizur Holyoke.

William Branch against Mary Parsons

William Branch of Springfield testifies on oath that when I lived at the Long Meadow and Joseph Parsons lived there, a certain time Joseph Parsons told me, that where ever he laid the key his wife could find it: and would go out in the night and that when she went out a woman went out with her and came in with her: but says Joseph Parsons God preserves his with his angels: and further the said William Branch sayeth that while they lived together in the Long Meadow; George Colton told me that he following Mary Parsons in her fit, he followed her through the water where he was up to the knees and she was not wet: this thing I told to old Mr. Pynchon when he was here: who wondered at it but said he could not tell what to say to it. Testified on oath before me Elizur Holyoke.

Thomas Stebbins against Mary Parsons

Thomas Stebbins testifies on oath that when Mr. William Pynchon dwelt in Springfield Joseph Parsons came to him and asked what he thought of such a thing as this: that when a person shall hide a thing and another shall find it wherever it is laid: as says he, wherever I hide the key of my door, my wife will find it and get out, and Mr. Pynchon wondering at it said he could not tell what to say to it, or what to think of it or words to that purpose. Testified on oath before me Elizur Holyoke.

Source: Middlesex County Court Records, folder 15 (MA). All these testimonies are written in the same booklet. The Harvard Law School owns another copy of these statements.

Margaret and John Bliss for Mary Parsons

Margaret Bliss and John Bliss testifieth that William Hannum and his wife said to them the 12 of August last that they had nothing against Mary Parsons. August 18, 1656 taken upon oath before us William Houlton Thomas Bascum.

Source: Middlesex County Court Records, folder 15 (MA).

William Houlton on Sarah Bridgman's suspicion

William Houlton testifieth upon oath that Sara Bridgman the wife of James Bridgman said to him she had such jealousies and suspicion of Mary Parsons that she could not be satisfied unless the said Mary were searched by women three times. August 18, 1656 in the presence of us Thomas Bascum Edward Elmer.

Ann Bartlett for Mary Parsons

The testimony of Ann Bartlett.

This deponent testifieth upon oath that the child of Sara Bridgman when she last lay in was sick as soon as it was born insomuch that it did groan something much and the said Ann Bartlett testifieth that a little while after she went to see the said Sara and asked how her child did and the said Sara told her that her child had the looseness still which it had at the first and if it continueth I fear it will be the death of my child. The said Ann Bartlett also testifieth upon oath that she watched the child of Sara Bridgman the same night the child died and then the child had a great looseness and the said Sara Bridgman said thus hath it been from the first. August 18, 1656 in the presence of us William Houlton Thomas Bascum.

Source: Middlesex County Court Records, folder 15 (MA).

John Mathews denies suspecting Mary Parsons

John Mathews affirmeth that he hath at present no grounds of jealousy for himself, of Mary Parsons the wife of Joseph Parsons, to be a witch, and that what he testified yesterday on oath was upon the earnest importuning of James Bridgman and his brother; further the said John Mathews affirmeth that when he was at work at Joseph Parsons's house there came a great clap of thunder suddenly, whereat Mary Parsons with the fright fell down in a swoon, in my sight: John Mathews further saith that he never spake a word to James Bridgman or his wife of that which I testified yesterday [ ] I [*word blotted*] spake it before the commisioners, and hereto I set my mark. Springfield, September 30, 1656 Before me John Pynchon.

Source: Middlesex County Court Records, folder 15 (MA).

Robert Bartlett on hearing from George Lancton

Robert Bartlett testifieth that George Lancton told him the last winter that Goody Bridgman and Goody Branch were speaking about Mary Parsons concerning her being a witch and the said George told to the said Robert that my wife being there, said she could not think [it] and the said Goody Bridgman seem[ed] to be distasted with us also they had hard thought[s] of the wife of the said Robert because she was intimate with the said Mary Parsons. June 20, 1656. Taken upon oath in the presence of us William Houlton Thomas Bascum.

Hannah Lancton verifies the above

Hanna Lancton the wife of George Lancton testifieth to the truth of this that Robert Bartlett [said] and saith it is the very truth in the presence of us William Houlton Thomas Bascum.

Source: Middlesex County Court Records, folder 15 (MA).

Hannah Lancton on the sickness of Sara Bridgman's child

Hanna Lancton testifieth upon oath that the child of Sara Bridgman when she last lay in she being her next neighbor came to dress her child not long after she had been brought abed and that then the child of the said Sara had a looseness and she thought it had taken cold and told the said Sara that her child was altered and that the clothes were loose about it and that she feared it had taken cold for the lower part of it was cold. August 18, 1656 in the presence of us William Houlton Thomas Bascum.

Hanna Broughton on the sickness of Sara Bridgman's child

Hanna Broughton testifieth upon oath that to the best of her remembrance the child of Sara Bridgman when she last lay in was sick before the time that the said Sara sat up for she being her next neighbor on the other side and the said Sara having no nurse she and Hanna Lancton were often there to look to the woman and the child. The said Hanna also testifieth that the child of the said Sara was ill as soon as it was born. August 18, 1656 in the presence of us William Houlton Thomas Bascum.

Source: Middlesex County Court Records, folder 15 (MA).

John Broughton on the death of William Hannum's cow

John Broughton testifieth that William Hannum came to him to have him skin his young cow that died about March last and when I had skinned his cow and came to open her there was a great quantity of water in the belly of the cow so much as I and Goodman Hannum judged it to be 4 or five gallons the said John testifieth that the said William Hannum called to his wife and told her they need not fear but the cow died of the water. August 18, 1656 testified upon oath before us William Houlton Thomas Bascum.

John Webb and others on the death of William Hannum's cow

John Webb and George Alexander testifieth that they asked William Hannum what he thought his cow died of and the said William told them that he thought his cow died of the water for she had a great quantity of water in her belly. August 18, 1656 testified upon oath before us William Houlton Thomas Bascum.

Source: Middlesex County Court Records, folder 15 (MA).

George Alexander and others
on the rattlesnake killing the ox

George Alexander Samuel Allen and Goody Webb testifieth that they were present when the ox of William Hannum was stung with the rattlesnake and they did conceive nothing but what might come to pass in an ordinary way and that they killed the rattlesnake. August 18, 1656. Testified upon oath before us William Houlton Thomas Bascum.

Source: Middlesex County Court Records, folder 15 (MA).

Margaret Bliss on Sara Bridgman's suspicions

Margaret Bliss testifieth that Sara Bridgman told her that she did hear that her daughter Parsons was suspected to be a witch and that she had heard there was some discontent between the blind man at Springfield and her daughter and that she had done him hurt and that there was some words between the blind man and her daughter and then the child of the blind man had a sounding fit. June 20, 1656 testified upon oath before us William Houlton Thomas Bascum.

Source: Middlesex County Court Records, folder 15 (MA).

John Webb and Hanna Broughton about Sara Bridgman

John Webb [and] Hanna Broughton testifieth upon oath that Sara Bridgman being summoned about last June before the three men at Northampton deputed by the honorable court for the trial of small cases they then desired to speak with her boy that had his knee sore[.] The said Sara said that her boy should not come. August 15, 1656 in the presence of us William Houlton Thomas Bascum.

Source: Middlesex County Court Records, folder 15 (MA).

Several witnesses on what Goody Parsons said, etc.

The testimony of Goodwife Wright the wife of Samuel Wright junior. Goodwife Wright saith that when she was at Goody Parsons's house she told her that Goodwife Molton said she would make her candles for her and half for the other.

Goodman Webb and his wife doth affirm the same that Goodwife Parsons said so to them.

Goodwife Molton was spoken to about this business in the presence of John Webb and his wife and denied it and said that she never speak word with Goodwife Parsons about it.

Richard Lyman doth affirm the same that Goodwife Molton denied it. So that it's a mad lie of Goodwife Parsons.

Richard Lyman and John Webb affirms that at that time when Goodman Elmore was swearing some witnesses concerning Goodwife Bridgman's businesses: Goodman Elmore urged them to swear and telling of them what they should say and did construe the meaning of their words and writ down what he thought good; and when he read it the witnesses denied what he writ.

John Webb affirms that Goodman Elmore said upon a time when he was examining something depending upon this business of Goodwife Bridgman's, that he stood for them and would stand for them meaning Goodwife Parsons.

Source: Middlesex County Court Records, folder 15 (MA).

Richard Sikes on Mary Parsons being in a fit

Richard Sikes affirmeth upon oath, that about four years ago, being at supper at Goodman Colton's: Samuel Bliss came in and said his sister, Mary Parsons was run down the meadow whereupon I went forth with Goodman Colton and we overtook her presently she being fallen down in one of her fits and we brought her in and laid her on the bed and she would look fearfully sometimes as if she saw something, and then bow down her head, as others did in their fits about that time. But I could [*torn*] and further saith not. Taken upon oath this September 27, 1656 before me John Pynchon.

John Mathews on Mary Parsons's fits

John Mathews testifies that about four years ago, being at Joseph Parsons's house making of barrels: upon occasion of some difference betwixt Joseph Parsons and his wife, he said to his wife that she was led by an evil spirit. Thereupon she said he was the cause of it, by locking her into the cellar and leaving her: Joseph Parsons said further that she went over the water and Colton after her, and she was not wet, only Goodman Colton was wet: she said also that when her husband locked her into the cellar, the cellar was full of spirits, and she threw the bedstaff at them and the bedclothes and her pillow and yet they would not be gone: and from this time she told one it was that she fell into her fits some few days after, she the said Mary Parsons told me, [that?] spirits appeared to her like poppets as she was washing her clothes at the brook, and then she fell into her fits: Mary Parsons the wife of Joseph Parsons further told me that in her fits, she had gone from her house in the Long Meadow through the great swamp in her shift, and when she came to herself she could not tell how she came thither. Taken upon oath this September 27, 1656 before me John Pynchon.

Source: Middlesex County Court Records, folder 15 (MA).

Hannah Lancton about Sara Bridgman's statements

Hanna Lancton the wife of George Lancton testifieth that Sara Bridgman the wife of James Bridgman told her, that her boy when his knee was sore cried out of the wife of Joseph Parsons and said that she did hurt him and that she would pull of[f] his knee and also the said Sara told her that she had heard other[s] say they were jealous that the wife of Joseph Parsons was not right and the said Hanna saith that by reason thereof she had some fear of the wife of Joseph Parsons but it hath pleased God to help her over them and doth believe there was no such cause and is sorry she should have hard thoughts of her upon no better grounds. Testified upon oath in the presence of us William Houlton Thomas Bascum. June 20, 1656.

Sara Bridgman acknowledges complaining about Mary Parsons

Sara Bridgman owned before us that she told Hanna Lancton that her boy cried out of the wife of Joseph Parsons and said she would hurt him and that she would pull of[f] his knee and that she had heard other[s] say that there were jealousies of Goody Parsons that she was not right. William Houlton Thomas Bascum. [*no date.*]

Source: Middlesex County Court Records, folder 15 (MA).

William Hannum on his sick cow

William Hannum being asked what he did with his cow when he had skinned her he said he let her lie in the yard the first day [ ] next day in the morning he drew part of the cow down toward the swamp before his house. August 16, 1656 in the presence of us William Houlton Thomas Bascum.

Source: Middlesex County Court Records, folder 15 (MA).

James Bridgman solicits witnesses

William Hannum and his wife said to us that James Bridgman hired them to [go] down to Springfield to give in their testimony or else they would not have gone but that he was very importunate with them. August 18, 1656 William Houlton Thomas Bascum.

Source: Middlesex County Court Records, folder 15 (MA).

John Pynchon defends Goodwife Parsons

Being requested by Goodwife Parsons to give this testimony which testifies of my hearing some report concerning Goodwife Parsons, that gave me occasion to say: if it were true, Goodwife Parsons could not be right, she the said Goodwife Parsons desiring me to declare whether I said so, and what reports I heard of her, I accordingly declare, that to my remembrance I never said any such word, neither do I remember any reports that I have heard, which have given me occasion to speak any such words of Goodwife Parsons: and here to I set my hand this 30th of September 1656. John Pynchon.

Source: Middlesex County Court Records, folder 15 (MA).

Mary Parsons and her fits

Simon Beamon testifies, that about the time the witches were apprehended to be sent to Boston Mr. Moxon's children[1] were taken ill in their fits (which we took to be bewitched) and at the same time was Mary Parsons, the wife of Joseph Parsons and others taken with the like fits so that they were all carried out of the meeting it being Sabbath day as Mr. Moxon's children acted so did Mary Parsons the wife of Joseph Parsons, just all one, and I have diverse times been with them all, and I could discern no difference in their fits[.] And once I carried Mary Parsons home to[2] the Long Meadow when she was in her fits, and when she was at home and came to herself she wondered how she came there, and by the way as I carried her behind me I was fain to hold her up upon the horse, and I discerned that she did not understand herself nor where she was, and she would often cry out of the witches and call to Hannah Smith that they might creep under Goodwife Warriner's bed (from whence I took her to carry her home) or else the witches would kill them, she said, and I have at other times been helping to hold her when she hath been in her fits and have found it as much as two men could do to hold her in her fits. Taken upon oath this September 19, 1656 before me John Pynchon.

1. The reference is to the minister's children whom Hugh Parsons of Springfield had been suspected of bewitching; see chap. 2.
2. He meant "from."
Source: Autograph File (John Pynchon), HLH.

Evidence about testimony

There was tendered to Goodman Parsons and his wife references about the business by James Bridgman in the presence of Samuel Wright senior and William Francis. And reference tendered the second time in the presence of Samuel Wright senior Richard Lyman William Francis John Webb and she refused it. And her answer was what the court would give her that she would stand to.

Source: Middlesex County Court Records, folder 15 (MA).

George Lancton on what he and several women thought

George Lancton's testimony what he spake to Goodman Bartlett. At a time when his wife [and] Goodwife Bridgman and Goodwife Branch was together they thought Goodwife Parsons was naught and was not right and this I told to Goodman Bartlett. This George Lancton can affirm upon oath.

Source: Middlesex County Court Records, folder 15 (MA).

Decision of the court in the slander suit

The court having read the attachments and perused the evidences respectively presented on both sides which are on file with the records of this court do find that the defendant hath without just ground raised a great scandal and reproach upon the plaintiff's wife: and do therefore order that the defendant shall make acknowledgment before the inhabitants of the places where the said parties dwell: viz. Northampton and also at Springfield at some public meeting at each place by order of Mr. Pynchon or Mr. Holyoke or either of them and in such words and manner as shall be suitable satisfaction for such an offence and the same to be testified under the hands of the said Mr. Pynchon and Mr. Holyoke, within 60 days next ensuing and in case of default having notice of the time at each place the said defendant viz. James Bridgman shall pay damages to the plaintiff ten pounds sterling: Also this court doth order that the defendant shall pay to the plaintiff his costs of court viz. seven pounds one shilling and eight pence. [October 7, 1656.]

Source: James R. Trumbull, *History of Northampton* (1898), *1*, p. 51.

Mary Parsons under suspicion for the death of Mrs. Bartlett

At a County Court held at Springfield September 29, 1674.

There being exhibited to this court diverse testimonies on oath from Northampton of many persons declaring causes of jealousies and suspicion of witchcraft in the town and diverse of the testimonies reflecting on the wife of Joseph Parsons senior, she having information that such things were bruited abroad and that she should probably be called in question for reason aforesaid she voluntarily made her appearance in court, desiring to clear herself of such an execrable crime, and the testimonies being read before her and she examined thereupon[,] the court, thought meet for special reason to refer the matter to further disposition when she should be called forth to make further answer and it being so declared to her she was for present dismissed.

Samuel Bartlett of Northampton having lately lost his wife to his great grief as he expresseth and the rather for that he strongly suspects that she died by some unusual means, viz., by means of some evil instrument he presented to this court diverse evidences to show the grounds of his fear and suspicion[.] Also Goodman Bridgman sending to the court and entreating that diligent inquisition may be made concerning the death of the said woman his daughter for that he also strongly suspects, she come to her end by some unlawful and unnatural means and for that diverse of the testimonies do reflect on Goodwife Parsons senior of Northampton the court having read the testimonies do think it meet that the case should be further looked into and therefore do refer the said case and all other things concerning the said Goodwife Parsons that have been now presented to the adjournment of this court which is to be kept at Northampton the 18th day of November next, for further disposition and do order that she be warned thereto attend to answer what shall be objected against her and the witnesses are to be warned to appear to testify before her viva voce what they have already given in upon oath concerning her.

Mary Parsons asserts her innocence; she is searched

At the County Court on the 18th of November.

Mary Parsons the wife of Joseph Parsons senior appeared also Samuel Bartlett whom this court ordered to produce the witnesses in the matter referring to Goodwife Parsons's suspicion of witchcraft: and the said Goodwife Parsons being called to speak for herself, she did assert her own innocency often mentioning it how clear she was of such a crime, and that the righteous God knew her innocency with whom she had left her cause. There having been many suspicions of witchcraft at Northampton and several testimonies concerning the same, of persons suspected, exhibited to the last County Court in September last at Springfield by persons then and there coming voluntarily some to give in evidence and others there appearing also without summons to clear themselves of so execrable a crime, also James Bridgman sending to the court that diligent inquisition might be made concerning the death of his daughter, Samuel Bartlett's wife, whom both Goodman Bridgman and Samuel Bartlett suspect she came to her end by some unnatural means, and for that diverse testimonies reflect upon Mary Parsons the wife of Joseph Parsons senior, it being also affirmed that there were many more witnesses that would come in in the case, the court then thought meet to order Mary Parsons to appear at the court now hither adjourned, who accordingly appearing as abovesaid, also Samuel Bartlett appeared, whom the court ordered to produce the testimonies in the case, which being brought in and the court finding them many and various, some of them being demonstrations of witchcraft and others sorely reflecting upon Mary Parsons as being guilty that way, though the trial of the case belongs not to this court, but to the Court of Assistants, yet considering the remoteness, and the season of the year and many difficulties if not incapabilities of persons there to appear some being so weak, this court took the more pains in inquiring into the case, appointed a jury of soberdized chaste women to make diligent search upon the body of Mary Parsons whether any marks of witchcraft might appear, who gave in their account to the court on oath of what they found (which) with all the testimonies in the case the court orders to be sent to Boston to our honored Governor by the first opportunity, leaving it to his wisdom and prudence in communicating the matter to the honorable magistrates for the further proceeding therein as they shall see cause, and the recorder of this court is accordingly to take care that all the writings and evidences in the case be ready and delivered to the worshipful Major Pynchon who is desired to write to the Governor concerning this matter.

It is further ordered that Mary Parsons shall make her appearance

before the Governor or magistrates or Court of Assistants to answer
to what she is suspected of in case she be called or required thereto
by authority and her husband Joseph Parsons to become bound in a
bond of 50 pounds for his wife's appearance accordingly if required
before the 13th May next.

[*Joseph Parsons made bond: document omitted*].[1]

Some testimonies being procured in court reflecting on John Parsons the court have read and considered them do not find in them any
such weight whereby he should be prosecuted on suspicion of witchcraft and therefore do discharge the said John Parsons of any further
attendance.

1. Printed in Trumbull, *History of Northampton, 1*, pp. 230–31.
Source: Northampton, Mass. (Hampshire County), Registry of Probate Books, *1*
(1660–1690), pp. 158–60. Microfilm, Harvard University Library.

The grand jury indicts Mary Parsons

The grand jury was called again and they perusing several evidences
sent down from the County Court at Northampton relating to Mary
Parsons the wife of Joseph Parsons they presenting an indictment
against her on suspicion of witchcraft leaving her to further trial[,] the
court ordered her committed to the prison in Boston there to remain
and be kept in order to her further trial.

Source: *Recs. Ct. Assistants, 1*, p. 31.

Mary Parsons is tried and acquitted

At this court Mary Parsons the wife of Joseph Parsons of Northampton
in the County of Hampshire in the Colony of the Massachusetts being
presented and indicted by the grand jury was also indicted by the
name of Mary Parsons the wife of Joseph Parsons for not having the
fear of God before her eys and being instigated by the devil hath at
one or other of the times mentioned in the evidences now before the
court entered into familiarity with the devil and committed several
acts of witchcraft on the person or persons of one or more[,] as in the
said evidences relating thereto reference being thereto had amply do-
eth and may appear and all this contrary to the peace of our sovereign
lord the King his crown and dignity the laws of God and of this jurisdiction[.] After the indictment and evidences in the case were read the
prisoner at the bar holding up her hand and pleading not guilty putting herself on her trial, the jury brought in their verdict they found
her not guilty—and so she was discharged. May 13, 1675.

Source: *Recs. Ct. Assistants, 1*, p. 33.

7. One Man's Many Accusers
(1658–1669)

▲

John Godfrey

John Godfrey is singular within the annals of New England witch-craft. Somehow he acquired a reputation for strange or suspicious actions and, like so many of the women who were brought to court, he was accused of witchcraft not once but several times. Godfrey seems to have arrived in New England in the mid-1630s while in his teens. In a deposition of 1659 a witness recalled hearing him talk about witchcraft and the devil's compact in 1640. He settled in Essex County, Massachusetts, and moved about from town to town. He was frequently in the county courts, sometimes as plaintiff and some-times as defendant.

Accusations of witchcraft arose in 1658–59. In 1658 Godfrey sued Abraham Whitaker of Haverhill for debt. A year later he himself was being charged with witchcraft; it is likely, though not certain, that he was indicted, tried, and acquitted. He won a suit for slander shortly thereafter.

Godfrey was in court again on charges of witchcraft in 1665 and 1666. The Whitaker family reappeared as witnesses against him; and John Remington, together with members of his family, described a quarrel with Godfrey.

In 1669 Godfrey filed suit for defamation against Daniel Ela of Haverhill for spreading stories that he was simultaneously in two Essex County towns, Ipswich and Salisbury. He did not win this case.

Godfrey never married. He may have earned his living as a herds-man. He had died by 1675.

*The extensive records relating to Godfrey's various suits for pay-
ment, and charges against him of drunkenness, stealing, and "cursing speeches," are not included in this collection. Nor does it include
bills of cost stemming from his suit against Daniel Ela.*[1]

*John P. Demos has reconstructed Godfrey's very complicated life
history in* Entertaining Satan: Witchcraft and the Culture of Early
New England *(New York, 1982), chapter 2.*

1. Some of these are printed in *Recs. Ct. Assistants, 3*, pp. 151–55.

Ambiguous verdict in Godfrey's suit of defamation

At a court held at Salem June 28, 1659.

John Godfrey plaintiff against William Symonds and Samuel his son
defendants in an action of slander that the said Samuel, son to William
Symonds hath done him in his name, charging him to be a witch, the
jury find for the plaintiff 2d damages and cost of court 29s yet notwithstanding do conceive that by the testimonies he is rendered suspicious.

Source: Essex County Court Records, *4*, p. 29 (EI).

Several persons complain against John Godfrey

Complaint against John Godfrey for witchcraft March, 1659.

To the honored court to be holden at Ipswich this twelfth month
1658 or 1659[.] Honored gentlemen[:]

Whereas divers of esteem with us and as we hear in other places
also have for some times have suffered losses in their estates and
some affliction on their bodies also: which as they suppose doth not
arise from any natural cause or any neglect in themselves but rather
from some ill-disposed person: that upon differences had betwixt
themselves and one John Godfrey resident at Andover or elsewhere
at his pleasure we whose names are underwritten do make bold to
sue by way of request to this honored court that you in your wisdom
will be pleased if you see cause for it, to call him in question and to
hear at present or at some after sessions what may be said in this
respect.

James Davis, Sr. in the behalf of his son Ephraim Davis.
John Haseltine and Jane his wife.
Abraham Whitaker for his ox and other things.
Ephraim Davis in the behalf of himself.
Some things we hear of and it may be they may be of consequence[:]
Benjamin Swet in the case of his child.

Isabelle Holdred hearing a voice and being afflicted in her body.

Job Tyler of Andover for a bird coming in to suck his wife.

Charles Brown for what he did see although we say no more at present.

Widow Ayres's daughter and Goodman Procter's daughter for a pail with some things in it.

Source: Essex County Court Papers, *5*: 7–1 (EI).

Thomas Hayne on a horse that frightened Goodwife Holderidge

Thomas Hayne testifieth that being with Goodwife Holderidge she told me that she saw a great horse and showed me where it stood: I then took a stick and struck on the place but felt nothing, and I heard the door shake and Goodwife said it was gone: out at the door immediately after she was taken with extremity of fear and pain so that she presently fell into a sweat and I thought she would swoon away: she trembled and shook like a leaf. Thomas Hayne.

Source: Essex County Court Papers *5*:7–2 (EI).

Nathan Gould and a snake that frightened Goodwife Holderidge

Nathan Gould being with Goodwife Holderidge one night there appeared a great snake as she said with open mouth and she being weak hardly able to go alone yet then ran and laid hold of Nathan Gould by the head and could not speak for the space of half an hour. Nathan Gould.

Source: Essex County Court Papers *5*:7–2a (EI).

Isabelle Holdred on shape-changing animals

The deposition of Isabelle Holdred who testifieth that John Godfrey came to the house [where] Henry Blaisdell her husband and herself were and demanded a debt of her husband and said a warrant was out, and Goodman Lord was suddenly to come[.] John Godfrey [*torn*]ed if we would not pay him[.] The deponent answered yes, tonight [or?] morrow if we had it: for I believe we shall no[t?][*torn*] we are in thy debt: John Godfrey answered that's a bitter word: [*torn*] said I must begin and must [send] Goodman Lord: the deponent answ[ered] [ ] when thou wilt I fear the[e] not nor all the devils in hell: and farther [the?] deponent testifieth that two days after this, she was taken with those stran[ge] fits with which she was tormented a fortnight together night and day and several apparitions appeared to the deponent in the night: The first night a bumble bee, the next night a bear appeared which ground the teeth and shook the claw, thou sayest thou art not afraid: thou thinkest Henry Blaisdell's house will save thee[.] The deponent answered I hope that Lord Jesus Christ will save me: the apparition then spake thou sayest thou art not afraid of all the devils in hell but I will have thy heart['s] blood within a few hours[.] The next was the apparition of a great snake at which the deponent was exceedingly affrighted and skipped to Nathan Gould who was in the opposite chimney corner and caught hold of the hair of his head and her speech was taken away for the space of half an hour: the next night appeared a great horse and Thomas Hayne being there the deponent told him of it: and showed him where: the said Thomas Hayne took a stick and struck at the place where [the?] apparition was: his stroke glanced by the side of it: and it went [under?] the table, and he went to strike again[.] Then the apparition fled to the [*torn*] and made it shake and went away: and about a week after the deponent [and her?] son were at the door of Nathan Gould and heard a rushing in the [*torn*] the deponent said to her son yonder is a beast: he answered 'tis one [of?] Goodman Cobbye's black oxen: and it came toward them: and came within [*torn*] yards of them the deponent her heart began to ache for it seemed to have [*torn*] great eyes: and spake to the boy let's go in: but suddenly the ox beat her up against the wall and struck her down and she was much hurt by it: not being able to rise up but some others carried me into the house: all my face being bloody being much bruised [the?] boy was much affrighted a long time after: and for the space of two hours [was?] in a sweat that one might have washed hands on his hair.

Further the deponent affirmeth that she hath been often troubled with [*torn*] black cat sometimes appearing in the house and sometimes in the night [*torn*] bed and lay on her and sometimes stroking her face the cat [*torn*] thrice as big as an ordinary cat.

Source: Essex County Court Papers, 5:8–1 (EI).

Charles Brown and wife report John Godfrey speaking of witches

The deposition of Charles Brown and his wife: This deponent saith about 6 or 7 years since in the meetinghouse of Rowley being in the gallery in the first seat there was one in the second seat (which he doth to his best remembrance think and verily believe it was John Godfrey) this deponent did see him yawning ope[n] his mouth and while he so yawned this deponent did see a small teat under his tongue. And further this deponent saith that John Godfrey was at this deponent's house about 3 year[s] since speaking about the power of witches he the said Godfrey spoke that if witches were not kindly entertained the devil will appear unto them and ask them if they were grieved or vexed with anybody and ask them what he should do for them and if they would not give them beer or victuals they might let all the beer run out of the cellar and if they looked steadfastly upon any creature it would die and it were hard to some witches to take away life either of man or beast yet when they once begin it then it is easy to them.

Source: Essex County Court Papers, 5:8–2 (EI).

William Osgood and John Godfrey's contract with the devil

William Osgood testifieth that in the year [16]40 in the month of August he being then building a barn for Mr. Spencer[,] John Godfrey being then Mr. Spencer's herdsman he on an evening came to the frame where divers men were at work: and said that he had gotten a new master against the time he had done keeping cows[.] The said William Osgood asked him who it was he answered he knew not[.] He again asked him where he dwelt, he answered he knew not: he asked him what his name was he answered he knew not: he then said to him how then wilt thou go to him when thy time is out: he said the man will come and fetch me: then William Osgood asked him hast thou made an absolute bargain[?] He answered that a covenant was made and he had set his hand to it: he then asked of him whether he had not a counter covenant: Godfrey answered no: William Osgood said what a mad fellow art thou to make a covenant in this manner: he said he's an honest man: how knowest thou said William Osgood[.] J[ohn] Godfrey answered he looks like one[.] William Osgood then answered I am persuaded thou hast made a covenant with the devil: he then skipped about and said I profess I profess.[1]

William Osgood

1. The word is a contraction in the manuscript and may possibly be "protest."
Source: Essex County Court Papers, 5:8–3 (EI).

Thomas Chandler against John Godfrey

Thomas Chandler testified that 'I going to Job Tyler's house to serve an attachment I did take John Godfrey with me and when I came to the said Tyler's house John Care being there said what come you hither for Godfrey you witching rogue. . . .' Copy of Ipswich Court record of March 25, 1662, in action of Job Tyler v. John Godfrey, made by Robert Lord, clerk.

Source: *Essex Ct. Recs.*, 2:410.

A case of slander: Godfrey v. Singletary

To the marshall of Ipswich or constable of Haverhill you are required in his Majesty's name to attach the body and goods of Jonathan Singletary to the value of an hundred pounds and take bond of him to the said value with sufficient security for his appearance at the next County Court to be holden at Ipswich the last 3d day of this present month there to answer the complaint of John Godfrey in an action of slander and defamation for calling him witch and said is this witch on this side [of] Boston gallows yet[?] And make return under your hand. Dated March 15, 1663, per curiam Anthony Somerby.

Source: Essex County Court Papers, 9:82–4 (EI).

John Remington and others testify about Godfrey

The deposition of John Remington and Edwa[rd Youmans][:] These deponents being at the last court held at Ip[swich *torn*] Jonathan Singletary being there in the court [*torn*] that John Godfrey came to him in the [*torn*] when the prison door was locked [*torn*] Jonathan, and said now I can speak [*torn*] pay the executions you are in prison for, you may soon [*torn*] forth, and farther Jonathan said before Godfrey came thus unto him and spake to him, he heard a noise and the prison shake and the locks and doors chattering as if they did open and shut at his coming in: and also that he see Godfrey's face as plain in the prison as he did in the court. Taken upon the oaths of John Remington and Edward Youmans 20th: 4th: 63: before me Simon Bradstreet. [*verso:*] John Godfrey Verdict.

[*the following has a line drawn through it:*] we find for the plaintiff that Jonathan Singletary shall make a public acknowledgment at Haverhill that he wronged John Godfrey by his words or pay ten shillings.

Source: Essex County Court Papers, 9:82–5 (EI).

What John Singletary heard and did in prison

Dated the fourteenth the twelfth month 1662.

The deposition of Jonathan Singletary aged about 23 who: testifieth that I being in the prison at Ipswich this night last past between nine and ten of the clock at night after the bell had rung I being set in a corner of the prison upon a sudden I heard a great noise as if many cats had been climbing up the prison walls and skipping into the house at the windows and jumping about the chamber and a noise as if boards ends or stools had been thrown about and men walking in the chambers and a crackling and shaking as if the house would have fallen upon me[.] I seeing this and considering what I knew by a young man that kept at my house last Indian harvest and upon some difference with John Godfrey he was presently several nights in a strange manner troubled and complaining as he did and upon consideration of this and other things that I knew by him I was at present something affrighted—yet considering what I had lately heard made out by Mr. Mitchell at Cambridge[1] that there is more good in God than there is evil in sin and that although God is the greatest good and sin the greatest evil yet the first being of evil cannot wear the scales or over power the first being of good so considering that the author of good was of greater power than the author of evil[,] God was pleased of his goodness to keep me from being out of measure frighted so: this noise abovesaid held as I suppose about a quarter of an hour and then ceased and presently I heard the bolt of the door shoot or go back as perfectly to my thinking as I did the next morning when the keeper came to unlock it and I could not see the door open but I saw John Godfrey stand within the door and said: Jonathan Jonathan so I looking on him said what have you to do with me[?] He said I come to see you are you weary of your place yet[?] I answered I take no delight in being here but I will be out as soon as I can[.] He said if you will pay me in corn you shall come out[.] I answered no if that had been my intent I would have paid the marshall and never have come hither[.] He knocking of his fist at me in a kind of a threatening way said he would make me weary of my part and so went away I know not how nor which way and as I was walking about in the prison I tripped upon a stone with my heel and took it up in my hand thinking that if he came again I would strike at him[.] So as I was walking about he called at the window Jonathan said he if you will pay me corn I will give you two years day and we will come to an agreement[.] I answered him saying why do you come dissembling and playing the devil's part here your nature is nothing but envy and malice which you will vent though to your own loss and you seek peace with no man[.] I do not dissemble said he I will give you my hand upon it I am in earnest so he put his hand in at the window and I took hold of it with my left hand and pulled him to me and with the stone in my right hand I thought I struck him and went to recover my hand to strike again and [*blotted*] his hand was gone and I would have struck but there was nothing to strike and how he went away I know not for I could neither feel when his hand went out of mine nor see which way he went. [*inscribed:*] Testimony (not as yet sworn) about Godfrey.

1. Jonathan Mitchell, minister in Cambridge.
Source: Essex County Court Papers, 9:83–1 (EI).

Abraham Whitaker and Edward Youmans on defamation of Godfrey

The deposition of Abraham Whitaker and Edward Youmans who testifieth that Jonathan Singletary meeting John Godfrey in the street at Haverhill Jonathan Singletary called John Godfrey witch and said to him is this witch a [on?] this side Boston gallows this was the latter end of the last summer. Sworn before me March 22, 1663 Daniel Denison.

Source: Essex County Court Papers, 9:83–2 (EI).

The verdict in Godfrey v. Singletary

At a court held at Salem the 30th: 4 mo: 1663.
John Godfrey plaintiff against Jonathan Singletary defendant in an action of defamation for a slander he hath done him in his name, reporting that the said Godfrey came into Ipswich prison in the night time, when the said Singletary was in the prison when the prison doors were locked and fast, with other defaming speeches, and for damages: According to attachment: the attachment with what the jury found for the defendant: Costs 20s: the plaintiff appealed.
John Godfrey and Mr. Edmond Batter do acknowledge themselves to stand bound in £4 bond to the [treasurer] of the county jointly and severally upon condition that the said Godfrey shall [present] his said appeal to effect.

Source: Essex County Court Records, 4, p. 113 (EI).

[At] the court held at Ipswich March 29, 1664.

John Godfrey plaintiff against Jonathan Singletary defendant in an action of slander and defamation for calling him witch and said is this witch on this side Boston gallows yet[.] The attachment and other evidences were read committed to the jury and are on file[.] The jury found for the plaintiff:[ ] acknowledgment at Haverhill with[in] a month that he hath done the plaintiff wrong in his words or 10s damages and costs of court £2. 16–0

Source: Essex County Court Records, *9*, p. 124 (EI).

Order to witnesses to appear at Court of Assistants

You are hereby required in his Majesty's name to [sum]mon and require Mathias Button and Sarah his daughter Edward Youmans and his wife Abraham Whitaker and Elizabeth his wife Robert Swan and Elizabeth his wife Abigail Remington wife to John Remington and John their son Joseph Johnson and the wife of William Holdridge Ephraim Davis William Symons Samuel Symons and Mary the wife of William Neasse all of Haverhill to make their several appearances before the next Court of Assistants to be held at Boston on the first Tuesday in March next at eight of the clock in the morning then and there to give in their particular and several evidences what they know of and concerning John Godfrey of Newbury being a witch or of any act of witchcraft done by him he being bound over to that court in order to his trial on the complaint of Job Tyler and John Remington making your return hereof to the Secretary at or before the time prefixed hereof you are not to fail[.] Dated in Boston February 6, 1665. By order of the County Court sitting in Boston February 4, 1665. Edward Rawson Secretary.

To the constable of Andover[:]

You are hereby required in his Majesty's name to summon and require Mr. Francis Dane[1] and Nathan Parker both of Andover to make their personal appearances before the next Court of Assistants to be held in Boston on the first Tuesday in March next then and there to give in their evidences what they know of and concerning John Godfrey of Newbury being [a] witch or of any act of witchcraft done by him [. . .] February 6, 1665 by order of the County Court sitting in Boston February 5, 1665. Edward Rawson Secretary.

[*on the back*] This warrant was served upon Mr. Dane and Nathan Parker the 22 of the 12 month 1665 by me Thomas Johnson constable.

1. Dane was the town minister.
Source: *Recs. Ct. Assistants, 2*, pp. 158–59.

Francis Dane cannot appear in court

To the honorable court at Boston.

May it please your worships, I received a warrant under Mr. Secretary's hand, for my appearance at Boston at this court, to give in evidence, about some words that Godfrey spoke to me, concerning witches, the which I understand were shown in the court under my own hand; but considering the necessity that is incumbent by reason of prevailing infirmity, I humbly crave your favor[able] interpretation of my absence; 'tis not disrespect, nor neglect of [duty] my conscience witnessing the frailty of nature; and the rawness of the weather, and now having presented the cause, I crave leave to draw a veil desiring almighty God to be with you, and to conduct you in paths of justice and righteousness: I rest [   ] your honors, obliged unto all due service in the Lord. Francis Dane. March 5, 1665.

Source: "Trials for Witchcraft in New England," HLH.

Job Tyler and family against John Godfrey

The deposition of Job Tyler aged about 40 years Mary his wife and Moses Tyler his son aged betwixt 17 and 18 years and Mary Tyler about 15 years old.

These deponents witness that they saw a thing like a bird to come in at the door of their house with John Godfrey in the night about the bigness of a blackbird or rather bigger to wit as big as a pigeon, and did fly about, John Godfrey laboring to catch it, and the bird vanished as they conceived through the chink of a jointed board, and being asked by the man of the house wherefore it came, he answered it came to suck your wife. This was as they remember about 5 or 6 years since. Owned in court March 7, 1665 by Job Tyler and Moses Tyler. Owned in court March 13, 1665 by Mary Tyler on her former oath. Taken upon oath of the 4 above mentioned parties this 27.4 1659 before me Simon Bradstreet. Edward Rawson Secretary.

Source: "Trials for Witchcraft in New England," HLH.

Nathan Parker on Godfrey's threat

The testimony of Nathan Parker 44 years.

John Godfrey came into my house and discussing of Job Tyler Godfrey said that he could afford to blow on Tyler and not leave him worth a groat.[1] Deposed in court March 7, 1665. Edward Rawson Secretary.

1. A coin of little value.
Source: *Recs. Ct. Assistants, 2*, p. 159.

Joseph Johnson on Godfrey's threatening speech

I Joseph Johnson of Haverhill being about 27 years of age went to John Remington's and there was John Godfrey and Goodman Button and I heard John Godfrey say that if John Remington's son was a man as he was a boy it had been worser for him. Sworn in court March 7, 1665. As attests Edward Rawson Secretary.

Source: *Recs. Ct. Assistants,* 2, p. 159.

William Howard on encountering John Godfrey many years ago

The deposition of William Howard aged about 56 years.

[The?] deponent witnesseth that about 26 years ago he going upon [New]bury plain towards Hampton he there spoke with a man that was following of cattle, who said he had been Mr. Spencer's [ap]prentice and his time was then out (or near out) and he then discovered that he wanted a service: and this deponent did then contract with that party to serve him for a considerable time (but how long that time was this deponent have forgot)[.] But he doth remember that he did give him a piece of money in part of payment and as this deponent doth suppose he did then write the agreement: which said person was like John Godfrey and as I suppose he [di]d then name himself by that name: and further this deponent sayeth not. Sworn in court March 7, 1665 as attests Edward Rawson Secretary.

Source: *Recs. Ct. Assistants,* 2, p. 159.

John Remington (Jr.) on his fall and John Godfrey's response

The deposition of John Remington.

This deponent testifieth that I heard John Godfrey say to my father that if he drived the cattle up the woods to winter then my father should say and have cause to repent that he did drive them up and these words he said in a great rage and passion and of [   ] this my father and I did drive up the cattle and I for the most part did tend them: and about the middle of December last as I was a coming home from the cattle about a mile from them: then the horse I rid[e] on begun to start and snort and the dog that was with me begun to whine and cry and it still[.] I made a shift to sit on the horse still for a matter of a quarter of a mile and then I smelt a sweet smell like cider and presently I looked up into the swamp and I see a crow come towards

me flying and perched upon a tree against me and she looked at me
and the horse and dog and it had a very great and quick eye and it had
a very great bill and then the said crow flew of[f] that tree to another
after me[.] Then I begun to mistrust and think it was no crow and
thought if it was not a crow it could not hurt my soul though it hurt
my body and horse and as I was a thinking thus to myself the horse I
was upon fell down [u]pon on[e] side in pain grown upon my leg and
as soon as I [   ] the horse was fallen then the crow came and flew
round me several times as if she would light upon me but she [should:
crossed out] did not touch me[.] Then the horse rise and went about
four rod and then stood still and I lay on the ground still and was not
able to follow him for the present[.] Then when I came a little [be]tter
to myself I made a shift to creep on my hands and knees the horse and
the crow scr[eeche]d and made a noise like a cat and the hallo'oing of
a man then I got upon the horse and went on[.] Then the crow appeared to me sometimes a great crow and sometimes like a little bird
and so continued with me about a mile and a half further and she flew
upon the dog and bite him to the last[.] All this while after I fell with
the horse I was taken very sick and thought I should have died till
such time the crow left me and then the dog made on me and re-
joiceth very much after the crow left us: and then the second day fowling I being at home John Godfrey came to my father's house in a great
rage and asked of me how I did and I told him pretty well only I was
lame with the horse falling on me two days before[.] Then said Godfrey every cockating[1] boy must rid[e] I unhorsed on[e] boy t'other day
I will unhorse the[e] shortly to[o] if the[e] rides my horse[.] Then said
I I am not able to carry victuals upon my back then said Godfrey 'tis a
sorry horse cannot carry his own provender[.] Then said Godfrey to
me John if the[e] hadst been a man as the[e] wast a boy the[e] hadst
died on the spot where the[e] got the fall[.] Then said my mother to
Godfrey how canst the[e] tell that there is none but God can tell that
and except the[e] be more than a[n] ordinary man the[e] canst not tell
that[.] Then Godfrey bid my mother hold her tongue he knew what he
said better than she and said I say again had he been [a man] as he
was a boy he had died on the spot where he fell.
[*margin*] Godfrey saith that he knows not that he said if he had been
a man [as he was a] boy he had died that he had knowledge of [   ]
the boy. This was deposed on his oath in this court March 7, 1665
Edward Rawson Secretary.

1. Not in *OED*, but surely meaning "cocky" or "boastful."

Abigail Remington on her son's injury and Godfrey's response

The deposition of Abigail Remington.

This deponent testifieth that John Godfrey came to our house the beginning of winter and said to my husband that if he drove the cattle up to the woods to winter then my husband should have cause to say and repent that he did drive them up and these words he said in a great rage and passion[.] Then after this the second day after my son John was lame with the fall of the horse upon him John Godfrey came to my house and asked my son John how he did in a very great rage and John made answer pretty well only he was lame with the horse falling on him two days before[.] Then said Godfrey every cockating boy must rid[e] I unhorsed on[e] boy t'other day and I will unhorse the[e] shortly to[o] if the[e] rides my horse[.] Then said John I am not able to carry my victuals on my back[.] Then said Godfrey 'tis a sorry horse cannot carry his own provender[.] Then said Godfrey to John: John if the[e] hadst been a man as the[e] wast a boy the[e] hadst died on the spot where the[e] got the fall[.] Then said I to Godfrey how canst the[e] tell that: there is none but God can tell that: and except the[e] beest more than a[n] ordinary man the[e] canst not tell that[.] Then Godfrey bid me hold my tongue he knew better what he said than I: and said: I say again had he been a man as he was a boy he had died on the spot where he fell.

Abigail Remington her mark.

Mathias Button on Godfrey's response

The deposition of Mathias Button.

This deponent testifieth coming into the house of John Remington two days after that John Remington's son being hurt with a fall of a horse: seeing him lie in the chimney corner asking him how he did his answer was to me that he had a fall of a horse: which hurt his leg[.] Godfrey being there made answer and said to John and said if thou hadst been a man thou hadst died upon the spot where he fell but seeing he was a boy he 'scaped the horse[.] These words was spoken by John Godfrey two or [three] times over: this was delivered in by Mathias Button on his oath took in court March 7, 1665. Edward Rawson Secretary.

Source: *Recs. Ct. Assistants, 2*, pp. 160–61.

John Godfrey is indicted and tried

At a Court of Assistants held at Boston 6th March 1665/6.

John Godfrey being bound over to this court by the County Court in January last in Boston on the complaint and accusation of Job Tyler and John Remington on suspicion of witchcraft, the said Job Tyler and John Remington being also bound over to prosecute against the said John Godfrey summons for witnesses being granted out and many appeared Edward Youmans Robert Swan Mathias Button William Symons and John Remington deposed in court that whatever evidence either of them shall give into the grand jury in relation to John Godfrey shall be the truth, whole truth, and nothing but the truth, and divers others with them being sworn in court before and against the prisoner which are on file John Godfrey being brought to the bar it was declared that the grand jury had found him guilty and putting him on trial for his life—the jury was impannelled the said John Godfrey holding up his hand at the bar, he was indicted by the name of John Godfrey of Newbury for not having the fear of God before your eyes did or have consulted with a familiar spirit, and being instigated by the devil have done much hurt and mischief by several acts of witchcraft to the bodies and goods of several persons as by several evidences may appear contrary to the peace of our sovereign lord the King his crown and dignity and the wholesome laws of this jurisdiction. To which he pleaded not guilty and referred himself for his trial to God and the country: The several evidences produced against the prisoner being read committed to the jury and remain on file with the records of this court the jury brought in their verdict i.e. we find him not to have the fear of God in his heart he have made himself [ ] to us being suspiciously guilty of witchcraft but not legally guilty, according to law and evidence we have received[.] The verdict was accepted and party discharged.

Source: *Recs. Ct. Assistants, 1*, p. 151–52; an order for payment of witnesses (p. 152) is omitted.

The case of Godfrey versus Remington decided for defendant

In the case now depending between John Godfrey, plaintiff, against John Remington and Abigail, his wife, defendants, coming to this court by disagreement of the bench, at the last Court of Assistants, from the verdict of the jury, the court, on a full hearing of the case, do find for the defendant confirmation of the judgment of the last County Court at Salisbury. October 9, 1667.

Source: *Mass. Bay Recs., 4*, pt. 2, p. 349.

Godfrey sentenced for suborning witnesses

At the County Court held at Salisbury April 13, 1669.

John Godfrey for his wicked and most pernicious suborning witnesses to the perverting of justice both by himself and others by his instigating of them: sometimes by hindering persons from giving evidence and sometimes to give false evidence as doth fully appear by many testimonies now on file with this court's records: This court for these horrible and destructive crimes doth sentence him to pay one hundred pound[s] as a fine to the county and to stand upon the pillory the space of one hour with this inscription written in capital letters upon a paper fastened upon him: viz.: in these words: (John Godfrey for suborning witnesses) and this is to be put in execution upon the next lecture day at Salisbury near the meetinghouse and he is utterly disabled from giving evidence in any case hereafter: unless he be restored by authority: and to pay costs and to stand committed to prison until this sentence be performed in all respects.

This is a true copy out of the court's book of records as attests Thomas Bradbury recorder.

Source: *Recs. Ct. Assistants*, 3, p. 153.

Godfrey v. Ela in a suit of defamation

At a County Court held at Salem this June 29, 1669.

John Godfrey plaintiff against Daniel Ela defendant in an action of defamation [. . .] dated 10: 4: 69 the jury find[s] for the defendant: costs of the court: 39s. 6d.[1]

1. In a previous action Godfrey had complained against Ela for seizing his body "under pretence of being the marshall's deputy." This case was decided in Godfrey's favor. He had also sued Mathias Button for molestation, but the jury decided for the defendant.
Source: Essex County Court Records, 5, leaf 23 (EI).

Andrew Grele and Abraham Whitaker on Godfrey's whereabouts

The depositions of Andrew Grele and Abraham Whitaker who testifieth and saith that we heard Daniel Ela say that John Godfrey was seen at Ipswich and at Salisbury at both places at on[e] time the first day of Salisbury Court last past as he heard at Ipswich. Taken upon oath 15 (4) 1669. Before me Simon Bradstreet.

Source: *Recs. Ct. Assistants*, 3, p. 154.

Abiel Sommerby and others on the judge's refusing bond

Abiel Sommerby aged 28 years. This deponent testifieth that he being at Salisbury Court heard James Ordway and one or two more say that they would have been bound for John Godfrey if the judge of the court had not said, if he were gone [into the farthest part of New England: *crossed out*] we would have him brought back again in chains or irons. And John Godfrey was pleading with the court to take his own bond for his appeal in Button's action, and he would have all his writings fetched, and they should be left in the court's hands, and the judge of the court made answer[,] we shall not take a thousand pound bond in this c[ase] then the voice of the people that stood by was that there should be no bond taken for him [which] did discourage those that was intended to be bound for him. Abiel Sommerby.

Peter Godfrey aged 38 years can evidence all above written. Peter Godfrey.

James Ordway aged about 45 years testifieth to all abovesaid. And further saith that he intended to be bound for him freely but the matter was made so odious by the court that afterward John Godfrey offered twenty pounds to him to be bound but he would not. And further this deponent saith that the judge of the court said, he did believe that no man will have the face to appear in this case to be bound for him. James Ordway. Sworn before me by James Ordway June 21, 1669. Daniel Denison.

Source: *Recs. Ct. Assistants, 3*, p. 155.

John Godfrey's whereabouts

At the county court held at Salisbury May 13, 1669 John Godfrey did own in court that his dwelling or usual abode is at one Francis Skerry's in Salem. This is a true copy out of the court's book of records as attests Thomas Bradbury recorder.

Source: *Recs. Ct. Assistants, 3*, p. 154.

An apparition of John Godfrey

Elizabeth Button aged 47 years or thereabout saith about 4 or 5 weeks after Salisbury Court last my daughter Sarah being in the house and it being a rainy time she and I sat together in a bed by the fireside[.] About twelve or one a clock there was a great noise about the house which this deponent took to be the cattle but when she was awake she saw a shape of a man and sit in a great chair and being a great fire near the bed and near the chair within a yard and a half I saw Godfrey sitting and I would fain a struck him but could not put forth my hand and I did what I could to wake the maid that was in bed with me but could not for I could neither speak nor stir and thus he continued for the space of two hours[.] I see him three or four times but as soon as I had come to settle myself in the bed he vanished away to my apprehension for he went strangely out and the door was fast and when I rise in the morning I went to the door and it was fast bolted[.] The time I saw Godfrey was about 12 or one of the clock in the night. Taken upon oath 22. 4. 1669 before me Simon Bradstreet.

Source: *Recs. Ct. Assistants, 3*, p. 154.

John Griffing on Godfrey's whereabouts

The deposition of John Griffing aged 28 years testifieth and saith that being at the house of Stephen Swett of Newbury the last winter was twelve month I did then and there see John Godfrey going towards Newbury meetinghouse at which time John Godfrey was in Boston prison as I was informed by John Godfrey himself about 2 months after[.] I do further testify that I saw John Godfrey the first night of Salisbury Court last at the house of John Severance's at Salisbury and many times more at the same court other days and further that John Godfrey told me this deponent that he was not at Ipswich any time that week of the court at Salisbury[.] I further testify that about seven years ago the last winter John Godfrey and this deponent went over Merrimack River on the ice to go to Andover[.] Godfrey on foot and this deponent on horseback and the horse was as good a one as ever he ride on and when I was at Goodman Gage his field I saw John Godfrey in the same field a little before me this deponent but when I had rid[den] a little further not seeing Godfrey nor any track at all and it was at a time when there had fallen a middling snow overnight and not seeing him nor his steps I run my horse all the way to Andover; and the first house I came into at Andover was Goodman Rust's house and when I came in I see John Godfrey sitting in the corner and Goody Rust told me that he had been there so long as that a maid that was in the house had made clean a kettle and hung on peas and pork to boil for Godfrey and the peas and pork was ready to boil and the maid was skimming the kettle. Taken upon oath 22 (4) 1669 before me Simon Bradstreet.

Source: *Recs. Ct. Assistants, 3*, pp. 155–56.

Susanna Roper on Godfrey's whereabouts

The deposition of Susanna Roper aged about 5[3] saith that the second Tuesday of April last standing at the door of my own house I saw John Godfrey going along in the street toward Rowley my two daughters being present and one of them speaking and saying there is Godfrey he turned his face towards the door and I spake to my daughters and said I wonder Godfrey was here now being Salisbury Court day and the reason I took the more notice of him was because I heard he was to be at Salisbury Court this being about the middle of the afternoon that day. Taken upon oath June 24, 1669 before me Samuel Symonds.

Source: *Recs. Ct. Assistants, 3*, p. 156.

Robert Lord on John Godfrey's whereabouts

The deposition of Robert Lord Marshall aged about 37 years.

This deponent testifieth that I being at Salisbury Court to wait upon the worshipful Mr. Symonds saw John Godfrey at Salisbury in Cornet Severance's house about twelve of the clock the first day of the court: and so every day of the court occasionally and [left] the said Godfrey there at Salisbury at the end of the court when we came home: and further saith not. Sworn before me Daniel Denison. June 24, 1669.

Source: *Recs. Ct. Assistants, 3*, p. 156.

Robert Pike on conversing with Godfrey about a lawsuit

The deposition of Robert Pike aged 52 year[s] or thereabout.

This deponent sayeth that at the last County Court held at Salisbury he see John Godfrey at the house of Goodman Severance in Salisbury and in the forenoon of that day being Tuesday he the said Godfrey and this deponent had a long discourse together upon the head of the stairs at the said Severance his house concerning an action which this deponent had against the said Godfrey in which this deponent promised the said Godfrey not to enter it: if the said Godfrey would do what the said deponent desired him to do: (but he did it not) and therefore this deponent entered his action at noon to save double entry having waited for his answer all the forenoon also farther testifies that he saw the said Godfrey there every day of the said court and when the court ended and farther sayeth not.

Deposed in the presence [of] God whom I call to witness to the truth thereof this 15 of the 4 month 1669. By me Robert Pike Commissioner.

Source: *Recs. Ct. Assistants, 3*, p. 157.

Edward Clark and others on John Godfrey's whereabouts

The deposition of Edward Clark who saith that I heard Daniel Ela say that John Godfrey was at Ipswich and at Salisbury both at one time the first day of Salisbury Court as he heard and further saith not. Edward Clark. Sworn in court at Salem 30 (4) 1669. Attests Hilliard Veren Clerk.

The deposition of Daniel Manning aged about 21 years[.] This deponent testifieth coming along in the street near our house [I saw?] John Godfrey coming from Rowley woods going into the town: The [   ] day after Goody Archer was buried about eleven or twelve of the [clock?]. The said Godfrey passed close by me in the street: the same [   ] Goody Roper and her daughters told me at night they saw Go[dfrey] by their house towards Rowley in the afternoon: and further saith [not]. June 28, 1669. Taken upon oath before me Daniel Denison.

The deposition of Sarah Roper and Elizabeth Roper saith that upon the middle of the afternoon on the second Tuesday of April last we saw John Godfrey going along the street toward Rowley and one of us speaking there is Godfrey the said Godfrey turned his face towards the door towards us standing at our father's door. Taken upon oath June 24, 1669 before me Samuel Symonds.

Source: *Recs. Ct. Assistants, 3*, pp. 157–58.

8. Mother and Daughter:
The Holmans of Cambridge
(1659–1660)

▲

Winifred and Mary Holman

*The family of John Gibson, who settled in Cambridge, Massachu-
setts, by 1635, lived across the street from the widow Winifred Holman and her daughter, Mary. Winifred may have been a healer. John
Gibson's oldest child, Rebecca, married Charles Stearns in 1654.
Some time later, after Rebecca had become the mother of a son, she
began to imagine that she and her child were afflicted by the Holmans, mother and daughter. In June 1659 Thomas Danforth, the
Cambridge magistrate, acted on the complaint of the Gibsons and
arrested the two women. No jury seems to have indicted them. In
March 1660 the Holmans filed suit "in an action of defamation and
slander" against John Gibson and Rebecca Stearns. The jury dismissed the suit against Mrs. Stearns on the grounds that she had
been "deprived of her natural reason when she expressed those
words charged on her." Gibson was ordered to apologize and remit
a fine. Mrs. Holman died in 1671 at the age of seventy-four; her
daughter died, unmarried, in 1673, at the age of forty-three. The
documents that follow stem from the Holmans' suit for defamation.
The facts of the case are narrated by Lucius R. Paige in* History of
Cambridge, Massachusetts *(1877), pp. 356–64.*

Order to apprehend Winifred and Mary Holman

To the Constable of Cambridge. You are required forthwith to apprehend the persons of Widow Holman and her daughter Mary, and im-

mediately bring them before the County Court now sitting at Charlestown, to be examined on several accusations presented, on suspicion
of witchcraft; and for witnesses John Gibson and his wife; you are
forthwith to bring them away, and not suffer them to speak one with
another after their knowledge of this warrant, and hereof you are not
to fail at your peril. 21 (4) 1659. Thomas Danforth. It will be convenient that you charge some meet person to bring away the maid first,
and then you may acquaint the mother also with this warrant respecting her also.

Source: Paige, *History of Cambridge*, p. 356.

John Gibson and his family against Winifred and Mary Holman

A relation of the passages between Mrs. Holman and her daughter
Mary and the wife of Charles Stearns now living in Cambridge. The
first thing that makes us suspect them is that after she had two extraordinary strange fits, which she never had the like before[,] Mary
Holman asked her why she did not get some help for them and she
answered she could not tell what to do she had used means by physicians and could have no help and the said Mary said that her mother
said if she would put herself into her hands that she would undertake
to cure her with the blessing of God[.] Our daughter telling us of it and
we not suspecting them we wished her to go and to see what she
would say to her and she said her daughter was a prating wench and
loved to prate but yet she did prescribe some herbs to her that she
should use in the spring[.]

After this my daughter's child grew ill and Mary Holman coming in
often asked her what her child ailed and she said moreover that her
mother and she took notice of it that the child declined ever since the
5 of January and will till it come to the grave but if you will put it into
my hands I will undertake to cure it: I cured one at Malden that had
the rickets and if you will take a fool's counsel you may if you will not
choose. She said also the child fell away in the lower parts and yet she
did not see the child opened[.] She said also that Mr. Mitchell's[1] child
had the rickets and it was easy to be seen for the face did shine but
since Mr. Mitchell sent to Lynn for a skillful woman to look on it and
she could not see no such thing[.]

After this, Mary Holman borrowed a skillet of her and when she
brought it home the child was asleep in the cradle and a boy a rocking
it and the mother of the child was gone for water and the boy said that

Mary Holman came to the child as it was asleep and took it by the nose and made the blood come and set it a crying that the mother heard it and before she came in Mary was gone out over the sill[.] When she came in and saw the child in such a case she chode[2] the boy for making the child cry and he said it was Mary Holman that did it and went away as fast as she could.

After this, she was taken with her ordinary fits 2 nights and 2 days and was pretty well again and sensible one day and then she was taken with a strange raving and marvellous unquiet night and day for the space of 3 or 4 days and nights together and took no rest and it was observed that all this time Mrs. Holman was walking about by her rails stooping down and picking of the ground along as she went and both of them walking up and down and [to?] and again that it was taken notice of by many and all this time she raged [and] could not be quiet till the last day of the week in the afternoon they were gone both from home and then she was quiet and was fast asleep till she came home and suddenly she sprung up out of her sleep and cried out with such rage against Mrs. Holman that she was a witch and that she must be hanged[.]

Her mother being amazed she went out and see her a coming towards the house and the nearer she came the more she raged and so she continued all night: and in the morning Mary Holman came in for fire as she did every morning and sometimes twice in a day[;] as soon as she came in she cried out on her that she was a witch so that we could not still her till my wife shoved her out of door and when they were out Mary asked my wife what her daughter ailed and said she was a quiet woman: another being by my wife answered she thought she was bewitched[.] Then said Mary Holman my mother said that she was not light headed nor her head did not ache but she continued [so still] and crying out to her mother and said Mrs. Holman she was working wickedness on the Lords day[.] With that, my wife looked out and saw Mrs. Holman a pecking by the rails as she did of other days.

When folks were gone to meeting about half an hour after two of the clock she went to meeting that is Mrs. Holman and by that time she got to meeting as we guessed she lay still about half an hour and then fell asleep and of a sudden, she flings up and cries out of Mrs. Holman[.] My wife not thinking they had been come [home] from meeting looked out and saw her at home[.] Anon after Mary Holman came to the house and said to my wife your daughter had a sleep had she not and she answered her why do you ask and she said because she slept yesterday afore this time and so she did but how she should come to know it we cannot tell for they were both times from home[.]

On the second day in the morning Mary came for fire and she cried out [on] her as before and continued raging almost all that day[.] On the third day Mary Holman was a coming again for fire and my wife prayed me that if I saw her come that I would not let her come in and so I did[.] I met with her at the sill with a bright skillet in her hand and she asked me how my daughter did and I said she is not well and I asked her whither she went with that and she said for fire[.] But I told her she should not have none here but bade her go to some other house: upon which we took notice that that day she was very quiet and there was such a sudden alteration to admiration to all that saw it and so continued but after she was more sensible of her weakness[.]

Some things were forgotten that my daughter before she was taken with her fits put a pair of stockings to her and she kept them a great while and upon the last day of the week at night she sent them home and she wore them on the Sabbath and that night she had her fits being free from them a great while before and as was said before when she had had them two days and two nights she fell into this strange condition as before mentioned[.] And all this time she cried out of Mrs. Holman and her daughter Mary that they were witches and they must be found out and said you must not suffer a witch to live [Exodus 22:18] and she said Mr. Danforth³ was chosen a magistrate to find out Mrs. Holman—and when my wife went to give her some refreshing she would not take it in she was so troubled with Mrs. Holman that she must be found out that my wife told her that she would get the magistrate to find her out, and it was taken notice of by my wife and others that her countenance was changed and [she] did eat[.]

Thus she lay taking on against Mrs. Holman and Mary to all that came to her that they were witches and must be hanged and so she told them to their faces and could not be stilled and many times she flung up with such rage and cried out with exceeding earnestness that Mrs. Holman was at the rails let me go out and I will show you her and it was so[,] for my wife and others looked out and saw her there[.] It seemed to us very strange for it was not possible that she could see her for she was kept so close on her bed and a covering hanging before her and another before the window[.] The first great trouble that she had she was affrighted with Satan and thought that she saw him stand by the bedside so that she cried out with a loud noise all night to the Lord for help saying Lord help me Lord help me that she was heard a great way off[.]

The second great trouble she had she was likewise troubled with Satan appearing to her that she was set of a great trembling that she shook the bed she lay on and striving mightly with her body and fighting with her hands that 2 men were fain to hold her[.] We asked her why she fought so and she said she fought with the devil: and ever and anon she called out of Mrs. Holman and would have her sent for and one that sat by said what would you say to her[?] And she said I will tell her that she is a witch[.] We then not suspecting her so to be we reproved her and wished her not to say so but the more we forbade her the more violent she was in so calling her and crying out of Mrs. Holman's black chest and Mrs. Holman's cake but what she meant by them we cannot tell[.]

But this last time she was troubled with Mrs. Holman and her daughter Mary and concerning the child it does decline and fall away daily according to Mary's words and yet we cannot perceive that it is sick at all but will suck and eat and in the time of the mother's trouble the child is set quite crooked in the body which before was a straight thriving child: also it was taken notice of that in the time of my daughter's trouble that her hands were set crooked that her husband could not get them open[.] A while after we were at the court she had another raging fit wherein she was carried with rage against her parents and her brothers and sisters and we desired one of our brethren to pray with her and she raged at him and bade him get him home or she would throw something at his head and she was so outrageous that we were fain to tie her hands[.] And she cried out and said a snake stung her under her arms and when she was out of her distemper she said she saw a thing like a great snake come into the house with a thing like a turtle upon the back and came upon the bed to her[.]

And another time when one of our elders was at prayer she barked like a dog and though we held her mouth close with our hands yet she would speak saying that Mrs. Holman and Mary Holman were witches and bewitched her and her child and sometimes she cried out against blood that it cried and that it stunk and we bade her hold her peace but she said she must speak and conscience must speak and at last she said there was a [hoale?] of blood by the cradle.

And there was many prayers made for her and it pleased God that suddenly she came out of it and was ravished at the sight of things: how they appeared to her even [as] they did before[.] Her mother being gone out she followed her and said Mother I am well but she could not believe her but she said go to work and she went about her work and she told her mother that she felt something come out of her at that instant and the next day she looked out of her window and saw Mary Holman running about as if she were catching a bird and presently she was taken sick almost struck dead as she thought and her mother got her to bed and gave her something to refresh her and then she told her this[.]

The next night after being in her senses she called to her husband and said that Mrs. Holman was here and she rose out of her bed and followed her to the window and then she told her husband that she was at the gate but he could not see her: the next night after she cried out and said her back was broke and felt as if a sword had been thrust into her back and the next night the child was taken very sick[.] A little while after this Mr. Danforth came by and asked how the child did and we prayed him to come in and see it and he saw how crooked it was and how it was pined away and said he thought it could not live long. But the child did eat well and suck well and yet wasted away as Mary Holman said it would do[.] The next day being Lord's day Mrs. Holman stayed at home in the forenoon and when folks were gone to meeting the said Mrs. Holman stand right before the door looking upon the cradle where the child lay while sermon was almost done and then she came home before us dressed in her best clothes and she seeing her was amazed seeing how a little before undressed: the week following they went out both of them to gleaning and suddenly the child was straight and pretty well insomuch that we thought it would have been well again and all that time the mother was pretty well but when they had done gleaning Mrs. Holman went up and down the common picking in her old clothes and sometimes in her best and so she did 3 or 4 times and 2 days after they both stood without their home looking upon her 2 or 3 hours together[.]

Her mother observing of them and their carriage was not as other times but before her fits she was persuaded that mischief was at hand and she begged prayers of her neighbors and wished her husband to pray hard and that night she had 5 or 6 fits[.] The third day after she was pretty well and went about her work till towards night that Mrs. Holman came out and sat down upon her knees to hoe and continued upon her knees hoeing near two hours we conceive[.] As soon as she begun to hoe the woman began to be ill and was fain to go to bed and begun to be distempered and when it was almost night her mother went to see what she had done and could not see no hole at all more than in any other place and she saw both of them stand in their [masters ?] and when it was too dark to work[.] And on the next morning they were at the same place hoeing as long and all that night and 2 or 3 nights after she could not [   ] but lay crying out that Mrs. Holman's imps were biting of her feet that she durst not put them down and when she was out of her bed we could not keep her from Mrs.

Holman's but would go thither and tell her that she had imps in a black chest[.]

And this have been observed that when Mrs. Holman and her daughter were gone abroad that she was pretty quiet and would eat her meat and when they came home she was distempered again and thus it was always[.] When she was in her trouble it pleased God to move some of the church to set a day apart to seek God for her in her distemper and it pleased God to release her the next day and was well a pretty while but soon time she had another fit but more moderate than before: before which we saw two strange things: the one was digging a hole in the common close by her rails and the other was she having a great heap of sand at her door she began to carry it away in a great dish[.] My wife going out in the morning saw Mrs. Holman carrying sand called to me to see her and said she was persuaded our daughter was sick[.] Presently her son Abraham spake to her and he went in[.] Then my wife went to see her daughter and she had a fit and when Abraham was gone out with his cart the old woman came out to carry sand and presently upon it she had another fit and while she continued carrying sand her husband and her mother stood looking on her till she went in and she kept in till day and all that time Mrs. Holman kept in she had no fire while it was dark and then her fits came again[.]

After this she fell into her distemper again but more moderate and slept well in the night but she was afflicted with fear and pain frighten[ed] out of her sleep twice in the night by Mrs. Holman [who] came in to her as she lay or by some other thing by her means and this continued 3 or 4 nights[.] After she was in her perfect senses she was so hurt in her body at these things that she was afraid that she should be made to miscarry[.] But this day she felt no pain at all[.] Concerning the child it was very badly handled as credible witnesses can make it appear how the ribs were bent in and the breast mixed up: and some of our creatures being strangely afflicted and strangely transported and thus it have been for a long time some times upon [one] and sometimes upon another[.]

Another time my wife observing Mrs. Holman doing some strange things my wife was much troubled for fear her daughter would be distracted on the second day night she had her ordinary fits and the next day she lay sick all day when Mrs. Holman was at home: on the Wednesday and Thursday Mrs. Holman went abroad and then she was well and about her work[.] On the next day of a sudden she begun to be distempered and lay down and her mother looked out and saw Mrs. Holman doing as was said before and was stirred up to seek the Lord that if she be a working of wickedness that the Lord would be pleased to prevent her and presently Mrs. Holman went away and of a sudden she found such a change that she called for her mother and said she was well and was freed from any further distemper at that time[.]

And this we have observed all along when she was in her distemper if Mrs. Holman be but gone from home she was presently in her right mind and if her son Abraham was about home she was well but if he were from home and his mother come home she presently fell into her distemper again and this was observed that most part of the last summer that one of them and sometimes both kept at home of the Lord's day[.] This also have been observed that the old woman have been seen to go out toward night into swamps and highways: examine why she goeth out at night to swamps and highways[.]

This wintertime she have kept in we have been well but the next time Mrs. Holman went to meeting being of a lecture day she stood by our daughter looking on her very often and at night she had her fits and since one of them will stand by her looking whereupon she is taken so sick that she can scarce sit on her seat and so it was with the child upon her looking on it it would groan as if it would die presently[.] Another time Mrs. Holman was seen going towards one of our neighbor's house within her own fence towards night it rained a pretty pace and walked two or 3 times close by the rails as near the house as she could[,] not having anything to do that we that saw her could conceive and when she saw us she returned home and she was without any hat on her head and presently upon it the woman was taken so sick that she sent for her husband to come to her[.] For this there is 2 or 3 witnesses[.]

The last fits she had were her ordinary fits for manner but more than ordinary for continuance[.] Formerly she had them one or two nights but now they continued almost a week together but her other distemper did not follow[;] through mercy her senses continued unless it was when she was affrighted by Satan's appearing to her sometimes in one shape and sometimes in another[.] And this we observed that these fits were when Mrs. Holman came out of her house to do something in her [   ] and when she went in again she was quiet and well[.] Myself my sister and sons can witness this[.]

The last winter before this I was afflicted with Mrs. Holman's hens[.] I could not keep them out of my barn from [de]stroying my corn[.] I being much troubled at it spake of it to my wife and she said it may be the poor woman cannot keep them at home[.] I being thus afflicted with them I flung a stone at one of them and killed it and laid it upon a hovel that stood upon the common[.] When my wife saw it she sent to Mrs. Holman to see if it were one of hers and her daughter fetched it home and after that they troubled me no more though they went abroad still which we wondered at being so constantly there every day before[.] After this my wife had a brood of chickens of fifteen which were like to do well and did thrive for the space of one fortnight and then they were taken with fits and they would turn their heads upward and turn round many times and run about the house as if they were mad and sometimes pecking towards the ground but not touch the ground and sometimes they would be pretty well and eat their meat but they died 2 or 3 at a time till they came to four[.] Likewise Mrs. Holman had a white cock that went a grazing about the common every day in the summertime between the pond and the houses without any hens with him and we taking notice of him asked Mary Holman wherefore that cock went so alone and she said that the hens did not care for him nor he cared not for them and she said moreover that he was seven years old[.] Then we asked her why they would keep him and she said she could not tell her mother would keep him and soon after that we saw him no more[.]

Also there was a bird that was taken notice of not only of us but of some others such a one as [ne]ither they nor we ever saw before[.] It was all milk-white save only a little gray on the wings[.] My son being told of such a bird did look to see if he could see it and did see it and threw stones at it but could not hit it although it were very near him and when it rose up it would fly to Mrs. Holman's house[.] So likewise when those that saw it first flung stones at it it would always fly thither and sometimes they said they saw it fly into the house[.] They had taken notice of it a week before we did and when [my] son and I went to mend up the fence that was before my daughter's house the bird was skipping about the rails[.] My son said here is the devilishest bird that ever I saw in my life and I asked him why he did [say] so and he said I never threw half so often at a bird in his life but he did hit it but this I cannot hit and he flung again at it but could not hit it and we both of us see it fly to Mrs. Holman's house[.] The same day my son and the other persons saw it again and they hunted it about and flung stones at it and it flying thither again one of them called out saying the bird was gone home and two of them resolved the next day to get their guns and see if they could shoot it[.] Mrs. Holman came out of her house and looked on them and in likelihood heard what they said for they were near the house but since that time the bird have not been seen[.] In this time my daughter Stearns going out of her house within evening saw this bird under her house sill[.] She thought at first it had been a cat but she going towards it perceived it was a white bird and it did fly along by the house side and so away to Mrs. Holman's[.] It was seen another evening when it was too late for birds to be abroad between my daughter's house and the rails.

My wife have been much troubled with her wheel when she have set herself to spin for the necessity of her family[.] Sometimes she could not make no work of it she thought at first it might be out of kilter and we both used what means we could with it but it was never the better but was fain to set it away and go about some other work[;] and when she took it again it would go very well and thus it was very often; and sometimes when she could make no work with it she would set it away and not so much as unband it and take it again and not alter it at all and it would go very well[.] One time amongst the rest she set herself to work and was much troubled that she could make no work of it[.] She began to fear that there might be something that might be the cause of it[;] she set her wheel away and went out and saw Mary Holman at the oak turning round and when she saw my wife she catched up a chip and that caused her to fear that it might be by their means[.] Another time she was a spinning and as it was wont so it did again that she was so affected with it that she could have cried and sitting still with her wheel before her saying thus to herself Lord thou hast commanded me to labor but I am hindered[;] good Lord if there be any hand of Satan in it prevent it with some other words and went to spinning again and it went as well as ever[.]

At another time when my daughter was not very well my wife went out and saw Mary Holman sitting on her knees at a hole of water[.] She took up water in a dish and held it up a pretty height and drained [it] into another thing[.] My wife went presently to her daughter and found her crying so immoderately that the tears fell so fast from her eyes that my wife was fain to stand and wipe them off her face with her apron and her mother asked her wherefore she cried and she said she could not tell but she said she could not forbear it[.] Concerning what our daughter have seen and felt in the time of her affliction she can declare if she be called to it[.][4]

1. Jonathan Mitchell, minister in Cambridge.
2. Past tense of *chide.*
3. Thomas Danforth, resident of Cambridge and a magistrate (Assistant) in the government.
4. This document has no signatures. The Middlesex County Court records include, however, a draft version to which is appended the following: "John Gibson Sen. Rebecca Gibson John Gibson Jr. Rebecca Stearns Charles Stearns Steven Francis 4(1660) sworn in court to the respective evidences as attest Thomas Danforth."
Source: Middlesex County Court Records, folder 25 (MA). Partially printed in Paige, *History of Cambridge*, pp. 357–63.

Warrants to attach John Gibson, Jr., John Gibson Sen. and his wife in an action of defamation

To the constable of Cambridge or his deputy[:] You are hereby required to attach the goods and in want thereof the person of John Gibson Jr. of Cambridge and take hold of him to the value of twenty pounds with sufficient surety or sureties for his appearance at the next County Court holden at Cambridge upon the third day of April next, then and there to answer the complaint of Winifred Holman of Cambridge in an action of slander and so make a true return hereof under your hand, dated this 26 of March 1659/60. By the court Samuel Green.

To the constable of Cambridge or his deputy[:] You are hereby required to attach the goods and in want thereof the persons of John Gibson of Cambridge Sr. and his wife, and take bond of them to the value of ten pounds with sufficient surety or sureties for their appearance at the next County Court holden at Cambridge upon the third day of April next, then and there to answer the complaint of Winifred Holman of Cambridge in an action of defamation and slander. Hereof you are to make a true return under your hand, dated this 28 of March 1660. By the court Samuel Green.

Source: Middlesex County Court Records, folder 25 (MA).

Warrant to attach goods or person of Rebecca Stearns

To the constable of Cambridge or his deputy: You are hereby required to attach the goods or in want thereof the person of Rebecca the wife of Charles Stearns of Cambridge and take bond of her to the value of ten pounds with sufficient surety or surieties for her appearance at the next County Court holden at Cambridge, upon the third day of April next then and there to answer the complaint of Winifred Holman of Cambridge, in an action of defamation and slander, hereof you are to make a true return under your hand. Dated this 28 of March 1660 By the court: Samuel Green.

Source: Middlesex County Court Records, folder 25 (MA).

Neighbors support Mrs. Holman

We, whose names are underwritten, we do here testify that Winifred Holman, we having been acquainted with her this many years, she being near neighbor unto us, and many times have had occasion to have dealings with her, and we have not indeed in the least measure perceived, either by words or deeds, any thing whereby we could have any grounds or reason to suspect her for witchery or any thing thereunto tending. And this is evident unto us that she is diligent in her calling, and frequents public preaching, and gives diligent attention thereunto.

John Palfrey, Matthew Bridge, Richard Eccles, Francis Whitmore, John Greene, Nathaniel Green, William Dickson.

We, who have here subscribed our names, do testify that we have known this Winifred Holman, widow, this many years, but never knew any thing in her life concerning witchery. But she hath always been a diligent hearer of and attender to the word of God.

Mary Patten, Mary Hall, Jane Willows, Anna Bridge, Elizabeth Bridge, Elizabeth Green, Jeane Dickson, Elizabeth Winship, Thomas Fox, Ellen Fox, William Towne, Martha Towne, Mary Eccles, Isobell Whitmore, John Bridge, Rebecca Wyeth, Gregory Stone, Lydia Stone.

Source: Paige, *History of Cambridge,* pp. 363–64.

Elizabeth Bowers explains the Holmans' going for water

Elizabeth Bowers being at the court this afternoon and hearing that part about pouring the water out of a dish into another [ ] she think[s] she is bound to speak to give light to the court and [   ]. She had sought to speak herein [   ] but she was taken off but that which she can say she have heard Mary Holman and her mother complain for want of water and being so under suspicion she could not well tell how to go to a neighbor's house for water lest there should be [   ] of her to some as they said. [   ] were faint to get water any way [   ] a dish her well being [   ] and purpose she speak and they said they could be content to carry a pail of water from my house home which was near half a mile.

Source: Middlesex County Court Records, folder 25 (MA).

Elizabeth Bowers and other witnesses to defamation

Elizabeth Bowers aged 25 years witnesseth that she being present heard Abraham Holman ask Goody Gibson if she did not say his mother was a witch and she sayeth she would not say his mother was a witch but she had cause to suspect her for her daughter had been very grievously handled and she had seen her at very strange things[.]

Abraham Holman and Jeremiah Johnson witnesseth the same. April 4, 1660. Sworn in court as attests Thomas Danforth.

Source: Middlesex County Court Records, folder 25 (MA).

The testimony of Abraham Holman and [Mary Holman: *crossed out*] that they heard Rebecca Stearns say: Mrs. Holman your chest is full of imps. But whether she was in her fits whereby at sundry seasons she rageth, and is deprived of the [use] of her reason, we dare not affirm for the contrary [*inserted:* in anno 1659]. Sworn in court April 4, 1660 as attests Thomas Danforth.

Source: Middlesex County Court Records, folder 25 (MA).

The testimony of Beth Holman is as followeth that she also heard Rebecca Stearns say that Mrs. Holman is a witch and it was about whether she was in one of her raging fits at the time she cannot tell. Sworn in court April 4, 1660 as attests Thomas Danforth.

Source: Middlesex County Court Records, folder 25 (MA).

The testimony of Thomas Andrews seventeen years of age Daniel Andrews sixteen years of age and Samuel Burke aged about seventeen years do say being coming from meeting on the Lord's day that they heard John Gibson say of Mary Holman that there cometh the young witch. And Daniel Andrews saith it is more than you know[.] And John Gibson said I am sure of it. Dated June 15, 1659. Sworn in court April 4, 1660 as attests Thomas Danforth.

Source: Middlesex County Court Records, folder 25 (MA).

Elizabeth Bowers being at Goody Gibson's house about ten days since and she heard Goody Gibson say that her daughter did call another woman witch and she reproved her daughter and said do you know what you say and she answered her mother as she sayeth that it was Mrs. Holman she meant[.] Then Abraham Holman replied to Goody Gibson does your daughter know what she sayeth and she sayeth sometimes she doth and sometimes she doth not. Sworn in court April 4, 1660 as attests Thomas Danforth.

Source: Middlesex County Court Records, folder 25 (MA).

9. The Hartford Witch-hunt (1662–1665)

▲

The largest witch-hunt in mid-seventeenth-century New England occurred in Hartford, Connecticut. It resulted in accusations against at
least eight persons, three of whom, Nathaniel and Rebecca Greensmith and Mary Barnes, were executed; a fourth, Mary Sanford,
probably died as well. The origins of this witch-hunt may be traced
to a Hartford woman, Ann Cole, who in 1662 began to suffer what
was deemed "diabolical possession." She named Elizabeth Seager
as one of the persons responsible for tormenting her, and neighbors
came forward with testimony to support the accusation. She also
named another resident of Hartford, Rebecca Greensmith, the aged
wife of a farmer of modest means, Nathaniel Greensmith.

Accusations of witchcraft came from a second source, Elizabeth
Kelly, an eight-year-old girl who accused Goodwife Ayres of causing
her sickness. Few documents are as moving as the description John
and Bethia Kelly, Elizabeth's parents, provided of their daughter's
fatal illness. Mrs. Ayres's husband, who was questioned along with
his wife, also accused Rebecca Greensmith. The Greensmiths were
indicted in December 1662. Rebecca confessed to having "familiarity
with the devil" and made statements that told against her husband.
She described attending meetings in the woods with Elizabeth
Seager, Goodwife Sanford, Goodwife Ayres, and four others: James
Wakeley, Peter Grant's wife, Henry Palmer's wife, and Judith Varlet.
The Greensmiths were executed in early 1663. Mary Barnes of Farmington was probably executed at the same time. The Ayres and Judith Varlet escaped to New York. Elizabeth Seager was tried (apparently two different times) in 1663 for adultery and witchcraft and

convicted of the former crime; she was finally convicted of witchcraft in another trial in 1665, but Governor John Winthrop, Jr., refused to carry out the sentence. The documents pertaining to Elizabeth include the unique record of a jury's deliberations. According to Increase Mather, two of the suspects in this witch-hunt, in all likelihood the Greensmiths, were subjected to the swimming test.

    Kinship, and possibly a disputed inheritance, were involved in the Hartford witch-hunt. Bethia (Wakeman) Kelly had one brother and two sisters; one sister married James Wakely. Hannah, the other, married Francis Hackleton. These children were orphaned while they were minors, and the estate passed to a trustee, who was made responsible for distributing Samuel Wakeman's estate to his children when they turned eighteen. Whether this happened peacefully, or only because the children sued or the courts intervened, is unclear. It is striking that Hannah Hackleton was charged in 1665 with adultery, murder, and blasphemy. The jury convicted her of adultery and blasphemy. But at the same session of the Court of Assistants in 1666 she and Elizabeth Seager had their capital sentences suspended.[1]

    Information about the Hartford witch-hunt, and some of the relevant documents, appears in John M. Taylor, The Witchcraft Delusion in Colonial Connecticut (New York, 1908). John Whiting, who reported Ann Cole's possession to Increase Mather, was a minister in Hartford.

1. Some of the documents pertaining to the Wakeman inheritance are printed in Charles W. Manwaring, comp., *A Digest of the Early Connecticut Probate Records* (Hartford, Conn., 1904), *1*, pp. 39–40. Although Mrs. Hackleton was acquitted of the capital crime, she was ordered to be whipped and to "stand at gallows with a rope about her neck for one hour." Court of Assistants Records, *56*, p. 52 (CSL).

John Whiting describes the "possession" of Ann Cole

These for the Rev. Mr. Increase Mather, Teacher of a church in Boston.

    An account of a remarkable passage of divine providence that happened in Hartford in the year of our Lord 1662.

    The subject was, Ann Cole (the daughter of John Cole, a godly man among us then next neighbor to the man and woman that afterward suffered for witchcraft) who had for some time been afflicted and in some fears about her spiritual estate; two of her brethren also were very lame, one of them so continuing to this day, his knee-joint of one leg having no motion, but otherwise well for many years. She hath been and is a person esteemed pious, behaving herself with a pleasant mixture of humility and faith under her heavy sufferings, professing (as she did sundry times) that she knew nothing of those things that were spoken by her, but that her tongue was improved to express what was never in her mind which was matter of great affliction to her. Since the abatement of her sorrows she is joined to the church and therein [has] been a humble walker for many years[.] And since also married to a good man, hath born him several children, and in her constant way approved herself truly godly to the charity of all observers.

The matter is, that anno 1662 this Ann Cole (living in her father's family) was taken with strange fits, wherein she (or rather the devil, as 'tis judged, making use of her lips) held a discourse for a considerable time. The general purport of it was to this purpose, that a company of familiars of the evil one (who were named in the discourse that passed from her) were contriving how to carry on their mischievous designs against some and especially against her, mentioning sundry ways they would take to that end, as that they would afflict her body, spoil her name, hinder her marriage, etc. wherein the general answer made among them was, She runs to her rock. This method having been continued some hours; the conclusion was, Let us confound her language [so] she may tell no more tales. And then after some time of unintelligible muttering the discourse passed into a Dutch tone (a family of Dutch then living in the town) and therein an account was given of some afflictions that had befallen diverse, among the rest a young woman (next neighbor to that Dutch family) that could speak but very little (laboring of that infirmity from her youth), had met with great sorrow, as pinchings of her arms in the dark, etc. whereof she had before informed her brother (one of the ministers in Hartford): In that Dutch-toned discourse there were plain intimations given, by whom and for what cause such a course had been taken with her. Judicious Mr. Stone[1] (who is now with God) being by, when this latter discourse passed, declared it in his thoughts impossible that one not familiarly acquainted with the Dutch (which Ann Cole had not at all been) should so exactly imitate the Dutch tone in the pronunciation of English: Sundry times such kind of discourse was uttered by her, which was very awful and amazing to the hearers: Mr. Samuel Hooker[2] was present the first time, and Mr. Joseph Haynes,[3] who wrote what was said, so did the relator also, when he came into the house, some time after the discourse began—extremely violent bodily motions she many times had, even to the hazard of her life in the apprehensions of those that saw them: And very often great disturbance was given in the public worship of God by her and two other women who had also strange fits. Once in special on a day of prayer kept on that account, the motion and noise of the afflicted was so terrible, that a godly person fainted under the appearance of it.

The consequent was, that one of the persons presented as active in the aforementioned discourse (a lewd, ignorant, considerably aged woman)[4] being a prisoner upon suspicion of witchcraft, the court sent for Mr. Haynes and myself to read what we had written; which when Mr. Haynes had done (the prisoner being present) she forthwith and freely confessed those things to be true, that she (and other persons named in the discourse) had familiarity with the devil. Being asked whether she had made an express covenant with him, she answered she had not, only as she promised to go with him when he called (which she had accordingly done sundry times). But that the devil told her, that at Christmas they would have a merry meeting, and then the covenant should be drawn and subscribed: Thereupon the forementioned Mr. Stone (being then in court) with much weight and earnestness laid forth the exceeding heinousness and hazard of that dreadful sin, and therewith solemnly took notice (upon the occasion given) of the devil's loving Christmas.[5]

A person at the same time present being desired, the next day more particularly to inquire of her about her guilt, it was accordingly done, to whom she acknowledged that though when Mr. Haynes began to read, she could have torn him in pieces, and was as much resolved as might be to deny her guilt (as she had done before), yet after he had read awhile, she was as if her flesh had been pulled from her bones (such was her expression) and so could not deny any longer. She also declared that the devil first appeared to her in the form of a deer or fawn, skipping about her, wherewith she was not much affrighted, but by degrees he contrived [to] talk with her; and that their meetings were frequently at such a place (near her own house) that some of the company came in one shape, and some in another, and one in particular in the shape of a crow came flying to them.

Amongst other things she owned that the devil had frequent use of her body with much seeming (but indeed horrible, hellish) delight to her.

This with the concurrent evidence, brought the woman and her husband to their death as the devil's familiars, and most of the other persons mentioned in the discourse made their escape into another part of the country.

After this execution of some and escape of others, the good woman had abatement of her sorrows, which hath continued sundry years, and she yet remains maintaining her integrity, walking therein with much humble comfort after her so sore and amazing affliction: The works of the Lord are great sought out of all them that have pleasure therein.

Reverend and dear sir[:] I had thoughts of sending the precedent account before now, but I could not (nor yet can) find my papers wherein I wrote what came from Ann Cole in her fits. However I have gathered up the main sum, and now send it: if you think fit to insert the whole or anything of it, not varying the substance, it is left with you.

There are some other remarkables I have some acquaintance with, wherein I have moved others that know them more fully to give an information: The Lord be with you, succeeding at your holy labors to his honor and the good of souls: Forget not yours sincerely in our dear Savior, John Whiting. Hartford, December 4, 1682.

1. Samuel Stone, minister in Hartford.
2. Minister in Farmington, Connecticut.
3. Minister in Hartford.
4. The colonists rejected Christmas as a pagan invention.
5. Rebecca Greensmith.
Source: John Whiting to Increase Mather, Mather Papers, Prince Collection, BPL. Printed in *Coll. MHS*, 4th ser., *8* (1868), pp. 466–69.

The swimming test

There were some that had a mind to try whether the stories of witches not being able to sink under water, were true; and accordingly a man and woman mentioned in Ann Cole's Dutch-toned discourse, had their hands and feet tied, and so were cast into the water, and they both apparently swam after the manner of a buoy, part under, part above the water. A bystander imagining that any person bound in that posture would be so born up, offered himself for trial, but being in the like manner[1] gently laid on the water, he immediately sunk right down. This was no legal evidence against the suspected persons; nor were they proceeded against on any other account; [. . .] Whether this experiment were lawful, or rather superstitious and magical, we shall inquire afterwards.[2]

1. Changed from "mattered" in the original, an apparent error.
2. The origins and history of the swimming test are described in George Lyman Kittredge, *Witchcraft in Old and New England* (Cambridge, Mass., 1929), chap. 15; he remarks (p. 232) that "there is manifest connection with the ancient and all-but-universal belief that water . . . dissolves a spell or interposes an obstacle to the passage of uncanny beings."
Source: Increase Mather, *An Essay for the Recording of Illustrious Providences* (Boston, 1684), p. 139.

The Greensmiths are indicted; the jury convicts them

At a Particular Court held at Hartford December 30, 1662.

The indictment of Nathaniel Greensmith and of Rebecca his wife.

Nathaniel Greensmith thou are here indicted by the name of Nathaniel Greensmith for not having the fear of God before thine eyes[;] thou hast entertained familiarity with Satan the grand enemy of God and mankind and by his help hast acted things in a preternatural way beyond human abilities in a natural course for which according to the law of God and the established law of this commonwealth thou deservest to die.

The jury return that they find the prisoner at the bar Nathaniel Greensmith guilty of the indictment.

Respecting Rebecca Greensmith the prisoner at the bar the jury find her guilty of the indictment.

The said Rebecca confesseth in open court that she is guilty of the charge laid in against her.

Source: *Coll. CHS, 22 (1928)*, p. 258.

The Kellys describe their daughter's fatal illness

The testimony and relation of John Kelly and Bethia his wife concerning the sickness and death of their daughter Elizabeth Kelly aged 8 years and upwards.

Witnesseth[:]

That our said daughter on the 23d of March 1661 being the Lord's day was in good health as she was also a long time before to our apprehension and had neither then nor before done anything that we know that might be prejudicial to her health. And on the said Lord's day was in the forenoon at her grandmother's house and with her came to our house the wife of William Ayres who going to eat did take broth hot out of the boiling pot and did immediately eat thereof and did require our said child to eat with her of the same, which we did forbid telling her it was to[o] hot for her but the child did eat with her out of the same vessel whereupon she began to complain of pain at her stomach for which pain I gave her a small dose of the powder of angelica root which gave her some present ease, we did at that present wonder the child should eat broth so hot having never used so to do but we did not then suspect the said Ayres. In the afternoon on the same day the child went to the meeting again and did not much complain at her return home but about 3 hours in the night next following the said child being in the bed with me John Kelly and asleep did suddenly start up out of her sleep and holding up her hands cried Father Father help me help me Goodwife Ayres is upon me she chokes me, she kneels on my belly, she will break my bowels, she pinches me, she will make me black and blue, oh! Father will you not help me, with some other expression of like nature to my great grief and astonishment[.] My reply was lie you down and be quiet do not disturb your mother, whereupon she was a little quiet but presently she starts up again and cried out with greater violence than before against Goodwife Ayres using much the expressions aforesaid. Then rising I lighted a candle and took her up and put her into the bed with her mother from which time she was in great extremity of misery crying still out against the said Ayres and that we would give her drink and on the Monday crying out against the said Ayres saying Goody Ayres torments me she pricks me with pins she will kill me, Oh! Father set on the great furnace and scald her, get the broad axe and cut of[f] her head; if you cannot get a broad axe get the narrow axe and chop off her head, with many the like expressions continually proceeding from her, we used what physical helps we could obtain and that without delay, but could neither conceive nor others for us that her malady was natural in which sad condition she continued till Tuesday on which day I Bethia Kelly being in the house and with me the wife of Thomas Whaples and the wife of Nathaniel Greensmith, the child being in great misery the aforesaid Ayres came in whereupon the child asked her Goodwife Ayres why do you torment me and prick me, to which Goodwife Whaples said to the child you must not speak against Goody Ayres she comes in love to see you, while the said Ayres was there the child seemed indifferent well and fell asleep, the said Ayres said she will be well again I hope[.] The same Tuesday at night the child told us both that when Goody Ayres was with her alone she asked me Betty why do you speak so much against me I will be even with you for it before you die, but if you will say no more of me I will give you a fine lace for your dressing. I Bethia Kelly perceiving her while being with the child and thinking she promised her something I asked her what it was[.] The said Ayres answered a lace for a dressing, the said Ayres departing the child was more quiet till midnight and then she broke out afresh as before against Goody Ayres, moreover on the same Tuesday the child said Father why do you not go to the magistrates and get them to punish Goody Ayres pray father go to the magistrates and if I could go myself I would complain to them of her how she misuses me: in this plight she continued till Wednesday night and then died[.] The last words she spake was Goodwife Ayres chokes me and then she was speechless.

The woman takes oath to all the particulars except that about the dose of angelica and the first time of the child's crying out.

Taken upon oath by John Kelly and his wife May 13, 1662
in open court. D[aniel?] Clark Secretary.

[*inscribed on first page*]: The evidences of sundry persons respecting Goody Ayres killing Kelly's daughter.

Source: Wyllys Papers, AMBL.

Witnesses to the appearance of the Kellys's child

We whose names are underwritten, were called forth and desired to take notes, of the dead child of John Kelly, do hereby testify, what we saw as followeth: the child was brought forth, and laid upon a form, by the Goodwife Ayres, and Goodwife Whaples, and the face of it being uncovered, Goodwife Ayres was desired by John Kelly to come up to it and to handle it; the child having purged a little at the mouth. The[n] Goodwife Ayres wiped the corner of the child's mouth with a cloth, and then she was desired, to turn up the sleeve of the arm and she did endeavor to do it; but the sleeve being somewhat straight she could not well do it. Then John Kelly himself ripped up both sleeves of the arms, and upon the backside of both the arms from the elbow to the top of the shoulders were black and blue, as if they had been bruised, or beaten; after this the child was turned over, upon the right side, and so upon the belly, and then there came such a scent from the corpse, as that it caused some to depart the room, as Gregory Molterton, and George Grant, then the child being turned again, and laid into the coffin, John Kelly desired them to come into the room again, to see the child's face, and then we saw upon the right cheek of the child's face, a reddish tawny great spot, which covered a great part of the cheek, it being on the side next to Goodwife Ayres where she stood, this spot or blotch was not seen before the child was turned: and the arms of the child did appear to be very limber, in the handling of them. Thomas Catting, Thomas Butt, Joseph Water, Gregory Molterton, Nathaniel Willett, George Graves Thomas [   ].

Source: Samuel Wyllys Papers, CSL.

An autopsy report on John Kelly's child

Testified upon oath before the magistrates by Mr. Rossiter[1] and Mr. Pitkins. Attests March 31, 1662 Daniel Clark Secretary.

All these 6 particulars underwritten I judge preternatural—upon the opening of John Kelly's child at the grave I observed[:]

1. The whole body, the musculous parts, nerves, and joints, were all pliable, without any stiffness, or contraction, the gullet only excepted: experience of dead bodies renders such symptoms unusual.

2. From the costall ribs to the bottom of the belly in the whole latitude of the womb; both the scarfskin and the whole skin with the enveloping or covering flesh had a deep blue tincture; w[he]n the inward part thereof was fresh, and the bowels under it in true order, without any discoverable peccunry,[2] to cause such an effect or symptom.

3. No quantity or appearance of blood was in either vortex or cavity of belly or breast, but in the throat only at the very swallow where was a large quantity, as that part could well [contain][3] both fresh and fluid, no way [congelated][4] or clotted as it come[s] from a vein opened that I stroke it out with my finger as water.

4. There was the appearance of pure fresh blood in the backside of the arm, affecting the skin as blood itself without bruising, or [congelating].[5]

5. The bladder of gall was all broken, and curded, without any tincture in the adjacent parts.

6. The gullet or swallow was contracted, like a hard fishbone that hardly a large pease could be forced through.

Dr. Rossiter.

[*inscribed*] Mr. Rossiter's and Mr. Pitkin's observation about Kelly's child.

1. Dr. Thomas Rossiter of Windsor, Connecticut.
2. Not in *OED*, but probably related to "peccant," meaning corrupted, diseased.
3. The word in the manuscript is probably "entoyme."
4. The word in the manuscript may be "congrated."
5. The word in the manuscript may be "congrating."
Source: Wyllys Papers, AMBL.

Joseph Marsh testifies against Goodwife Ayres

I Joseph Marsh coming in to John Kelly's house on the Tuesday morning after his child was taken sick I heard her say father bring hither the broad axe or else the narrow axe and her mother being by her asked her what to do and she answered to cut off Goody Ayres's head then her mother asked her why whe[re] is she and she said there she comes over the mat[.] This I Joseph Marsh can safely testify: moreover I Joseph Marsh can testify that I coming into John Kelly's house there sat Goody Ayres upon the bed where Betty Kelly lay and I heard her speak to her saying if she would be quiet and hold her tongue and lie still and go to sleep and say no more to her father about her she would come tomorrow morning and bring her a [brary?] lace to set upon her dress upon which she replied saying will you and she said yes indeed I will and if I [   ]. March 31, 1661 this I Joseph Marsh can safely testify.

Source: Samuel Wyllys Papers, CSL.

A tale of the devil

Goody Burr and her son Samuel can testify such an expression as this: being both together in my house that Goody Ayres said when she lived at London in England that there came a fine young gentleman a suiting to her and when they were discoursing together the young gentleman made her promise him to meet him at that place another time: the which she engaged to do so: but looking down upon his foot she perceived it was the devil: then she would not meet him as she promised him but he coming there and found her not: she said that he carried away the iron bars. The mark of Goody Burr[;] Samuel Burr.

Source: Samuel Wyllys Papers, CSL.

Robert Stern sees women in the woods

Robert Stern testifieth as followeth.

I saw this morning Goodwife Seager in the woods with three more women and with them I saw two black creatures like two Indians but taller[.] I saw likewise a kettle there over a fire[.] I saw the women dance round those black creatures and whiles I looked upon them one of the women Goodwife Greensmith said look who is ayonder and then they ran away up the hill. I stood still and the black things came towards me and then I turned to come away: He further saith I knew the persons by their habit or clothes having observed such clothes on them not long before.

Source: Samuel Wyllys Papers, CSL.

Maria Screech on suing about a dead sow

Mrs. Maria Screech deposed testifieth I had a sow lay dead in the frame of Richard Howard's house under a piece of timber so somebody came to calling and I went out of the house with Mrs. Blackledge and I did look upon the sow and it was my girl's sow. Now afterwards Goodwife Stedman came to my house and was troubled and said she saw this sow a day or two before in Mr. Blackledge his lot and did believe that they had hurt the sow and she would have had me have gone to the court to have sued Mr. Blackledge for the sow and she said that she would come in to witness against him[.] She said she had several hogs hurt and one pig dead and I asked her why did not she sue[.] She answered why should she sue when I and others would not[.] And I could not perceive that the sow had received hurt from anybody and Goodman Howard said he could not perceive that any- body had hurt her. [January 2, 1662]. Taken upon oath before Daniel Clark.

Source: Wyllys Papers, AMBL.

Hanna Robbins reports her father's suspicions of Goody Palmer

Hanna the daughter of Mrs. Robbins aged about 24 years affirmeth that Goody Palmer and Katherine Harrison[1] were present at Mr. Rob- bins his house in the time of that sickness whereof her mother de- parted this life, and Mrs. Robbins very much complained against Goody Palmer as one that caused her afflictions and cried out that she saw her and saith that Mr. Robbins 2 or 3 times forewarned the said Palmer not to come to his house, yet nevertheless the said Palmer would thrust herself into the company, and further Hanna saith that Mr. Robbins had drawn out a writing relating to prove witchcraft oc- casioning the death of his wife, but now she knoweth not where it is. And further the said Hanna saith that, in the time of the sickness whereof her said sister Mary died she the said Mary complained of witches as occasioning her sickness and Hanna heard her sister say[,] the tears running down her cheeks[,] you tell me it is fancy that I complain that I am afflicted by some evil, evil persons, but it is true, and she the said Hanna further saith that she heard Mary say they thought she the said Mary was bewitched to death. [*undated*]

1. Seven years later, Katherine Harrison was accused of witchcraft. See chap. 11.
Source: Wyllys Papers, AMBL.

Alice Wakely on Mrs. Robbins's body

Alice the wife of James Wakely aged about or above 50 years testifieth that being present with Mrs. Robbins in the time of the sickness whereof Mrs. Robbins died, she did see and know that the body of Mrs. Robbins was stiff so that both she and Goodwife Miggat senior could not move either her arms or legs although both of them tried to move them, and the same day Mrs. Robbins died, then her whole body was limber extraordinary after her death. [*cut off*]

Source: Samuel Wyllys Papers, CSL. This deposition may concern Katherine Harrison; it is reprinted on p. 176.

Why the jury convicted Goody Seager

The causes why half the jury or more did in their vote cast Goody Seager (and the rest of the jury were deeply suspicious, and were at a great loss and staggering whereby; they were sometimes likely to come up in their judgments to the rest; whereby she was almost gone and cast as the foreman expressed to her at giving in of the verdict) are these[:] first it did appear by legal evidence that she had intimate familiarity, with such, as had been witches, viz. Goody Sanford and Goody Ayres[.] Secondly[.] This she did in open court stoutly deny saying the witnesses were prejudiced persons, and that she had no more intimacy than they themselves, and when the witnesses questioned with her about frequent being there, she said she went to learn to knit; this also she stoutly denied, and said of the witnesses they belie me, then when Mr. John Allyn said did she not teach you to knit. She answered sturdily and said, I do not know that I am bound to tell you and at another turn being pressed to answer she said, nay I will hold what I have if I must die. Yet after this she confessed that she had so much intimacy with one of them as that they did change work one with another.

Thirdly[.] She having said that she did hate Goody Ayres it did appear that she bore her great yea more than ordinary good will as appeared by relieving her in her trouble, in a covert way, and was troubled that it was discovered; likewise when Goody Ayres said in court; this will take away my life, Goody Seager shoved her with her hand and said hold your tongue what grind my teet[h?]: Mr. John Allyn being one witness hereto when he had spoken; she said they seek my innocent blood; the magistrate replied, Who[?] She said everybody.

Fourthly[.] Being spoken to about trial by swimming; she said the devil that caused me to come here can keep me up[.] About the business of flying the most part brought it was not legally proved.

Lastly the woman and Robert Stern being both upon oath their witness was judged legal testimony or evidence. Only [some?] in the jury because Robert Stern's first words upon his oath were I saw these women and as I take it Goody Seager was there though after that he said, I saw her there I knew her well I know God will require her blood at my hands if I should testify falsely. Also because he said he saw her kettle, then being at so great a distance; they doubted that these things did not only weaken and blemish testimony; but also in a great measure disable it for standing to take away life. [January 16, 1662].

Walt Tyler.

Source: Wyllys Papers, AMBL.

The indictment and verdict: guilty of adultery

A court held at Hartford, July 2, 1663.

Elizabeth Seager thou art here indicted by the name of Elizabeth Seager for not having the fear of God before thine eyes thou hast entertained familiarity with Satan the grand enemy of God and mankind, and by his help hast acted things in a preternatural way beyond the ordinary course of nature, as also for that thou hast committed adultery, and hast spoken blasphemy against God, contrary to the laws of God, and the established laws of this corporation for all or any of which crimes by the said laws thou deservest to die.

The prisoner pleaded not guilty of the indictment and referred herself to the trial of the jury.

The jury return that they find the prisoner guilty of the indictment in that particular of adultery.

Source: Court of Assistants Records, *56*, p. 5, CSL.

Indictment of Elizabeth Seager in 1665

Elizabeth Seager thou art here indicted by the name of Elizabeth Seager the wife of Richard Seager not having the fear of God before thine eyes thou hast entertained familiarity with Satan the grand enemy of God and mankind and hast practiced witchcraft formerly and continuest to practice witchcraft for which according to the law of God and the established law of this corporation thou deservest to die[.] The prisoner answered not guilty, and refers herself to be tried by God and the country[.] The jury being called to return their verdict upon the indictment of Elizabeth Seager the foreman declares that they find the prisoner guilty of familiarity with Satan. June 26, 1665.

Source: Court of Assistants Records, *56*, pp. 35–36 (CSL).

Testimony of Mrs. Miggat against Goody Seager

I[1] being desired by the magistrates the last day of the session of the General Court in May, to hear the complaint of Mrs. Miggat,

Mrs. Miggat saith she went out to give her calves meat, about five weeks since, and Goodwife Seager came to her and shaked her by the arm, and said how do you, how do you, Mrs. Miggat.

Second: Mrs. Miggat also saith: a second time Goodwife Seager came to her towards the little river, a little below the house: which she now dwelleth in, and told her, that God was naught, God was naught, it was very good to be a witch and desired her to be one, she should not need fear, going to hell, for she should not burn in the fire.

Third time, Mrs Miggat affirmeth that Goodwife Seager came to her at the hedge corner belonging to their house lot, and there spake to her but what, she could not tell, which caused Mrs Miggat (as she saith) to [torn] away with great fear. . . .

[*in left-hand margin, alongside the following statement, is written:* "place this to the second particular"]:

Mrs. Miggat said to her at this time that she did not love her: she was very naught, and Goodwife Seager shaked her by the hands and bid her farewell, and desired her, not to tell anybody what she had said unto her.

1. One of the magistrates, or perhaps a local justice of the peace.

An apparition of Goodwife Seager

Mrs. Miggat saith a little before the flood this spring, Goodwife Seager, came into their house, on a moon shining night, and took her by the hand and struck her on the face as she was in bed with her husband, whom she could not wake, and then Goodwife Seager went away, and Mrs Miggat went to the door but darst not look out after her.

These particulars Mrs. Miggat charged Goodwife Seager with being face to face, and at Mr. Miggat's new dwelling house, per John Talcott. [May, 1663 or 1665]

[*inscribed:*] Testimonies concerning witchcraft and Goody Seager 1663 G. Greensmith['s] testimony to it[.] Testimonies about Seager touching witchcraft 1665.

Source: Wyllys Papers, AMBL.

Daniel and Margaret Garrett describe rejected parsnips, and Goody Seager's reaction to Ann Cole

The testimony of Daniel Garrett senior and the testimony of Margaret Garrett: In reference to Goodwife Seager:

Goodwife Garrett saith that Goodwife Seager said there was a day kept at Mr. Wyllys's in reference to Ann Cole: and she further said she was in great trouble even in agony of spirit, she propound[ed] as follows that she sent her own daughter Eliza[beth] Seager to Goodwife Hosmer to carry her a mess a parsnips; Goodwife Hosmer was not home she was at Mr. Wyllys's at the fast:[1] Goodman Hosmer and her son was at home, Goodman Hosmer bid the child carry the parsnips home again he would not receive them and if her mother desired a reason, bid her send her father and he would tell him the reason: Goodwife Seager upon the return of the parsnips was much troubled and sent for her husband and sent him up to Goodman Hosmer to know the reason why he would not receive the parsnips, and he told Goodman Seager it was because Ann Cole at the fast at Mr Wyllys's cried out against his wife as being a witch: and he would not receive the parsnips, lest he should, be brought in hereaft[er] as a testimony against his wife, then Goodwife Seager said that Mr. Haynes[2] had writt[en] a great deal of hodgepodge that Ann Cole had said that she was under suspicion for a witch: and then she went to prayer, and did adventure to bid Satan go and tell them she was no witch[:] This deponent after she had a little paused said, who did you say, then Goodwife Seager said again she had sent Satan to tell them, she was no witch[.] This deponent asked her why she made use of Satan to tell them, why did she not beseech God to tell them she was no witch[.] She answered because Satan knew she was no witch.

Goodman Garrett testifies, that before him and his wife Goodwife Seager said, that she sent Satan to tell them that she was no witch.

Three witnesses to Goodwife Seager's reasoning about Satan

We underwritten do testify, that Goodwife Seager said upon the relating of Goodwife Garrett['s] testimony in reference to her sending Satan, that the reason why she sent Satan was because he knew she was no witch, and to prove that she brought that place in the 19 Acts 14.[3] Edward Stebbing Steven Hart senior Josiah Willard.

Further Goodwife Garrett saith that Will[iam] Edwards told Goodwife Seager that she did fly, the said Seager replied that William Edwards made her fly, then Goodwife Garrett said then you own you did fly, then Goodwife Seager replied if I did fly William Edwards made me fly.

Goodman Garrett saith the same.

Further Goodwife Garrett saith, that she made a cheese better than ordinary, the which upon a time (when Goodwife Seager was in their barn a husking Indian corn), the said Goodwife Garrett desired her husband to fetch her down that cheese, which she had marked with several notches, her husband fetched that cheese to her; when he brought it, she found all on[e] side of the cheese full of maggots: the other side very sound and good, this deponent cut out the maggoty side into a tray and flung it into the fire, suddenly upon which Goodwife Seager cried out exceedingly in the barn insomuch as this deponent heard her into the house and after a short time Goodwife Seager came into the house, cried out she was full of pain, and sat wringing of her body and crying out what do I ail what do I ail.

To this also Goodman Garrett testifies.

What is in this paper on this side and the other side Margaret Garrett upon her oath testified that it was the truth before the prisoner and jury and before Mr. James Richards and myself, this: June 17, 1665 as attests John Allyn.

Daniel Garrett upon his oath in what he testifies in this paper to be the truth.

John Allyn

Goodwife Watson tells Seager about Ann Cole

The testimony of Goodwife Watson.

Goodwife Watson saith she told Seager['s] wife, that Goodwife Cole said, she desired to speak with her daughter, and Seager's wife said, she heard, Ann Cole cried out of her, Goodwife Watson answered her, in her fits she mentioneth many, but no more you than others, and out of her fits she saith no more to you, than to any other, and Seager's wife said, they missed their mark: they aimed at me why do they not lay hold of others as well as me, why do they lay hold of the chief (actor herself said), Goodwife Watson answered her, if you know others to be chief why do you not discover them, Seager['s] wife said she would in due time. Goodwife Seager owned this testimony before Deacon Stebbins.

Deacon Hart John Horton John Loomis.

[*inscribed:*] Testimonies upon the trial of Elizabeth Seager June 15, 1665.

1. A fast held to pray for the healing of Ann Cole.
2. We know from John Whiting's letter that Joseph Haynes, minister in Hartford,

prepared a written summary of Ann Cole's statements. These statements implicated Goody Seager, who, not surprisingly, responded as is indicated here.
3. The scriptural reference is to an attempted exorcism by "several sons of one Sceva, a Jew, and chief of the priests."
Source: Wyllys Papers, AMBL.

Seager quotes Scripture to prove she is no witch

We underwritten do testify, that Goodwife Seager said (upon the relating of Goodwife Garrett's testimony, in reference to Seager sending Satan[ )], that the reason why she sent Satan, was because he knew she was no witch, we say Seager said Dame you can remember part of what I said, but you do not speak of the whole you say nothing of what I brought to prove that Satan knew I was no witch, I brought that place in the Acts,[1] about the sons that spake to the evil spirits in the name of Jesus whom Paul preacheth I have forgot their names. Stephen Hart, Josiah Willard, Daniel Pratt.

1. Acts 19:13–16.
Source: Samuel Wyllys Papers, CSL.

The governor delays sentencing

The Governor and magistrates being met to consider of the issue of the case respecting the prisoners Hannah Hackleton and Elizabeth Seager that by the verdict of the jury are found guilty of their respective indictments the Governor declared that it was his desire that the matter might be respited to a further consideration for advice in those matters that were to him so obscure and ambiguous and the issue is deferred to the Quarter Court in September next. July 8, 1665.

Source: Court of Assistants Records, *56*, p. 38, CSL.

Elizabeth Seager is set free

At a special Court of Assistants[:]
Respecting Elizabeth Seager this court considering the verdict of the jury and finding that it doth not legally answer the indictment do therefore discharge and set her free from further suffering or imprisonment. May 18, 1666.

Source: Court of Assistants Records, State Archives, *56*, p. 52, CSL.

10. A Father's Battle
(1666–1667)
▲

William Graves

William Graves of Stamford, Connecticut, had refused to pay over to his daughter Abigail her "portion" or inheritance after she married Samuel Dibble. When Dibble "got an attachment to try by a course of law" for the inheritance, his father-in-law told him he "should repent the bringing that attachment as long as" he lived. As happened in so many similar situations, the anger Graves expressed toward his daughter and son-in-law made them fear that he would do them some harm. Abigail experienced a difficult labor, and attributed her sufferings to a visit from her father during which he seems to have voiced the spiritual counsel that she "fit thy self to meet the Lord." A hearing on charges of witchcraft was held in February 1666. No action seems to have been taken against Graves. Somewhat paradoxically, he suspected that "some one in this town that I and mine have suffered much wrong by" was causing his daughter's troubles.

Ann Smith describes William Graves's fears
about his daughter's health

The testimony of Ann Smith saith that she being at Samuel Dibble's house a helping his wife in her labor in her extremity and misery; and likewise she said Goody Smith persuaded her to lie still and she said she could not lie still and I asked her the reason why and she said she was so bitten she could not lie still; I asked her where she was so bitten and she said in her back and everywhere; and she continuing in such misery; Goodman Graves helping her to hold her, and she said Goody Smith said that she thought it was not an ordinary distemper that she was troubled withal, Goodman Graves said that he and his family had suffered upon that account, and he said if his daughter died, he would bring out one in this town that he never thought to do; and he said that she should not be buried presently for he would have all the town lay their hands on her[.][1] The reason was demand[ed] of him why and he said because no one should take offence; and he said he was there on Thursday the 17th of this month—a sitting in the house with his daughter all alone and of a sudden he said she rised up out of her chair and gave him such an ugly look and went to bed: and then he said he concluded that she would not live: and if so be she was not delivered quickly he thought she would not [ ] and further saith not—but is ready to be deposed of this. Stamford January 30, 1666/7.

Mary Scholfield describes William Graves' advice to his daughter

The testimony of Mary Scolfield she being at Samuel Dibble's house: William Graves said he had counseled his daughter to prepare herself to meet the Lord and said if she was not delivered suddenly she would die[.] Upon these words he said she changed her countenance and went sick to bed and being asked whether it was at noon or at night, he answered it was at noon; and more he said if my child die in this condition she shall not be buried a good whiles: for all the town shall touch her[.] The said Scolfield asked William Graves whether he knew the party that was the cause of it, he said though there was one in the town that both I and mine was the worse for him; yet the whole town shall touch her and then none will take offence: And further said not but is ready to be deposed of what is above written. Stamford January 31, 1666/7.

Thomas Steedwell remembers William Graves's advice

The testimony of Thomas Steedwell[:] he heard William Graves confess before him and his wife: that he wished Abigail Dibble his said daughter to prepare herself to meet the Lord for if she did not fall in labor suddenly it was a question whether ever she would or no[.] He said she rise up and gave me an ugly look and went sick to bed this was said on the 17th day of January last: and she continued so before she was delivered, and when she was delivered it was with much difficultness where was but little hopes of her life and taken in strange fits[.] Her father being by her said if my daughter die in these fits she shall not be buried a good whiles for I will bring some out in this town that I and mine have suffered much wrong by: and this he is ready to be deposed of.

The midwife testifies about Abigail's labor

The testimony of Mary Holmes being midwife to Samuel Dibble's wife in her labor testifies that she had a kindly labor as other women had, until the child came to the breath[.] Then she was taken with a trembling and striving that we was not able to deal with her; and after she came to herself again, she had her labor kindly and was delivered as well as any women could be, and as soon as she was in her bed, her fits came again astriving: and further saith not but is ready to be deposed of this whenever she is called to it. Stamford February 4, 1666/7.

Mary Scholfield describes the delivery, and the mother's fits

The testimony of Mary Scolfield being in assistance and aiding help by the desire of the midwife in the labor of the said Goody Dibble both for skill and experience in such matters presenting the midwife's place[.] Just upon the delivery of the child into the world the midwife's strength failing of her she desired the said Goody Scolfield to supply her place as joining with her before by desire, and then immediately as to give the cry; one part of her mouth was drawed up and the other down: with her lips turning black: and her eyes staring out in a ghastly manner and likewise her tongue hanging out and a dumb voice: and upon this the child was drawn away up into her body in likeness to the belly of a whale, and this continuing for the space of half an hour only the child lay quivering within her body, and about an hour after as she apprehended with the pangs of death and not by the former course of labor as other women have: the child came trembling into the world and before we could get her into bed she flung herself upon the feet of the bed, and said she was well enough: and as soon as she was in the bed she had a very strange fit as formerly she had: and further says not: but this she is ready to be deposed of when she is called to it.

Thomas Steedwell describes Abigail Dibble's fits

The testimony of Thomas Steedwell: he being at the house of Samuel Dibble one Saturday in the forenoon presently after the delivery of his wife; continuing there while Sabbath day in the morning helping to hold her his said wife in her raging fits and presently falling of them fits into sounding fits, with her tongue fleering out of her mouth near a handful long: and about as thick as his wrist and as black as possible might be; and her eyes out of her head in a ghastly manner and when those fits went of[f], her tongue went in again, but there was such a smell with her breath that none in the room were able to abide the steam thereof: The ghastly sight and hideousness thereof he is not able to express, never knowing or seeing any in such fits and with such noisome smell in his life: and further saith not: But this he is ready to be deposed of what is above written[.] Mary Scolfield and Ann Smith testify the same as is above alleged etc. Stamford February 4, 1666/7.

Thomas Steedwell and others on what Goodman Graves said

And further the above said Thomas Steedwell and Ann Smith say that Goodman Graves said my child will die; and I shall be hanged for her and further said in the said Steedwell's hearing presently good people be merciful to me: and further they said not; but are ready to be deposed of all I [have] above written.

The testimony of Zachariah Dibble[:] he said he heard William Graves say: my child will die; and I shall be hanged shall I for her and further saith you will take away my life with my daughter's.

The testimony of Elizabeth Steedwell[:] she said she heard William Graves say my child will die and I shall be hanged for her shall I and further saith not.

1. Another folk belief: a dead body, if touched by the murderer, will make a physical response. This belief colors a deposition from the Hartford witch-hunt in which several witnesses described the corpse of Elizabeth Kelly. Interestingly, Graves rejected any direct accusation of someone in the town. For the context, see David D. Hall, *Worlds of Wonder, Days of Judgment: Popular Religious Belief in Early New England* (New York, 1989), p. 176.
Source: Wyllys Papers, AMBL.

Zachariah Dibble and others on what William Graves said

The testimony of Zachariah Dibble he says he heard William Graves say that if his child die in these fits everyone in the town shall touch her that none may take offence at it and further said he would bring somebody upon their trial: and further says not[.] But this he is ready to be deposed of.

Testimony[:] Ann Hardy deposeth the same as is above mentioned and further she says that William Graves said if my child die in this condition, I will discover the person that is the cause of it, and further saith not.

The testimony of Sarah Bates concerning some words she heard between Mary Scolfield and William Graves: he said that everyone in the town shall touch her the said Abigail Graves—Mary Scolfield asked him why he would do so if he did suspect any person why he did not bring them out[.] He said everyone should touch her and then none would take offence and further saith not: But is ready to be deposed of this.

Further the said Sarah Bates testifieth that I heard William Graves say at Samuel Dibble's house my child is dying: and they would take away my life with hers and to that purpose he spoke these words two or three times: and further saith not but is ready to be deposed of this. Stamford, February 4, 1666/7.

The husband, Samuel Dibble, describes a quarrel

The testimony of Samuel Dibble saith that he made a demand of his father Graves for his wife's portion[:] He answered me I should have nothing: I should carry better to him: I asked wherein I had offended him; he told me because I would not help him reap: I told him I never reaped: then I got an attachment to try by a course of law for my wife's portion: he asked me where I thought I should gain anything by it[.] I told him I should gain my due[.] His answer was he never engaged anything to me; he told me I should repent the bringing that attachment as long as I lived: my answer was good now father do not threaten: for threaten[ed] folks live long his answer was; but you shall live never the longer for it: In the summertime my wife being afraid she would have me yield myself to her father in anything it would be the better for us: I told her I feared no man: she said maybe so but you do not know what they can do to us: about a fortnight before my wife's labor father Graves came to my house: and suddenly began to counsel his daughter saying Abigail fit thyself to meet the Lord: for if thou dost not fall in labor properly: she would die and so went away: on that the Thursday fortnight after he came again and I heard him repeated over the same words as is above last mentioned: saying Abigail fit thyself to meet the Lord for if thou are not delivered suddenly thou wilt die: and he said she rose up and gave me an ugly look and went sick to bed: and came again another time and said if my child die in these fits I will discover the party that is the cause of it: and so went away and came again to my house after I had served a warrant upon him to appear at Mr. Lane's house and said my child will die and I shall be hanged for her and further saith not: this he can be deposed of. Stamford, February 4, 1666/7.

[*inscribed:*] These to Mr. Nathaniel Gold at Fairfield with care present.

Source: Wyllys Papers, AMBL.

11. One "Cunning Woman":
At Odds With All
(1668–1670)

▲

Katherine Harrison of Wethersfield

A widow and a resident of Wethersfield, Connecticut, at the time she was charged with witchcraft in 1668, Katherine Harrison was the subject of extraordinary suspicions and aggression by her neighbors. She had been married to John Harrison, a well-to-do farmer who at his death in 1666 left an estate of £929 to Katherine and their three daughters. In September 1668, about the time that she was first accused of witchcraft, one of Katherine's neighbors, Michael Griswold, charged her with slandering his wife, and another, John Chester, accused her of "unjust detaining of land."[1] These suits went against her. Shortly thereafter, Katherine petitioned the government for relief from vandalism and the fine of £15 that was levied in the case of slander. These petitions (which are not included in this volume)[2] reveal her as fearful that, between them, neighbors and the civil courts would take away her "estate." Katherine's determination to preserve some of that estate for her children may account for her request that certain men (including John and Jonathan Gilbert) become guardians of her children and her property.

A jury indicted her for witchcraft the following May. The depositions submitted at this time suggest that Katherine was a healer and a fortune-teller. If the statements of her neighbors can be trusted, she was familiar with a book or books written by the English astrologer William Lilly.[3]

The judicial response to the accusations against her was essen-

tially one of finding a middle ground between guilt and innocence. One jury could not agree on a verdict. Another found her guilty, but the magistrates dissented. Instead, they ordered her to leave the colony of Connecticut. By 1670 she had moved to New York, where, once again, she was complained of for witchcraft.[4] She returned to Connecticut in 1672 to handle further matters relating to her estate. It is possible she remained for good; she may have died in 1682. Her life history is analyzed in Carol Karlsen, The Devil in the Shape of a Woman *(New York, 1987), pp. 84–89, from which much of the information in this note is derived.*

1. Court of Assistants Records, State Archives, *56*, pp. 79–80, CSL. Two months later, she filed suit against Ann Latimore, charging her with "not securing to her land that was bought of her." Ibid., p. 81. The two parties eventually reached an agreement that seems to have favored Harrison.
2. They may be found in "Crimes and Misdemeanors," Vol. 1, pt. 1, State Archives, CSL.
3. William Lilly's career is described in Keith Thomas, *Religion and the Decline of Magic* (New York, 1971).
4. These documents are printed in George L. Burr, ed., *Narratives of the Witchcraft Cases* (New York, 1914), pp. 48–52.

Katherine Harrison describes the attacks on her property

A complaint of several grievances, of the Widow Harrison's which she desires the honored court to take cognizance of and as far as may be to give her relief in.

May it please this honored court, to have patience with me a little; having none to complain to, but the fathers of the commonweal; and yet meeting with many injuries; which necessitates me, to look out; for some relief: I am bold to present you with those few lines; as a relation of the wrongs, that I suffer humbly craving, your serious consideration of my state a widow; of my wrongs (which I conceive) are great, and that as far as the rules of justice and equity will allow, I may have right, and a due recompense; that what I would present to you in the first place is we had a yoke of oxen one of which spoiled at our stile before our door, with blows upon the back and side, so bruised that he was altogether unserviceable; about a fortnight or three weeks after the former, we had a cow spoiled, her back broke and two of her ribs, nextly I had a heifer in my barnyard; my earmark of which was cut out, and other earmarks set on; nextly I had a sow that had young pigs earmarked (in the sty) after the same manner; nextly I had a cow at the side of my yard, her jawbone broke, and one of her hooves, and a hole bored in her side, nextly I had a three-year-old heifer in the meadow stuck with a knife or some weapon and wounded to death:

nextly I had a cow in the street wounded in the bag as she stood before my door, in the street, nextly, I had a sow went out into the woods, came home with ears luged[1] and one of her hind legs cut off[.] Lastly my corn in Mile meadow much damnified with horses, they being staked upon it; it was wheat; all which injuries as they do savor of envy so I hope they will be looked upon, by this honored court according to their nature and judged according to their demerit, that so your poor suppliant may find some redress; who is bold to subscribe

Your servant, and suppliant Katherine Harrison.

Postscript: I had my horse wounded in the night, as he was in my pasture no creature, save three calves with him: more I had one two-year-old steer the back of it broke, in the barnyard; more I had, a matter of 30 poles of hops cut and spoiled: all which things, have happened since my husband['s] death, which was last August was two year; there is witness to the oxen Jonathan and Josiah Gilbert: to the cows being spoiled: Enock Buck: Josiah Gilbert to the cow that had her jawbone broke: Daniel Rose John Bromson: to the heifer, one of Widow Stodder['s] sons, and William Taylor; to the corn John Beckly: to the wound of the horse Anthony Wright Goodman Higby: to the hops cutting: Goodwife Standish and Mary Wright; which things being added; and left to your serious consideration, I make bold again to subscribe

Yours Katherine Harrison

[*inscribed:*] Widow Harrison's Grievances presented to the court October 6, 1668.

1. Pulled, rougly pulled *(OED)*.
Source: Wyllys Papers, AMBL.

Rebecca Smith against Katherine Harrison

Rebecca Smith aged about 75 years testifieth as followeth that formerly being at Jonathan Gilbert his house about 14 days together: Goodwife Gilbert the wife of Jonathan Gilbert had a black cap which she had lent to Katherine Harrison, and Katherine Harrison desired to have the said cap, but Goody Gilbert refused to sell it to Katherine, after Goodwife Gilbert wore the said cap and when she had the cap on her head her shoulders and head was much afflicted; after the cap being pulled off, Goody Gilbert said she was well, again a certain time after Goody Gilbert wore, or put on the said cap: then she was afflicted as before; the said cap being again pulled off, Goody Gilbert again said she was well. Thus being afflicted several times, it was suspected to be by witchcraft after the said Rebecca Smith heard say the cap was burned.

And further the said Rebecca affirmeth that she hath been afflicted near a year last past, being suddenly taken her thigh and leg being stiff like a stick, and dreadful sick, having strange fits insomuch that she the said Rebecca often said in the hearing of her married daughter and others, she thought or doubted that some evil person had bewitched her, but this both she the said Rebecca and the family do affirm that since Friday last past she hath been much better, her fits of[f], the aforesaid afflictions have been quite eased and taken away and whereas on the Lord's day since her said first affliction she and her family have observed, that she was usually the most afflicted on the Sabbath day: but now this Lord's day last, she hath not only been freed of the fits aforesaid, but also hath found herself well, excepting such infirmities as do accompany old age. Dated October 12, 1668 this they affirmed in my hearing [*cut off*].

Source: Samuel Wyllys Papers, CSL.

William Warren against Katherine Harrison

William Warren testified in open court that Katherine Harrison was a common and professed fortune teller, and some other matters concerning Katherine Harrison needful to be considered of: because they were not (as I conceive) taken in writing. October 27, 1668.

Source: Samuel Wyllys Papers, CSL.

William Warren says that Katherine Harrison did express that she was a fortune teller and did tell him and Simon Sackett and Elizabeth Batemen and my master's daughter our fortunes. She said she had her skill from Lilly [and she looked on my hands].[1] This was about 17 years ago. Exhibited in court and sworn October 30, 1668. Attest John Allyn Secretary.

1. Crossed out in the manuscript.
Source: Samuel Wyllys Papers, CSL.

John Wells sees Katherine Harrison

When my father lived in the house where Joseph Wright liveth some mornings our cows were late before they came home and my mother sent me to see if I could meet them[.] I went once or twice but the second time I was sent I went about halfway cross the street and could go no further my legs were bound to my thinking with a napkin but [I] could see nothing I looked toward the cattle that were in the street by Goodman Not's shop and I saw Goodwife Harrison rise from a cow that was none of her own with a pail in her hand and made haste home and when she was over her own stile I was loosed. June 29, 1668. This was about 7 or 8 years ago. John Wells. This was owned and acknowledged by John Wells before me Samuel Wells.

Source: Samuel Wyllys Papers, CSL.

A witness describes Harrison as knowing magic

Thomas Waples aged about 50 years testifieth that Katherine the late wife of John Harrison deceased, was a noted liar and did report she had read Mr. Lilly's book in England and one that did spin more than he doth judge could be spun without some unlawful help: which yarn did not well prosper as Mrs. Cullick said and that the said Katherine told fortunes matters that were in future time to be accomplish[ed] and further saith that Captain Cullick did turn the said Katherine out of his service for her evil conversation. And further the said Thomas Waples testifieth that Goody Greensmith did before her condemnation accuse Katherine Harrison to be a witch. Dated August 7, 1668. Sworn and exhibited in court October 24, 1669. Attest John Allyn secretary Thomas Waples his mark.

Source: Samuel Wyllys Papers, CSL.

Mary Olcott describes apparent fortune-telling

Mary Olcott the wife of Thomas Olcott testifieth that when Elizabeth the new wife of Simon Smith was servant to Captain Cullick, the said Elizabeth thought she should have been married to William Chapman, although the said Elizabeth affirmed that Katherine, afterwards the wife of John Harrison affirmed that she should not be married to William, for Katherine said that Elizabeth should be married to one named Simon. Dated August 8, 1668 Mary Olcott.

Source: Samuel Wyllys Papers, CSL.

Richard Montague and Katherine Harrison's recovering of bees

Richard Montague aged about 52 years testifieth as follows that meeting with Goodwife Harrison in Wethersfield the said Katherine Harrison said that a swarm of her bees flew away out her neighbor Bore-man's lot, and into the great meadow and thence over the great river to [Nabucd?] side, but the said Katherine said that she had fetched them again, this seemed very strange to the said Richard because this was acted in a little time and he did believe the said Katherine neither went nor used any lawful means to fetch the said bees as aforesaid. Dated August 13, 1668. Hadley taken upon oath before us Thomas Clark Samuel Smith exhibited in court October 29, 1668 as attest John Allyn Secretary.

Source: Samuel Wyllys Papers, CSL.

Katherine Harrison predicts the death of two men

The deposition of Samuel Martin senior aged about fifty years testifieth that being at Katherine Harrison her house in March last: we spake in due course about Mr. Josiah Willard and Samuel Hale senior: then and there she said I shall shortly see them gone both them and theirs: I asked her why and she said: do you not know. There was one almost gone the other day: I asked who was almost gone she said Mr. Willard: for he had been sick and further sayeth not. Sworn in court May 25, 1669 attest John Allyn Secretary.

Source: Samuel Wyllys Papers, CSL.

Two men reject being cited as witnesses by Katherine Harrison

Whereas we are informed that Katherine Harrison hath given in a writing into court against Josiah Gilbert and inserted our names to it this may testify that we know nothing of that matter nor gave any consent that our hands should be set to any such thing but do utterly disclaim it. Samuel Hurlbut Alexander Rony his mark. May 26, 1669.

Source: Samuel Wyllys Papers, CSL.

These deponents say that they heard Josiah Gilbert say that Goodwife Harrison called him cousin but he know no such matter but she was one that followed the army in England. Alexander Rony Samuel Hurlbut.

Source: Samuel Wyllys Papers, CSL.

Katherine Harrison is suspected of causing someone's death

Eleazer Kinnerly aged about 28 years affirmeth that he and his late wife in her lifetime [did] oft say that she suspected or [   ] that her mother was bewitched, and so it was reported and judged [by?] many others, and also Mr. Kinnerly saith that he heard his late wife affirm that upon some discourse about Master Robbins his death Katherine Harrison let fall these words (in the presence of sundry persons) when your father [*above the line:* Mr. Robbins] was killed this seized on and took deep impression in the heart of the said Mary that her father was killed and further saith that Goodman Cole of Hartford hearing the words aforesaid it took deep impresion upon his spirit as suspicious of murder. [*signatures cut off*]

Source: Samuel Wyllys Papers, CSL.

Alice Wakely on a strange death

Alice the wife of James Wakely aged about or above 50 years testifieth that being present with Mrs. Robbins in the time of the sickness whereof Mrs. Robbins died, she did see and know that the body of Mrs. Robbins was stiff so that both she and Goodwife Wright senior could not move either her arms or legs although both of them tried to move them, and the same day Mrs. Robbins died, then the whole body was limber extraordinary after her death. [*signatures cut off*]

Source: Samuel Wyllys Papers, CSL.

Thomas Bracy on a curious task of tailoring

Thomas Bracy aged about 31 years testifieth as follows that formerly James Wakely would have borrowed a saddle of the said Thomas Bracy which Thomas Bracy denied to lend to him, he threatened Thomas and said, it had been better he had lent it to him, also Thomas Bracy being at work the same day making a jacket and a pair of breeches, he labored to his best understanding to set on the sleeves aright on the jacket and seven times he placed the sleeves wrong, setting the elbows on the wrong side and was fain to rip them of[f] and new set them on again, and also the breeches going to cut out the breeches, having two pieces of cloth of different colors, he was so bemoidered[1] in that matter, that he cut the breeches one of one color, and the other of another color, in such a manner he was bemoidered in his understanding or acting, yet nevertheless the same day and time he was well in his understanding, and health in other matters and so was forced to leave working that day.

Katherine Harrison threatens Thomas Bracy for saying she is a witch

The said Thomas being at Sergeant Hugh Wells his house over against John Harrison's house in Wethersfield, he saw a cart coming towards Joh[n] Harrison's house loaden with hay, on the top of the hay he saw perfectly a red calf's head, the ears standing pert up, and keeping his sight on the cart till the cart came to the barn, the calf vanished, and Harrison stood on the cart, which appeared not to Thomas before, nor could Thomas find or see any calf there at all though he sought to see the calf—after this Thomas Bracy giving out some words, that he suspected Katherine Goody Harrison [*in margin:* Goody Katherine Harrison] of witchcraft[,] Katherine Harrison met Thomas Bracy and threatened Thomas telling him that she would be even with him.

After that Thomas Bracy aforesaid, being well in his senses and health and perfectly awake, his brothers in bed with him, Thomas aforesaid saw the said James Wakely and the said Katherine Harrison stand by the bedside, consulting to kill him the said Thomas, James Wakely said he would cut out his throat, but Katherine counseled to strangle him, presently the said Katherine seized on Thomas striving to strangle him, and pulled or pinched him so as if his flesh had been pulled from his bones, therefore Thomas groaned, at length his father Martin heard, and spake, then Thomas left groaning and lay quiet a little, and then Katherine fell again to afflicting and pinching, Thomas again groaning Mr. Martin heard, and arose and came to Thomas who could not speak till Mr. Martin laid his hand on Thomas, then James and Katherine aforesaid went to the bed's feet, his father Martin and his mother stayed watching by Thomas all that night after, and the next day Mr. Martin and his wife, saw the marks of the said affliction, and pinching, dated 13th: of August one thousand six hundred sixty and eight. Hadley. Taken upon oath before us Henry Clarke Samuel Smith.

1. Based on "moider," meaning confused or perplexed *(OED).*
Source: Wyllys Papers, AMBL.

Elizabeth Smith on Katherine Harrison as fortune-teller

Elizabeth the wife of Simon Smith of 30 mile Island aged about 34: years testifieth as followeth, viz. that Katherine Harrison formerly living with her in Captain Cullick his house, the said Katherine was noted by the said Elizabeth, and others, the rest of the family to be a great or notorious liar, a Sabbath breaker, and one that told fortunes, and told the said Elizabeth her fortune, that her husband's name should be Simon, and also told the said Elizabeth some other matters, that did come to pass, and also the said Katherine would oft speak and boast, of her great familiarity with Mr. Lilly one that told fortunes, and foretold many matters that in future time were to be accomplished, and also the said Katherine did often spin, so great a quantity of fine linen yarn, as the said Elizabeth did never know, nor hear of any other woman that could spin so much, and further the said Elizabeth saith that Captain Cullick observing the evil conversation in word and deed of the said Katherine, therefore he turned the said Katherine out of his service, one matter or cause was because the said Katherine, told fortunes, such matters as were to be accomplished in after times, dated July 29, 1668: taken upon oath September 28, 1668 before me John Allyn Assistant.

Source: Wyllys Papers, AMBL.

Joseph Dickinson on strange events connected with Widow Harrison

The deposition of Joseph Dickinson of Northampton aged about 32 years testifieth and saith that he and Phillip Smith of Hadley went down early in the morning to the great dry swamp, and there we heard a voice call Hoccanum Hoccanum come Hoccanum and coming further into the swamp we see that it was Katherine Harrison, that called as before, we saw Katherine go from thence homewards the said Phillip parted from Joseph, and a small time after Joseph met Phillip again, and then the said Phillip affirmed that he had seen Katherine's cows near [a] mile from the place where Katherine called them, the said Joseph went homewards and going homeward met Samuel Belden riding into or down the meadow, Samuel Belden asked Joseph whether he had seen Katherine Harrison her cows, then Joseph asked Samuel aforesaid whether he had seen the said Katherine Harrison. The said Samuel told Joseph aforesaid that he saw her near the meadow gate going homeward, and also more told him that he saw Katherine Harrison her cows, running with great violence tail on end, homewards and said he thought the cattle would be at home so soon as Katherine aforesaid, if they could get out at the meadow gate.

And further this deponent saith not. Northampton 13: 6: 1668 Taken upon oath before me William Clarke David Wilton.

Exhibited in court October 29, 1668 attests John Allyn Secretary.

Source: Wyllys Papers, AMBL.

John Graves on his cows' strange behavior

John Graves aged about 39 years testifieth as followeth that formerly going to reap in the meadow at Wethersfield his land he was to work on, lay near to John Harrison's and Katherine Harrison their land. It came into the thoughts of the said John Graves that the said John Harrison and Katherine his wife being rumored to be suspicious of witchcraft, therefore he would graze his cattle on the rowing of the land of Goodman Harrison aforesaid, thinking that if the said Harrisons aforesaid were witches then something would disturb the quiet feeding of the cattle: He thereupon, adventured, and tieth his oxen to his cartrope one to one end the other to the other end making the oxen surely fast as he could tying 3 or 4 fast knots at each end, and tying his yoke to the cartrope about the middle of the rope between the oxen[;] and himself went about 10: or 12 pole distant to see if the cattle would quietly feed, as in other places, the cattle stood staring and fed not and looking steadfastly on them he saw the cartrope of it[s] own accord untie and fall to the ground, thereupon he went and tied the rope more fast and more knots at an end, and stood apart as before to see the issue, in a little time the oxen as affrighted fell to running and ran with such violence that he judgeth that the force and speed of their running made the yoke so tied as aforesaid fly above six foot high to his best discerning. The cattle were used ordinarily before to be so tied and fed peaceably in other places, and presently after being so tied on other men's ground they fed peaceably as at other times, dated August 13, 1668. Hadley; taken upon oath before us Henry Clark Samuel Smith.

Exhibited in court October 29, 1668 attests John Allyn Secretary.

Source: Wyllys Papers, AMBL.

Joan Francis on an apparition of Katherine Harrison

Joan Francis her testimony[:] About 4 years ago about the beginning of November in the night just before my child was stricken ill Goodwife Harrison or her shape appeared, and I said the Lord bless me and my child here is Goody Harrison and the child lying on the outside

I took it and laid it between me and my husband the child continued strangely ill about three weeks wanting a day and then died had fits we felt a thing run along the sides or side like a whetstone: Robert Francis saith he remembers his wife said that night the child was taken ill, the Lord bless me and my child, here is Goody Harrison.

Joan Francis saith that this summer Goody Harrison's daughter, came for some emptyings, I told her I had none, quickly after I brewed a barrel of beer, and I had drawed but a little of it, and the barrel was not bunged, but the head flew out of one end, and all the hops from the bunge[d] of[f] that end, the barrel was almost a new barrel. We had it of Joseph Wright, the head and hops flew to the end of the hall, and gave such a report as scared or feared the children. Goodwife Francis saith that when Goodwife Harrison appeared to her she saw her by a light, there being then a fire on the hearth and she stood with her back to the fire and her face towards her, she lying in another room, the door being just against her bed, and against the fire. Sworn in court October 29: [16]68 attests John: Allyn Secretary.

[*inscribed:*] Robert Francis's evidence about Katherine Harrison a witch.

Source: Wyllys Papers, AMBL.

Mary Kercum sees the apparition of Katherine Harrison

The relation of Mary the wife of Thomas Kercum: She saith that a night or two after that Mrs. Wickam had seen Goodwife Harrison and her husband as they told me, she watched with Mrs. Wickam, and in the middle room to her understanding she did see Goodwife Harrison and her black dog, there, and being frighted came back into the other room again, this was about midnight, as I thought. October 29, 1668. She also saith that there was a kind of light that she did see by which to her apprehension was moonlight. Sworn in court October 29, 1668 attests John Allyn Secretary.

Source: Wyllys Papers, AMBL.

Goodwife Johnson against Katherine Harrison

May 27, 1668: The relation of the wife of Jacob Johnson, she saith that her former husband was employed by Goodman Harrison to go to Windsor with a canoe for meal and he told me as he lay in his bed at Windsor, in the night he had a great box on the ears, and after when he came home he was ill, and Goodwife Harrison did help him with diet drink and plasters[.] But after awhile we sent to Captain Atwood to help my husband in his distress [b]ut the same day that he came at night, I came in at the door, and to the best of my apprehension, I saw the likeness of Goodwife Harrison, with her face towards my husband, and I turned about to lock the door and she vanished away, then my husband's nose fell a bleeding in an extraordinary manner, and so continued, if it were meddled with to his dying day. Sworn in court October 29, 1668 attests John Allyn Secretary.

Source: Wyllys Papers, AMBL.

Mary Hale hears the voice of Katherine Harrison

Mary Hale aged about 20 years testifieth that about the latter end of November: being the 29 day 1668 the said Mary Hale lying in her bed a good fire giving such light that one might see all over that room we heard the said Mary then was the said Mary heard a noise and presently some things fell on her legs with such violence that she feared it would have broken her legs, and then it came upon her stomach and oppressed her so as if it would have pressed the breath out of her body then appeared an ugly shaped thing like a dog, having a head such that I clearly and distinctly know to be the head of Katherine Harrison who was lately imprisoned upon suspicion of witchcraft, Mary saw it walk to and fro in the chamber, and went to her father's bedside then came back and disappeared: that day seven night next after at night lying in her bed something came upon her in like manner as is formerly related first on her legs and feet and then on her stomach crushing and oppressing her very sore, she put forth her hand to feel (because there was no light in the room so as clearly to discern), Mary aforesaid felt a face which she judged to be a woman's face, presently then she had a great blow on her fingers which pained her 2 days after which she complained of to her father and mother, and made her fingers black and blue, during the former passages Mary called to her father and mother but could not wake them till it was gone. After this the 19: day of December in the night (the night being very windy) something came again and spoke thus to her saying to Mary aforesaid you said that I would not come again, but are you not afraid of me, Mary said no, the voice replied I will make you afraid before I have done with you, and then presently Mary was crushed and oppressed very much then Mary called often to her father and mother, they lying very near, then the voice said though you do call they shall not hear, till I am gone, then the voice said you said that I preserved my cart to carry me to the gallows, but I will make it a [death?] cart to you (which said words Mary remembered she had only spoke in private to her sister a little before, and to no other)[.] Mary replied she feared her not, because God had kept her, and would keep her still[.] The voice said she had a commission to kill her, Mary asked who gave you the commission, the voice replied God gave me the commission, Mary replied the devil is a liar from the beginning for God will not give commission to murder, therefore it must be from the devil, then Mary was again pressed very much then the voice said you will make known these things abroad when I am gone, but if you will promise me to keep these aforesaid matters secret, I will come no more to afflict you. Mary replied I will tell it abroad, whereas the said Mary mentioneth divers times in this former writing that she heard a voice, the said Mary affirmeth that she did and doth know that it was the voice of Katherine Harrison aforesaid, and also Mary aforesaid affirmeth that the substance of the whole relation is the truth.

[*margin:*] Sworn in court May 25, 1669 attests John Allyn Secretary about the cat.

Source: Wyllys Papers, AMBL.

The ministers address evidentiary questions in witch-hunting

The answer of some ministers to the questions propounded to them by the honored magistrates, October 20, 1669.

To the first question whether a plurality of witnesses be necessary, legally to evidence one and the same individual fact: we answer,

That, if the proof of the fact do depend wholly upon testimony, there is then a necessity of a plurality of witnesses, to testify to one and the same individual fact; and without such a plurality, there can be no legal evidence of it. John 8:17 the testimony of two men is true; that is legally true, or the truth of order, and this chapter alleges to vindicate the sufficiency of the testimony given to prove that individual truth, that he himself was the Messiah or Light of the world. v. 12. Matthew 26:59–60.

To the second question whether the preternatural apparitions of a person, legally proved, be a demonstration of familiarity with the devil? We answer, that it is not the pleasure of the most high, to suffer the wicked one to make, an undistinguishable representation, of any innocent person in a way of doing mischief, before a plurality of witnesses. The reason is because, this would utterly evacuate all human testimony; no man could testify, that he saw this person do this or that thing, for it might be said, that it was the devil in his shape.

To the third and fourth questions together: whether a vicious person's foretelling some future event, or revealing of a secret, be a demonstration of familiarity with the devil? We say this much,

That those things, whether past, present or to come, which are indeed secret, that is cannot be known by human skill in arts, or strength of reason arguing from the course of nature, nor are made known by divine revelation either mediate or immediate, nor by information from man, must needs be known (if at all) by information from the devil: and hence the communication of such things, in way of divination (the person pretending the certain knowledge of them) seems to us, to argue familiarity with the devil, inasmuch as such a person, doth thereby declare his receiving of the devil's testimony, and yield up himself as the devil's instrument to communicate the same to others.

Source: Wyllys Papers, AMBL.

The indictment of Katherine Harrison

Court of Assistants at Hartford, May 25, 1669.

Katherine Harrison thou standest here indicted by the name of Katherine Harrison (of Wethersfield) as being guilty of witchcraft for that thou not having the fear of God before thine eyes hast had familiarity with Satan the grand enemy of God and mankind and by his help hast acted things beyond and besides the ordinary course of nature and hast thereby hurt the bodies of divers of the subjects of our sovereign lord the King for which by the law of God and of this corporation thou oughtest to die. What sayest thou for thyself guilty or not guilty. May 11, 1669.

Source: Court of Assistants Records, State Archives, *53*, pp. 1–2, CSL. Printed in John M. Taylor, *The Witchcraft Delusion in Colonial Connecticut, 1647–1697* (1908), pp. 47–48.

The jury struggles to reach a verdict

The prisoner returned not guilty and referred herself to a trial by the jury present.

The jury finding difficulty in the matter given them in reference to the indictment of Katherine Harrison cannot as yet agree to give in a verdict upon which the court see cause to adjourn until the next session of the Court of Assistants in October at which the jury are to appear to give in their verdict and the prisoner to remain in durance till that time.

Source: Court of Assistants Records, State Archives, *53*, p. 2, CSL.

Court of Assistants held at Hartford, October 12, 1669.

The jury recalled in court and did appear who were by the court ordered to pass upon the consideration of the indictment of Katherine Harrison formerly committed to them[.] This court orders that those that were summoned from Wethersfield to attend this court about Katherine Harrison's business by warrant did appear shall be allowed by the said Harrison the men 2s apiece and the women 18p apiece[.] Upon the motion of Marshall Gilbert and Katherine Harrison her attorney this court desires any two of the Assistants in Hartford to appoint those indebted to the said Harrison to appear before them upon three days' warning to clear up their accounts: and such as do not appear and clear up their accounts to the satisfaction of the Assistants present being warned to attend the same of aforesaid, the debts of it stands in the said aforesaid Katherine Harrison shall be deemed to be due to her upon account.

Source: Court of Assistants Records, State Archives, *53*, p. 4, CSL.

The jury being called to give in their verdict upon the indictment of Katherine Harrison return that they find the prisoner guilty of the indictment[.] This court sees cause to allow Daniel Garrad for attending Katherine Harrison at the special court twelve shillings to be paid out of the estate of the said Harrison[. . .]

Source: Court of Assistants Records, State Archives, *53*, p. 5, CSL.

The court rejects the jury verdict

A Court of Assistants by Special Order from the General Court May 30, 1670 held at Hartford.

This court having considered the verdict of the jury respecting Katherine Harrison cannot concur with them so as to sentence her to death or to a longer continuance in restraint but do dismiss her from her imprisonment she paying her just fees[.]

Willing her to mind the fulfillment of removing from Wethersfield which is that will tend most to her own safety and the contentment of the people who are her neighbors.

Source: Court of Assistants Records, State Archives, *53*, p. 7, CSL.

12. Three Ambiguous Cases (1669–1681)

▲

Ann Burt

Ann Burt had come to Massachusetts with her husband in 1635. The family settled in Lynn. She was a widow by 1669, when she was indicted and presumably tried for witchcraft. No record of a trial has survived, which may mean she was acquitted. Widow Burt practiced healing. Like certain other women who had this skill (for example, Jane Hawkins, Margaret Jones, and Elizabeth Morse), she was vulnerable to accusations of witchcraft from disappointed patients or suspicious neighbors. One of the witnesses against her, Phillip Read,[1] practiced medicine himself and was known as a doctor. Ann Burt died in 1673.

1. Presumably, this was the same Phillip Read who in the early 1670s was accused of "blasphemously" cursing, "the Divill take you & your prayers." David D. Hall, *Worlds of Wonder, Days of Judgment: Popular Religious Belief in Early New England* (New York, 1989), p. 294.

Bethiah Carter on Goodwife Burt as healer

The testimony of Bethiah Carter aged 23 years or thereabouts[:] Testifieth that she heard Sara Townsend say when she was a maid and lived with Goodwife Burt that the said Goodwife Burt told her if she could believe in her god she would cure her body and soul and farther she said Goodwife Burt told her she could not cure her own husband because he would not believe in her god: but her maid did believe in her god and she was cured: this she heard Sara Townsend say when she was in good health and sense[.] A while after this the said Sara Townsend being sorely afflicted with sad fits crying out and railing against me saying my father carried me to Boston but carried her to Lynn to an old witch[.] And farther the said Sara hath told to me and others that she hath seen the said Burt appear often at her bed's feet and at divers other places in the day and also at night, this she hath often related as well in health as in sickness [and] farther saith not. November 1, 1669.

Source: Essex County Court Papers, *15*:61–1 (EI).

Phillip Read on the sickness of Sara Townsend

Mr. Phillip Read physician aged 45 years or thereabouts testifieth that he being sent for 3 several times to see the above said Sara Townsend and her sister Carter: being both very ill but especially the said Sara Townsend being in a more sadder condition he had no opportunity to examine her condition but did plainly perceive there was no natural cause for such unnatural fits[.] But being sent for the fourth time and finding her in a meet capacity to give information of her aggrievance and cause of her former fits she told me the above said Burt had afflicted her and told her if ever she did relate it to anyone she would afflict her worse[.] One hour after she had a sadder fit than any ever she had afore: then I asked her who afflict[s] her now and what the matter was[.] She replied with a great screech she had told me already and that she did now suffer for with it much more now. Not related at present. Witness my hand 15th: 9 month 1669 Phillip Read.

Source: Essex County Court Papers, *15*: 61–1 (EI).

John Knight against Goody Burt

The testimony of John Knight about forty seven years of age saith he was going to fetch some things for his wife and he saw old Goody Burt coming out of a swamp and she was in her smock sleeves and a black hancather and black cap on her head and he looked up and suddenly she was gone out of sight and I looked about and could not see her go[.] When I came into the house I found her in the same habit as I saw her and he said unto her did I not see you in the swamp even now and she said no I was in the house[.] And he told her then she was a light-headed woman and further saith not.

Source: Essex County Court Papers, *15*:61–1 (EI).

Jacob Knight on Goody Burt as specter

The testimony of Jacob Knight aged about 24 or 25 years: I boarded in the house of Mr. Cobbet with my brother Wormwood: in which house Widow Burt lived at that time, my brother, and sister being gone to Boston: there being no fire in my brother's room, I went into Widow Burt's room to light my pipe, and told her I had a pain in my head, and so went into my lodging room which was through five doors (and stooping down to loose my shoes looking upward there was Widow Burt with a glass bottle in her hand, and she told me there was something would do my head good, or cure my head, and gave me the bottle in my hand, and when I had drunk of it, I was worse in my head) but concerning the five doors I passed through into my room I think they were all shut after me, but however there is one floor, that must be passed over to come into my room, that was so loose that it would make such a noise, that might, in an ordinary way be heard when any passed over it, but I heard nothing and her sudden being with me put me into a fright, and so remained while the next morning though she presently left me, and so the next morning but one, I being to go to Salem, intended to tell my sister Wormwood of it, before I went, but Widow Burt coming into my sister Wormwood's room, said I had a mind to say something to my sister of her that I would not have her hear, and this was before I had said anything, and so went out of the house, and then I told my sister, and going to Salem, I saw a cat, which being out of sight again, I presently saw a dog it being likewise presently out of sight, I saw one before me, like unto Widow Burt, going before me down a hill as I was going up it, and so I lost sight of her[.] The night following I lodged at my brother Knight's at Salem, I looking out of the chamber, it being a clear moonlight night, I saw Widow Burt upon a gray horse or mare in my brother's yard, or one in her shape, and so I waked my cousin John Knight that lodged with me, and told him of it, then neither he nor I could see anything, so when he was asleep again she appeared to me in the chamber, and then I took up a piece of a barrel head and threw it at her, and as I think hit her on the breast: and then could see her no more at that time.

Source: Essex County Court Papers, *15*:62–1 (EI). [*on reverse:*] Against Goody Burt several evidences.

John Pearson and Mary Burnop against Goody Burt

The testimony of John Pearson aged about nineteen years and Mary Burnop aged about 26 years testifieth that Goodwife Burt coming into the room where Sarah Pearson was asked her how she did. She said the worse for her the said Burt sat down and laughed at the said Sarah[.] She coming towards her said dost thou laugh and knowest thou hast done me a mischief[?] I could find in my heart to baste thy sides[.] The said Burt said do if thou durst and I will pay thy sides.

Further the abovesaid John Pearson saith that he heard Goodwife Burt abovesaid did say that the abovesaid Sarah should speak as much against her friends as ever she did against her.

Furthermore that the abovesaid Mary Burnop saith she heard the abovesaid Sarah speak telling Bethiah Carter that her father had her to Boston: but carried me to Lynn to an old witch [and] further saith not.

Source: Essex County Court Papers, *15*:62–2 (EI).

Madeleine Pearson against Goody Burt

The testimony of Madeleine Pearson aged fifty years or thereabouts saith she heard Sarah Pearson say when her father had her down to Goodwife Burt to be cured of her sore throat the first night she was there the said Burt put her to bed: and told the said Sarah if she would believe in her god she would cure her body and soul: but if she told of it she should be as a distracted body as long as she lived: and further that her husband did not believe in her god and should not be cured and that her maid did believe in her god and was cured[.] This she said being in her right mind she being some time in good health the said Burt said to her Sarah will you smoke it and giving of her the pipe she smoked it: and the said Sarah fell into her fits again and said that Goodwife Burt brought the devil to her to torment her [and] farther saith not.

Source: Essex County Court Papers, *15*:63–1 (EI).

Thomas Farrar blames sickness in his family on Goody Burt

Thomas Farrar aged above fifty years saith that my daughter Sarah and my daughter Elizabeth were in former time sorely afflicted and in their greatest extremity they would cry out and roar and say that they did see Goody Burt and say there she is do you not see her[?] Kill her there she is[.] And that they said several times and I have a son now in extreme misery much as the former hath been and the doctor says he is bewitched to his understanding.

Source: Essex County Court Papers, *15*:63–2 (EI).

Nicholas Disborough

*Nicholas Disborough of Hartford, Connecticut, experienced the
"strange providence" of having stones and bricks hurled at him and
members of his family. His barn also burned down. This chain of
events, which probably occurred in the late 1670s, made him wonder if a grandson's death by drowning was accidental. Disborough
arrived in New England in the 1630s and was an early settler of
Hartford. He and his wife had four daughters. A widower when
these events occurred, Disborough died in 1683. The minister in Hadley, Massachusetts, John Russell, sent a description of Disborough's
troubles to Increase Mather, who had solicited examples of "remarkable providences" for* An Essay for the Recording of Illustrious
Providences *(1684). As so often happened, a quarrel was involved:
Disborough and a son-in-law named Andross (probably a corruption of Andrews) each claimed ownership of a "chest" of clothes. The
quarrel did not turn into accusations of witchcraft; instead, it was
arbitrated by two of the colony's political leaders, who told Disborough to return the chest to Andross. Mather included a summary
of Russell's letter in* An Essay.

A strange providence

Hadley August 2, 1683
Reverend and dear sir[:]
I have not been unmindful of what you wrote to me in your last
though my long delay might minister occasion of imputing neglect to
me in not returning a more speedy answer. But the reason of it was
that (although I accounted my information that I had formerly concerning the solemn providence to be good) I knew by writing to Hartford I might receive such account of the matter as would be more
distinct and every way satisfactory. I therefore wrote to a friend there
and received not his answer till the evening before Mr. Chaun[c]y
came down and he going early in the morning I had not time to write
then nor have since had opportunity till now. The account I have now
received is as followeth. There liveth at Hartford an aged man called
Nicholas Disborough; whose wife's daughter being married to one
John Andross has born to the said Andross one daughter and deceased
or at least left one daughter whether she had more children I know
not. Some time after the mother's decease Andross sends his daughter
to live with Disborough and her grandmother his wife. The child having lived with them some years is drowned in a pond near the house

being about 7 or eight years old. To this child had Andross given her mother's cloth[e]s: and sent them in a chest to Disborough. The child dead the father demands the clothes; Disborough pleads a right to them having kept the child three or four years. Thus matters continued from about the beginning of June till the end of August or beginning of September when Disborough who had formerly said he would consider and take advice about the matter resolves he will keep the cloth[e]s till fetched out of his hands. Within two or three days after this resolve declared to Andross; the said Disborough began to be visited with a strange providence, stones and dirt being thrown at him at first small pieces. A son of the said Disborough's being with him his father examines him about it; he saith himself had met with the like; he thought it was Mr. Lord's Indian for he saw him and spake with him that day in the lot. The man went to Mr. Lord and was satisfied that his Indian was in a place far distant that day. This providence becomes amazing: things being thrown at him and his boy, night and day in house and field: sometimes in open places where one might see a quarter of a mile about and no appearance of hand or person to throw them. The things were stones dirt brickbats, cobs of Indian corn. When in the house and doors shut they would come down the chimney and fall upon them and upon others that were in the house. Sometime they would come in at the door sometime at the window not hurting anybody though they fell on their hats and cloth[e]s. Though most commonly they fell on him and his son; which was his wife's son. One thing was very remarkable a piece of clay of the bigness of a man's two thumbs came down the chimney; fell on the table which stood out of the chimney they threw it on the hearth where it lay a considerable time; they went to supper; and while at supper that piece of clay lift up itself; and fell on the table they took it up found it hot havin[g] lain so long on the hearth as to make it hot[.] This asserted by the man; his wife, and wife's son. One stone that hit him on the arm put him to some little pain. Another on his leg drew a little blood which appeared through his stocking[.] Thus it continued till November, about which time the said Disborough's barn was burnt no man knew how but very strangely; and considerably to his loss. After this burning from Tuesday to Thursday nothing thrown; and then went on as formerly till December: when upon more discourse of the clothes, the matter was referred to Major Talcott and Captain Allyn. Who upon hearing the case determined the cloth[es] be returned to Andross which done, the next day two or three small stones or pieces of d[irt] fell upon the hat of the said Disborough since which time he hath not been troubled in like manner. Some of the stones and brickbats above a pound weight that fell down by them; yet they received no considerable hurt. It was a strange and awful providence in the rounds of it and more than natural which occasioned great thoughts of heart whether the child's death were merely casual or etc. But how and what the cause of these motions was the Lord only knows. This is the account I received from Captain Allyn; a near neighbor to Disborough, a diligent and wise observer of the providence; and one that by hearing the case as an arbitrator was acquainted with the thing in its full compass; as to what openly appeared matter of much instruction it contains to let us see what our preserving unseen mercies are[. . . .]

Your obliged friend and servant
John Russell

Source: John Russell to Increase Mather, August 2, 1683. Mather Papers, Prince Collection, BPL. Printed in *Coll. MHS*, 4th ser., *8* (1868), pp. 86–88.

Rachel Fuller and Isabelle Towle

Rachel Fuller was accused of witchcraft in July 1680, when "suspicion" fell on her of causing the death of the infant Moses Godfrey. Rachel had married John Fuller of Hampton, New Hampshire, in 1677; she was already the mother of two children, and in her new marriage she had several more. Rachel may have practiced as a "cunning woman," or healer. John and Mary Godfrey, parents of the deceased baby, were the leading witnesses, though others also testified against Rachel. A second woman, Isabella Towle, about whom almost nothing is known, was arrested in the summer or fall of 1680. Both women were released from imprisonment sometime in 1681. In their depositions the Godfreys described using the countermagic of sweet bays (a species of laurel) and urine. According to two witnesses, Rachel Fuller said that other men and women in the town were "witches and wizards" and named some of them, including Eunice Cole, who had frequently been accused of witchcraft since the 1660s. It is indicative of the changing dynamics of witch-hunting that the authorities did not follow up on Rachel's comments. The case is described in John P. Demos, Entertaining Satan: Witchcraft and the Culture of Early New England *(New York, 1982), pp. 330–32.*

Witnesses to the physical appearance of John Godfrey's child

We, whose names are underwritten, being called by authority to view a dead child of John Godfrey's, being about a year old upon the 13th of July, 1680, which was suspected to be murdered, we find grounds of suspicion that the said child was murdered by witchcraft: first, in part by what we saw by the dead corpse; second, something we perceived by the party suspected, which was then present, and was examined by authority; and, third, by what was said by the witness.

The names of the jury of inquest:

Thomas Marston,
William Marston,
Foreman, Henry Roby,
Abraham Drake,
Abraham Perkins,
Anthony Taylor,
John Smith,
Thomas Leavitt,
Aratus Leavitt,
Gershom Elkens,
Henry Derbond,
John Sanborne.

This true list was given in upon oath the 13th of July, 1680, before me,

Samuel Dalton, of the Council.

John Fuller gives bond for his wife Rachel

John Fuller owns himself to stand bound in the sum of one hundred pounds unto the Treasurer of the Province of New Hampshire, that Rachel, his wife, shall appear before the authority of this Province of New Hampshire, to answer to what shall be charged against her in point of witchcraft, and that she shall abide the order of the court, and not depart without license, and shall appear whenever she is called.

Owned before me, July 14, 1680. Christopher Lux, Samuel Dalton, of the Council.

Mary and Sarah Godfrey against Rachel Fuller

The deposition of Mary Godfrey, the wife of John Godfrey, and of Sarah Godfrey, her daughter, aged about 16 years. These deponents saith that, about three weeks or a month ago, the same day that Mr. Buff went through the town, these deponents took care to save some of the sick child's urine, to show it to Mr. Buff; and they could not save it, for, though we put a pewter dish under the child, yet all its water ran on the floor; and Sarah Godfrey took some embers out of the fire and threw them upon the child's water; and by and by Rachel Fuller came in and looked very strangely, bending, daubed her face with molasses, as she judged it, so as that she had almost daubed up one of her eyes, and the molasses ready to drop off her face; and she sat down by Goody Godfrey, who had the sick child in her lap, and took the child by the hand; and Goodwife Godfrey, being afraid to see her come in in that manner, put her hand off from the child and wrapped the child's hand in her apron. Then the said Rachel Fuller turned her about, and smote the back of her hands together sundry times, and spat in the fire. Then she, having herbs in her hands, stood and rubbed them in her hand and strewed them about the hearth by the fire. Then she sat her down again, and said, Woman, the child will be well! and then went out of the door. Then she went behind the house; and Mehitable Godfrey told her mother that Goody Fuller was acting strangely. Then the said Mary Godfrey and Sarah, looking out, saw Rachel Fuller standing with her face towards the house, and beat herself with her arms, as men do in winter to heat their hands, and this she did three times; and stooping down and gathering something off the ground in the interim between the beating of herself, and then she went home.

Sworn July 14, 1680 before me. Samuel Dalton, of the Council. Owned in court of Hampton, September 7, 1680, by the deponent.

Elias Stileman, Secretary.

Elizabeth Denham and May Godfrey report Rachel Fuller on witches

The deposition of Elizabeth Denham and Mary Godfrey, who saith that we, being in discourse with Rachel Fuller, she told us how those that were witches did so go abroad at night, they did lay their husbands and children asleep, and she [the] said Rachel Fuller told us of several persons that she reckoned for witches and wizards in this town, to the number of 7 or 8. She said eight women and two men, some of whom she expressed by name, and Eunice Cole, Benjamin Evans's wife, and daughters, Goodwife Coulter and her daughter Prescott, and Goodwife Towle, and one that is now dead.

Sworn July 14, 1680 before me, Samuel Dalton, of the Council.

Mary Godfrey describes countermagic against Rachel Fuller

Mary Godfrey, the wife of John Godfrey, further saith, that the next day after that Rachel Fuller had been there with her face daubed with molasses, the children told their mother that Rachel Fuller had told them that if they did lay sweet bays under the threshold, it would keep a witch from coming in; and, said one of the girls' mother, "I will try," and she laid bays under the threshold of the back door all the way, and halfway of the breadth of the fore door, and soon after Rachel Fuller came to the house, and she always had formerly come in at the back door, which is next her house, but now she went about to the fore door, and, though the door stood open, yet she crowded in on that side where the bays lay not, and rubbed her back against the post so as that she rubbed off her hat, and then she sat her down and made ugly faces, and nestled about, and would have looked on the child, but I not suffering her, she went out rubbing against the post of the door as she came in, and beat off her hat again, and I never saw her in the house since; and I do further testify that while she was in the house she looked under the door where the bays lay. Mehitable Godfrey, aged about 12 years, affirms to the truth hereof.

Sworn July 14, 1680, before me, Samuel Dalton, of the Council.

Nathaniel Smith against Rachel Fuller

The deposition of Nathaniel Smith, aged about twenty years, who saith, that he, going to the house of John Fuller, as he was coming home with his herd, and the said Fuller's wife asked him what news there was in the town, and the said Smith said he knew none, and then she told him that the other night there was a great row at Goodman Roby's; this was at the first time when Doctor Reed was at this town; and the said Rachel Fuller told me that they had pulled Doctor Reed out of the bed, and with an enchanted bridle did intend to lead a jaunt, and he got her by the coat, but could not hold her, and I asked her who it was, and she turned from me, and as I thought did laugh.

Sworn July 14, 1680, before me, Samuel Dalton, of the Council.

John and Mary Godfrey against Rachel Fuller

The deposition of John Godfrey, aged about 48 years, and his wife, aged about 36 years, who saith that Rachel Fuller, coming into our house about 8 or 9 o'clock in the day, and sitting down by my wife, my wife having the child that was ill in her lap. The child being exceedingly ill, and the said Fuller seeing my wife much troubled and grieved, Rachel Fuller said that this would be the worst day with the child—tomorrow it will be well. And the said Fuller took the child by the hand, and my wife snatched the hand from her and wrapped it in her apron. Mary Godfrey, the wife of John Godfrey, further saith, that at the same time, I, seeing the said Fuller patting the child's hand, drew the child's hand from her; and then the said Rachel Fuller arose from the place where she did sit, and turned her back to my husband, and did smite the back side of her hands together, and did spit in the fire.

Sworn July 14, 1680, before me, Samuel Dalton, of the Council. Sworn by the deponent in court at Hampton, September 7, 1680.

Elias Stileman, Secretary.

Elizabeth Denham against Rachel Fuller

The deposition of Elizabeth Denham, who saith that, about three weeks since, I was at John Fuller's house, and there, she and I being speaking about John Godfrey's child that was then ill, Rachel Fuller was then very inquisitive to know of me what I thought ailed the child; and after I told her what I thought, she still continued asking me what I thought was the matter with the child; and she then kept calling her own child Moses, after the name of the sick child. Sworn July 14, 1680, before me, Samuel Dalton, of the Council.

The deponent, in court held in Hampton, September 7, 1680, appeared and owned the above testimony. Elias Stileman, Secretary.

Hezron Leavitt against Rachel Fuller

The deposition of Hezron Leavitt, aged about thirty-six years, testifieth, that as he was riding up to his lot the last Thursday in July last, at night, about sun half an hour high, he saw John Fuller's wife upon her hands and knees, scrabbling to and fro, first one way and then another, and seemed to him to be mighty lazy; but after she espied him she left off that manner of acting, and seemed to take up her apron with one of the hands, and with the other hand to gather up something; and as I drew near her it seemed to me as if she laid something upon a log, and come back and fetched a little child, that stood by her when she was in her former actions, and went through at her own gate, as he thought, the aforesaid log being near to her gate; and when she was in her gate she went toward her garden, and as soon as she was come up to her gate she turned and went toward the door, with a child and a little basket in her hand, as it seemed to your deponent; and your deponent looking on her she gave him a frowning look at first, but as your deponent was passing from her, she laughed on him, as seemed to him; and after your deponent was gone some way thence, she was gotten to the place first mentioned, as near as your deponent can guess, and in the same manner of acting as first named; and your deponent quickly returning again found her still in the same actions; and as soon as I apprehended she discerned him she left off and went away, as before, and presently there came from her gate to the place a thing like a little dog, as to the seeming of your deponent, and went to the place where she was so acting as before; and there, walking to and fro, went back again.

Source: *N.H. Prov. Court Papers, 1*, pp. 415–19. These are nineteenth-century transcriptions, and the punctuation has undoubtedly been modified from the original manuscript.

Bond is given and released

The court having heard the case of Rachel Fuller and Isabella Towle being apprehended and committed upon suspicion of witchcraft do order that they still continue in prison till bond be given for their good behavior of £100 apiece during the court's pleasure testimony put on file.

John Fuller acknowledgeth to owe and stand indebted to the Treasurer of this province in the sum of £100 for Rachel Fuller for her good appearance: and Isaac Marston and John Redman senior stand bound in like sum for Isabella Towle's good appearance. September 7, 1680.

At a court held in Dover June 7, 1681, the persons above bounden appeared and desired their bonds might be taken off, proclamation being then made and nothing appearing to the contrary the court declares the persons are all free of their bonds.

Source: *N.H. Ct. Recs., 1*, p. 368.

13. A Servant "Possessed"
(1671–1672)
▲

Elizabeth Knapp

In 1671 the household of Samuel Willard (1640–1707), minister of Groton, Massachusetts, included sixteen-year-old Elizabeth Knapp, a servant. Elizabeth was the only child of James and Elizabeth (Warren) Knapp, whose families had participated in the founding of Massachusetts in the 1630s. James, a farmer who was frequently chosen one of Groton's selectmen, came to the newly founded town in 1662. For three months in 1671–72 (mid-October to mid-January), Elizabeth acted strangely—having fits, barking like a dog, speaking rudely in a gruff voice to the minister. Initially, a physician prescribed "physic," but he soon conceded that "the distemper was diabolical." Thereafter the responsibility for healing Elizabeth passed to Willard and several of his colleagues in the ministry. The crux of the healing process became Elizabeth's confession of sin. Willard described the case in a "brief account" that Increase Mather summarized in An Essay for the Recording of Illustrious Providences *(1684). Some two and a half years after her recovery, Elizabeth married. She became the mother of at least six children.*

Willard instructed the townspeople of Groton on the spiritual significance of Elizabeth's "possession" in a fast-day sermon. It was printed as part of Useful Instructions for a Professing People in Times of Great Security and Degeneracy *(Cambridge, 1673). He urged the townspeople to respond to the event as "an awakening word of Counsel": they should engage in self-examination and consider "what sins . . . have given Satan so much footing in this poor place" (pp. 32, 42). He admonished them not to focus on witchcraft*

*per se, but to "remember that God sits and rules over Men and Dev-
ils" (p. 31).*

    *Elizabeth blamed an older woman for her bewitchment. It is note-
worthy that Willard and others in the town rejected this accusation
after talking with the woman and reviewing the evidence. The devil's compact, Elizabeth's confusion about religious obligations, and
her fantasies about "money" are other important aspects of the text.
John P. Demos has interpreted the episode from a psychoanalytical
perspective in* Entertaining Satan: Witchcraft and the Culture of
Early New England *(New York, 1982), chapter 4. Carol Karlsen sets
it in the context of Elizabeth's "ambivalence about the kind of
woman she wanted to be":* The Devil in the Shape of a Woman:
Witchcraft in Colonial New England *(New York, 1987), chapter 7.*

Samuel Willard describes the "possession" of Elizabeth Knapp

A Brief Account of a Strange and Unusual Providence of God Befallen
to Elizabeth Knapp of Groton.

    This poor and miserable object about a fortnight before she was
taken, we observed to carry herself in a strange and unwonted manner. Sometimes she would give sudden shrieks, and if we inquired a
reason, would always put it off with some excuse, and then would
burst forth into immoderate and extravagant laughter, in such wise,
as sometimes she fell onto the ground with it: I myself observed oftentimes a strange change in her countenance, but could not suspect the
true reason, but conceived she might be ill, and therefore divers times
inquired how she did, and she always answered well; which made me
wonder: but the tragedy began to unfold itself upon Monday, October
30, 1671, after this manner (as I received by credible information, being that day myself gone from home). In the evening, a little before
she went to bed, sitting by the fire, she cried out, oh my legs! and
clapped her hands on them, immediately, oh my breast! and removed
her hands thither; and forthwith, oh I am strangled, and put her hands
on her throat: those that observed her could not see what to make of
it; whether she was in earnest or dissembled, and in this manner they
left her (excepting the person that lay with her) complaining of her
breath being stopped[.]

    The next day she was in a strange frame (as was observed by di-
vers), sometimes weeping, sometimes laughing, and [making] many
foolish and apish gestures. In the evening, going into the cellar, she
shrieked suddenly, and being inquired of the cause, she answered,

that she saw 2 persons in the cellar; whereupon some went down with her to search, but found none; she also looking with them; at last she turned her head, and looking one way steadfastly, used the expression, what cheer old man? which, they that were with her took for a fancy, and so ceased; afterwards (the same evening), the rest of the family being in bed, she was (as one lying in the room saw, and she herself also afterwards related) suddenly thrown down into the midst of the floor with violence, and taken with a violent fit, whereupon the whole family was raised, and with much ado was she kept out of the fire from destroying herself[.] After which time she was followed with fits from thence till the Sabbath day; in which she was violent in bodily motions, leapings, strainings and strange agitations, scarce to be held in bounds by the strength of 3 or 4: violent also in roarings and screamings, representing a dark resemblance of hellish torments, and frequently using in these fits, divers words, sometimes crying out money, money, sometimes sin and misery with other words. On Wednesday [November 1], being in the time of intermission questioned about the case she was in, with reference to the cause or occasion of it, she seemed to impeach one of the neighbors, a person (I doubt not) of sincere uprightness before God, as though either she, or the devil in her likeness and habit, particularly her riding hood, had come down the chimney, stricken her that night she was first taken violently, which was the occasion of her being cast into the floor; whereupon those about her sent to request the person to come to her, who coming unwittingly, was at the first assaulted by her strangely, for though her eyes were (as it were) sealed up (as they were always, or for the most part, in those fits, and so continue in them all to this day), she yet knew her very touch from any other, though no voice were uttered, and discovered it evidently by her gestures, so powerful were Satan's suggestions in her[.] Yet afterward God was pleased to vindicate the case and justify the innocent, even to remove jealousies from the spirits of the party concerned, and [to the] satisfaction of the bystanders[.] For after she had gone to prayer with her she confessed that she believed Satan had deluded her, and hath never since complained of any such apparition or disturbance from the person.

These fits continuing (though with intermission), divers (when they had opportunity) pressed upon her to declare what might be the true and real occasion of these amazing fits. She used many tergiversations and excuses, pretending she would [declare it] to this and that young person, who coming, she put it off to another, till at the last, on Thursday night [November 2], she brake forth into a large confession in the presence of many, the substance whereof amounted to thus much: That the devil had oftentimes appeared to her, presenting the treaty of a covenant and proffering largely to her: viz. such things as suited her youthful fancy, money, silks, fine clothes, ease from labor to show her the whole world, etc.: that it had been then three years since his first appearance, occasioned by her discontent: that at first his apparitions had been more rare, but lately more frequent; yea, those few weeks that she had dwelt with us almost constant[ly], that she seldom went out of one room into another, but he appeared to her urging of her: and that he had presented her a book written with blood of covenants made by others with him, and told her such and such (of some whereof we hope better things) had a name there; that he urged upon her constant temptations to murder her parents, her neighbors, our children, especially the youngest, tempting her to throw it into the fire, on the hearth, into the oven; and that once he put a bill-hook into her hand, to murder myself, persuading her I was asleep, but coming about it, she met me on the stairs at which she was affrighted[.] The time I remember well, and observed a strange frame in her countenance and saw she endeavored to hide something, but I knew not what, neither did I at all suspect any such matter; and that often he persuaded her to make away with herself and once she was going to drown herself in the well, for, looking into it, she saw such sights as allured her, and was gotten within the curb, and was by God's providence prevented[.]

Many other like things she related, too tedious to recollect: but being pressed to declare whether she had not consented to a covenant with the devil, she with solemn assertions denied it, yea asserted that she had never so much as consented to discourse with him, nor had ever but once before that night used the expression, what cheer, old man? and this argument she used, that the providence of God had ordered it so, that all his apparitions had been frightful to her; yet this she acknowledged (which seemed contradictory, viz.:), that when she came to our house to school, before such time as she dwelt with us, she delayed her going home in the evening, till it was dark (which we observed), upon his persuasion to have his company home, and that she could not, when he appeared, but to go to him[.]

One evident testimony whereof we can say something to, viz.: the night before the Thanksgiving, October 19,[1] she was with another maid that boarded in the house, where both of them saw the appearance of a man's head and shoulders, with a great white neckcloth, looking in at the window, at which they came up affrighted both into the chamber, where the rest of us were[.] They declaring the case, one of us went down to see who it might be; but she ran immediately out of the door before him, which she hath since confessed, was the devil coming to her; she also acknowledged the reason of her former sudden shriekings, was from a sudden apparition, and that the devil put these excuses into her mouth, and bid her so to say, and hurried her into those violent (but she saith feigned and forced) laughters: she then also complained against herself of many sins, disobedience to parents, neglect of attendance upon ordinances, attempts to murder herself and others; but this particular of a covenant she utterly disclaimed: which relation seemed fair, especially in that it was attended with bitter tears, self-condemnations, good counsels given to all about her, especially the youth then present, and an earnest desire of prayers: she sent to Lancaster for Mr. Rowlandson,[2] who came and prayed with her, and gave her serious counsels; but she was still followed, all this notwithstanding, with these fits: and in this state (coming home on Friday) I found her; but could get nothing from her, whenever I came in [her] presence she fell into those fits, concerning which fits, I find this noteworthy, she knew and understood what was spoken to her, but could not answer, nor use any other words but the forementioned, money, etc.: as long as the fit continued, for when she came out of it, she could give a relation of all that had been spoken to her: she was demanded a reason why she used those words in her fits, and signified that the devil presented her with such things, to tempt her, and with sin and misery to terrify her; she also declared that she had seen the devils in their hellish shapes, and more devils than anyone there ever saw men in the world. Many of these things I heard her declare on Saturday at night: On the Sabbath [November 5] the physician came, who judged a main part of her distemper to be natural, arising from the foulness of her stomach and corruptness of her blood, occasioning fumes in her brain, and strange fantasies; whereupon (in order to further trial and administration) she was removed home, and the succeeding week she took physic, and was not in such violence handled in her fits as before; but enjoyed an intermission, and gave some hopes of recovery; in which intermission she was altogether senseless (as to our discovery) of her state, held under security and hardness of heart, professing she had no trouble upon her spirits, she cried Satan had left her. A solemn day[3] was kept with her, yet it had then (as I apprehend) little efficacy upon her; she that day again expressed hopes that the devil had left her, but there was little ground to think so, because she remained under such extreme senselessness of her own estate.

And thus she continued, being exercised with some moderate fits, in which she used none of the former expressions, but sometimes fainted away, sometimes used some strugglings, yet not with extremity, till the Wednesday following [November 15], which day was spent in prayer with her, when her fits something more increased, and her tongue was for many hours together drawn into a semicircle up to the roof of her mouth, and not to be removed, for some tried with the fingers to do it: From thence till the Sabbath seven night following: she continued alike, only she added to former confessions of her twice consenting to travel with the devil in her company between Groton and Lancaster, who accompanied her in [the] form of a black dog with eyes in his back, sometimes stopping her horse, sometimes leaping up behind, and keeping her (when she came home with company) 40 rod at least behind, leading her out of the way into a swamp, etc.: but still no conference would she own, but urged that the devil's quarrel with her was because she would not seal a covenant with him, and that this was the ground of her first being taken.

Besides this nothing observable came from her, only one morning she said God is a father, the next morning God is my father, which words (it is to be feared) were words of presumption, put into her mouth by the adversary. I suspecting the truth of her former story, pressed whether she never verbally promised to covenant with him, which she stoutly denied; only acknowledged that she had had some thoughts so to do: but on the forenamed November 26 she was again with violence and extremity seized by her fits in such wise that 6 persons could hardly hold her, but she leaped and skipped about the house perforce roaring and yelling extremely, and fetching deadly sighs, as if her heartstrings would have broken, and looking with a frightful aspect, to the amazement and astonishment of all the beholders, of which I was an eyewitness: the physician being then again with her, consented that the distemper was diabolical, refused further to administer, [and] advised to extraordinary fasting; whereupon some of God's ministers were sent for: she meanwhile continued extremely tormented night and day, till Tuesday about noon; having this added on Monday and Tuesday morning that she barked like a dog, and bleated like a calf, in which her organs were visibly made use of: yea (as was carefully observed) on Monday night and Tuesday morning, whenever any came near the house, though they within heard nothing at all, yet would she bark till they were come into the house.

On Tuesday [November 28], about 12 of the clock, she came out of the fit, which had held her from Sabbath day about the same time, at least 48 hours, with little or no intermission, and then her speech was restored to her, and she expressed a great seeming sense of her state: many bitter tears, sighings, sobbings, complainings she uttered, bewailing of many sins forementioned, begging prayers, and in the hour of prayer expressing much affection: I then pressed if there were anything behind in reference to the dealings between her and Satan, when she again professed that she had related all. And declared that in those fits the devil had assaulted her many ways, that he came down the chimney, and she essayed to escape him, but was seized upon by him, that he sat upon her breast, and used many arguments with her, and that he urged her at one time with persuasions and promises of ease and great matters, told her that she had done enough in what she had already confessed, [that] she might henceforth serve him more securely; anon told her her time was past and there was no hopes[4] unless she would serve him; and it was observed in the time of her extremity, once when a little moment's respite was granted her of speech, she advised us to make our peace with God and use our time better than she had done[.] The party advised her also to bethink herself of making her peace, [and] she replied, it is too late for me.

The next day was solemnized, when we had the presence of Mr. Buckley, Mr. Rowlandson, and Mr. Estabrook,[5] whither coming, we found her returned to a sottish and stupid kind of frame, much was pressed upon her, but no affection at all discovered: though she was little or nothing exercised with any fits, and her speech also continued: though a day or two after she was melancholy and being inquired of a reason, she complained that she was grieved that so much pains were taken with her, and did her no good, but this held her not long: and thus she remained till Monday [December 4], when to some neighbors there present she related something more of her converse with the devil, viz., that it had been five years or thereabouts, since she first saw him, and declared methodically the sundry apparitions from time to time, till she was thus dreadfully assaulted, in which the principal [matter] was, that after many assaults she had resolved to seal a covenant with Satan, thinking she had better do it than be thus followed by him, [she also declared] that once, when she lived at Lancaster, he presented himself and desired of her blood, and she would have done it, but wanted a knife[.] In the parley she was prevented by the providence of God interposing my father;[6] a second time in the house he met her, and presented her a knife, and as she was going about it my father stepped in again and prevented [it], [so] that when she sought and inquired for the knife it was not to be found, and that afterward she saw it sticking in the top of the barn, and some other like passages[.]

She again owned an observable passage which she also had confessed in her first declaration, but is not there inserted, viz. that the devil had often proferred her his service, but she accepted not; and once in particular [he offered] to bring her in chips for the fire, [and] she refused, but when she came in she saw them lie by the fireside, and was afraid, and this I remark; I sitting by the fire spake to her to lay them on, and she turned away in an unwonted manner: She then also declared against herself her unprofitable life she had led, and how justly God had thus permitted Satan to handle her, telling them, they little knew what a sad case she was in. I after[ward] asked her concerning these passages, and she owned the truth of them, and declared that now she hoped the devil had left her, but being pressed, whether there were not a covenant, she earnestly professed, that by God's goodness she had been prevented from doing that, which she of herself had been ready enough to assent to; and she thanked God there was no such thing.

The same day she was again taken with a new kind of unwonted fit in which after she had been awhile exercised with violence, she got her a stick, and went up and down, thrusting and pushing here and there, and anon looking out a window, and cried out of a witch appearing in a strange manner in [the] form of a dog downward, with a woman's head, and [she] declared the person, other whiles that she appeared in her whole likeness, and described her shape and habit, [and] signified that she went up the chimney and went her way: What impression we read in the clay of the chimney, in [the] similitude of a dog's paw, by the operation of Satan, and in the form of a dog's going in the same place she told of, I shall not conclude; though something there was, as I myself saw, in the chimney in the same place where she declared the foot was set to go up. In this manner was she handled that night and the two next days, using strange gestures, complaining by signs when she could not speak, explaining that she was sometimes in the chamber, sometimes in the chimney; and anon assaults her, sometimes scratching her breast, beating her sides, strangling her throat, and she did oftentimes seem to our apprehension as if she would forthwith be strangled.

She declared that if the party were apprehended she should forthwith be well, but never till then; whereupon her father went and procured the coming of the woman impeached by her, who came down to her on Thursday night [December 7], where (being desired to be present) I observed that she was violently handled, and lamentably tormented by the adversary, and uttered unusual shrieks at the instant of the person's coming in, though her eyes were fast closed: but having experience of such former actings, we made nothing of it but waited the issue. God therefore was sought to, to signify something whereby the innocent might be acquitted or the guilty discovered; and he answered our prayers, for by two evident and clear mistakes she was cleared, and then all prejudices ceased, and she never more to this day hath impeached her of any apparition: in the aforementioned allegation of the person she also signified that sometimes the devil also, in the likeness of a little boy, appeared together with the person.

Friday was a sad day with her, for she was sorely handled with fits, which some perceiving pressed that there was something yet behind not discovered by her; and she after a violent fit, holding her between two and 3 hours did first to one, and afterwards to many acknowledge that she had given of her blood to the devil, and made a covenant with him; whereupon I was sent for to her; and understanding how things had passed, I found that there was no room for privacy[.] In another, already made by her so public, I therefore examined her concerning the matter; and found her not so forward to confess,[7] as she had been to others, yet thus much I gathered from her confession: That after she came to dwell with us, one day as she was alone in a lower room, all the rest of us being in the chamber, she looked out at the window, and saw the devil in the habit of an old man, coming over a great meadow lying near the house, and suspecting his design, she had thoughts to have gone away, yet at length resolved to tarry it out, and hear what he had to say to her; when he came he demanded of her some of her blood, which she forthwith consented to, and with a knife cut her finger, he caught the blood in his hand, and then told her she must write her name in his book, she answered [that] she could not write, but he told her he would direct her hand, and then took a little sharpened stick, and dipped in the blood and put it into her hand, and guided it, and she wrote her name with his help.

What was the matter she set her hand to I could not learn from her; but thus much she confessed, that the term of time agreed upon with him was for 7 years; one year she was to be faithful in his service, and then the other six he would serve her and make her a witch. She also related, that the ground of contest between her and the devil which was the occasion of this sad providence, was this, that after her covenant [was] made the devil showed her hell and the damned, and told her if she were not faithful to him, she should go thither and be tormented there; she desired of him to show her heaven, but he told her that heaven was an ugly place, and that none went thither but a company of base rogues whom he hated; but if she would obey him, it should be well with her: but afterward she considered with herself, that the term of her covenant was but short, and would soon be at an end, and she doubted [not] (for all the devil's promises) [that] she must at last come to the place he had shown her, and withal feared, [that] if she were a witch, she should be discovered and brought to a shameful end; which was many times a trouble on her spirits; this the devil perceiving, [he] urged upon her to give him more of her blood, and set her hand again to his book, which she refused to do, but partly through promises, partly by threatenings, he brought her at last to a promise that she would sometime do it; after which he left not incessantly to urge her to the performance of it, once he met her on the stairs, and often elsewhere, pressing her with vehemence, but she still put it off; till the first night she was taken, when the devil came to her, and told her he would not tarry any longer: she told him she would not do it[;] he answered she had done it already, and what further damage would it be to do it again, for she was his sure enough. She rejoined she had done it already, and if she were his sure enough, what need [had] he to desire any more of her; whereupon he struck her the first night, again more violently the second, as is above expressed.

This is the sum of the relation I then had from her; which at that time seemed to be methodical. These things she uttered with great affection, overflowing of tears, and seeming bitterness: I asked of the reason of her weeping and bitterness, she complained of her sins, and some in particular, profanation of the Sabbath, etc.: but nothing of this sin of renouncing the government of God and giving herself up to the devil: I therefore (as God helped) applied it to her and asked her whether she desired not prayers with and for her; she assented with earnestness, and in prayer seemed to bewail the sin as God helped, then in the aggravation of it, and afterward declared a desire to rely on the power and mercy of God in Christ: she then also declared, that the devil had deceived her concerning those persons impeached by her, that he had in their likeness or resemblance tormented her, persuading her that it was they, that they bore her a spleen, but he loved her, and would free her from them, and pressed on her to endeavor to bring them forth to the censure of the law.

In this case I left her; but (not being satisfied in some things) I promised to visit her again the next day which accordingly I did, but coming to her, I found her (though her speech still remained) in a case sad enough, her tears dried up and senses stupefied, and (as was observed) when I could get nothing from her, and therefore applied myself in counsel to her, she regarded it not, but fixed her eye steadfastly upon a place, as she was wont when the devil presented himself to her, which was a grief to her parents, and brought me to a stand; in this condition I left her.

The next day [December 10], being the Sabbath, whether upon any hint given her, or any advantage Satan took by it upon her, she sent for me in haste at noon[.] Coming to her, she immediately with tears told me that she had belied the devil, in saying she had given him of her blood, etc.: professed that the most of the apparitions she had spoken of were but fancies, as images represented in a dream, earnestly entreated me to believe her, called God to witness to her assertion[.] I told her I would willingly hope the best, and believe what I had any good grounds to apprehend; if therefore she would tell a more methodical relation than the former, it would be well, but if otherwise, she must be content that everyone should censure according to their apprehension[.] She promised so to do, and expressed a desire that all that would might hear her; that as they had heard so many lies and untruths, they might now hear the truth, and engaged that in the evening she would do it[.] I then repaired to her, and divers more then went. She then declared thus much, that the occasion of it was her discontent, that the devil had sometimes appeared to her; that her condition displeased her; her labor was burdensome to her, she was neither content to be at home nor abroad; and had oftentimes strong persuasions to practice in witchcraft, had often wished the devil would come to her at such and such times, and resolved that if he would, she would give herself up to him soul and body: but (though he had oft times appeared to her, yet) at such times he had not discovered himself, and therefore she had been preserved from such a thing[.] I declared a suspicion of the truth of the relation, and gave her some reasons; but by reason of the company did not say much, neither could anything further be gotten from her.

But the next day I went to her, and opened my mind to her alone, and left it with her, declared (among other things) that she had used preposterous courses, and therefore it was no marvel that she had been led into such contradictions, and tendered her all the help I could, if she would make use of me, and more privately relate any weighty and serious case of conscience to me[.] She promised me she would if she knew anything; but said that then she knew nothing at all: but stood to the story she had told the foregoing evening: and indeed what to make of these things I at present know not, but am waiting till God (if he see meet) wind up the story, and make a more clear discovery. It was not many days before she was hurried again into violent fits after a different manner, being taken again speechless, and using all endeavors to make away with herself, and do mischief unto others; striking those that held her, spitting in their faces; and if at any time she had done any harm or frightened them she would laugh immediately; which fits held her sometimes longer, sometimes shorter[.] Few occasions she had of speech; but when she could speak, she complained of a hard heart, counselled some to beware of sin, for that had brought her to this, bewailed that so many prayers had been put up for her, and she still so hard-hearted and no more good wrought upon her; but being asked whether she were willing to repent, shaked her head, and said nothing.

Thus she continued till the next Sabbath [December 17] in the afternoon; on which day in the morning, being something better than at other times, she had but little company tarried with her in the afternoon, when the devil began to make more full discovery of himself: It had been a question before, whether she might properly be called a demoniac, or person possessed of the devil, but it was then put out of question[.] He began (as the persons with her testify) by drawing her tongue out of her mouth most frightfully to an extraordinary length and greatness, and [making] many amazing postures of her body; and then by speaking, vocally in her, whereupon her father and another neighbor were called from the meeting, on whom (as soon as they came in), he railed, calling them rogues, charging them for folly in going to hear a black rogue, who told them nothing but a parcel of lies, and deceived them, and many like expressions.

After exercise I was called, but understood not the occasion till I came and heard the same voice, a grum, low, yet audible voice it was. The first salutation I had was, oh! you are a great rogue. I was at first something daunted and amazed, and many reluctances I had upon my spirits, which brought me to a silence and amazement in my spirits, till at last God heard my groans and gave me both refreshment in Christ and courage: I then called for a light to see whether it might not appear a counterfeit, and observed not any of her organs to move, the voice was hollow, as if it issued out of her throat. He then again called me a great black rogue. I challenged him to make it appear [so]; but all the answer was, you tell the people a company of lies. I reflected on myself, and could not but magnify the goodness of God not to suffer Satan to bespatter the names of his people with those sins which he himself hath pardoned in the blood of Christ. I answered, Satan, thou art a liar and a deceiver, and God will vindicate his own truth one day: he answered nothing directly, but said, I am not Satan, I am a pretty black boy, this is my pretty girl; I have been here a great while[.] I sat still and answered nothing to these expressions; but when he directed himself to me again, oh! you black rogue, I do not love you: I replied through God's grace I hate thee; he rejoined, but you had better love me. These manner of expressions filled some of the company there present with great consternation, others put on boldness to speak to him, at which I was displeased, and advised them to see their call clear, fearing lest by his policy and [the] many apish expressions he used, he might insinuate himself, and raise in them a fearlessness of spirit of him. I no sooner turned my back to go to the fire, but he called out again, where is that black rogue gone?

I seeing little good to be done by discourse, and questioning many things in my mind concerning it, I desired the company to join in prayer unto God; when we went about that duty and were kneeled down, with a voice louder than before something he cried out, hold your tongue, hold your tongue, get you gone you black rogue, what are you going to do, you have nothing to do with me, etc.: but through God's goodness was silenced, and she lay quiet during the time of prayer, but as soon as it was ended, began afresh, using the former expressions, at which some ventured to speak to him: Though I think imprudently, one told him God had him in chains:[8] he replied, for all my chain, I can knock thee on the head when I please: he said he would carry her away that night. Another answered, but God is stronger than thou. He presently rejoined, that's a lie, I am stronger than God; at which blasphemy I again advised them to be wary of speaking, counselled them to get serious persons to watch with her, and left her, commending her to God.

On Tuesday [December 19] following she confessed that the devil entered into her the second night after her first taking, that when she was going to bed, he entered in (as she conceived) at her mouth, and had been in her ever since, and professed that if there were ever a devil in the world there was one in her, but in what manner he spoke in her she could not tell. On Wednesday night, she must forthwith be carried down to the Bay in all haste, she should never be well, till an assembly of ministers was met together to pray with and for her, and in particular Mr. Cobbett:[9] her friends advised with me about it; I signified to them, that I apprehended Satan never made any good motion, but it was out of season, and that it was not a thing now feasible, the season being then extremely cold, and the snow deep, that if she had been taken in the woods with her fits she must needs perish. On Friday [December 22] in the evening she was taken again violently, and then the former voice (for the sound) was heard in her again, not speaking, but imitating the crowing of a cock, accompanied with many other gestures, some violent, some ridiculous, which occasioned my going to her, where by signs she signified that the devil threatened to carry her away that night. God was again then sought for her, and when, in prayer, that expression was used, that God had proved Satan a liar, in preserving her once when he had threatened to carry her away that night, and was entreated so to do again, the same voice, which had ceased 2 days before, was again heard by the by-standers 5 times distinctly to cry out, oh, you are a rogue, and then ceased: but the whole time of prayer, sometimes by violence of fits sometimes by noises she made, she drowned her own hearing from receiving our petition, as she afterwards confessed.

Since that time she hath continued for the most part speechless, her fits coming upon her sometimes often, sometimes with greater inter-mission, and with great varieties in the manner of them, sometimes by violence, sometimes by making her sick, but (through God's good-ness) so abated in violence that now one person can as well rule her, as formerly 4 or 5. She is observed always to fall into her fits when any strangers go to visit her, and the more go the more violent are her fits: As to the frame of her spirits she hath been more averse lately to good counsel than heretofore, yet sometimes she signifies a desire of the company of ministers. On Thursday last [January 11, 1671–72], in the evening, she came [in] a season to her speech, and (as I received from them with her) again disowned a covenant with the devil, disowned that relation about the knife forementioned, declared the occasion of her fits to be discontent, owned the temptations to murder; declared that though the devil had power of her body, she hoped he should not of her soul, that she had rather continue so speechless than have her speech, and make no better use of it than formerly she had, expressed that she was sometimes disposed to do mischief, and [it] was as if some had laid hold of her to enforce her to it, and had double strength to her own, that she knew not whether the devil were in her or no if he were she knew not when or how he entered[.] That when she was taken speechless, she feared as if a string was tied about the roots of her tongue and reached down into her vitals, and pulled her tongue down, and then most when she strove to speak: On Friday [January 12], in the evening, she was taken with a passion of weeping and sigh-ing, which held her till late in the night, at length she sent for me, but the unseasonableness of the weather and my own bodily indisposition prevented: I went the next morning, when she strove to speak some-thing but could not, but was taken with her fits, which held her as long as I tarried, which was more than an hour, and I left her in them: and thus she continues speechless to this instant, January 15, and fol-lowed with fits: concerning which state of hers I shall suspend my own judgment, and willingly leave it to the censure of those that are more learned, aged, and judicious: only I shall leave my thoughts in respect of 2 or 3 questions which have risen about her: viz.

1. Whether her distemper be real or counterfeit: I shall say no more to that but this, the great strength appearing in them, and great weakness after them, will disclaim the contrary opinion; for though a person may counterfeit much, yet such a strength is beyond the force of dissimulation.

2. Whether her distemper be natural or diabolical, I suppose the premises will strongly enough conclude the latter, yet I will add these 2 further arguments: 1. the actings of convulsion, which these [fits] come nearest to, are (as persons acquainted with them observe) in many, yea the most essential parts of them quite contrary to these actings. 2, she hath no ways wasted in body, or strength by all these fits, though so dreadful; but [she hath] gathered flesh exceedingly, and hath her natural strength when her fits are off, for the most part.

3. Whether the devil did really speak in her. To that point, which some have much doubted of, thus much I will say to countermand this apprehension: 1. The manner of expression I diligently observed, and could not perceive any organ, any instrument of speech (which the philosopher makes mention of) to have any motion at all. Yea her mouth was sometimes shut without opening sometimes open without shutting or moving, and then both I and others saw her tongue (as it used to be when she was in some fits, when speechless) turned up circularly to the roof of her mouth. 2. The labial letters, divers of which were used by her, viz. B. M. P. which cannot be naturally expressed without motion of the lips, which must needs come within our ken, if observed, were uttered without any such motion, if she had used only linguals, gutturals, etc., the matter might have been more suspicious. 3. The reviling terms then used, were such as she never used before nor since in all this time of her being thus taken: yea, hath been always observed to speak respectfully concerning me. 4. They were expressions which the devil (by her confession) aspersed me, and others withal, in the hour of temptation, particularly she had freely acknowledged that the devil was wont to appear to her in the house of God and divert her mind, and charge her she should not give ear to what that black-coated rogue spoke. 5. We observed when the voice spake, her throat was swelled formidably, as big at least as one's fist. These arguments I shall leave to the censure of the judicious.

4. Whether she have covenanted with the devil or no: I think this is a case unanswerable, her declarations have been so contradictory, one to another, that we know not what to make of them, and her condition is such as administers many doubts; charity would hope the best, love would fear the worst, but thus much is clear she is an object of pity, and I desire that all that hear of her would compassionate her

forlorn state. She is (I question not) a subject of hope, and therefore all means ought to be used for her recovery. She is a monument of divine severity; and the Lord grant that all that see or hear, may fear and tremble. Amen.

Samuel Willard.

1. Thanksgiving: a day of special religious observance, to give thanks for favorable providences.
2. Joseph Rowlandson, the minister of nearby Lancaster.
3. A fast day.
4. The "devil" was reiterating a theme in many sermons, especially those addressed to young people; David D. Hall, *Worlds of Wonder, Days of Judgment: Popular Religious Belief in Early New England* (New York, 1989), p. 135.
5. Edward Buckley and Joseph Estabrook, ministers in Concord.
6. Simon Willard.
7. Interpreting Elizabeth's malaise to be caused by unrepented and unacknowledged sin, Willard was urging her to confess and thereby cleanse herself. The role of confession in witch-hunting and the religious system is described in Hall, *Worlds of Wonder*, chap. 4.
8. That Satan was not an independent power in the world, but ultimately under God's control (and hence used by God to accomplish his purposes), was standard ministerial doctrine—and possibly a reassuring idea.
9. Thomas Cobbett, minister in Ipswich and author of a treatise on prayer.

Source: Mather Papers, Prince Collection, BPL. Printed verbatim in Samuel A. Green, *Groton in the Witchcraft Times* (1883), pp. 7–21; *Coll. MHS,* 4th ser., *8* (1868), pp. 555–69, and in a modernized version in *Remarkable Providences, 1600–1760,* ed. John Demos (New York, 1972), pp. 358–71. The dates in brackets are Willard's.

14. Vehement Suspicion: Eunice Cole of Hampton (1656–1680)

▲

Eunice Cole

The charge of being a witch disrupted the life of Eunice Cole for more than two decades. A resident of Hampton in present-day New Hampshire, Mrs. Cole had been in and out of the courts of Essex and Norfolk counties, Massachusetts, since the 1640s. She was tried on charges of witchcraft for the first time in 1656. It is probable that she was convicted; instead of ordering her execution, the court sentenced Mrs. Cole to imprisonment in Boston and a public whipping. She was in and out of prison for the next decade, during which time, in 1662, her aged husband William died. Eunice was charged again with witchcraft in 1673; the court criticized her, though the formal verdict was innocence. In the years before and after this trial she lived in Hampton in a destitute condition. Her third court hearing on charges of witchcraft occurred in 1680; though not indicted, she was put in prison. The depositions from 1673, which are the fullest surviving records of community suspicions, describe Eunice Cole as attempting to persuade a ten-year-old girl, Ann Smith, to live with her. This episode in particular, and Eunice Cole's life history in general, are fully analyzed in John P. Demos, Entertaining Satan: Witchcraft and the Culture of Early New England *(New York, 1982); another important account that explores the finances of the Cole family is Carol Karlsen's in* The Devil in the Shape of a Woman: Witchcraft in Colonial New England *(New York, 1987). Most of the documents* relating to Cole's financial circumstances are not included in this collection.

Eunice Cole complains of her care

The deposition of Thomas Coleman and Abraham Drake[:]

These deponents saith about a year and half ago they being at Robert Drake's house at a meeting with the selectmen Eunice Cole came in to the said house and demand[ed] help of the selectmen for wood or other things and the selectmen told her she had an estate of her own and needed no help of the town[.] Whereupon Eunice answered they could help Goodman Robe being a lusty man and she Cole have none but Eun[ ] said all could not or should not do and about two or three days after this said Robe lost a cow and a sheep very strangely and one of the men there present told Eunice Cole she should look at a hand of God in it, for withdrawing the people's hearts from helping of her[.] Eunice Cole answered, no 'twas the devil did it.

Deposed in court September 5, 1656. Edward Rawson Secretary.

Thomas Coleman and John Redman deposed to the evidence and particularly to the word[s] should not do. September 1656 Edward Rawson Secretary.

Source: "Trials for Witchcraft in New England," HLH.

Joanna Sleeper on a cat that afflicted Goodman Wedgewood

Joanna Sleeper aged 33 years or thereabouts testifieth that last winter was a twelve month this deponent went into Goodman Wedgewood's to see him he being sick when I came in he was very cheer[i]ly over what he had been, and when I arose up to go away yet standing by his bedside I saw a cat come down from the plancher[1] (of a gray color) over his bed to my best thinking and she came upon his breast: and he cried out Lord have mercy upon me the cat hath killed me, and broken my heart, and his wife asked me if that were the cat (which she showed me), and I thought the cat which I saw as aforesaid was bigger than the cat she showed me although she was like that cat for color, and it was the same evening the which Goodwife Cole was there about noon before, and farther saith not. Sworn in court September 4, 1656 Edward Rawson Secretary.

1. Planking or platform.
Source: Suffolk County Court Files, 2:256a (MA).

Goody Marston and Goodwife Palmer against Eunice Cole

The deposition of Goody Marston and Goodwife Susannah Palmer—who being sworn saith that Goodwife Cole said that she was sure there was a witch in the town, and she knew where he dwelt and who they are and that thirteen years ago she knew one bewitched as Goodwife Marston's child was and she said she was sure that party was bewitched, for it told her so and it was changed from a man to an ape as Goody Marston's child was and she had prayed this thirteen years that God would discover that witch and farther that deponent saith not. Taken upon oath before the commissioners of Hampton the 8th of the 2d month: 1656 William Fuller Henry Dow. Vera Copia per me Thomas Bradbury.

Sworn in court September 4, 1656 per Edward Rawson Secretary.

Source: MA *135*:2.

Thomas Philbrick against Eunice Cole

The deposition of Thomas Philbrick[:] this deponent saith that Goodwife Cole said that if this deponent's calves if they did eat any of her grass she wished it might poison them or choke them and one of them I never see it more and the other calf came home and died about a week after. Taken upon oath before me, Thomas Wiggin Vera Copia per me Thomas Bradbury recorder. Sworn in court September 4, 1656 Edward Rawson Secretary.

Source: MA *135*:2.

Thomas Moulton's wife and Goodwife Sleeper describe strange sounds

The deposition of Thomas Moulton's wife and Goodwife Sleeper[:] These deponents testifieth that we being talking about Goodwife Cole, and Goodwife Marston's child and on the sudden we heard something scrape against the boards of the window and we went out and looked about and could see nothing and then we went in again and began to talk the same also again concerning she and Goodwife Marston's child and then we heard the scraping again and then we went out again and looked about and could see nothing, and the scraping was so loud that if a dog or a cat had done it we should have seen the marks in the boards and we could see none. The house where we were was Thomas Sleeper's house and farther these deponents saith not. Taken upon oath before us the commissioners of Hampton the 10th 2d month 1656. Vera Copia per me Thomas Bradbury recorder William Fuller Henry Dow. Sworn in court September 4, 1656 Edward Rawson Secretary.

Source: MA *135*:2.

Mary Coleman on words spoken in private

The deposition of Mary Coleman the wife of Thomas Coleman[:] This deponent witnesseth that Goody Cole came to her house and said that her husband had made a great complaint against this deponent to Nathaniel Boulton of some words that were spoke betwixt this deponent and her husband in their own house in private and Goody Cole did repeat the words to this deponent that she and her husband spake together which [were] words of discontent but these words were never spoken to any person neither by this deponent nor her husband as he saith and to this they will take their oaths of. Thomas Coleman also affirms that he never spake the words to any person. Sworn in court Thomas Bradbury Vera Copia per me Thomas Bradbury recorder. Sworn in court September 4, 1656 Edward Rawson Secretary.

Source: MA *135*:2.

Richard Ormsby and others on what they saw when Eunice Cole was whipped

The deposition of Richard Ormsby constable of Salisbury. That being about to strip Eunice Cole to be whipped (by the judgment of the court at Salisbury) looking upon her breasts under one of her breasts (I think her left breast) I saw a blue thing like unto a teat hanging downward about three quarters of an inch long not very thick, and having a great suspicion in my mind about it (she being suspected for a witch) [I] desired the court to send some women to look of it and presently hereupon she pulled or scratched it of[f] in a violent manner, and some blood with other moistness did appear clearly to my apprehension and she said it was a sore. John Goddard doth testify that he saw her with her hand violently scratch it away. Sworn in the court at Salisbury. 12th, 2d. month 1656, Thomas Bradbury Vera Copia per me Thomas Bradbury recorder. Sworn in the court September 4, 1656.

Edward Rawson affirmed I stood by and saw the constable rip her shift down and saw the place raw and fresh blood where Good[y] Cole [*ends abruptly*].

The court presently stepping to her saw a place raw with some fresh blood but no appearance of any old sore: Thomas Bradbury recorder in the name of the court. Sworn in court September 4, 1656 Richard Ormsby Edward Rawson Secretary.

Also Abraham Perkins and John Redman affirmed on oath that they stood by and saw the constable tear down her shift and saw the place raw and where she had [tore?] of[f?] her teat and fresh blood come from it and saw her [ ] her hand to tear of[f] it was torn off. Sworn in court September 4, 1656 Edward Rawson Secretary.

Source: MA *135*:3.

Abraham Drake blames a loss of cattle on his quarrel with Eunice Cole

The deposition of Abraham Drake[:] This deponent saith about this time twelve month my neighbor Cole lost a cow and when we had found it I and others brought the cow home to his house and he and she desired me to flea this cow, and presently after she charged me with killing her cow and said they should know that he had killed her cow for the just hand of God was upon my cattle and forthwith I lost two cattle and the latter end of summer I lost one cow more. Sworn in court Thomas Bradbury recorder. Sworn in court September 4, 1656 Edward Rawson.

Source: MA *135*:3.

Eunice Cole calls someone a whore

To the constable of Hampton—Also you are to give notice to William Cole to bring his wife to the said court to answer a presentment against her for unseemly speeches in saying to Hulda Hussie where is your mother Mingay that whore: she is a bed with your father that whore master: And for witnesses the wife of Jasper Blake and Alexander Denum. Dated the 19th day of the 12th month 1660.

Source: Norfolk County Court Papers, 18b (EI); paper 16 is essentially a duplicate and is not included here.

The court grants Eunice Cole's petition for release from prison

In answer to the petitions of Eunice Cole, the inhabitants of Hampton, as also the petition of William Salter, all in relation to the said Eunice Cole, the court do order, that the said Eunice Cole pay what is due on arrears to the keeper, and be released the prison, on condition that she depart, within one month after her release, out of this jurisdiction, and not to return again on penalty of her former sentence being executed against her. October 8, 1662.

Source: *Mass. Bay Recs., 4*, pt. 2, p. 70.

Eunice Cole is released and required to depart

In answer to the petition of Eunice Cole, it is ordered, that she may have her liberty upon her security to depart from and abide out of this jurisdiction, according to the former favor of this court. May 3, 1665.

Source: *Mass. Bay Recs., 4*, pt. 2, p. 149.

A new trial (1673): Eunice Cole has enticed Ann Smith

The deposition of Ann Huggins aged about 14 years[:] This deponent testifieth that as she and this other girl was a coming by the place where Goody Cole lives she came out of her house and asked this Ann Smith to live with her, and she said that there was a gentle man within [who] would give her some plums and the girl not being willing to go with her she laid hold on her to pull to her and then this deponent said that she should go about her business for she had nothing to do with her: and Goody Cole said that she would ask her mother if she would let her live with her, and farther this deponent saith not. Given the 12: 8 month 1672 before me Samuel Dalton Commissioner.

Source: MA *135*:4.

Sarah Clifford on Eunice Cole's enticing of Ann Smith

The deposition of Sarah Clifford aged about thirty years[:] This deponent testifieth that she heard Ann Smith cry and she going out found this Ann in the orchard with her mouth bloody and blood on the paths, and this deponent asked her several questions and asked her how she came so: and Ann answered she knew not how and after she came into the house those that were with her asked her whether that she knew any body and by what they did perceive she knew none there and after this deponent took her in her arms and carried her into another house, and then the child told her that there came a old woman into the garden with a blue coat and a blue cap and a blue apron and a white neck cloth and took this girl as she told us up by the hand and carried her into the orchard and threw her under a pearmain tree, and she was asked to live with this old woman and she said if she would live with her she would give her a baby and some plums, and the girl told her that she would not, and then this old woman said that she would kill her if she could, and then the old woman took up a stone and struck her on the head, and when she had so done she turned into a little dog and run upon this pearmain tree, and so then she was like an eagle: and further this deponent saith that this girl as we thought [was] very ill on the last sixth day at night, and we asked her what she ailed and the girl complained of cats and she said that she was pricked with pins. Sworn the 12: 8 month 1672 before me Samuel Dalton Commissioner.

Source: MA *135*:5.

Ann Smith on her enticement by Eunice Cole

The deposition of Ann Smith about the age of 9 years[:] This deponent testifieth that when she was in the cabbage yard that there came a woman to her in a blue coat and a blue cap and a blue apron, and a white neckcloth, and the woman took her by the hand and carried her into the orchard under the pearmain tree, and there she took up a stone and knocked her on the head, then she turned into a little dog and run upon the tree then she flew away like an eagle, and farther this deponent saith that if she came again she would kill her, and at another time since that, she sitting in the corner that there came a thing like a grey cat and spake to her and said to her that if she would come to her on the very day she would give her fine things and further this deponent saith not. Ann Smith affirmed to this above written the 12: 8 month 1672; before me Samuel Dalton.

Source: MA *135*:6.

Witnesses against Eunice Cole

The names of such witnesses as gave testimony against Eunice Cole last Salisbury Court: 2 month 1673[:]
viz. Abraham Perkins senior and Mary his wife
Abraham Drake and Alexander Dummer
Bridget Clifford and Sarah Clifford
and John Mason and Ann Smith of Salisbury Ephraim [   ].
    At Boston there was information given at court that Mistress Pearson the wife of Mr. George Pearson [and] the wife of Captain Edward

Huchinson could evidence that which was very material against her.

Source: MA *135*:7.

Mary Perkins on Eunice Cole's animal familiar

The deposition of Mary Perkins the wife [of] Abraham Perkins senior who saith that many years since one Sabbath day when Mr. Dalton was preaching this deponent saw a small creature about the bigness of a mouse fall out of the [ ] of Eunice Cole and fall into her lap it being of [ ] color and as soon as it was in her lap it ran away and [*four words*] startled at it took up her [ ] and went away [*tear?*] another place in a fright and Eunice Cole [ing] it draw off [ ] together and to [ ] at it; and this deponent further testifieth that at another time being appointed [*two or three words*] by Captain Wiggins to search Eunice Cole she found a strange place in her legs being a conjunction of blue veins [*blot*] were [ ] with blood and [ ] met together where was a strange [ ] of all these [ ] as the deponent did judge. Sworn the 7: the 2 month 1673 before me Samuel Dalton Commissioner.

Source: MA *135*:8.

The court orders Eunice Cole to jail to await trial

At the County Court held at Salisbury April 29, 1673
Second Session.
The court upon the hearing of the evidences against Eunice Cole now presented; and consideration of former things against her, do judge that she shall be committed to Boston Goal there to be kept in order to her further trial[.] And the constable of Hampton is ordered by this court to carry down Eunice Cole by the first opportunity to Boston Goaler: to be secured according to the court's order.
This is a true copie as attests Thomas Bradbury recorder.

The grand jury presentment

The presentment of the grand jury of Norfolk, at Hampton 1672: October the 9th[:] We present Eunice Cole widow for enticing Ann Smith to come to live with her; from John Clifford senior who hath the charge of her by her father: witness John Clifford senior and Anne Huggins and Ann Smith: Vera Copia per me Thomas Bradbury recorder.

Source: MA *135*:9.

Brigit Clifford describes the enticing of Ann Smith

The deposition of Brigit Clifford aged about 56 years who saith that the last summer when she sent Ann Smith into the cabbage yard she see her go into the cabbage yard and some [time] after my daughter Sarah said that she heard her cry in the orchard and this deponent wondering how she came there when she came crying out of the orchard I asked her what she ailed and she said she knew not but as she came she spake these words she will knock me on the head she will kill me, and the child crying out in this manner my daughter Sarah took her up and carried her into her house which was near mine: and when she had laid her in the cradle the child related to us two that when she was in the cabbage yard there came an old woman to her in a blue coat and a blue cap and a blue apron and a white neckcloth and took her up and carried her under the pearmain tree and told her that if she would live with her she would give her a baby and some plums and the child said she told her that she would not live with her: then said she the old woman struck me on the head with a stone and then she turned into a little dog and run up the tree and then flew away like an eagle and further this deponent saith that the sixth day at night before Hampton Court last she sitting in the chimney corner the said Ann Smith fixing her eyes into the other corner she perceived that her color or countenance changed and by and by she cried out I won't change and this deponent asked her what she ailed she being very well before she said that there was a thing in the corner like a grey cat which spoke to her and said that if she would come to her upon the very day she would give her fine things: and upon that she said she would not, and immediately she was taken very ill and continued in a strange fit until 2 of the clock in the morning and would shriek out and say there is the cat do you not see her, mother, and she said she doth prick me she doth wring me and so she continued till one or two of the clock the next morning in this strange fit.

Brigit Clifford under oath to all above written the 21: 6 month 1673 before me Samuel Dalton Commissioner.

Source: MA *135*:11.

The court appoints persons to prepare the case

Whereas the County Court last held at Salisbury did commit Eunice Cole to Boston Goal until she might come to her trial at the Court of Assistants for having familiarity with the devil as in the court's mittimus[1] doth more fully appear but it being omitted by the court to appoint any meet person to prepare the evidences and present testimony to the Court of Assistants, we underwritten have thought meet by the advice of some of our honored magistrates to appoint our trusty and much esteemed friends Mr. John Sherborn or Mr. Ware to be employed as a trustee in the behalf of the country to prepare all the evidences relating to the said case and to present them to the next Court of Assistants and to manage and improve the same, and to implead the said Eunice so far as the honorable Court of Assistants think so meet to employ him or them in that affair to which we set our hands the 22th of August 1673: Samuel Dalton.

1. A warrant delivering someone into custody.
Source: MA *135*:12.

Robert Smith on Eunice Cole's complaints about her supplies and problems with his bread

The deposition of Robert Smith constable of Hampton in the year 1672 who saith that the last year when he was constable he having order from the selectmen to supply Eunice Cole with provisions, and did attending to what supply the town brought in to him, and the said Eunice Cole would be often finding fault with him about her provision and complaining that it was not so good as was brought in to him and [upon?] a time when I was going to mill she asked him if he did grind rye to which I or my wife answered her that they did [not: *crossed out?*] usually grind English with their Indian in the summer time and when that grist was ground we could never make any bread of the English meal at home but it would stink and prove loathsome before it was 24 hours old and would corrupt in spots like rotten cheese, and if we did bake it over again it would be as bad as it was and stink in the same manner, and upon this we baked some Indian bread with our neighbor Goodwife Wedgwood and the Indian bread proved good but the English that was baked with it at the same time did stink and prove loathsome as before[.] The next day after it was baked, and being suspicious that Goody Cole had enchanted our oven we took of the same meal and the same yeast and carried it to our daughter Page and our daughter Page made us some bread of it and it lasted six or seven days

and was sweet and good as any other bread use[d] to be, and after this
we baked of the same meal again at home and it would stink and
corrupt as soon as ever it was cold and prove[d] so loathsome from
time to time that we were faint to give it to the swine and to the dog
and further these deponents testify viz. Robert Smith and Susan his
wife that one night there was such a loathsome stink in the room
where they lay that the said Goody Smith could not endure her bed
but thought she should have been poisoned and it was the same kind
of stink that the bread had before and she was faint to rise in the night
and desire her husband to go to prayer to drive away the devil and he
rising went to prayer and after that the stink was gone so that they
were not troubled with it and the same evening they had baked an
Indian loaf of bread which did stink on the outside as the English had
done before, and after this they carried meal to their daughter Page's
again and she made them bread and then that bread proved naught
and did stink like the other and the bread which their daughter Page
baked with it proved naught likewise that these deponents were at
such great straits they dare not bake with anybody for fear of spoiling
their bread. Deposed by Robert Smith and Susan his wife the 29 6
month 1673 before me Samuel Dalton Commissioner.

Source: MA *135*:13.

The Court summarizes actions concerning Eunice Cole

In the case of Eunice Cole
1. Take out a warrant from the secretary for Jonathan Thing and for
Mrs. Pearson and for Captain Hutchinson's wife.
2. Take out of the records of the Court of Assistants a copy of the
evidence of Richard Ormsby constable of Salisbury and Samuel Winslow's evidence concerning her pulling of[f] her teat at Salisbury
when she was going to be whipped which doth concur with Ephraim
Winslow's evidence now in the case.
Thirdly. Concerning the evidence of Alice Perkins and Alice Dunsten
if it be objected that it is old evidence it may be such unfounded that
though it speaks of what was done many years since yet it was never
brought in against her before: Secondly. When she was examined
about it at Salisbury Court last being demanded who she spake to she
said that she spake to God in prayer: which answer was inconsistent
with truth, because they testified that she went up and down the
house and clapped the door after her which was not a prayer [ges-
ture?]. Thirdly. The voice that spake to her was strange-like and

speaking out of the earth, which showeth that if her God answered her it was the devil as appears John 29:4: As one that hath a familiar spirit out of the ground.

Fourthly. Concerning the evidence of Ann Smith Ann Huggins Brigit and Sarah Clifford: the sum of what they testify is that Eunice Cole did appear to the said Ann Smith in sundry forms sometimes like a woman then like a dog and afterward like an eagle and lastly like [a] grey cat and all tending to entice her to live with her: and it was her design formed to insinuate herself into young ones as was testified by Ruth Roby when she was upon her last trial how many ways and in how many forms she did appear to her and that have been her [ ] from time to time which caused John Clifford to complain of her to the grand jury for enticing away of a child which was committed to his jurisdiction.

Fifthly. The [concurrence?] of the evidence of Mary Perkins senior and that of Elizabeth Shaw and the wife of Jacob Perkins[:] the first testifieth that she found a place in her leg which was provable where she had been sucked by imps or the like, the second testifieth that they heard the whining of puppies or such like under her coats as though she had a desire to suck.

Source: MA *135*:15.

Presentment by the grand jury

We the grand jury for the Massachusetts jurisdiction in New England do present and indict Eunice Cole of Hampton [now] widow for not having the fear of God before her eyes and being instigated by the devil did on the 24th of November in the year 1662 and since [entered] into covenant with the devil and then and since have had familiarity with the devil contrary to the peace of our sovereign [and Lord] the King his crown and dignity the law of God and of this jurisdiction. [*endorsed:*] We find this bill thus far that she had had familiarity with the devil and put her upon further trial. William Alford in the name of the rest of the jury.

Source: MA *135*:16.

The Court orders the jailkeeper to hold Eunice Cole

To William Saltern goalkeeper of Boston prison: you are hereby required in his Majesty's name by order of the County Court held at Salisbury the 29th of April 1673 by adjournment to take into your custody the body of Eunice Cole and there safely to keep her until she come to a legal trial upon suspicion of having familiarity with the devil, as appears by former and latter evidence, and hereof you are not to fail at your peril. Dated May 1, 1673 by the court Thomas Bradbury recorder.

Source: Suffolk County Court Files, *13*:1228 (MA).

Abraham Perkins on hearing voices at Eunice Cole's

Abraham Perkins senior testifieth that when William Gifford now constable the night before that he carried Eunice Cole down to Boston this deponent being one of the selectmen desired to carry a pair of knitting pins to Eunice Cole and when I came there I heard a discoursing in her house and hearkening I heard the voice of Eunice Cole and a great hollow voice answer her and the said Eunice seemed to rant and to be displeased with something finding fault and the said hollow voice spake to her again in a strange and unworldly manner but I could not understand any sentence but as if one had spoken out of the earth or in some hollow vessel it being an astonishing voice that answered her: and I being much amazed to hear th[at] voice: I went and called Abraham Drake and Alexander Dummer and we three went to her house and hearkened and heard the said Eunice Cole speak and the said strange voice answer her divers times, and the said Eunice Cole went up and down in the house and cl[atter]ed the door to and again and spake as she went and the said voice made her answer in a strange manner as is above said and there was the shimmering of a red color in the chimney corner and upon that we went and informed Mr. Dalton of what we had heard and seen and so we went to her house again and [*torn*] and asked who it was that did talk to her and she said that there was nobody there and we asked her if there had been nobody with her that night and she said no there had been nobody that night and we asked her who it was that she spake to and discoursed with and she answered that she did not talk to anybody. Abraham Perkins senior and Alexander Dummer made oath to this as above written the 7 [*torn*] 1673 before me Samuel Dalton Commissioner.

Source: Suffolk County Court Files, *13*:1228 (MA).

Ephraim Winslow on seeing Eunice Cole whipped

The deposition of Ephraim Winslow who sayeth that at that time when Goodwife Cole was whipped at Salisbury in Captain Higgins's time

Richard Ormsby being constable as he was taking of[f] her clothes when she was naked about her breasts Richard Ormsby spake after this manner is there no good woman will come hither—she turning her about from the magistrates and did take hold of something about her breast and with her fingers did wring of[f] something and it did bleed and drop blood I saw it when she was a whipping so bled there and her breast was ill-colored as it had been beaten black and blue-ish[.] Some years after in Captain Higgins's time I saw her whipped at Hampton by John Huggins and I did take good notice of her breast and then it was not of that color but there as the other or the rest of her body that was naked: farther when she pulled it of[f] her breast she said it was an old sore. Sworn before the court held at Salisbury April 29, 1673 second session: Thomas Bradbury recorder. Sworn in Cambridge September 3, 1673 attest Edward Rawson Secretary.

Source: Suffolk County Court Files, *13*: 1228 (MA).

John Mason was cursed by Eunice Cole and fell sick

The deposition of John Mason aged about 20 years who saith that be-ing upon the watch the last summer one Sabbath day at night coming near the house of Eunice Cole where she dwelleth, and hearing of her mutter in the house I went to the door with James Bunse and the said Eunice Cole called me devil and said she would split out my brains and the next day I took sick and lay sick about a fortnight after[.] Sworn the 7:2 mo 1673 before me Samuel Dalton Commissioner.

Source: Suffolk County Court Files, *13*:1228 (MA).

Elizabeth Pearson on refusing Eunice Cole and falling sick

Elizabeth Pearson aged about thirty [*corner torn*] testifieth and sayeth that: I laying in of [*corner torn*] Sisters Nanneys and my nurse came and to[ld] [me?] old Goodwife Cole of Hampton desired [*corner torn*] and the women that was in the chamber was not [*corner torn*] she should come up [*tear*] nurse told me that she gave this answer that I was not willing she should come up that night or the next I fell into an ague and fever and the child was taken sick in an unusual manner and at six weeks' end died and further sayeth not. Deposed in court September 5, 1673 the prisoner at the bar as attests Edward Rawson Secretary.

Source: Suffolk County Court Files, *13*:1228 (MA).

Hopestill Austin on Goody Cole and a woman newly delivered

The deposition of Hopestill Austin aged twenty-nine years or thereabout saith that about seven year ago: living in the house of Mrs. Nanneye: did see Goody Cole at the said Mrs. Nanneye's house: where the said Goody Cole hearing that Mrs. Pearson was lately brought to bed in the said house: had a desire to go see the said Mrs. Pearson and her little one; whereupon Mrs. Pearson's nurse replied that her mistress was not very well: and did not desire any more company: But she the said Goody Cole pressed to go up the stairs: but this deponent pulled her down again, saying that she should not go up: whereupon the said Goody Cole replied that it had been better she had gone up: so went away muttering; what she said this deponent cannot tell: but in a very little time both Mrs. Pearson and her child was taken very ill; and in a very sad manner: whereof the child died; Goody Cole said is there gentle folk above: this deponent said, gentle or simple you shall not go up: whereupon she went away muttering as abovesaid and further saith not. Deposed in court September 5, 1673 the prisoner at the bar. Edward Rawson Secretary.

Source: Suffolk County Court Files, *13*:1228 (MA).

Jonathan Thing and the strange appearances of Eunice Cole

Jonathan Thing aged about 56 years testifieth that about 16 or 17 years ago I going in the street at Hampton I saw one that I did judge was Eunice Cole about 20 rod: behind or in a triangle sideways of me and in a short time sooner than any man could possibly go it I saw her as I did judge was she about 20 rods or more before me upon that I went apace wondering at the thing and when I came to her as I did judge was she I talked with her and found her to be Eunice Cole[.] Also about that time coming out of my gate I saw nobody nor there was nobody near: as I could see and presently she the said Eunice Cole was before me looking into the house among my cattle, I asked her what she did there[?] She answered what is that to you, sawsbox, I hastened to come up to her and she seemed as it were to swim away I could not catch her[.] I then being strong and in health I followed her 20 or about 30 rod. Sworn to in court September 5, 1673 the prisoner at the bar. Edward Rawson Secretary.

Source: Suffolk County Court Files, *13*:1228 (MA).

Abraham Perkins Sen. confirms the testimony of Goodman Ormsby

The deposition of Abraham Perkins senior age 60[.]

This deponent witnesseth that divers [cases times?] being at Salisbury Court when Eunice Cole had her trial when Goodman Ormsby was constable and saw her teat plucked of[f] as he saith and myself saw the blood run down where the said constable saw the teat and called others to see it and at the same time Eunice Cole being whipped the next night after as Goodman Ormsby was in bed as he saith something like a cat leaped upon his face and very much changed him[.] The next morning coming to court Captain Wiggins asked him how his face came to be so scared he said something in the night came and scared him and told the court all the story and they all wondered at it[.] And further saith that about nine or ten years ago he had several of his lambs lying dead Eunice Cole coming by and would hem and when the deponent looking up said what do you there and she would say it is so and shall be so do what you will. Also about the same time he had 3 or 4 swine a fatting that at first they fed on the corn well but after a time would eat no corn meal pease or [else?] but [ ] [ ] which I killed them and being opening of them myself and wife found the[re] nothing but [ ] in them [ ][ ][ ] Goody Eunice Cole coming by [ ] [ ] [ ] said it must be so it shall be so do what you will[.] And further saith that his wife and family was present [and] heard th[ese] words of [ ] etc. Deposed in court September 5, 1673 attests Edward Rawson Secretary.

Source: Suffolk County Court Files, *13*:1228 (MA).

Elizabeth Shaw on Eunice Cole's animal familiars

The deposition of Elizabeth Shaw the wife of Joseph Shaw who saith that the latter end of the last summer the same day that the wife of Joseph Dow was brought to bed of her last child being the Sabbath day that the same day in the afternoon this deponent being in the same seat[1] where Eunice Cole did sit: and Mr. Cotton[2] being at prayer this deponent did hear a noise like to the whining of puppies when they have a mind to suck and this deponent sitting next to Eunice Cole did to her best discerning judge that the noise of whining was under the said Eunice and the said Eunice being sitting in the seat this deponent hearing such a noise for some time together did turn her head and look on Eunice Cole and then the said Eunice did stir herself or nestle a little as she sat and I heard no more of the noise of whining which I had heard before and this deponent looked diligently about in the seat to see that there were any dog but could see none nor any other creature that should make such a noise there being nobody in the seat at that time but Eunice Cole and this deponent and the wife of Jacob Perkins and after that this deponent had turned her head from Eunice Cole she turned to the wife of the said Jacob Perkins and she was stooping to look towards Eunice Cole and she smiled on this deponent whereby I considered that she might also hear the noise as I did. Sworn the 28: 1 month 1673 before me Samuel Dalton Commissioner.

1. Elizabeth Shaw was sitting in a "seat" (probably a bench) reserved for women.
2. Seaborn Cotton, minister of Hampton, New Hampshire.
Source: Suffolk County Court Files, *13*:1228 (MA).

Mary Perkins on Eunice Cole's animal familiars

Mary Perkins the wife of Jacob Perkins doth testify that she did hear the same noise above mentioned when Eunice Cole went by her into the seat and at that time when she smiled on Goody Shaw and [I] could see no creature in or about the seat [*smudged*] make such a noise. Sworn the 8: 2 month 1673 upon oath in open [court] before me Samuel Dalton Commissioner September 5, 1673 the prisoner [   ] Elizabeth Shaw only present at the bar. Edward Rawson Secretary.

Source: Suffolk County Court Files, *13*:1228 (MA).

Verdict of not guilty yet suspicious

In the case of Eunice Cole now prisoner at the bar not legally guilty according to indictment but just ground of vehement suspicion of her having had familiarity with the devil. Jonas Clarke in the name of the rest. [1673]

Source: Dow, *Hist. Hampton, 1*, p. 80.

Another imprisonment and ambiguous verdict

Eunice Cole of Hampton being by authority committed to prison on suspicion of being a witch and upon examination of testimonies the court vehemently suspects her so to be but not full proof is sentenced and confined to imprisonment and to be kept in durance until this court take further order with a lock to be kept on her leg. In [the] meanwhile the selectmen of Hampton to take care to provide for her as formerly that she may be relieved. September 7, 1680.

Source: *N.H. Ct. Recs., 1*, p. 368.

15. Two Grandparents, One Grandson, and a Seaman (1679–1681)

▲

Elizabeth Morse and Caleb Powell

In 1679 Elizabeth and William Morse were elderly residents of Newbury, Massachusetts; a shoemaker by trade, William had lived in the town since 1635. The Morses were members of the church, and William could both read and write. Their household included a grandson, John Stiles. Strange events began to happen within the Morses' house—furniture moving about, tools falling down the chimney, pigs loose in the kitchen. Were these "preternatural" events or was their grandson playing tricks on them?[1] Caleb Powell, a seaman, came to the Morses and volunteered to take the boy away. Powell had a local reputation for knowledge of the occult; he may have been a "cunning person." William Morse complained that Powell was a witch, but on March 30, 1680, the Essex County Court refused to indict him, though in doing so it declared "that he hath given such ground of suspicion . . . that we cannot so acquit him, but that he justly deserves to bear his own shame and the costs of prosecution of the complaint." All this while, some of Elizabeth's neighbors had apparently felt (and said) that she was a witch. Early in 1680 the local magistrate, John Woodbridge, began to collect testimony. The depositions show that she was reputedly a healer; as in other cases, this skill may have made her vulnerable to accusations of witchcraft.

Elizabeth Morse was brought to trial before the Court of Assistants in Boston in May 1680. The jury found her guilty and the governor sentenced her to execution. Three days later, on June 1, the governor

*and the Assistants voted a temporary reprieve. The lower house of
the General Court urged her execution, but to no avail. William
Morse, who actively protested the evidence brought against her, continued to petition the government on her behalf. In the summer of
1680 Elizabeth was in Boston jail, and William urged that she be
allowed the use of a private chamber in order to escape the "hot"
conditions. A year later she was allowed to return to Newbury.*

*Important light is thrown upon her reprieve by what John Hale
had to say about the case in* A Modest Enquiry Into the Nature of
Witchcraft *(Boston, 1702). His commentary refers to doubts among
the magistrates about the use of "spectral" evidence in witchcraft
trials. Increase Mather publicized the bewitching of the Morses'
house in* An Essay for the Recording of Illustrious Providences
*(1684); he barely mentioned the legal proceedings against Eliza-
beth.[2] The documents that follow omit the description in Mather's
Essay along with warrants for service on the jury and vouchers of
expenses by the witnesses who came to Boston from Newbury.[3] Two
local histories include useful accounts of the case.[4]*

1. See the deposition by Mary Tucker and Mary Richardson that follows. At
a session of the Essex County Court on May 3, 1680, John Stiles confessed to
stealing a silver spoon and to having lied about it beforehand; his grand-
father posted bond. Essex County Court Papers, *33*:26–2 (EI).
2. Mather had received from Joshua Moody, the minister in Portsmouth, New
Hampshire, a description in William Morse's handwriting of events at the
possessed house. This document, which is printed below for the first time, is
substantially briefer than the account in *Illustrious Providences*. Mather (but
not Morse) described John Stiles, the grandson, as exhibiting symptoms of
possession that he blamed on Caleb Powell. According to Mather, the Morses
had also heard a "voice, singing, 'Revenge! Revenge! Sweet is revenge!' "
Mather, *Essay*, p. 154.
3. These warrants and vouchers may be found in "Trials for Witchcraft in
New England," HLH.
4. Joshua Coffin, *A Sketch of the History of Newbury* (Boston, 1845), pp. 122–
32; John Currier, *History of Newbury* (Boston, 1902), *1*, pp. 186–89.

William Morse describes his enchanted house

The testimony of William Morse and his wife which they both saw:

On last Thursday night my wife and I being in bed we heard a great
noise about the house of knocking against the roof with sticks and
stones throwing against the house with great violence: whereupon I
myself arose and my wife and saw not anybody but was forced to return into the house again the stones being thrown so violently against
us[;] we going to bed again and the same noise on the house we
locked the door fast and about midnight we heard a great noise of a

hog in the house and I arose and found a great hog in the house and the door being shut: I opened the door the hog running violently out.

The next morning a stick of links hanging in the chimney fast I saw come down violently and not anybody near to them and jumped up on a chair before the fire. I hanged them up again and they come down again into the fire[.] The next day I had an awl in the window which was taken away I know not how: and come down the chimney: I took the same awl and put [it] into a cupboard and fastened the door[.] The same awl came down 3 or 4 times[.] We had a basket in the chamber come down the chimney I locked it up myself and laid it before me: it was suddenly taken away I know not how and come down the chimney again: I then took a brick and put into it and said it should carry that away if it did go up again[.] It was taken away I know not how and come down the chimney and the brick a little after it: on Saturday next some sticks on light fire down the chimney and stones: and then my awls taken away from me 4 times as I used them and come down the chimney 4 times my nails in a cover of a firkin come down the chimney[.] Again the door being locked I heard a hog in the house I let him alone until day and found it to be one of my own: willing to go out[.]

The next day being Sabbath day sticks and stones were thrown down violently the chimney: on Monday next Mr. Richardson and another saw many things [*tear*] I sent my boy to go off nothing was amiss in my barn: I not being able to tie my cattle up [at?] nights but still being untied with many other strange things: the frame being thrown down upon the boy: we all run out to help him in[.] When we come in we saw a cotton wheel turned with the legs upward and many things set upon it as a stick and a spade like the form of a ship[,] pots hanging over the fire dancing one against the other I being forced to unhang them[.]

We saw an andiron dance up and down: many times and into a pot and out again and up atop of a table: the pot turning over and spilling all in it[.] I sending my boy to fetch my tools which I do make ropes with so soon as the door being opened they come violently down of themselves again[.] A tub of bread come down from a shelf and turned over: my wife went to make the bed the clothes did fly off many times of themselves and a chest opened and shut and doors fly together my wife going into the cellar: things tumbling down and the door flinging together violently: I being at prayer my head being covered with a cloth: a chair did oftentimes bow to me and then struck me on the side: my wife come out of the other room a wedge of iron being thrown at her and a space but not reach her and a stone which hurt her much: and sitting by the fire with my wife and two more neighbors with us: a stone struck against the lamp and struck it out many times and a shoe which we saw in chamber before come down the door being shut and struck me a blow on the head which did me much hurt[.] A mate of a ship coming often to me and said he was much grieved for me and said the boy was the cause of all my trouble and my wife was much wronged and was no witch and if [I] would let him have the boy but one day he would warrant me no more trouble[.] I being persuaded to it he come the next day at the break of day and the boy was with him until night and I had not any trouble since. December 3, 1679.

Source: Mather Papers, Prince Collection, BPL.

William Morse describes his enchanted house for the court

The testimony of William Morse which sayeth together with his wife, aged both about 65 years. That Thursday night being the 27th day of November we heard a great noise without round the house of knocking the boards of the house, and as we conceived throwing of stones against the house: whereupon myself and wife looked out, and saw nobody, and the boy all this time with us, but we had stones and sticks thrown at us that we were forced to retire into the house again, afterwards we went to bed and the boy with us, and then the like noises was upon the roof of the house.

2. The same night about midnight the door being locked when we went to bed, we heard a great hog in the house grunt and make a noise as we thought willing to get out and that we might not be disturbed in sleep I rose and let him out and I found a hog in the house, and the door unlocked[;] the door was firmly locked when we went to bed.

3. The next morning a stick of links hanging in the chimney, they were thrown out of their place and we hanged them up again; and they were thrown down again and some into the fire.

4. The night following I had a great awl lying in the window, the which awl we saw fall down out of the chimney into the ashes by the fire.

5. After this I bid the boy put the same awl into the cupboard, which we saw done, and the door shut too: this same awl came presently down the chimney again in our sight and I took it up myself: again the same night we saw a little Indian basket that was in the loft before come down the chimney again: and I took the same basket and put a piece of brick into it, and the basket with the brick was gone, and

came down again the third time with the brick in it, and went up again the fourth time, and came down again without the brick: and the brick came down a little after.

6. The next day being Saturday, stones, sticks and [*torn*] of bricks came down so that we could not quietly dress or breakfast, and sticks of fire also came down at the same time.

7. That day in the afternoon my thread 4 times taken away and came down the chimney, again my awl and a gimlet wanting came down the chimney: again my leather taken away came down the chimney: again my nails being in the cover of a firkin taken away came down the chimney. Again the same night the door being locked a little before day hearing a hog in the house I rose and saw the hog to be mine, I let him out.

8. The next day being Sabbath day, many stones and sticks and pieces of bricks came down the chimney: on the Monday Mr. Richardson[1] and my brother being there, the frame in my cowhouse they saw very firm. I sent my boy out to scare the fowls from my hog's meat: he went to the cowhouse and it fell down my boy crying with hurt of the fall: in the afternoon, the pots hanging over the fire did dash so vehemently one against the others: we set down one that they might not dash to pieces: I saw the andiron leap into the pot and dance, and leap out, and again leap in and dance and leap out again, and leap on a table and there abide, and my wife saw the andiron on the table: also I saw the pot turn itself over and throw down all the water: again we saw a tray with wool leap up and down and throw the wool out, and so many times and saw nobody meddle with it: again a tub his hoop fly off of itself and the tub turn over and nobody near it: again the woolen wheel turned upside down and stood upon its end, and a spade set on it: Stephen Greenleaf saw it, and myself and my wife; again my rope tools fell down upon the ground before my boy could take them being sent for them, and the same thing of nails tumbled down from the loft into the ground, and nobody near. Again my wife and boy making the bed, the chest did open and shut the bed cloths could not be made to lie on the bed but fly of[f] again. Again Caleb Powell came in and being affected to see our trouble did promise me and my wife that if we would be willing to let him keep the boy we should see ourselves that we should be never disturbed while he was gone with him: he had the boy and had him quiet ever since.

Thomas Rogers and George Hardy being at William Morse his house affirm that the earth in the chimney corner moved and scattered on them: that Thomas Rogers was hit with somewhat, Hardy with an iron ladle as is supposed. Somewhat hit William Morse a great blow but it was so swift that they could not certainly tell what it was, but looking down after they heard the noise they saw a shoe. The boy was in the corner at the first, afterwards in the house. [*Undated*]

1. John Richardson, minister in Newbury.
Source: Essex County Court Papers, *32*:131–1 (EI).

Other witnesses to these events, and to Powell's black arts

Mr. Richardson on Saturday testifieth that a board flew against his chair and he heard a noise in another room, which he supposed in all reason to be diabolical.

Anthony Morse affirmeth, that he saw the board before tacked with nails to the window, but his evidence is drawn at large by himself.

John Dole saw a pin and stick of candlewood to fall down, a stone, a firebrand, and these things he saw not what way they came till they fell down by him.

The same affirmed by John Tucker: the boy was in one corner when they saw and observed all the while and saw no motion in him.

Elizabeth Titcomb affirmeth that Powell said that he could find the witch by his learning if he had another scholar with him, this she saith were his [im?]pressions to the best of her memory.

Stephen Greenleaf, and Edward Richardson affirm the motion of the [*hole*] [ ] in the [ ].

John Tucker affirmeth that Powell said to him he saw the boy throw the shoe while he was at prayer.

John Badger's oath is drawn out by itself.

John Emerson affirmeth that Powell said he was brought up under Norwood, and it was judged by the people there, that Norwood studied the black art. [*Undated*].

Source: Essex County Court Papers, *32*:132–1 (EI).

More testimony by the Morses

A farther testimony of William Morse and his wife[.]

We saw also a keeler of bread turn over against me and st[r]uck me not any being near it and so overturned. I saw a chair standing in the house and not anybody near it did often bow towards me and so rise up again.

My wife also being in the chamber the chamber door did violently fly together not anybody being near it. My wife going to make a bed the bed did move to and fro not anybody being near it. I also saw an iron wedge and spade was flying out of the chamber on my wife and did not strike her. My wife going into the cellar a drum standing in the house did roll over the door of the cellar and being take up again the door did violently fly down again. My barn's door 4 times unpinned I know not how. I going to shut my barn door looking for the pin the boy being with me (as I did judge) the pin coming down out of the air and did fall down near to me.

Again Caleb Powell came in as beforesaid and seeing our spirits very low by the sense of our great affliction began to bemoan our condition and said that he was troubled for our affliction, and said that he had eyed this boy and drawed near to us with great compassion, poor old man, poor old woman this boy is the occasion of your grief, for he hath done these things, and hath caused his good old grandmother to be counted a witch[.] Then said I how can all these things be done by him[?] Said he, although he may not have done all yet most of them, for this boy is a young rogue, a vile rogue, I have watched him, and see him do things as to come up and down.

Caleb Powell also said he had understanding in astrology, and astronomy, and knew the working of spirits, some in one country, and some in another, and looking on the boy said you young rogue to begin so soon. Goodman Morse if you be willing to let me have this boy, I will undertake you shall be free from any trouble of this kind while he is with me: I was very unwilling at the first and my wife, but by often urging me to it he told me whither, and what employment and company he should go, I did consent to it and this was before John Badger came: and we have been freed from any trouble of this kind ever since that promise made, on Monday night last to this time being Friday in the afternoon: then we heard a great noise in the other room oftentimes, but looking after it, could not see any thing: but afterwards looking into the room we saw a board hanged to the press: then we being by the fire, sitting in a chair my chair often would not stand still but ready to throw me backward often times: afterward my cap almost taken off my head 3 times: again a great blow in my pate, and my cat did leap from me into the chimney corner: presently after this cat was thrown at my wife: we saw the cat to be ours we put her out of the house and shut the door: presently the cat was throwed into the house: we went to go to bed suddenly my wife being with me in the bed the lamp light by our side my cat again throwed at us 3 times jumping away presently into the floor, and one of those times, a red waistcoat throwed on the bed, and the cat wrapped up in it: again the lamp standing by us on the chest, we said it should stand and burn out, but presently was beaten down, and all the oil shed, and we left in the dark: again a great noise a great while very dreadful: again in the morning a great stone being 6 pound weight did remove from place to place we saw it: two spoons throwed off the table, and presently the table throwed down: and being minded to write my inkhorn was hid from me, which I found covered with a rag, and my pen quite gone: I made a new pen and while I was writing one ear of corn hit me in the face and firesticks and stones throwed at me and my pen brought to me while I was writing with my new pen, my inkhorn taken away and not knowing how to write any more, and there found him, and so I was able to write again: again my wife her hat taken from her head sitting by the fire by me the table almost thrown down: again my spectacles thrown from the table and thrown almost into the fire by me and my wife: and the boy: again my book of all my accounts thrown into the fire, and had been burnt presently if I had not taken it up: again boards taken off a tub and set upright by themselves, and my paper do what I could hardly keep it while I was writing this relations and things thrown at me while a writing presently before I could dry my writing a mammoth hat rubbed along it but I held so fast that it did blot but some of it: my wife and I being much afraid that I should not preserve it for the public use did think best to lay it in the Bible and it lay safe that night, again the next I would lay it there again but in the morning it was not there to be found, the bag hanged down empty, but after was found in a box alone: again while I was writing this morning, I was forced to forbear writing any more I was so disturbed with so many things constantly thrown at me. This relation brought in, December 8.

Source: Essex County Court Papers, *32*:132–1 (EI).

John Badger says that Caleb Powell spoke of knowing astrology

John Badger affirmeth that being at William Morse his house: and heard Caleb Powell say that he thought by astrology: and I think he said by astronomy too with it: he could find out whither or no there were diabolical means used about the said Morse his trouble and that the said Caleb said he thought to try to find it out.

Source: Essex County Court Papers, *32*:133–1 (EI).

Mary Tucker and Mary Richardson on Powell's breaking the enchantment

The deposition of Mary Tucker aged about 20[.] She remembreth that Caleb Powell came in to her house and said to this purpose that he coming to William Morse his house, and the old man being at prayer, he thought not fit to go in but looked in at the window, and he said he had broken the enchantment, for he saw the boy play tricks while he was at prayer, and mentioned some and among the rest that he saw him to fling the shoe at the said Morse's head.

Taken on oath March 29, 1680 before me John Woodbridge Commissioner.

Mary Richardson confirmed the truth of the above written testimony on oath at the same time.

Source: Essex County Court Papers, *32*:133–2 (EI).

Anthony Morse on the strange events at his brother's house

I Anthony Morse: occasionally being at my brother's Morse['s] house my brother showed me a piece of a brick which had several times come down the chimney: I sitting in the corner I took the piece of brick in my hand: within a little space of time the piece of brick was gone from me I knew not by what means: Quickly after the piece of brick came down the chimney: Also in the chimney corner I saw a hammer on the ground: there being no person near the hammer it was suddenly gone: by what means I know not: but within a little space after the hammer came down the chimney: and within a little space of time after that came a piece of wood down the chimney about a foot long: and within a little after that came down a firebrand: the fire being out: this was about 10 days ago. Newbury: 8: 9: 1679 Taken on oath December 8, 1679 before me John Woodbridge Commissioner.

Source: Essex County Court Papers, *32*:133–3 (EI).

Complaint against Caleb Powell for witchcraft

Caleb Powell being complained of for suspicion of working with the devil to the molesting of William Morse and his family, was by warrant directed to the constable brought in by him. The accusation and testimonies were read, and the complaint respited till the Monday following. December 3, 1679.

December 8, 1679. Caleb Powell appeared according to order and farther testimony produced against him by William Morse, which being read and considered it was determined that the said William Morse should prosecute the case against the said Powell at the County Court to be held at Ipswich the last Tuesday in March ensuing, and in order hereunto.

William Morse acknowledged himself indebted to the treasurer of the county of Essex, the full sum of £20.

The condition of this obligation is that the said William Morse shall prosecute his complaint against Caleb Powell at that court.

Caleb Powell was delivered as a prisoner to the constable till he could find security of £20 for the answering of the said complaint or else he was to be carried to prison. John Woodbridge Commissioner.

Source: Essex County Court Papers *32*:130–1 (EI).

Sarah Hall and Joseph Mirick on Caleb Powell as wizard

The testimony of Sarah Hall, about 33 years, and Joseph Mirrick about 19. Who affirm,

That John Moores boatswain of the vessel wherein Joseph Dole was [*blot*] and Caleb Powell was mate, hath often said in their hearing that if there were any wizards he was sure that Caleb Powell was a wizard. Which he affirmed oftentimes in their house. Taken on oath February 27, 1679 before me John Woodbridge Commissioner.

Source: Essex County Court Papers, *32*:130–2 (EI).

The county court disposes of Caleb Powell

Upon the hearing the complaint brought to this court against Caleb Powell for suspicion of working by the devil to the molesting of the family of William Morse of Newbury, though this court cannot find any evident ground of proceeding farther against the said Caleb Powell, yet we determine that he hath given such ground of suspicion of his so dealing, that we cannot so acquit him, but that he justly deserves to bear his own shame and the costs of the prosecution of the complaint.

Referred to Mr. Woodbridge to examine and determine what the charges.

Source: Essex County Court Papers, *32*:130–3 (EI).

Israel Webster on John Stiles saying he is going to hell

The testimony of Israel Webster aged about 35 years who testifieth upon oath that John Stiles being at his house he asked him whether, he said when he was going to meeting, that he was going to hell. He answered yes he asked him why, his answer was, because he was not going to heaven. He also asked him, whether he said that he could not read, on the Sabbath days, he said yes—because the devil would not let him.

Taken on oath January 7, 1679.

Source: Essex County Court Papers, *33*:26–1 (EI).

Thomas Titcomb on Stiles's bad language

The testimony of Thomas Titcomb aged about 18 years testifieth and sayeth that before the late troubles at William Morse's I was going to meeting upon a Sabbath day[.] I overtook Samuel Smith and John Stiles and other [lads?] against Robert Cracker's house; John Stiles used many foul words and seeing him so foul being asked whether he would go he replied he would go to hell and spoke the words 2 or 3 times [or?] before we could believe he would speak such wild words[.] Then I sharply reproved him for it. Then he said he would go to hell and farther sayeth not.

Taken on oath January 7, 1679. John Stiles in open court sayeth that he doth not know but that he did say the words charged by Thomas Titcomb.

Source: Essex County Court Papers, *33: 26–3* (EI).

Elizabeth Titcomb describes mysterious sounds

Elizabeth Titcomb aged about fifty, after the burning of apples at Ensign Greenleaf's I was soon troubled at my house with a noise knocking at the door which did awake me out of a sound sleep: the first knocking I lay still harkening for to hear a voice and none I heard: I thought somebody did want my help knocking a second time but I heard no voice: a third time I heard knocking then I went forth, and called to my daughter Lydia: asked her if she did hear the noise, she said yes then I opened my chamber door and said, who are you and what is your business but no voice so I considered that I had no call to go to the door, and begged of God to give me rest: but I was much disturbed by the violent motion of a creature which I did never know before nor since.

Lydia Titcomb affirmeth the same about the noise. The same Peniel Titcomb affirms.

Jonathan Woodman and a cat that he identifies as Elizabeth Morse

The deposition of Jonathan Woodman aged about thirty five years who testifieth and saith that about seven years ago being going home in a dark night from Ensign Greenleaf's upon the green at Walch's cellar I met with a white thing like a cat which did play at my legs and I did often kick at it having no weapon in my hand at last struck it with my foot against the fence near Israel Webster's house and there it stopped with a loud cry after the manner of a cat and I see it no more: I further testify that William Morse of Newbury did own that he did send for a doctor for his wife the same night and same time of night that I was troubled with that cat above mentioned which was some grounds of suspicion but there was nothing in it—because her hurt in her head was done two or three days before they sent for the doctor by something falling out of the chimney[.] He further said that she seem[ed] to make little of it till that night above mentioned and then grew very bad that he was forced to send for the doctor. Taken on oath, January 7, 1679.

Benjamin Richardson on strange events at William Morse's

The testimony [of] Benjamin Richardson aged about twenty-one years testifieth and saith that as I came in the morning from Cousin Tucker's about three weeks or a month ago by the corner of Goodman Morse's house I heard the boy John Stiles cry out and [he] said the house is afire the house is afire[.] Then Goodman Morse see me made signs and winked to me to come to see where I could spy anything[.] Then I went in and went up the stairs and then he barked like a dog and yowled like [a] cat and then he growled and his hair stood up on end and then he jumped out of that bed and went into another bed and there was a board that leaned against the chest and flew from the chest and struck the boy and further I see a shriveled hand to strike the boy. Taken on oath, January 7, 1679.

David Wheeler and a sick heifer

The testimony of David [Wheeler] aged about 54 years or thereabouts testifieth that I took notice of several passages: as first of her actions that she would usually be digging and crobbing the ground with the end of a staff which I never took notice of any person that acted in the like manner further the said David Wheeler having a heifer about 3 or

4 years old that came home out of the woods one day was chawed upon the back about the breadth of a hand: and about a fortnight after was chaw[ed] on the other side by that about as much more: and the said heifer grew ill and would sometimes go into the river so deep until the water touch[ed] her nose and she stayed there until some of our family were forced to wade to fetch her out to save her from drowning—and the same heifer that is above mentioned being missing we could not find her some considerable time: afterwards we found her in an out house that had no other passage any other way but a small gap we had cut for small calves: and I was verily persuaded that the heifer was bewitched, and Goodwife Morse was the occasion of it. Taken on oath, January 7, 1679.

Joshua Richardson and sick sheep

The deposition of Joshua Richardson: aged about thirty years testifieth and saith that about five years ago then I had three sheep to drive to Hampton: and when I came down the street I thought it best to cache my sheep at Goodman Morse's barn because it was near my canoe that was to carry them over the river and Goodman Morse's cowhouse door stood open next [to] the highway and I looked in and I saw nothing there: so I drove my sheep into the cowhouse and as I was a caching the sheep Goody Morse came out and was mighty with me and said I had better ask leave and I went away with my sheep and when I came to Hampton about two hours after the sheep were all sick and did foam at the mouths and one of them died presently and they asked me where I cached the sheep and I told them in Morse's cowhouse and they said they did believe they were bewitched and so do I to[o]. Taken on oath, January 7, 1679.

Caleb Moody on quarrels with the Morses

The testimony of Caleb Moody aged 42 years testifieth and sayeth that I having lived near to Elizabeth Morse about twenty years I have lost several cattle in an [un]usual manner, about 16 years ago I had some difference with the said Morse the next morning one of my best hogs lay dead in the yard and no natural cause that I know of[.] Another time the said Elizabeth Morse came to me late of a Saturday night and desired me to go to Mr. Woodbridge his store to see after her husband[.] I told her I did not apprehend any danger of him. The next morning I sent my eldest son to the house to inquire whether her husband was come home[.] The lad came home and told me that he

was come home and that she the said Elizabeth Morse told him that
[if] I had been as good I had gone to look after her husband, that very
morning as I was afterwards informed by John Ordway that as he was
driving out the flock of sheep that he then kept one of my sheep lay
down and died, at another time I had a cow [that] was suddenly taken
in a very strange manner and tumbled over logs that laid in the yard
and strived to turn reared upon her head and so continued a while
and rose up again and went away[.] After this I saw the same cow
coming down the hill by William Morse's house and I saw the said
Elizabeth Morse stand without the door and my cow fall into the like
strange condition as she did before and tumbled into a gutter or gully
that was worn with the running of the water[.] After[ward] she recovered and went away home: at another time of a Sabbath day morning
one of my cows great with calf was turned into the stall with her head
under her stone dead in such a manner that I could not think it possible for a cow to put herself into such a place but conclud[ed] the
devil by some instrument did it and several that saw it did say they
were of the same mind or words to that purpose: at another time
about three or four years ago in the summertime I had a four year old
heifer that was brought out of the woods with a calf about three weeks
old and I [put] them into my pasture near to the said Morse's house
and let her go there 2 or 3 days with her calf to user to the place[.]
Then I went to take away the calf to kill it [and] the heifer seemed to
take no notice of the calf when I fetched it away which made me to
marvel because she was very fond of her calf[.] After the calf was
killed I went to see what was the matter with the heifer and she was
laid down in a shady place among thorn bushes and would neither eat
nor chew her cud for several days and as I was trying to get her up I
saw the said Elizabeth Morse within about 5 or 6 rods of [me] so I
drove the heifer away but she would not feed[;] afterwards I went
again to see what would become of her, and she was laid down again
in the same place and I looked up and saw the said Elizabeth Morse
near the same place where I had seen her before and this I did to the
best of my memory 3 or four times the heifer lay near the same place
and the said Elizabeth Morse was within sight[.] I do not remember
that I did see her come or go away but saw her at once which did make
me very much suspect she had bewitched my heifer, further I do testify that about a month or five weeks ago William Fanning borrowed
my mare to go to mill and being in my pasture near to the said Morse's
house after sunset I heard William Fanning at the said Morse's barn
talking with him about John Stiles and I heard the said Fanning
threaten to break his bones[.] The next morning John Hall came over

to my house and told me that William Fanning had called at his house before day and told him that he was much frighted with a cat in Captain Pierce's pasture. Taken on oath, January 7, 1679.

William Fanning describes strange events

The testimony of William Fanning aged about 36 years testifieth and sayeth that about a month or five weeks ago living near to William Morse's in the evening quickly after sunset I saw John Stiles standing by Mr. Denison's cowhouse and I asked him what was the best news at their house, and he told me that there was several hundreds of devils in the air and they would be at their house by and by and they would be at my house anon: and that very night I went to Sargeant Moody's house which is my neighbor and borrowed his mare to go to mill, and I went to mill with two bushels of corn and got it ground, and when I came back again in John Hall's pasture the mare began to startle and snort and reared up on end so that I could not get her forward and I looked down upon the mare's head [where] I spied a great white cat without a tail upon my breast and she had fast hold of my neckcloth and coat[.] I having a good stick in my hand I struck her off, and again the cat was a coming up upon my left side I took my stick in my left hand and struck her down again then I alighted, and as soon as I alighted the cat came playing between my legs so that I could not well go forward, and watching my opportunity I struck her a very great blow up against a tree and after that I struck her another blow which made her lay for dead and I went presently to John Hall's house, and he was abed[.] I called to him and desired him that he would go to such a tree and there I thought he would find a dead cat, and I went straight away home and told my wife and told her what I had met withal. Taken on oath January 7, 1679.

John Mighill and his sick cattle

John Mighill aged about 44 years testifieth that about ten years since I went to William Morse's house to work by the order of Jonathan Morse the son of William Morse[.] I went to hew shingle[s] and at night when I was going home Goody Morse did very much urge me to stay all night and help her son the next day insomuch that I was glad to make any [ex]cuse that I had tied a young mare up in the house and must go home to water her[.] Then she said, be sure to come again tomorrow[.] So I went home but came there no more and she sent to me several times to come to work and at the last there was word came to me that she was very angry with me and suddenly after there was a great alteration in my cattle there was one of my cows that had a calf about a fortnight old and at night he was wet when I put him up and in the morning I went to fetch him out to suck and the hair and skin was gone of[f] his back and it was red like a burn and would never heal but grew worse and worse[.] At the last his eyes came out of his head and then I thought it was time to knock him on the head and another of my cows got a little push with another beast and the dung ran out of her side and another of my cows stood in the middle of the yard when I went to tie them up [at] night and she could not go of[f] the place where she stood but I was glad to let her stand in the middle of the yard all night and my mare was drowned and thus my creatures were that I had scarce any creature tha[t] was well and Goody Morse being angry with me and having been talked of for a witch I was afeared that she had some hand in this. Taken on oath January 7, 1679.

Robert Earle reports conversations with Elizabeth Morse

The deposition of Robert Earle aged 45 years or thereabouts. Sayeth that on Tuesday night last about two of the clock at night, going into the chamber where Elizabeth Morse was shut in finding her sitting upright in her bed. She said to me that she was very glad that I was come in for she was in great trouble and that she thought she should die for it now for they were going to find out another way for blasphemy. And I went near her bedside and I heard a strange kind of noise which was like a whelp sucking of her dam (or kittens sucking) which made me to think whether any of the cats had laid any of their kittens upon the side of the bed. Or whether it might be some strange kind of hissing within her. Further I testify that yesterday when I went to fetch her to the court she said that now they say abroad I shall die. I asking of her why she said so and who it was that said so. She said my husband and I have been talking together of it. And she said that I did know what they did say if I would speak, and such as I that do know such things spoke of abroad[.] Then I remembering there was some did ask me what I thought would be done with her, I said I did not know but that she might die for it which made me have the more suspicion of her calling to mind what I had said abroad.

He further adds that on Wednesday night last going into the room where the said Elizabeth Morse was alike sitting up as beforesaid [he] heard the like noise, though not so loud. And this was near about the same time of night. [*Undated*]

Order to the constable to seize Elizabeth Morse

To Joseph Pike constable of Newbury. March 6, 1679/80.

In his Majesty's name you are required to seize on the person of Elizabeth Morse the wife of William Morse and her forthwith safely convey and deliver her to the keeper of the prison at Ipswich by him safely to be kept till the Court of Assistants on its adjournment to the 20th of May next who will give further order she being presented and left by the grand jury for trial as to witchcraft and hereof you are not to fail. Dated in Boston: from the 6th of March, 1679. This warrant received in Boston April 1, 1680. And the person within specified was delivered to the prison keeper in Ipswich April 20, 1680. Per me Joseph Pike constable of Newbury.

By the court, Edward Rawson, Secretary.

Esther Wilson reports her mother's fear of Elizabeth Morse

The testimony of Esther Wilson aged about 28.

That she living with her mother Goodwife Chandler when she was ill, she would often cry out and complain that Goodwife Morse was a witch, and had bewitched her, and every time she came to see her she was the worst for her. Though to meet were often forbidden yet she would not refrain coming. One coming to the house asked why we did not nail a horseshoe on the threshold (for that was an experiment to try witches) my mother the next morning, with her staff made a shift to get to the door, and nailed on a horseshoe as well as she could, Goodwife Morse, while the horseshoe was on, would never be persuaded to come into the house, and though she were persuaded by the deponent, and Daniel Rolfe to go in, she would not, and being demanded the reason, she would not tell me now, and said it was not her mind to come in: but she would kneel down by the door and talk and discourse, but not go in, though she would come often times in a day, yet that was her practice. William Moody coming to the house and understanding that there was a horseshoe, nailed on to the door, said it was a piece of witchery and knocked it off and laid it by; very shortly after the same day Goodwife Morse came in, and thrust into the parlor where my mother lay before she was up; and my mother complained of her, and I earnestly desired her that she would be gone, and I could very hardly with my importunity intreat her to do it: The horseshoe was off about a week and she would very often come in that time. About a week after my mother to keep her out of the house, got Daniel Rolfe to nail on the shoe again, which continued for about 7 or 8 days, and at that time she would not come over the threshold to come in though often importuned to do it. Then William Moody coming again took off the horseshoe, and put it in his pocket and carried it away: then the said Goodwife Morse came as before and would go in as before. In a short time after I being at home on a Sabbath day alone with my mother, I had been dressing her head, and she cried out on a sudden, Goody Morse, Goody Morse is coming into the house, I said I could not see her, my mother said I see her, there she is. Then I run to the door twice, but I could not see her; but my mother cried out, that wicked woman would kill her, be the death of her, she could not bear it: and fell into a grievous fit, and I took her and carried her in and laid her on a bed: and having so done, I went out to see if anybody were coming from meeting, and there (though I saw her not before) she rushed in and went into the parlor to my mother, and I stepping out and seeing my father coming lift up my hand to him to come and he made great haste, and I called in some of the neighbors, and so my mother continued a considerable time before she recovered. In this fit my mother's mouth was drawn awry, and she foamed at [the] mouth, and I wiped it of[f], but I was very much frighted to see her so till the neighbors came in. This is all that at the present she remembereth. Taken on oath, May 17, 1680, before me John Woodbridge, Commissioner. Read in court, 20 May, 1680. Edward Rawson, Secretary.

Elizabeth Titcomb describes pains and strange sensations

The testimony of Elizabeth Titcomb aged about 50 years.

That she being lately with Susanna Tappan aged about 74 years the said Tappan related to her that when Elizabeth Morse was in examination for witchcraft, and she being summoned gave in her testimony among others. When she went away the said Elizabeth Morse came after her and took her about the wrist, as if she would inquire what was the evidence she gave in against her. Who answered nothing but what you spake yourself; the said Tappan went home, and in the night she felt a cold damp hand, clasping her about her wrist, which affrighted her very much, and put her into a very great and dropping sweat. And from that time she continued ill, and an itching and pricking rose upon her body. Which afterwards came to such a dry scurse, that she could scrape it off as it were scales from an alewife, and that side which she was touched in was most out of frame, and she is smitten in the lower parts of her body after the same manner that she had testified against the said Morse what she heard her speak: and from that time she hath continued very ill, but little from her bed, and hath not been able to go abroad ever since to the public meeting. Who also sayeth that the very night when she being desired to go and inquire of the said Tappan what her evidence was, she had a beast strangely hanged in a harrow and dead. Taken on oath May 14, 1680. John Woodbridge, Commissioner. Sworn in court May 20, 1680. Edward Rawson Secretary.

Elizabeth Titcomb says Elizabeth Morse affirmed her innocence

Elizabeth Titcomb, formerly seriously telling Goodwife Morse of the report that went of her as touching her name for witchcraft and endeavoring to convince her of the wickedness for it, she seemed to be much affected with it and fell on weeping, and said she was as innocent as herself or the child newborn or as God in heaven. Sworn, Edward Rawson Secretary.

Lydia Titcomb describes a shape-changing animal

Lydia Titcomb aged about 17 years testifieth that she heard the discourse between her mother and the said Goodwife Morse, and the words which her mother hath expressed. And also that a little while after she and her brother and sister going home from the pond where they fetched water, there flew somewhat out of the bushes, in her opinion like an owl, and it came up presently to her and was turned into the shape of a cat, and quickly after turned into the shape of a dog, sometimes would be all black, then have a white ring about the neck sometimes would have long ears sometimes scarce any to be discerned, sometimes a very long tail sometimes a short one scarce discernible, and in such manner it followed us some time as if it would leap upon our backs, and frightened us very much, and accompanied us till they came near the house. And the last time we saw it we left it playing about a tree and we went in and left it. Taken on oath, May 14, 1680, before me, John Woodbridge Commissioner. Sworn in court May 20, 1680. Edward Rawson Secretary.

Susan Tappan clarifies the testimony of Elizabeth Titcomb

Susan Tappan being examined about the testimony of Elizabeth Titcomb, before written, testifieth that for the substance it is true, only there is a mistake that Goodwife Morse took her by the wrist not at that time when she came home from that meeting when the said

Morse was examined, but on a Sabbath day after when she came from the public meeting, which she might easily mistake her, and she sayeth that the said Morse came very hastily after her, as if she run. And she cannot directly tell the night when the cold hand clasped her wrist but it was not the night that she came home from the examination. In everything else the relation is exactly true. Taken on oath, May 17, 1680, before me John Woodbridge Commissioner.

Thomas Knowlton on Elizabeth Morse

Thomas Knowlton sayeth that when he brought down the prisoner Elizabeth Morse from Ipswich, she said she was accused about witchcraft she said she was as clear of the accusation as God in heaven. Sworn in court per Thomas Knowlton May 20, 1680. Edward Rawson Secretary.

Thomas Knowlton further testifies, that as I brought Goody Morse down she owned to me that she stroked Goodwife Ordway'[s] child over the head when it was sick, and the child died. Sworn in court, May 20, 1680. Edward Rawson Secretary.

John Chase on testifying against Morse and falling ill

John Chase[:] And as an addition to my former testimony I testify and say that the very day to the best of my knowledge that Caleb Powell came to take my testimony against Goodwife Morse that I was taken with the bloody flux and so it held me till I came to the court and charged her with it, that at that very instant of time it left me and I have not been troubled with it since, and that my wife has been sorely troubled with sore breasts, that she have lost them both and one of them rotted away from her. Sworn to in court, May 20, 1680. Edward Rawson Secretary.

Jane Sewall on Elizabeth Morse as a healer

The testimony of Mrs. Jane Sewall aged about 54 years. Who saith that some years since William Morse being at my house began of his own accord to say that his wife was accounted a witch, but he did wonder that she should be both a healing and a destroying witch, and gave this instance. Thomas Wells his wife being come to the time of her delivery was not willing (by the motion of his sister in whose house she was) to send for Goodwife Morse though she were the next neighbor, and continued a long season in strong labor and could not be delivered but when they saw the woman in such a condition and without any hopeful appearance of delivery determined to send for the said Goodwife Morse, and so Thomas Wells went to her and desired her to come, who at first made a difficulty of it, as being unwilling not being sent for sooner. Thomas Wells said he would have come sooner but [his wife's] sister would not let him, so at last she went, and quickly after her com[ing] the woman was delivered. This as she remembereth was the substance [of the] discourse though she doth not remember his very words: and she supposed [that] Thomas Wells and his wife living both at Boston can give more full testi[mony] concerning this thing. Taken on oath May 18, [1680]. Before me, John Woodbridge Commissioner. Read in court, May 20, 1680. Edward Rawson Secretary.

Elizabeth Titcomb on requesting Elizabeth Morse to help a pregnant woman

Elizabeth Titcomb saith that as to that part of this testimony relating to the sending for Elizabeth Morse she was present and was one of those [who] second[ed] sending for and saw Goody Morse when she [came there] and see a present speedy delivery of the woman. Sworn to in court May 20, 1680 by Elizabeth Titcomb. Edward Rawson Secretary.

John March on strange events and a conversation of Goody Morse

The testimony of John March aged 22 year testifieth that about 6 years since I lived with John Wells he working then at Boston and I with him there he sent me home to Newbury about some business and when I came home the wife of John Wells told me that she did not question but that as I should see something in the chamber at night and at night I went to bed and Daniel Greenleaf with me and after we had been at bed a little while we heard a great noise in the chamber[.] I looked up and saw several cats and rats at play together in the chamber running one after another the rats after the cats and I was very much amazed at it and a little while after I flung several things at them but could not strike them[.] The next morning before we came out of the chamber I heard Goody Morse and my dame Wells a talking together without the door several words they had which was very loud and I heard my dame Wells call Goody Morse witch and several such words which I could not tell the meaning of, before I came down, and [when] I came down my dame Wells came in again[.] She asked me if I saw such things as are before expressed[.] I asked her why she asked me she told me that Goody Morse told her that I had seen cats and rats that night[.] Then Goody Wells told me that she asked her how she knew it she told her that she heard so, though neither I nor Daniel Greenleaf who only knew it, had not been out of the chamber to tell anybody of it, nor seen anybody but only overheard them talking.

The said Goodwife Wells has professed before me several times, that often going to Goodwife Morse her house to fetch water, she hath seen some small creatures, like mice or rats run, into the house after her, and run under her coats. Taken on oath May 12, 1680.

This last Daniel Thurston, and Richard Woolworth have heard the said Goodwife Wells affirm, as they testify. Sworn in court May 20, 1680 per John March. Edward Rawson Secretary.

[The testimony of John March] He heard John Wells his wife say she saw imps go into said Morse's house. She being prosecuted would not own it, and was judged to pay damages, and now this is brought in.

James Brown on Goody Morse's reputation as a witch, and her response

The deposition of James Brown aged about 32 years testifieth that about 15 years ago I going from my father's to Mr. Woodman's of an errand met with Goody Morse and George Wheeler was under sail[.] Goody Morse asked me what vessel it was I said George Wheeler's she replied he goes out bravely but words to this effect that he should not return for a trick she knew: [he] further testifieth that I was one night at Salisbury and the next day was at Goody Morse's she told me of several misdemeanors among the rest of what I did the night before and I asked her how she could tell of [them?] She said everybody said it was true, I replied to her everybody says you are a witch, she said to me again our Savior Christ was belied and so is you and I: John March testifieth that he heard Goody Morse own before Mr. Woodbridge that she met with James Brown when George Wheeler was gone out: Jonathan Haynes testifieth that he heard Goody Morse own that she did reproach James Brown for his misdemeanors. The addition of James Brown and Jonathan Haynes with former oaths was by them sworn in court May 20, 1680. Edward Rawson Secretary.

David Wheeler on Elizabeth Morse's strange doings

The testimony of David Wheeler of Newbury aged fifty-five years or thereabouts testifieth and saith that having lived next neighbor to

Elizabeth Morse the wife of William Morse of Newbury aforesaid he took notice of many strange actions of her the said Elizabeth Morse more than ever he saw in any other woman, part whereof I have given in my evidence under oath before Mr. Woodbridge concerning a heifer whereunto I would farther add that all the rest of the breed of cattle have generally miscarried by strange accidents ever since till this present time which is the space of fifteen years or thereabouts, as also that the said Elizabeth Morse desired me one time to do a small piece of work for her which I neglected to do so soon as she desired, and I going many days on fowling at that time always as to the generality came home with lost labor which my neighbor Moody took notice of as well as myself, and he told me I would get no geese until I had finished her work which accordingly I speedily did and afterwards I had success as I used to have formerly, moreover several other accidents have befallen me which I believe that she the said Morse through the malice and envy of her heart against me might be the author of by witchcraft and farther saith not.

This addition to his former oath sworn to in court May 21, 1680. Edward Rawson Secretary.

Margaret Mirick on Goody Morse's knowledge of hidden events

The deposition of Margaret Mirick aged about 56. This deponent testifieth that about a letter that came from Piscataqua by Mr. Thomas Wiggins, we got Mr. Wiggins to read the letter and he went his way, and I promised to conceal the letter after it was read to my husband and myself and we both did conceal it, nevertheless in [a] few days after Goody Morse met me and clapped me on the back and said I commend you for sending such an answer to the letter: I presently asked her what letter why said she hadst not thee such a letter from such a man at such a time and sent such and such an answer at such a time and I came home presently and examined my husband about it[.] My husband said presently what is she a witch or a cunning woman; whereupon we examined our family and they said they knew nothing of the letter: afterwards I met with Goody Morse and asked her how she came to know it and desired her to tell me any one person that told her and I should be satisfied she asked me why I was so inquisitive and told me she could not tell. My husband testifieth that I presently told him the same. Sworn to in court May 21, 1680. Edward Rawson Secretary.

Source: "Trials for Witchcraft in New England," HLH. Printed in Samuel G. Drake, *Annals of Witchcraft in New England* (1869; repr. New York, 1972), pp. 258–96.

Zachariah Davis describes the strange behavior of a calf

When I lived at Salisbury William Morse's wife asked of me whether I could let her have a small parcel of wings and I told her I would [and?] so she would have me to bring them over for her the next time I came over, but I came over and did not think of the wings but met Goody Morse, she asked me where I had brought [them] and I told her no I did not think of it so I came 3 and 4 times and had them in my mind a little before I came over but still forgot them at my coming away[.] So meeting with her every time that I came over without them after that I had promised her the wings so she told me she wonder[ed] at it that my memory should be so bad but when I came home I went to the barn and there was 3 calves in a pen. One of them fell a dancing and roaring and was in such a condition as I never see one calf in before but being almost night the cattle came home and we put him to his dam and he sucked and was well 3 and 4 days and one of them was my brother's then come over to Newbury but we did not think to send the wings but when he came home and went to the barn this calf fell a dancing and roaring again so we put him to the cow but he would not suck but ran aroaring away so we catch[ed] him again with much ado and put him into the barn and we heard him roar several times in the night and in the morning I went to the barn and there he was sitting upon his tail like a dog, and I never see no calf sit after that manner before and so he remained in these fits while he died. Taken on oath, January 7, 1679.

Source: MA *135*:14. Printed in Coffin, *Sketch*, pp. 129–30.

A question of evidence is resolved

Question whether several distinct single testimonies of preternatural and diabolical actions by the prisoner at the bar, though not any two concurring to prove the same individual act is to be accounted legal evidence to convict of witchcraft[?] This is resolved on the affirmative by the court as attests Edward Rawson Secretary May 22, 1680.

Source: "Trials for Witchcraft in New England," HLH.

The indictment, trial, and reprieve of Elizabeth Morse

At a Court of Assistants on adjournment held at Boston May 20, 1680:
   The grand jury presenting Elizabeth Morse the wife of William Morse, she was indicted by the name of Elizabeth Morse for that she

not having the fear of God before her eyes being instigated by the devil and having familiarity with the devil contrary to the peace of our sovereign lord the King his crown and dignity the laws of God and of this jurisdiction: after the prisoner was at the bar and pleaded not guilty and put herself on God and the country for trial the evidences produced were read and committed to the jury;

The jury brought in their verdict and they found Elizabeth Morse the prisoner at the bar guilty according to indictment. The Governor on 27th May after the lecture pronounced the sentence[:] Elizabeth Morse you are go from hence to the place from whence you came to the place of execution and there to be hanged by the neck till you be dead: And the Lord have mercy on your soul.

The court was adjourned diem per diem: and on 1 June 1680 the Governor and magistrates voted the reprieving of Elizabeth Morse, condemned[,] till the next session of the court in October.

Attest Edward Rawson Secretary

Source: MA *135*:18(1).

William Morse asks for better living conditions for his jailed wife

To the honorable Governor and Council now sitting in Boston June 4, 1680 the petition of William Morse humbly showeth,

That whereas his dear wife was by the jury found guilty of witchcraft, and by the honorable court condemned to die: Yet since God hath been pleased to move your honors' hearts, to grant her a reprieve until October next, your petitioner humbly prays that your honors will be pleased to show her so much pity as to grant her liberty in the daytime to walk in the prison yard, and to the prison house, and that in the night she may have the privilege of a chamber in the common goal and be freed from the dungeon which is extreme close and hot in this season and also liberty on the Sabbath to go to meeting, he and his children giving security for her safe imprisonment. So shall he be ever obliged to pray as in duty bound. William Morse.

Source: "Trials for Witchcraft in New England," HLH.

The deputies protest the reprieve

The deputies on perusal of the acts of the honorable Court of Assistants as relating to the woman condemned for witchcraft, do not understand the reason why execution of the sentence given against her by said court is not executed, and that her second reprieval seems to us to be beyond what the law will allow, and do therefore judge meet to declare ourselves against it with reference to the concurrence of our honored magistrates hereto. William Torrey Clerk. November 3, 1680.

Not consented to by the magistrates. Edward Rawson Secretary.

Source: MA *135*:18(2). Printed in Currier, *History of Newbury*, p. 187.

Why the magistrates rejected the verdict of the jury

About 16 or 17 years since was accused a woman of Newbury, and upon her trial the jury brought her in guilty. Yet the Governor Simon Bradstreet Esq. and some of the magistrates reprieved her, being unsatisfied in the verdict upon these grounds.

1. They were not satisfied that a specter doing mischief in her likeness, should be imputed to her person, as a ground of guilt.

2. They did not esteem one single witness to one fact, and another single witness to another fact, for two witnesses, against the person in a matter capital. She being reprieved, was carried to her own home, and her husband (who was esteemed a sincere and understanding Christian by those that knew him) desired some neighbor ministers, of whom I was one, to meet together and discourse his wife; the which we did: and her discourse was very Christian among us, and still pleaded her innocence as to that which was laid to her charge. We did not esteem it prudence for us to pass any definitive sentence upon one under her circumstances, yet we inclined to the more charitable side.

In her last sickness she was in much darkness and trouble of spirit, which occasioned a judicious friend to examine her strictly, whether she had been guilty of witchcraft, but she said no: But the ground of her trouble was some impatient and passionate speeches and actions of hers while in prison, upon the account of her suffering wrongfully; whereby she had provoked the Lord, by putting some contempt upon his word. And in fine, she sought her pardon and comfort from God in Christ, and died so far as I understood, praying to and resting upon God in Christ for salvation.

Source: Hale, *A Modest Enquiry*, pp. 21–22.

William Morse on behalf of his wife pleads her innocence

To the honored Governor, Deputy Governor, magistrates and deputies now assembled in court May 18, 1681.

The most humble petition and request of William Morse in behalf of his wife (now a condemned prisoner) to this honored court is that they would be pleased so far to hearken to the cry of your poor prisoner who am a condemned person upon the charge of witchcraft and for a witch, to which charge your poor prisoner have pleaded not guilty, and am by the mercy of God and the goodness of the honored Governor, reprieved and brought to this honored court at the foot of which tribunal I now stand humbly praying your justice in hearing of my case and to determine therein as the Lord shall direct: I do not understand law nor do I know how to lay my case before you as I ought: for want of which [I] humbly beg of your honors that my request may not be rejected but may find acceptance with you it being no more but your sentence upon my trial whether I shall live or die, to which I shall humbly submit unto the Lord and you.

William Morse in the behalf of his wife: and his wife Elizabeth Morse prisoner[.]

The deputies judge meet to grant the petitioner a hearing the next 6th day, and that warrants go forth to all persons concerned from this court, then to appear in order to her further trial our honorable magistrates hereto consenting.

May 24, 1681 William Torrey clerk[.]

Not consented to by the magistrates Edward Rawson Secretary.

Source: MA *135*:19. Printed in Coffin, *Sketch*, p. 130.

William Morse criticizes the testimony against his wife

To the honored General Court now sitting in Boston.

The humble petition of William Morse in behalf of his wife Elizabeth Morse your distressed prisoner, humbly begging this that you would be pleased to give your petitioner leave to present to your consideration what may clear up the truth in those evidences which hath been presented and what is otherwise as[:]

First. To Joseph Bayley his testimony. We are ignorant of any such thing. Had it been then spoken of we might have cleared ourselves he might have observed some other as my wife, it being a frequent thing for cattle to be at a stand.

To Jonathan Haynes. As to his cattle or himself not making good work at such a time when cattle are haggled out to place it on such account that his neglect in not bringing us a bow of malt was the cause which had it been spoken of we might have given full satisfaction.

To Caleb Moody. As to what befell him in and about his not seeing my wife[,] that his cow making no haste to her calf, which we are ignorant of it being so long since and being in church communion with us should have spoken of it like a Christian and then proceeded so as we might have given an answer in less time than ten years; we were ignorant that he had a sheep so died[.] And his wife known to be a precious godly woman that hath often spoken to her husband not to be so uncharitable and have and do carry it like a Christian with a due respect in her carriage towards my wife all along.

To John Mighill. About the loss of his cattle was that he came one day to work, and would have had him come another day to finish it because the rain came in so upon us, and his not coming, judges my wife was angry and therefore had such loss, which we never knew of it, this being 12 years ago did amaze us now to hear of it.

To Zachariah Davis. To censure my wife now for not bringing quills about sixteen years ago that his loss of calves was for that when his father being in communion with us[1] did profess it to us that he judged it a hand of God and was far from blaming us but rather troubled his son should so judge.

To Joshua Richardson losing a sheep and his taking it forth off our yard my wife should say you might have asked leave, and whether overdriving it or what, now to bring it in I hope will be considered.

To John March['s] testimony. He heard John Wells his wife say she saw imp[s] go into said Morse's house. She being prosecuted would not own it and was adjudged to pay damages, and now this is brought in.

To James Brown['s] testimony. That one [day] George Wheeler going forth, my wife should say for a trifle she knew he should not come in again, which my wife knows not of it, nor doth some of the owners ever remember such a thing as to judge or charge it on her, but now is brought forth 16 years after when his wife said to Goody Hale that said Brown was mistaken her husband did come home well that voyage; and that James Brown should say to Robert Biddle that Powell, whom we sued did put in these words and not himself in the test[imony] and that said Brown did own to his uncle Mr. Nicholas Noyes that he could not swear to such a test[imony]; and did refuse to do it before Mr. John Woodbridge, and Mr. Woodbridge did admit to this he had sworn to it: and for his seeing my wife amongst troopers what condition he might be in we leave it to consideration we were ignorant of such a thing till now brought in so many years ago as he saith.

To Goodwife Ordway. Her child being long ill my wife coming in and look on it pitying of it did fear it would die and when it died Israel

Webster [our] next neighbor heard not a word of it at the time nor spoken of by others nor any of the family but her conceit and now brought in.

As for William Chandler's test[imony] about his wife's long sickness and my wife's visiting her, she through her weakness acted uncivilly and yet now to bring in against my wife when for so many years being in full communion with us never dealt with us about any such thing but had as loving converse with him as Christians ought and knew no otherwise till now.

To Widow Goodwin having her child sick gave forth that it was bewitched by my wife as she thought; we hearing of it dealt with her about it and she broke forth in tears craving forgiveness and said it was others that put her upon it to say as she did but now urged by Powell to say as she now saith.

To John Chase so saying that he saw my wife in the night coming in at a little hole and the like when he himself hath said he did not know but he was in a dream and that unto several persons he hath so said though now as he test[ifies] when my wife disowns any such thing.

To John Gladding that saw half of my wife about two a clock in the daytime if so might then have spoken and not reserved for so long a time which she utterly denies it nor knew of any such thing where she should be at that time as to clear herself.

To William Fanning should say my boy said the devil was at his house[.] Upon Fanning's saying to the boy the devil was at their house, and he would have me chide the boy which I told said Fanning the boy might be instructed to know the devil was everywhere though not as at our house and should not in time of affliction upbraid him, to our grief.

To Jonathan Woodman seeing a cat etc. he struck at it and it vanished away and I sending for Doctor Dole to see a bruise my wife had by the fall of a piece reaching down some bacon in our chimney which was many days before this time as Doctor Dole affirms it was no green wound though neglected to send for said Dole till then.

To Benjamin Lowell about my boy's catching a pigeon; my boy desired of me to see to catch a pigeon by throwing a stone, or the like, and he brought a pigeon, which I affirm was wounded, though alive.

To Goodwife Mirick about a letter. My wife telling her somewhat of the letter which she judges could not be and my wife hearing of it there was a discourse about this love letter, [she] might speak something about it by guess and not by any such way as she judged, and many have spoken, guessing at things which might be.

As to our troubles in the house it hath been dreadful and afflictive and to say it ceased upon her departure when it ceased before for a time and after she was gone there was trouble again.

As to rumors of some great wickedness committed in the house, which should cause the devil so to trouble us our conscience is clear of the knowledge of any such thing more than our common frailties and I reverence the holy sovereignty of God in laying such affliction on us and so that God's servants may be so afflicted in this manner as hath been known. And that Mr. Wilson of Ipswich, where she hath been twenty-eight weeks, did declare to me that my wife's conversation was christian-like as far as he observed. Thus praying for you in this and all other your concerns, am your distressed servant, William Morse. Newbury, May 14, 1681.

1. Member of the same congregation. Throughout this petition Morse was invoking the ethic of brotherly watchfulness among members of the gathered (congregational) church.

Source: MA *135*:19. Printed in Coffin, *Sketch,* pp. 127–28.

16. The Strange Death
of Philip Smith
(1683–1684)

▲

Mary Webster and Philip Smith

Mary (Reeve) Webster lived in the Hampshire County town of Hadley, Massachusetts. She married fifty-three-year-old William Webster in 1670; according to a nineteenth-century antiquarian, the two "became poor" and had to depend on the town for aid.[1] Mary was examined on suspicion of witchcraft by the county magistrates in Northampton on March 27, 1683. The case was referred to the Court of Assistants, which acquitted her. Thomas Hutchinson reported an episode (it is reproduced below) of village brutality that occurred in or about 1684. It is on the authority of Hutchinson's account that I include Cotton Mather's description, taken from Memorable Providences, Relating to Witchcrafts and Possessions *(Boston, 1689), of the fatal illness of Philip Smith. Mather tells a story of presumed bewitchment that is filled with bits of witch lore, from the strange smell in the air to the presumed animal familiar. Philip Smith died in 1685; Mary Webster died in 1696.[2]*

1. Sylvester Judd, *History of Hadley* (1863), p. 236.
2. Samuel G. Drake indicates that Philip Smith had testified against Mrs. Webster in 1683: *Annals of Witchcraft in New England* (1869; repr. New York, 1972), p. 175.

Mary Webster's case is referred to the Court of Assistants

Mary Webster of Hadley, being under strong suspicion of having familiarity with the devil, or using witchcraft, and having been in examination, and many testimonies brought in against her, or that did seem to center upon her, relating to such a thing; and the worshipful Mr. Tilton binding her to appear at this court, and having examined her yet further, and the testimonies aforenamed, look upon her case a matter belonging to the Court of Assistants to judge of, and have therefore ordered said Mary to be, by the first convenient opportunity, sent to Boston Goal, and committed there as a prisoner, to be further examined there, and the clerk is to gather up all the evidences and fit them to be sent down by the worshipful Mr. Tilton to our honored Governor.

Source: Drake, *Annals of Witchcraft*, pp. 169–70.

Mary Webster is indicted

Court of Assistants in Boston, May 22, 1683.
At this court Mary Webster wife to William Webster of Hadley being sent down upon suspicion of witchcraft and committed to prison in order to her trial was brought to the bar the grand jury being impanneled the grand jury on perusal of the evidences returned that as the grand jury for our sovereign lord the King they did indict Mary Webster wife to William Webster of Hadley for that she not having the fear of God before her eyes and being instigated by the devil hath entered into covenant and had familiarity with him in the shape of a warraneage[1] and had her imps sucking her and teats or marks found in her secret parts as in and by several testimonies may appear contrary to the peace of our sovereign lord the King his crown and dignity the laws of God and of this jurisdiction on their serious consideration of the testimonies did leave her to further trial.

1. An Indian word for black cat: Drake, *Annals of Witchcraft*, p. 170.
Source: *Recs. Ct. Assistants*, 2, pp. 229–30.

The court acquits Mary Webster

Court of Assistants June 1, 1683.
Mary Webster wife to William Webster of Hadley having been presented for suspicion of witchcraft by a grand jury in Boston 22nd of May last and left to further trial was now called and brought to the bar and was indicted by the name of Mary Webster wife to William Webster for that she not having the fear of God before her eyes and being instigated by the devil had entered into covenant and had familiarity with him in the shape of a warraneage and had her imps sucking her

and teats or marks found in her secret parts[. . . .] After the indictment and evidences in the case were read committed to the jury and are on file the jury brought in their verdict they found her not guilty.

Source: *Recs. Ct. Assistants, 2*, p. 233.

Cotton Mather describes Philip Smith's suspicious death

Sect. I. Mr. Philip Smith, aged about fifty years, a son of eminently virtuous parents, a deacon of the church at Hadley, a member of our General Court, an Associate in their county court, a selectman for the affairs of the town, a lieutenant in the troop, and, which crowns all, a man for devotion and gravity, and all that was honest, exceeding exemplary; such a man in the winter of the year, 1684, was murdered with a hideous witchcraft, which filled all those parts with a just astonishment. This was the manner of the murder.

Sect. II. He was concerned about relieving the indigencies of a wretched woman in the town; who being dissatisfied at some of his just cares about her, expressed herself unto him in such a manner, that he declared himself apprehensive of receiving mischief at her hands; he said, he doubted she would attempt his hurt.

Sect. III. About the beginning of January he began to be very valetudinarious, laboring under those that seemed Ischiadick pains. As his illness increased on him, so his goodness increased in him; the standers-by could in him see one ripening apace for another world; and one filled not only with grace to a high degree, but also with exceeding joy. Such weanedness from, and weariness of the world, he showed, that he knew not (he said) whether he might pray for his continuance here. Such assurance had he of the divine love unto him, that in raptures he would cry out, *Lord, stay thy hand, it is enough, it is more than thy frail servant can bear!* But in the midst of these things, he uttered still a hard suspicion, that the ill woman who had threatened him, had made impressions on him.

Sect. IV. While he remained yet of a sound mind, he very sedately, but very solemnly charged his brother to look well after him. Though he said he now understood himself, yet he knew not how he might be; *but be sure* (said he) *to have a care of me for you shall see strange things, there shall be a wonder in* Hadley! *I shall not be dead when it is thought I am!* This charge he pressed over and over; and afterwards became delirious.

Sect. V. Being become delirious, he had a speech incessant and voluble beyond all imagination, and this in divers tones and sundry voices, and (as was thought) in various languages.

Sect. VI. He cried out not only of sore pain, but also of sharp pins, pricking of him: sometimes in his toe, sometimes in his arm, as if there had been hundreds of them. But the people upon search never found any more than one.

Sect. VII. In his distresses he exclaimed very much upon the woman aforementioned, naming her, and some others, and saying, *Do you not see them; There, There, There they stand.*

Sect. VIII. There was a strong smell of something like musk, which was divers times in the room where he was, and in the other rooms, and without the house; of which no cause could be rendered. The sick man as well as others, complained of it; and once particularly, it so seized an apple roasting at the fire, that they were forced to throw it away.

Sect. IX. Some that were about him, being almost at their wits' end, by beholding the greatness and the strangeness of his calamities, did three or four times in one night, go and give disturbance to the woman that we have spoken of: all the while they were doing of it, the good man was at ease, and slept as a weary man; and these were all the times they perceived him to take any sleep at all.

Sect. X. A small gallery pot of alkermes, that was near full, and carefully looked after, yet unto the surprise of the people, was quite emptied, so that the sick man could not have the benefit of it.

Sect. XI. Several persons that sat by him, heard a scratching, that seemed to be on the ticking near his feet, while his feet lay wholly still; nay, were held in the hands of others, and his hands were far off another way.

Sect. XII. Sometimes fire was seen on the bed, or the covering, and when the beholders began to discourse of it, it would vanish away.

Sect. XIII. Diverse people felt something often stir in the bed, at some distance from his body. To appearance, the thing that stirred was as big as a cat: some tried to lay hold on it with their hands, but under the covering nothing could be found. A discreet and sober woman, resting in the beds feet, felt as [if] it were a hand, the thumb and the finger of it, taking her by the side, and giving her a pinch; but turning to see what it might be, nothing was to be seen. [. . .]

Sect. XVII. The night after he died, a very credible person, watching of the corpse, perceived the bed to move and stir, more than once; but by no means could find out the cause of it.

Sect. XVIII. The second night, some that were preparing for the funeral, do say, that they heard diverse noises in the room, where the corpse lay; as though there had been a great removing and clattering of stools and chairs.

Upon the whole, it appeared unquestionable that witchcraft had brought a period unto the life of so good a man.

Source: Cotton Mather, *Memorable Providences*, pp. 54–59. The omitted sections concern strange signs of life in the body after Smith had presumably died.

Thomas Hutchinson on the hazing of Mary Webster

[. . .] in 1684, Philip Smith, a judge of the court, a military officer and a representative of the town of Hadley, upon the same river (an hypocondriac person), fancied himself under an evil hand, and suspected a woman, one of his neighbors, and languished and pined away, and was generally supposed to be bewitched to death. While he lay ill, a number of brisk lads tried an experiment upon the old woman. Having dragged her out of her house, they hung her up until she was near dead, let her down, rolled her sometime in the snow, and at last buried her in it and there left her, but it happened that she survived and the melancholy man died.

Source: Thomas Hutchinson, *History of the Colony and Province of Massachusetts Bay*, ed. Lawrence Shaw Mayo (1936), 2, p. 14.

17. The "Possession" of the Goodwin Children (1688)

▲

Mary Glover (EXECUTED)

In 1688 four of the children of John Goodwin, a mason who lived in Boston, began to display the symptoms of what was later judged to be diabolical "possession." The Goodwins were members of the Charlestown church. The minister of that church, Charles Morton, joined the young minister of Boston Second Church, Cotton Mather, and several others in praying for the children: Martha, aged thirteen; John, eleven; Mercy, seven; and Benjamin, five. Some time prior to these outbreaks of "possession," Martha had accused the woman who did the family's laundry of stealing linens from them. Mary Glover, the mother of the laundress and herself a washerwoman, did not take kindly to these accusations and "gave the girl harsh language." Mother and daughter were arrested and the mother was put on trial for witchcraft. She confessed to practicing image magic (a search of her house supposedly turned up several poppets) and to being in league with the devil. The evidence against her included testimony that, six years before the Goodwin children became ill, she had bewitched a woman to death. Mrs. Glover was Irish and probably a Catholic (though not a practicing one in Puritan Boston); her native language was "Irish" (Gaelic). She was executed by hanging on November 16, 1688. The fits of the children continued, and Cotton Mather took Martha into his home in order to observe her more closely and pursue a spiritual healing. He described the children's behavior in Memorable Providences, Relating to Witchcrafts and

Possessions *(1689). Martha told him that three other women in Bos-ton were witches, and Mrs. Glover may also have named several confederates. But Mather kept these names to himself.*

The Goodwin children were notably rebellious against the values of the adult religious culture, in a manner that resembles Elizabeth Knapp's reactions. Their father, John Goodwin, regarded the chil-dren's illness as an "affliction" on himself for not being adequately pious.[1] *His statement, which Mather included in* Memorable Provi-dences *under the heading* Mantissa, *is charged with the tension be-tween two understandings of witchcraft. Some of Goodwin's neigh-bors urged him to pursue the methods of countermagic instead of relying on prayer and fasting, as Cotton Mather advised.*[2]

1. The structure of his piety and its relation to conceptions of the devil are discussed in Anne Kibbey, "Mutations of the Supernatural: Witchcraft, Re-markable Providences, and the Power of Puritan Men," *American Quarterly 34* (1982), pp. 125–48.
2. This tension is explored in Richard Godbeer's forthcoming study of magic and religion in early New England.

Joshua Moody reports on the Goodwins to Increase Mather[1]

We have a very strange thing among us which we know not what to make of except it be witchcraft, as we think it must needs be[.] 3 or 4 children of one Goodwin a mason that have been for some weeks grievously tormented, crying out of head, eyes, tongue, teeth breaking their neck, back, thighs, knees, legs, feet, toes etc. and then they roar out, Oh my head, oh my neck and from one part to another the pain runs almost as fast as I write it. The pain is (doubtless) very exquisite, and the cries most dolorous and affecting, and this is notable that two or more of them cry out of the same pain in the same part, at the same time, and as the pain shifts to another place in one, so in the other, and thus it holds them for an hour together and more, and when the pain is over they eat, drink, walk play, laugh as at other times, they are generally well a night. A great many good Christians spent a day of prayer there, Mr. Morton came over, and we each spent an hour in prayer since which the parents suspecting an old woman and her daughter living hard by, complaint was made to the justices, and com-passion had so far that the women were committed to prison, and are there now. Yesterday I called in at the house and was informed by the parent that since the women were confined the children have been well while out of the house, but as soon as any of them come into the house then taken as formerly, so that now all their children keep at their neighbors' houses, if any step home they are immediately afflicted, and while they keep out are well. I have been a little larger in this narrative because I know you have studied these things. We cannot but think the devil has a hand in it by some instrument. It is an example in all the parts of it not to be paralleled. You may inquire further of Mr. Oakes whose uncle administered physic to them at first, and he may probably inform you more fully. There are also sundry in the country that remain distracted since the measles last spring. Some have lately made away with themselves, one Redcoat and another man. I remember Dr. Owen on Luke 13:5 etc.[2] they are solemn warnings and presages. Boston, 4 (8) 1688.

1. Increase Mather was in England at the time.
2. John Owen, noted Puritan minister in England; the reference is to one of his commentaries on Scripture.
Source: Joshua Moody to Increase Mather, October 4, 1688, Mather Papers, Prince Collection, BPL. Printed in *Coll. MHS*, 4th ser., *8* (1868), pp. 367–70.

The Goodwin children as "possessed"

Section I. There dwells at this time, in the south part of Boston, a sober and pious man, whose name is John Goodwin, whose trade is that of a mason, and whose wife (to which a good report gives a share with him in all the characters of virtue) has made him the father of six (now living) children. Of these children, all but the eldest, who works with his father at his calling, and the youngest, who lives yet upon the breast of its mother, have labored under the direful effects of a (no less palpable than) stupendous witchcraft. Indeed that exempted son had also, as was thought, some lighter touches of it, in unaccountable stabs and pains now and then upon him; as indeed every person in the family at some time or other had, except the godly father, and the sucking infant, who never felt any impressions of it. But these four children mentioned, were handled in so sad and strange a manner, as has given matter of discourse and wonder to all the country, and of history not unworthy to be considered by more than all the serious or the curious readers in this new English world.

Section II. The four children (whereof the eldest was about thirteen, and the youngest was perhaps about a third part so many years of age) had enjoyed a religious education, and answered it with a very towardly ingenuity. They had an observable affection unto divine and sacred things; and those of them that were capable of it, seemed to have such a resentment of their eternal concernments as is not altogether usual. Their parents also kept them to a continual employment, which did more than deliver them from the temptations of idleness, and as young as they were, they took a delight in it, it may be as much as they should have done. In a word, such was the whole temper and carriage of the children, that there cannot easily be any thing more unreasonable, than to imagine that a design to dissemble could cause them to fall into any of their odd fits; though there should not have happened, as there did, a thousand things, wherein it was perfectly impossible for any dissimulation of theirs to produce what scores of spectators were amazed at.

Section III. About midsummer, in the year 1688, the eldest of these children, who is a daughter, saw cause to examine their washerwoman, upon their missing of some linen, which 'twas feared she had stolen from them; and of what use this linen might be to serve the witchcraft intended, the thief's tempter knows! This laundress was the daughter of an ignorant and a scandalous old woman in the neighborhood; whose miserable husband before he died, had sometimes complained of her, that she was undoubtedly a witch, and that whenever his head was laid, she would quickly arrive unto the punishments due to such a one. This woman in her daughter's defense bestowed very bad language upon the girl that put her to the question; immediately upon which, the poor child became variously indisposed in her health, and visited with strange fits, beyond those that attend an epilepsy, or a catalepsy, or those that they call the diseases of astonishment.

Section IV. It was not long before one of her sisters, and two of her brothers, were seized, in order one after another, with affects like those that molested her. Within a few weeks, they were all four tortured everywhere in a manner so very grievous, that it would have broke a heart of stone to have seen their agonies. Skillful physicians were consulted for their help, and particularly our worthy and prudent friend Dr. Thomas Oakes, who found himself so affronted by the distempers of the children, that he concluded nothing but a hellish witchcraft could be the original of these maladies. And that which yet more confirmed such apprehension was, that for one good while, the children were tormented just in the same part of their bodies all at the same time together; and though they saw and heard not one another's complaints, though likewise their pains and sprains were swift like lightning, yet when (suppose) the neck, or the hand, or the back of one was racked, so it was at that instant with t'other too.

Section V. The variety of their tortures increased continually; and though about nine or ten at night they always had a release from their miseries, and ate and slept all night for the most part indifferently well, yet in the daytime they were handled with so many sorts of ails, that it would require of us almost as much time to relate them all, as it did of them to endure them. Sometimes they would be deaf, sometimes dumb, and sometimes blind, and often, all this at once. One while their tongues would be drawn down their throats; another while they would be pulled out upon their chins, to a prodigious length. They would have their mouths opened unto such a wideness, that their jaws went out of joint; and anon they would clap together again with a force like that of a strong spring lock. The same would happen to their shoulder blades, and their elbows, and handwrists, and several of their joints. They would at times lie in a benumbed condition; and be drawn together as those that are tied neck and heels; and presently be stretched out, yea, drawn backwards, to such a degree that it was feared the very skin of their bellies would have cracked. They would make most piteous outcries, that they were cut with knives, and struck with blows that they could not bear. Their necks would be broken, so that their neck bone would seem dissolved unto them that felt after it; and yet on the sudden, it would become again so stiff that there was no stirring of their heads; yea, their heads would be twisted almost round; and if main force at any time obstructed a dangerous motion which they seemed to be upon, they would roar exceedingly. Thus they lay some weeks most pitiful spectacles; and this while as a further demonstration of witchcraft in these horrid effects, when I went to prayer by one of them, that was very desirous to hear what I said, the child utterly lost her hearing till our prayer was over.

Section VI. It was a religious family that these afflictions happened unto; and none but a religious contrivance to obtain relief, would have been welcome to them. Many superstitious proposals were made unto them, by persons that were I know not who, nor what, with arguments fetched from I know not how much necessity and experience; but the distressed parents rejected all such counsels, with a gracious resolution, to oppose devils with no other weapons but prayers and tears, unto him that has the chaining of them; and to try first whether graces were not the best things to encounter witchcrafts with. Accordingly they requested the four ministers of Boston, with the minister of Charlestown to keep a day of prayer at their thus haunted house; which they did in the company of some devout people there. Immediately upon this day, the youngest of the four children was delivered, and never felt any trouble as afore. But there was yet a greater effect of these our applications unto our God!

Section VII. The report of the calamities of the family for which we were thus concerned, arrived now unto the ears of the magistrates, who presently and prudently applied themselves, with a just vigor, to inquire into the story. The father of the children complained of his neighbor, the suspected ill woman, whose name was Glover; and she being sent for by the justices, gave such a wretched account of herself, that they saw cause to commit her unto the jailer's custody. Goodwin had no proof that could have done her any hurt; but the hag had not power to deny her interest in the enchantment of the children; and when she was asked, whether she believed there was a God? her answer was too blasphemous and horrible for any pen of mine to mention. An experiment was made, whether she could recite the Lord's Prayer; and it was found, that though clause after clause was most carefully repeated unto her, yet when she said it after them that prompted her, she could not possibly avoid making nonsense of it, with some ridiculous depravations. This experiment I had the curiosity since to see made upon two more, and it had the same event. Upon the commitment of this extraordinary woman, all the children had some present ease; until one (related unto her) accidentally meeting one or two of them, entertained them with her blessing, that is, railing, upon which three of them fell ill again, as they were before.

Section VIII. It was not long before the witch thus in the trap, was brought upon her trial; at which, through the efficacy of a charm, I suppose, used upon her, by one or some of her crew, the court could receive answers from her in none but the Irish, which was her native language; although she understood the English very well, and had accustomed her whole family to none but that language in her former conversation; and therefore the communication between the bench and the bar, was now chiefly conveyed by two honest and faithful men that were interpreters. It was long before she could with any direct answers plead unto her indictment; and when she did plead, it was with confession rather than denial of her guilt. Order was given to search the old woman's house, from whence there were brought into the court, several small images, or puppets, or babies, made of rags, and stuffed with goat's hair, and other such ingredients. When these were produced, the vile woman acknowledged, that her way to torment the objects of her malice, was by wetting of her finger with her spittle, and stroking of those little images. The abused children were then present, and the woman still kept stooping and shrinking as one that was almost pressed to death with a mighty weight upon her. But one of the images being brought unto her, immediately she started up after an odd manner, and took it into her hand; but she had no sooner taken it, than one of the children fell into sad fits, before the whole assembly. This the judges had their just apprehensions at; and carefully causing the repetition of the experiment, found again the same event of it. They asked her, whether she had any to stand by her: She replied, she had; and looking very pertly in the air, she added, No, he's gone. And she then confessed, that she had one, who was her prince, with whom she maintained, I know not what communion. For which cause, the night after, she was heard expostulating with a devil, for his thus deserting her; telling him that because he had served her so basely and falsely, she had confessed all. However to make all clear, the court appointed five or six physicians, one evening to examine her very strictly, whether she were not crazed in her intellectuals, and had not procured to herself by folly and madness the reputation of a witch. Diverse hours did they spend with her; and in all that while no discourse came from her, but what was pertinent and agreeable: particularly, when they asked her, what she thought would become of her soul? she replied, You ask me a very solemn question, and I cannot well tell what to say to it. She owned herself a Roman Catholic; and could recite her Pater Noster in Latin very readily; but there was one clause or two always too hard for her, whereof she said, She could not repeat it, if she might have all the world. In the upshot, the doctors returned her compos mentis; and sentence of death was passed upon her.

Section IX. Diverse days were passed between her being arraigned and condemned. In this time one of her neighbors had been giving in her testimony of what another of her neighbors had upon her death related concerning her. It seems one Howen about six years before, had been cruelly bewitched to death; but before she died, she called one Hughes unto her, telling her that she laid her death to the charge of Glover; that she had seen Glover sometimes come down her chimney; that she should remember this, for within this six years she might have occasion to declare it. This Hughes now preparing her testimony, immediately one of her children, a fine boy, well grown towards youth, was taken ill, just in the same woeful and surprising manner that Goodwin's children were. One night particularly, the boy said he saw a black thing with a blue cap in the room, tormenting of him; and he complained most bitterly of a hand put into the bed, to pull out his bowels. The next day the mother of the boy went unto Glover, in the prison, and asked her why, she tortured her poor lad at such a wicked rate. This witch replied that she did it because of wrong done to herself and her daughter. Hughes denied (as well as she might) that she had done her any wrong. Well then, says Glover, let me see your child and he shall be well again. Glover went on, and told her of her own accord, I was at your house last night. Says Hughes, In what shape? Says Glover, As a black thing with a blue cap. Says Hughes, What did you do there? says Glover, With my hand in the bed I tried to pull out the boy's bowels, but I could not. They parted; but the next day Hughes appearing at court, had her boy with her; and Glover passing by the boy, expressed her good wishes for him; though I suppose, his parent had no design of any mighty respect unto the hag, by having him with her there. But the boy had no more indispositions after the condemnation of the woman.

Section X. While the miserable old woman was under condemnation, I did myself twice give a visit unto her. She never denied the guilt of the witchcraft charged upon her; but she confessed very little about the circumstances of her confederacies with the devils; only, she said, that she used to be at meetings, which her prince and four more were present at. As for those four, she told who they were; and for her prince, her account plainly was, that he was the devil. She entertained me with nothing but Irish, which language I had not learning enough to understand without an interpreter; only one time, when I was representing unto her that and how her prince had cheated her, as herself would quickly find; she replied, I think in English, and with passion too, If it be so, I am sorry for that! I offered many questions unto her, unto which, after long silence, she told me, she would fain give me a full answer, but they would not give her leave. It was demanded, They! Who is that they? and she returned, that they were her spirits, or her saints (for they say, the same word in Irish signifies both). And at another time, she included her two mistresses, as she called them in that [they][1] but when it was inquired, who those two were, she fell into a rage, and would be no more urged.

I set before her, the necessity and equity of her breaking her covenant with hell, and giving herself to the Lord Jesus Christ, by an everlasting covenant: to which her answer was, that I spoke a very reasonable thing, but she could not do it. I asked her whether she would consent or desire to be prayed for; to that she said, if prayer would do her any good, she could pray for herself. And when it was again propounded, she said, she could not unless her spirits (or angels) would give her leave. However, against her will I prayed with her, which if it were a fault it was in excess of pity. When I had done, she thanked me with many good words; but I was no sooner out of her sight, than she took a stone, a long and slender stone, and with her finger and spittle fell to tormenting it; though whom or what she meant, I had the mercy never to understand.

Section XI. When this witch was going to her execution, she said, the children should not be relieved by her death, for others had a hand in it as well as she; and she named one among the rest, whom it might have been thought natural affection would have advised the conceal-ing of. It came to pass accordingly, that the three children continued in their furnace as before, and it grew rather seven times hotter than it was. All their former ails pursued them still, with an addition of ('tis not easy to tell how many) more, but such as gave more sensible dem-onstrations of an enchantment growing very far towards a possession by evil spirits.

Section XII. The children in the fits would still cry out upon, [they] and [them] as the authors of all their harm; but who that [they] and [them] were, they were not able to declare. At last, the boy obtained at some times, a sight of some shapes in the room. There were three of four of 'em, the names of which the child would pretend at certain seasons to tell; only the name of one, who was counted a sager hag than the rest, he still so stammered at, that he was put upon some periphrasis in describing her. A blow at the place where the boy be-held the specter was always felt by the boy himself in the part of his body that answered what might be stricken at; and this though his back were turned; which was once and again so exactly tried, that there could be no collusion in the business. But as a blow at the ap-parition always hurt him, so it always helped him too; for after the agonies, which a push or stab of that had put him to, were over (as in a minute or two they would be), the boy would have a respite from his fits a considerable while, and the hobgoblins disappear. It is very cred-ibly reported that a wound was this way given to an obnoxious woman in the town, whose name I will not expose: for we should be tender in such relations, lest we wrong the reputation of the innocent, by stories not enough inquired into.

Section XIII. The fits of the children yet more arrived unto such motions as were beyond the efficacy of any natural distemper in the world. They would bark at one another like dogs, and again purr like so many cats. They would sometimes complain, that they were in a red-hot oven, sweating and panting at the same time unreasonably: anon they would say, cold water was thrown upon them, at which they would shiver very much. They would cry out of dismal blows with great cudgels laid upon them; and though we saw no cudgels nor blow, yet we could see the marks left by them in red streaks upon their bodies afterward. And one of them would be roasted on an invisible spit, run into his mouth, and out at his foot, he lying, and rolling, and groaning as if it had been so in the most sensible manner in the world; and then he would shriek, that knives were cutting of him. Sometimes also he would have his head so forcibly, though not visibly, nailed unto the floor, that it was as much as a strong man could do to pull it up.

One while they would all be so limber, that it was judged every bone of them could be bent. Another while they would be so stiff, that not a joint of them could be stirred. They would sometimes be as though they were mad, and then they would climb over high fences, beyond the imagination of them that looked after them. Yea, they would fly like geese; and be carried with an incredible swiftness through the air, having but just their toes now and then upon the ground, and their arms waved like the wings of a bird. One of them, in the house of a kind neighbor and gentleman (Mr. Willis) flew the length of the room, about 20 foot, and flew just into an infant's high-armed chair; (as 'tis affirmed) none seeing her feet all the way touch the floor.

Section XIV. Many ways did the devils take to make the children do mischief both to themselves and others; but through the singular providence of God, they always failed in the attempts. For they could never essay the doing of any harm, unless there were somebody at hand that might prevent it; and seldom without first shrieking out, *They say, I must do such a thing!* Diverse times they went to strike furious blows at their tenderest and dearest friends, or to fling them down stairs when they had them at the top, but the warnings from the mouths of the children themselves, would still anticipate what the devils did intend. They diverse times were very near burning or drowning of themselves, but the children themselves by their own pitiful and seasonable cries for help, still procured their deliverance: which make me to consider, whether the little ones had not their angels, in the plain sense of our Savior's intimation. Sometimes, when they were tying their own neckclothes, their compelled hands miserably strangled themselves, till perhaps, the standers-by gave some relief unto them. But if any small mischief happened to be done where they were; as the tearing or dirtying of a garment; the falling of a cup, the breaking of a glass, or the like; they would rejoice extremely, and fall into a pleasure and laughter very extraordinary. All which things compared with the temper of the children, when they are themselves, may suggest some very peculiar thoughts unto us.

Section XV. They were not in a constant torture for some weeks, but were a little quiet, unless upon some incidental provocations; upon which the devils would handle them like tigers, and wound them in a manner very horrible. Particularly, upon the least reproof of their parents for any unfit thing they said or did, most grievous woeful, heartbreaking agonies would they fall into. If any useful thing were to be done to them, or by them, they would have all sorts of troubles fall upon them. It would sometimes cost one of them an hour or two to be undressed in the evening, or dressed in the morning. For if any one went to untie a string, or undo a button about them, or the contrary; they would be twisted into such postures as made the thing impossible. And at whiles, they would be so managed in their beds, that no bedclothes could for an hour or two be laid upon them; nor could they go to wash their hands, without having them clasped so oddly together, there was no doing of it. But when their friends were near tired with waiting, anon they might do what they would unto them. Whatever work they were bid to do, they would be so snapped in the member which was to do it, that they with grief still desisted from it. If one ordered them to rub a clean table, they were able to do it without any disturbance; if to rub a dirty table, presently they would with many torments be made incapable. And sometimes, though but seldom, they were kept from eating their meals, by having their teeth set when they carried any thing unto their mouths.

Section XVI. But nothing in the world would so discompose them as a religious exercise. If there were any discourse of God, or Christ, or any of the things which are not seen and are eternal, they would be cast into intolerable anguishes. Once, those two worthy ministers Mr. Fisk and Mr. Thatcher,[2] bestowing some gracious counsels on the boy, whom they then found at a neighbor's house, he immediately lost his hearing, so that he heard not one word, but just the last word of all they said. Much more, all praying to God, and reading of his word, would occasion a very terrible vexation to them: they would then stop their own ears with their own hands; and roar, and shriek; and holler, to drown the voice of the devotion. Yea, if anyone in the room took up a Bible to look into it, though the children could see nothing of it, as being in a crowd of spectators, or having their faces another way, yet would they be in wonderful miseries, till the Bible were laid aside. In short, no good thing must then be endured near those children, which (while they are themselves) do love every good thing in a measure that proclaims in them the fear of God.

1. Mather's brackets, a typographical device he repeated in section XII as a sign of his refusal to reveal the names of the persons mentioned by the children.
2. Moses Fisk and Thomas Thacher, two local ministers.
Source: Cotton Mather, *Memorable Providences*, pp. 1–18.

Mantissa

To the foregoing narrative, we have added an account given us, by the godly father of these haunted children; who upon his reading over so much of our history, as was written of their exercise before their full deliverance, was willing to express his attestation to the truth of it;

with this further declaration of the sense which he had of the unusual miseries, that then lay upon his family. 'Tis in his own style; but I suppose a pen hath not commonly been managed with more cleanly discourse by a hand used only to the trowel; and his condition hath been such, that he may fairly have leave to speak.

In the year 1688, about midsummer, it pleased the Lord to visit one of my children with a sore visitation; and she was not only tormented in her body, but was in great distress of mind, crying out, that she was in the dark concerning her soul's estate, and that she had misspent her precious time; she and we thinking her time was near at an end. Hearing those shrieks and groans which did not only pierce the ears, but hearts of her poor parents; now was a time for me to consider with myself, and to look into my own heart and life, and see how matters did there stand between God and my own soul, and see wherefore the Lord was thus contending with me. And upon inquiry I found cause to judge myself, and to justify the Lord. This affliction continuing some time, the Lord saw good then to double the affliction in smiting down another child, and that which was most heartbreaking of all, and did double this double affliction was, it was apparent and judged by all that saw them, that the devil and his instruments had a hand in it.

The consideration of this was most dreadful: I thought of what David said, 2 Samuel 24:14. If he feared so to fall into the hands of men, oh! then to think of the horror of our condition, to be in the hands of devils and witches! This our doleful condition moved us to call to our friends to have pity on us, for God's hand had touched us. I was ready to say, that no one's affliction was like mine; that my little house that should be a little Bethel for God to dwell in, should be made a den for devils; that those little bodies, that should be temples for the Holy Ghost to dwell in, should be thus harassed and abused by the devil and his cursed brood. But now this twice doubled affliction is doubled again. Two more of my children are smitten down, oh! the cries, the shrieks, the tortures of these poor children! Doctors cannot help, parents weep and lament over them, but cannot ease them. Now I considering my affliction to be more than ordinary, it did certainly call for more than ordinary prayer. I acquainted Mr. Allen, Mr. Moody, Mr. Willard, and Mr. C. Mather, the four ministers of the town with it, and Mr. Morton of Charlestown;[1] earnestly desiring them, that they, with some other praying people of God, would meet at my house, and there be earnest with God, on the behalf of us and our children; which they (I thank them for it) readily attended with great fervency of spirit; but as for my part, my heart was ready to sink to hear and see those doleful sights. Now I thought that I had greatly neglected my duty to my children, in not admonishing and instructing of them; and that God was hereby calling my sins to mind, to slay my children. Then I pondered of that place in Numbers 23:23: *Surely there is no enchantment against Jacob, neither is there any divination against Israel.* And now I thought I had broke covenant with God, not only in one respect but in many, but it pleased the Lord to bring that to mind in Hebrews 8:12: *For I will be merciful to their unrighteousness, and their sins and iniquities will I remember no more.* The consideration how the Lord did deal with Job, and his patience and the end the Lord made with him was some support to me. I thought also, on what David said, that he had sinned, but what have these poor lambs done? But yet in the midst of my tumultuous thoughts within me, it was God's comforts that did delight my soul. That in the 18 of Luke, and the beginning [ver. 1], where Christ spake the parable for that end, that *men ought always to pray and not faint.* This, with many other places, bore up my spirit. I thought with Jonah [Jonah 2:4] that I would yet again look towards God's holy temple; the Lord Jesus Christ. And I did greatly desire to find the Son of God with me in this furnace of affliction, knowing hereby that no harm shall befall me. But now this solemn day of prayer and fasting being at an end, there was an eminent answer of it: for one of my children was delivered, and one of the wicked instruments of the devil discovered, and her own mouth condemned her, and so accordingly executed. Here was food for faith, and great encouragement still to hope and quietly wait for the salvation of the Lord; the ministers still counselling and encouraging me to labor to be found in God's way, committing my case to him, and not to use any way not allowed in God's word. It was a thing not a little comfortable to us, to see that the people of God was so much concerned about our lamentable condition, remembering us at all times in their prayers, which I did look at as a token for good; but you must think it was a time of sore temptation with us, for many did say (yea, and some good people too), were it their case, that they would try some tricks, that should give ease to their children: But I thought for us to forsake the counsel of good old men, and to take the counsel of the young ones, it might ensnare our souls, though for the present it might offer some relief to our bodies;[2] which was a thing I greatly feared; and my children were not at any time free for doing any such thing. It was a time of sore affliction, but it was mixed with abundance of mercy, for my heart was many a time made glad in the house of prayer. The neighborhood pitied us, and were very helpful to us: Moreover, though my children were thus in every limb and joint tormented by those children of the devil, they also using their tongues at their pleasure, some-times one way, sometimes another; yet the Lord did herein prevent them, that they could not make them speak wicked words, though they did many times hinder them from speaking good ones; had they in these fits blasphemed the name of the Holy God, this you may think would have been a heart-breaking thing to us the poor parents; but God in his mercy prevented them, a thing worth taking notice of. Like-wise they slept well a nights: And the ministers did often visit us, and pray with us, and for us; and their love and pity was so great, their prayers so earnest and constant, that I could not but admire at it. Mr. Mather particularly; now his bowels so yearned towards us in this sad condition, that he not only prays with us, and for us, but he taketh one of my children home to his own house; which indeed was but a trou-blesome guest, for such a one that had so much work lying upon his hands and heart: he took much pains in this great service, to pull this child, and her brother and sister out of the hand of the devil.⁵ Let us now admire and adore that fountain the Lord Jesus Christ, from whence those streams come. The Lord himself will requite his labor of love. Our case is yet very sad, and doth call for more prayer; and the good ministers of this town, and Charlestown readily came, with some other good praying people to my house, to keep another day of solemn fasting and prayer; which our Lord saith this kind goeth out by. My children being all at home, the two biggest lying on the bed, one of them would fain have kicked the good men while they were wrestling with God for them, had not I held him with all my power and might; and sometimes he would stop his own ears. This you must needs think was a cutting thing to the poor parents. Now our hearts were ready to sink, had not God put [us] under his everlasting arms of mercy [Deuteronomy 33:27] and helped us still to hope in his mercy, and to be quiet, knowing that he is God, and that it was not for the potsherds of the earth to strive with their Maker. Well might David say [Psalms 1:2], that had not the law of his God been his delight, he had perished in his affliction. Now the promises of God are sweet; God having promised, to hear the prayer of the destitute, and not to despise their prayer; and he will not fail the expectation of those that wait on him; but he heareth the cry of the poor and needy. These Jacobs came and wrestled with God for a blessing on this poor family, which indeed I hope they obtained, and may be now worthy of the name Israel, who prevailed with God, and would not let him go till he had blessed us. For soon after this, there were two more of my children delivered out of this horrible pit. Here was now a double mercy, and how sweet was it, knowing it came in answer of prayer! Now we see and know, it is not a vain thing to call on the name of the Lord. For he is a present help in the time of trouble [Psalms 46:1]; and we may boldly say the Lord has been our helper. I had sunk, but Jesus put forth his hand and bore me up. My faith was ready to fail, but this was a support to me that Christ said to Peter [Luke 22:32], *I have prayed for thee that thy faith fail not.* And many other promises were as cordials to my drooping soul. And the consideration of all those that ever came to Christ Jesus for healing, that he healed their bodies, pardoned their sins, and healed their souls too; which I hope in God may be the fruit of this present affliction. If God be pleased to make the fruit of this affliction to be to take away our sin, and cleanse us from iniquity, and to put us on with greater diligence to make our calling and election sure, then, happy affliction! The Lord said that I had need of this to awake me. I have found a prosperous condition a dangerous condition. I have taken notice and considered more of God's goodness in these few weeks of affliction, than in many years of prosperity. I may speak it with shame, so wicked and deceitful, and ungrateful is my heart, that the more God hath been doing for me, the less I have been doing for him. My returns have not been according to my receivings. The Lord help me now to praise him in heart, lip, and life. The Lord help us to see by this visitation, what need we have to get shelter under the wing of Christ, to hast[e] to the rock, where we may be safe. We see how ready the devils are to catch us, and torment our bodies, and he is as diligent to ensnare our souls, and that many ways; but let us put on all our spiritual armor, and follow Christ the captain of our salvation; and though we meet with the cross, let us bear it patiently and cheerfully, for if Jesus Christ be at the one end, we need not fear the heft of it: if we have Christ we have enough; he can make his rod as well as his staff to be a comfort to us; and we shall not want if we be the sheep of Christ [Psalm 23]. If we want afflictions we shall have them, and sanctified afflictions are choice mercies.

Now I earnestly desire the prayer of all good people; that the Lord would be pleased to perfect that work he hath begun, and make it to appear that prayer is stronger than witchcraft.

December 12, 1688. John Goodwin

1. Thomas Allen, Joshua Moody, Samuel Willard, Cotton Mather, Charles Morton.
2. An intriguing comment that suggests Goodwin's confidence in countermagic.
3. In a section of *Memorable Providences* not included in this collection, Mather described the behavior of Mercy Goodwin after he took her into his home.
Source: Cotton Mather, *Memorable Providences*, pp. 45–53.

18. The Salem Witch-hunt
(1692)

▲

The most extensive witch-hunt in New England unfolded in Salem Village (now Danvers), a semi-independent jurisdiction of the town of Salem, Massachusetts. The witch-hunt passed through several phases; midway, its scope expanded far beyond the village where, during the winter of 1691–92, certain girls and young women began to experience the symptoms of diabolical "possession." Under the leadership of the minister Samuel Parris, and with assistance from other clergy, the villagers initially applied the spiritual remedies of penitential prayer and fasting that Samuel Willard had used in the case of Elizabeth Knapp, and Cotton Mather in that of the Goodwins. But as the symptoms intensified, onlookers began paying more attention to hints that certain people in the village were responsible. Three women were arrested at the end of February: Sarah Good, Sarah Osborne, and a West Indian slave named Tituba. More arrests and court examinations occurred in late March and early April. A former minister in the village, Deodat Lawson, described this phase in A Brief and True Narrative of Some Remarkable Passages Relating to Sundry Persons Afflicted by Witchcraft *(Boston, 1692). This text follows. On March 24, 1692, Lawson preached the lecture sermon at Salem Village. It was promptly published as* Christ's Fidelity the Only Shield against Satan's Malignity *(Boston, 1693).*

A special court of Oyer and Terminer convened in Salem Town on June 2 and condemned Bridget Bishop to be executed by hanging; she died on June 10. Five more (Sarah Good, Rebecca Nurse, Susannah Martin, Elizabeth How, and Sarah Wild) were tried and convicted on June 29 and executed on July 19. Early on, the evidence seemed to indicate that the devil and his agents had organized a major conspiracy complete with meetings in the woods, the black sacrament of the witches' sabbath, and signings of a covenant. A former minister of Salem Village, George Burroughs, was brought back from Maine and examined early in May. Cotton Mather deemed him the master conspirator. Burroughs and five others (Martha Carrier, George Jacobs, John and Elizabeth Procter, and John Willard) were tried and condemned to death in early August; with the exception of Elizabeth, who was pregnant, this group was executed on August 19. Now the witch-hunt included the extraordinary phenomenon of "confessing witches," persons who more or less of their own free will acknowledged covenanting with the devil.[1] In doing so they often implicated others, including members of their families. And by now, the witch-hunt had spread to adjacent towns, especially Andover, in a veritable explosion of accusations and confessions. In September, at two different sessions, the court condemned another fifteen. Some of these sentences were delayed, but eight were executed on the twenty-second: Samuel Wardwell, Martha Corey, Mary Easty, Alice Parker, Ann Pudeator, Mary Parker, Margaret Scott, Wilmot Reed.

As early as June the procedures of the court were beginning to trouble certain ministers and influential laymen. In October the governor of Massachusetts, Sir William Phips, ordered the trials temporarily suspended. Though the court reconvened in January 1693 and sentenced three more persons to death, no further executions occurred, and those still in prison or under sentence were soon released under a general pardon. Four years later Massachusetts observed a fast day to repent the taking of innocent lives.

Cotton Mather (1665–1729), co-minister of Second Church, Boston, with his father, Increase, included summaries of five of the trials in Wonders of the Invisible World *(Boston, 1692).[2] This book appeared as public opinion turned sharply against the judges and witnesses who led the witch-hunt. Mather's sharpest critic was a colonist named Robert Calef, who in 1700 published* More Wonders of the Invisible World; *Calef spoke frankly (and sceptically) about some of the inner workings of the witch-hunt. Historians continue to debate Mather's role in causing—or in bringing to a close—these tragic events. That debate lies outside the scope of this documentary history. The summaries Mather published in* Wonders *do, however, reveal most of the main characteristics of the Salem witch-hunt: the presumption of a grand conspiracy; the actings out of the "possessed" or afflicted witnesses; the assumption that apparitions and specters (what we might colloquially refer to as ghosts) were valid evidence; the vulnerability of "cunning" persons, or anyone who practiced healing and fortune-telling.*

It should not be surprising to find that here, as so often before, neighbors came forward to describe quarrels (old and recent) between themselves and the accused, or that several of the women who were executed in 1692 had been accused of witchcraft earlier in their lives. The complicated structure of interfamily feuds that fed the witch-hunt is described and analyzed in Charles W. Upham, Salem Witchcraft: With an Account of Salem Village *(1867), and Paul Boyer and Stephen Nissenbaum,* Salem Possessed: The Social Origins of Witchcraft *(Cambridge, 1974). But only at Salem did confessions spread so widely (more than fifty persons made them), and only at Salem was witch-hunting so animated by the idea of the devil as conspirator.*

Anyone interested in the full documentation should turn to Paul Boyer and Stephen Nissenbaum, eds., The Salem Witchcraft Papers: Verbatim Transcripts of the Legal Documents of the Salem Witchcraft Outbreak of 1692 *(New York, 1977). This collection does not include the statements (private and public) critical of the court proceedings.*

1. The meaning of "confession" in the religious culture of New England is described in David D. Hall, *Worlds of Wonder, Days of Judgment: Popular Religious Belief in Early New England* (New York, 1989), chapter 4. The pressures brought to bear on persons to confess are indicated in the documents Robert Calef included in *More Wonders of the Invisible World* (London, 1700), and in Boyer and Nissenbaum, eds., *Salem Witchcraft Papers, 3,* p. 777.
2. The circumstances under which Mather composed *Wonders of the Invisible World,* and the reaction to it, are admirably sketched in Thomas J. Holmes, *Cotton Mather: A Bibliography of His Works* (1940). Calef's *More Wonders of the Invisible World* is excerpted in George L. Burr, ed., *Narratives of the Witchcraft Cases 1648–1706* (New York, 1914).

A Brief and True Narrative

The Bookseller to the Reader.

The ensuing narrative being, a collection of some remarkables, in an affair now upon the stage, made by a credible eyewitness, is now offered unto the reader, only as a taste, of more that may follow in God's time. If the prayers of good people may obtain this favor of God, that the mysterious assaults from hell now made upon so many of our friends may be thoroughly detected and defeated, we suppose the curious will be entertained with as rare a history as perhaps an age has had; whereof this narrative is but a forerunner.

Benjamin Harris

On the nineteenth day of March last I went to Salem Village, and lodged at Nathaniel Ingersoll's near to the minister Mr. P's. house,[1] and presently after, I came into my lodging Capt. Walcot's daughter

Mary came to Lieutenant Ingersoll's and spake to me, but, suddenly after as she stood by the door, was bitten, so that she cried out of her wrist, and looking on it with a candle, we saw apparently the marks of teeth both upper and lower set, on each side of her wrist.

In the beginning of the evening, I went to give Mr. P. a visit. When I was there, his kinswoman, Abigail Williams (about 12 years of age),[2] had a grievous fit; she was at first hurried with violence to and fro in the room (though Mrs. Ingersoll, endeavored to hold her), sometimes making as if she would fly, stretching up her arms as high as she could, and crying *Whist, whist, whist!* several times; presently after she said there was Goodwife N.[3] and said, *Do you not see her? Why there she stands!* And she said Goodwife N. offered her the book, but she was resolved she would not take it, saying often, *I wont, I wont, I wont, take it, I do not know what book it is: I am sure it is none of God's book, it is the devil's book, for ought I know.* After that, she run to the fire, and begun to throw firebrands, about the house; and run against the back, as if she would run up [the] chimney, and, as they said, she had attempted to go into the fire in other fits.

On Lord's day, the twentieth of March, there were sundry of the afflicted persons at meeting, as, Mrs. Pope, and Goodwife Bibber, Abigail Williams, Mary Walcot, Mary Lewis, and Doctor Griggs' maid. There was also at meeting, Goodwife C.[4] (who was afterward examined on suspicion of being a witch): They had several sore fits, in the time of public worship, which did something interrupt me in my first prayer; being so unusual. After psalm was sung, Abigail Williams said to me, *Now stand up, and name your text:* and after it was read, she said, *It is a long text.* In the beginning of sermon, Mrs. Pope, a woman afflicted said to me, *Now there is enough of that.* And in the afternoon, Abigail Williams, upon my referring to my doctrine said to me, *I know no doctrine you had, if you did name one, I have forgot it.*

In sermon time when Goodwife C. was present in the meetinghouse Abigail W. called out, *Look where Goodwife C. sits on the beam suckling her yellow bird betwixt her fingers!* Anne Putnam another girl afflicted said *there was a yellow bird sat on my hat as it hung on the pin in the pulpit:* but those that were by, restrained her from speaking loud about it.

On Monday the 21st of March, the magistrates of Salem appointed to come to examination of Goodwife C. And about twelve of the clock, they went into the meetinghouse, which was thronged with spectators: Mr. Noyes[5] began with a very pertinent and pathetical prayer; and Goodwife C. being called to answer to what was alleged against her, she desired to go to prayer, which was much wondered at, in the presence of so many hundred people: the magistrates told her, they would not admit it; they came not there to hear her pray, but to examine her, in what was alleged against her. The worshipful Mr. Hathorne[6] asked her, *Why she afflicted those children!* She said she did not afflict them. He asked her, who did then? She said, *I do not know; how should I know?* The number of the afflicted persons were about that time ten, viz. four married women, Mrs. Pope, Mrs. Putnam, Goodwife Bibber, and an ancient woman, named Goodall, three maids, Mary Walcot, Mercy Lewis, at Thomas Putnam's, and a maid at Dr. Griggs's, there were three girls from 9 to 12 years of age, each of them, or thereabouts, viz. Elizabeth Parris, Abigail Williams and Ann Putnam; these were most of them at Goodwife C's examination, and did vehemently accuse her in the assembly of afflicting them, by biting, pinching, strangling, etc. And that they did in their fit, see her likeness coming to them, and bringing a book to them, she said, she had no book; they affirmed, she had a yellow bird, that used to suck betwixt her fingers, and being asked about it, if she had any familiar spirit, that attended her, she said, *She had no familiarity with any such thing.* She was a gospel woman: which title she called herself by; and the afflicted persons told her, ah! *She was, a gospel witch.* Ann Putnam did there affirm, that one day when Lieutenant Fuller was at prayer at her father's house, she saw the shape of Goodwife C. and she thought Goodwife N. praying at the same time to the devil, she was not sure it was Goodwife N. she thought it was; but very sure she saw the shape of Goodwife C. The said C. said, they were poor, distracted, children, and no heed to be given to what they said. Mr. Hathorne and Mr. Noyes replied, it was the judgment of all that were present, they were bewitched, and only she the accused person said, they were distracted. It was observed several times, that if she did but bite her underlip in time of examination the persons afflicted were bitten on their arms and wrists and produced the marks before the magistrates, ministers and others. And being watched for that, if she did but pinch her fingers, or grasp one hand, hard in another, they were pinched and produced the marks before the magistrates, and spectators. After that, it was observed, that if she did but lean her breast, against the seat, in the meetinghouse (being the bar at which she stood), they were afflicted. Particularly Mrs. Pope complained of grievous torment in her bowels as if they were torn out. She vehemently accused said C. as the instrument, and first threw her muff at her; but that flying not home, she got off her shoe, and hit Goodwife C. on the head with it. After these postures were watched, if said C. did but stir her feet, they were afflicted in their feet, and stamped fearfully. The afflicted persons asked her why she did not go to the company of witches which were before the meetinghouse mustering? Did she not hear the drum beat. They accused her of having familiarity with the devil, in the time of examination, in the shape of a black man whispering in her ear; they affirmed, that her yellow bird, sucked betwixt her fingers in the assembly; and order being given to see if there were any sign, the girl that saw it, said, it was too late now; she had removed a pin, and put it on her head; which was found there sticking upright.

They told her, she had covenanted with the devil for ten years, six of them were gone, and four more to come. She was required by the magistrates to answer that question in the Catechism, *How many persons, be there in the God-Head?*⁷ She answered it but oddly, yet was there no great thing to be gathered from it; she denied all that was charged upon her, and said, *They could not prove a witch;* she was that afternoon committed to Salem Prison; and after she was in custody, she did not so appear to them, and afflict them as before.

On Wednesday the 23 of March, I went to Thomas Putnam's, on purpose to see his wife: I found her lying on the bed, having had a sore fit a little before[.] She spake to me, and said, she was glad to see me; her husband and she, both desired me to pray with her, while she was sensible; which I did, though the apparition said, *I should not go to prayer.* At the first beginning she attended; but after a little time, was taken with a fit: yet continued silent, and seemed to be asleep: when prayer was done, her husband going to her, found her in a fit; he took her off the bed, to set her on his knees; but at first she was so stiff, she could not be bended; but she afterwards set down; but quickly began to strive violently with her arms and legs; she then began to complain of, and as it were to converse personally with, Goodwife N., saying, *Goodwife N. be gone! Be gone! Be gone! are you not ashamed, a woman of your profession, to afflict a poor creature so? what hurt did I ever do you in my life! you have but two years to live, and then the devil will torment your soul, for this your name is blotted out of God's book, and it shall never be put in God's book again, be gone for shame, are you not afraid of that which is coming upon you? I know, I know, what will make you afraid; the wrath of an angry God, I am sure that will make you afraid; be gone, do not torment me, I know what you would have* (we judged she meant, her soul) *but it is out of your reach; it is clothed with the white robes of Christ's righteousness.* After this, she seemed to dispute with the apparition about a particular text of scripture. The apparition seemed to deny it (the woman's eyes being fast closed all this time); she said, *She was sure there was such a text;* and she would tell it; and then the shape would be gone, for said she, *I am sure you cannot stand before that text!* then she was sorely afflicted; her mouth drawn on one side, and her body strained for about a minute, and then said, *I will tell, I will tell; it is, it is, it is!* three or four times, and then was afflicted to hinder her from telling, at last she broke forth and said, *It is the third chapter of the Revelations.* I did something scruple the reading it, and did let my scruple appear, lest Satan should make any superstitious lie to improve the word of the eternal God. However, though not versed in these things, I judged I might do it this once for an experiment. I began to read, and before I had near read through the first verse, she opened her eyes, and was well; this fit continued near half an hour. Her husband and the spectators told me, she had often been so relieved by reading texts that she named, something pertinent to her case; as Isaiah 40:1, Isaiah 49:1, Isaiah 50:1, and several others.

On Thursday the twenty-fourth of March (being in course the lecture day, at the village), Goodwife N. was brought before the magistrates Mr. Hathorne and Mr. Corwin,[8] about ten of the clock, in the forenoon, to be examined in the meetinghouse, the Rev. Mr. Hale[9] begun with prayer, and the warrant being read, she was required to give answer, *Why she afflicted those persons?* she pleaded her own innocency with earnestness. Thomas Putnam's wife, Abigail Williams and Thomas Putnam's daughter accused her that she appeared to them, and afflicted them in their fits: but some of the other[s] said, that they had seen her, but knew not that ever she had hurt them; amongst which was Mary Walcot, who was presently after she had so declared bitten, and cried out of her in the meetinghouse; producing the marks of teeth on her wrist. It was so disposed, that I had not leisure to attend the whole time of examination but both magistrates, and ministers, told me, that the things alleged, by the afflicted, and defences made by her, were much after the same manner, as the former was. And her motions, did produce like effects as to, biting, pinching, bruising, tormenting, at their breasts, by her leaning, and when, bended back, were as if their backs was broken. The afflicted persons said, the black man, whispered to her in the assembly, and therefore she could not hear what the magistrates said unto her. They said also that she did then ride by the meetinghouse, behind the black man. Thomas Putnam's wife, had a grievous fit, in the time of examination, to the very great impairing of her strength, and wasting of her spirits, insomuch as she could hardly, move hand, or foot, when she was carried out. Others also were there grievously afflicted, so that there was once such a hideous screech and noise (which I heard as I walked, at a little distance from the meetinghouse), as did amaze me, and some that

were within, told me the whole assembly was struck with consternation, and they were afraid, that those that sat next to them, were under
the influence of witchcraft. This woman also was that day committed
to Salem Prison. The magistrates and ministers also did inform me,
that they apprehended a child of Sarah G.[10] and examined it, being
between 4 and 5 years of age and as to matter of fact, they did unani-
mously affirm, that when this child, did but cast its eye upon the afflicted persons, they were tormented, and they held her head, and yet
so many as her eye could fix upon were afflicted. Which they did several times make careful observation of: the afflicted complained, they
had often been bitten by this child, and produced the marks of a small
set of teeth, accordingly, this was also committed to Salem Prison, the
child looked hale, and well as other children. I saw it at Lieutenant
Ingersoll's[.] After the commitment of Goodwife N. Thomas Putnam's
wife was much better, and had no violent fits at all from that 24th of
March, to the 5th of April. Some others also said they had not seen her
so frequently appear to them, to hurt them.

On the 25th of March (as Captain Stephen Sewall,[11] of Salem, did
afterwards inform me), Elizabeth Parris, had sore fits, at his house,
which much troubled himself, and his wife, so as he told me they were
almost discouraged. She related, that the great black man came to her,
and told her, if she would be ruled by him, she should have, whatso-
ever she desired, and go to a golden city. She relating this to Mrs.
Sewall, she told the child, it was the devil, and he was a *liar from the
beginning,* and bid her tell him so, if he came again: which she did
accordingly, at the next coming to her, in her fits.

On the 26th of March, Mr. Hathorne, Mr. Corwin, and Mr. Higginson,[12] were at the prison-keeper's house, to examine the child, and it
told them there, it had a little snake that used to suck on the lowest
joint of it[s] forefinger; and when they inquired where, pointing to
other places, it told them, not there, but there, pointing on the lowest
point of the forefinger; where they observed, a deep red spot, about
the bigness of a flea bite, they asked who gave it that snake? whether
the great black man, it said no, its mother gave it.

The 31st of March there was a public fast kept at Salem on account
of these afflicted persons. And Abigail Williams said, that the witches
had a sacrament that day at a house in the village, and that they had
red bread and red drink. The first of April, Mercy Lewis, Thomas Putnam's maid, in her fit, said, they did eat red bread like man's flesh,
and would have had her eat some: but she would not; but turned away
her head, and spit at them, and said, *I will not eat, I will not drink, it is
blood,* etc. She said, *That is not the bread of life, that is not the water of*

life; Christ gives the bread of life, I will have none of it! This first of April also Mercy Lewis aforesaid saw in her fit a white man and was with him in a glorious place, which had no candles nor sun, yet was full of light and brightness; where was a great multitude in white glittering robes, and they sung the song in the fifth of Revelation the ninth verse, and the 110 Psalm, and the 149 Psalm; and said with herself, *How long shall I stay here! let me be along with you:* She was loath to leave this place, and grieved that she could tarry no longer. This white man hath appeared several times to some of them, and given them notice how long it should be before they had another fit, which was sometimes a day, or day and half, or more or less: it hath fallen out accordingly.

The third of April, the Lord's day, being sacrament day, at the village, Goodwife C. upon Mr. Parris's naming his text, John 6:70, *One of them is a Devil,* the said Goodwife C.[15] went immediately out of the meetinghouse, and flung the door after her violently, to the amazement of the congregation: She was afterward seen by some in their fits, who said, *O Goodwife C. I did not think to see you here!* (and being at their red bread and drink) said to her, *Is this a time to receive the sacrament, you ran away on the Lord's day, and scorned to receive it in the meetinghouse, and, is this a time to receive it? I wonder at you!* This is the sum of what I either saw myself, or did receive information from persons of undoubted reputation and credit.

Remarks of things more than ordinary about the afflicted persons.

1. They are in their fits tempted to be witches, are showed the list of the names of others, and are tortured, because they will not yield to subscribe, or meddle with, or touch the Book, and are promised to have present relief if they would do it.

2. They did in the assembly mutually cure each other, even with a touch of their hand, when strangled, and otherwise tortured; and would endeavor to get to their afflicted, to relieve them.

3. They did also foretell when another's fit was a-coming, and would say, *Look to her!* she will have a fit presently, which fell out accordingly, as many can bear witness, that heard and saw it.

4. That at the same time, when the accused person was present, the afflicted persons saw her likeness in other places of the meetinghouse, suckling her familiar, sometimes in one place and posture, and sometimes in another.

5. That their motions in their fits are preternatural, both as to the manner, which is so strange as a well person could not screw their

body into; and as to the violence also it is preternatural being much beyond the ordinary force of the same person when they are in their right mind.

6. The eyes of some of them in their fits are exceeding fast closed, and if you ask a question they can give no answer, and I do believe they cannot hear at that time, yet do they plainly converse with the appearances, as if they did discourse with real persons.

7. They are utterly pressed against any person's praying with them, and told by the appearances, they shall not go to prayer, so Thomas Putnam's wife was told, *I should not pray;* but she said, *I should:* and after I had done, reasoned with the appearance, *Did not I say he should go to prayer.*

8. The aforementioned Mary W. being a little better at ease, the afflicted persons said, *She had signed the book;* and that was the reason she was better. Told me by Edward Putnam.

Remarks concerning the accused.

1. For introduction to the discovery of those that afflicted them, it is reported Mr. Parris's Indian man, and woman,[14] made a cake of rye meal, and the children's water, baked it in the ashes, and gave it to a dog, since which they have discovered, and seen particular persons hurting of them.

2. In time of examination, they seemed little affected, though all the spectators were much grieved to see it.

3. Natural actions in them produced preternatural actions in the afflicted, so that they are their own image without any poppets of wax or otherwise.

4. That they are accused to have a company about 23 or 24 and they did muster in arms, as it seemed to the afflicted persons.

5. Since they were confined, the persons have not been so much afflicted with their appearing to them, biting or pinching of them etc.

6. They are reported by the afflicted persons to keep days of fast and days of thanksgiving, and sacraments; Satan endeavors to transform himself to an angel of light, and to make his kingdom and administrations to resemble those of our Lord Jesus Christ.

7. Satan rages principally amongst the visible subjects of Christ's kingdom and makes use (at least in appearance) of some of them to afflict others; that Christ's kingdom may be divided against itself, and so be weakened.

8. Several things used in England at trial of witches, to the number of 14 or 15 which are wont to pass instead of, or in concurrence with

witnesses, at least 6 or 7 of them are found in these accused: see Keble's Statutes.[15]

9. Some of the most solid afflicted persons do affirm the same things concerning seeing the accused out of their fits as well as in them.

10. The witches had a fast, and told one of the afflicted girls, she must not eat, because it was fast day, she said, she would: they told her they would choke her then; which when she did eat, was endeavored.

Finis.

1. Samuel Parris, fourth minister in Salem Village, where he arrived in 1688, and the first to preside over a fully organized congregation. He was driven out of the Village in 1696. Boyer and Nissenbaum in *Salem Possessed* speculate about his personal history and its relationship to the witch-hunt.
2. A niece of Samuel Parris.
3. Rebecca Nurse, a seventy-one-year-old mother of eight children and wife of a substantial farmer; a church member, she responded to the accusations against her with a notable piety. She was executed, as were two of her sisters, Mary Easty and Sarah Cloyse.
4. Martha Corey, an older woman and the wife of Giles Corey; she was executed and her husband was pressed to death in a procedure known as *peine forte et dure*. Corey had refused to enter a plea, and the court used this procedure to force him to respond, which he chose not to do.
5. Nicholas Noyes, minister in Salem.
6. John Hathorne, a resident of Salem and a magistrate in the provincial government; Nathaniel Hawthorne was his direct descendant.
7. A question in the Shorter Westminster Catechism, which was commonly used in the New England churches.
8. Jonathan Corwin, a resident of Salem and a magistrate in the provincial government.
9. John Hale, the minister of nearby Beverly and author of *A Modest Enquiry Into the Nature of Witchcraft* (Boston, 1702).
10. Sarah Good of Salem Village, who was executed, and her daughter Dorcas.
11. Stephen Sewall, clerk of the courts in Salem; Samuel Parris had sent his daughter Elizabeth to live temporarily with the Sewalls.
12. John Higginson, senior minister of the Salem church.
13. Sarah Cloyse, an older woman and the sister of Rebecca Nurse; she was executed. If we can believe Robert Calef, she regarded this choice of text as reflecting on her sister. According to Calef, she "rose up and went out, the wind shutting the door forcibly, gave occasion to some to suppose she went out in anger." Burr, ed., *Narratives*, p. 346.
14. The "Indian woman" was Tituba. She and her fellow slave were attempting a classic experiment in countermagic. Heating something (in this case, urine) associated with an afflicted person or a suspected witch was supposedly a means of "discovering" the identity of the tormentor. Similar actions, and the same presumption of a cause-and-effect relationship, include the burning of the bewitched pudding in the Hugh and Mary Parsons case. Increase Mather condemned such tests in *An Essay for the Recording of Illustrious Providences* (1684) and again in *Cases of Conscience respecting Witchcraft* (1693).
15. Lawson meant to cite Joseph Keble's *An Assistance to Justices of the Peace* (London, 1683), for which point I am indebted to Burr, ed., *Narratives*, p. 163.

Source: Deodat Lawson, *A Brief and True Narrative of Some Remarkable Passages Relating to Sundry Persons Afflicted by Witchcraft* (1692).

Wonders of the Invisible World

I. The Trial of G. B. At a Court of Oyer and Terminer,
Held in Salem, 1692.

Glad should I have been, if I had never known the name of this man; or never had this occasion to mention so much as the first letters of his name. But the government requiring some account, of his trial, to be inserted in this book, it becomes me with all obedience, to submit unto the order.

I. This G. B.[1] was indicted for witchcrafts, and in the prosecution of the charge against him, he was accused by five or six of the bewitched, as the author of their miseries; he was accused by eight of the confessing witches, as being a head actor at some of their hellish rendezvous, and one who had the promise of being a king in Satan's kingdom, now going to be erected; he was accused by nine persons, for extraordinary lifting, and such feats of strength, as could not be done without a diabolical assistance. And for other such things he was accused, until about thirty testimonies were brought in against him; nor were these judged the half of what might have been considered, for his conviction: however they were enough to fix the character of a witch upon him, according to the rules of reasoning, by the judicious Gaule,[2] in that case directed.

II. The court being sensible, that the testimonies of the parties bewitched, use to have a room among the suspicions, or presumptions, brought in against one indicted for witchcraft, there were now heard the testimonies of several persons, who were most notoriously bewitched, and every day tortured by invisible hands, and these now all charged the specters of G. B. to have a share in their torments. At the examination of this G. B. the bewitched people were grievously harassed with preternatural mischiefs, which could not possibly be dissembled; and they still ascribed it unto the endeavors of G. B. to kill them. And now upon his trial, one of the bewitched persons testified, that in her agonies, a little black haired man came to her, saying his name was B. and bidding her set her hand unto a book which he showed unto her; and bragging that he was a conjurer above the ordinary rank of witches; that he often persecuted her, with the offer of that book, saying, *She should be well, and need fear nobody, if she would but sign it:* but he inflicted cruel pains and hurts upon her, because of her denying so to do. The testimonies of the other sufferers concurred with these; and it was remarkable, that whereas biting, was one of the ways which the witches used, for the vexing of the sufferers, when they cried out of G. B. biting them, the print of the teeth would be seen on the flesh of the complainers; and just such a set of teeth as G. B's would then appear upon them, which could be distinguished from those of some other men's. Others of them testified, that in their torments, G. B. tempted them, to go unto a sacrament, unto which they perceived him with a sound of trumpet summoning of other witches; who quickly after the sound would come from all quarters unto the rendezvous. One of them falling into a kind of trance, afterwards affirmed, that G. B. had carried her into a very high mountain, where he showed her mighty and glorious kingdoms, and said, *He would give them all to her, if she would write in his book;* but she told him, *They were none of his to give;* and refused the motions; enduring of much misery for that refusal.

It cost the court a wonderful deal of trouble, to hear the testimonies of the sufferers; for when they were going to give in their depositions, they would for a long while be taken with fits, that made them uncapable of saying anything. The Chief Judge asked the prisoner, who he thought hindered these witnesses from giving their testimonies? and he answered, *He supposed, it was the devil.* That honorable person, then replied, *How comes the devil so loathe to have any testimony born against you?* Which cast him into very great confusion.

III. It has been a frequent thing for the bewitched people, to be entertained with apparitions of ghosts of murdered people, at the same time, that the specters of the witches trouble them. These ghosts do always affright the beholders more, than all the other spectral representations; and when they exhibit themselves, they cry out, of being murdered by the witchcrafts or other violences of the persons who are then in specter present. It is further considerable,[3] that once or twice, these apparitions have been seen by others at the very same time that they have shown themselves to the bewitched; and seldom have there been these apparitions but when something unusual and suspected had attended the death of the party thus appearing. Some that have been accused by these apparitions, accosting of the bewitched people, who had never heard a word of any such persons, ever being in the world, have upon a fair examination freely, and fully, confessed the murders of those very persons, although these also did not know how the apparitions had complained of them. Accordingly several of the bewitched, had given in their testimony, that they had been troubled with the apparitions of two women, who said, that they were G. B's two wives; and that he had been the death of them; and that the magistrates must be told of it, before whom if B. upon his trial denied it, they did not know but that they should appear again in the court. Now, G. B. had been infamous for the barbarous usage of his two successive wives, all the country over. Moreover, it was testified, the specter of G. B. threatening of the sufferers told them, he had killed (besides others) Mrs. Lawson and her daughter Ann. And it was noted, that these were the virtuous wife and daughter, of one at whom this G. B. might have a prejudice for his being serviceable at Salem Village, from whence himself had in ill terms removed some years before: and that when they died, which was long since, there were some odd circumstances about them, which made some of the attendants there suspect something of witchcraft, though none imagined from what quarter it should come.

Well, G. B. being now upon his trial, one of the bewitched persons was cast into horror at the ghosts of B's two deceased wives, then appearing before him, and crying for, vengeance against him. Hereupon several of the bewitched persons were successively called in, who all not knowing what the former had seen and said, concurred in their horror, of the apparition, which they affirmed, that he had before him. But he, though much appalled, utterly denied that he discerned anything of it; nor was it any part of his conviction.

IV. Judicious writers, have assigned it a great place, in the conviction of witches, when persons are impeached by other notorious witches, to be as ill as themselves; especially, if the persons have been much noted for neglecting the worship of God. Now, as there might have been testimonies enough of G. B's antipathy to prayer: and the other ordinances of God, though by his profession singularly obliged thereunto; so, there now came in against the prisoner, the testimonies of several persons, who confessed their own having been horrible witches, and ever since their confessions had been themselves terribly tortured by the devils and other witches, even like the other sufferers; and therein undergone the pains of many deaths for their confessions.

These now testified, that G. B. had been at witch-meetings with them; and that he was the person who had seduced, and compelled them into the snares of witchcraft: that he promised them fine clothes, for doing it; that he brought poppets to them, and thorns to stick into those poppets, for the afflicting of other people: and that he exhorted them, with the rest of the crew, to bewitch all Salem Village, but be sure to do it gradually, if they would prevail in what they did.

When the Lancashire witches[4] were condemned, I don't remember that there was any considerable further evidence, than that of the bewitched, and then that of some that confessed. We see so much already against G. B. But this being indeed not enough, there were other things to render what had already been produced credible.

V. A famous divine, recites this among the convictions of a witch; the testimony of the party bewitched, whether pining or dying; together with the joint oaths of sufficient persons, that have seen certain prodigious pranks, or feats, wrought by the party accused. Now God had been pleased so to leave this G. B. that he had ensnared himself, by several instances which he had formerly given of a preternatural strength, and which were now produced against him. He was a very puny man; yet he had often done things beyond the strength of a giant. A gun of about seven foot barrel, and so heavy that strong men could not steadily hold it out, with both hands; there were several testimonies, given in by persons of credit and honor, that he made nothing of taking up such a gun behind the lock, with but one hand, and holding it out like a pistol, at arm's end. G. B. in his vindication was so foolish as to say, that an Indian was there, and held it out at the same time; Whereas, none of the spectators ever saw any such Indian; but they supposed the black man (as the witches call the devil; and they generally say he resembles an Indian) might give him that assistance. There was evidence, likewise, brought in, that he made nothing of taking up whole barrels filled with molasses, or cider, in very disadvantageous postures, and carrying of them through the difficultest places, out of a canoe to the shore.

Yea, there were two testimonies, that G. B. with only putting the forefinger of his right hand, into the muzzle of a heavy gun, a fowling-piece, of about six or seven foot barrel, did lift up the gun, and hold it out at arm's end; a gun which the deponents, though strong men, could not with both hands lift up, and hold out, at the butt end, as is usual. Indeed one of these witnesses, was overpersuaded by some persons, to be out of the way, upon G. B.'s trial; but he came afterwards, with sorrow for his withdraw, and gave in his testimony: Nor were either of these witnesses made use of as evidences in the trial.

VI. There came in several testimonies, relating to the domestic affairs of G. B. which had a very hard aspect upon him; and not only proved him a very ill man; but also confirmed the belief of the character, which had been already fastened on him.

E.g., 'twas testified, that keeping his two successive wives in a strange kind of slavery, he would when he came home from abroad, pretend to tell the talk which any had with them. That he has brought them to the point of death, by his harsh dealings with his wives, and then made the people about him to promise that in case death should happen, they would say nothing of it. That he used all means to make his wives write, sign, seal, and swear a covenant, never to reveal any of his secrets. That his wives had privately complained unto the neighbors about frightful apparitions of evil spirits, with which their house was sometimes infested; and that many such things have been whispered among the neighborhood. There were also some other testimonies, relating to the death of people, whereby the consciences of an impartial jury, were convinced, that G. B. had bewitched the persons mentioned in the complaints. But I am forced to omit several such passages, in this, as well as in all the succeeding trials, because the scribes who took notice of them, have not supplied me.

VII. One Mr. Ruck, brother-in-law to this G. B., testified, that G. B. and he himself, and his sister, who was G. B's wife, going out for two or three miles, to gather strawberries, Ruck, with his sister the wife of G. B. rode home very softly, with G. B. on foot in their company, G. B. stept aside a little into the bushes; whereupon they halted and halloo'd for him. He not answering, they went away homewards, with a quickened pace; without any expectation of seeing him in a considerable while: and yet when they were got near home, to their astonishment they found him on foot, with them, having a basket of strawberries. G. B. immediately, then fell to chiding his wife, on the account of what she had been speaking to her brother, of him, on the road: which when they wondered at, he said, *he knew their thoughts.* Ruck being startled at that, made some reply, intimating that the devil himself did not know so far; but G. B. answered, *my god, makes known your thoughts unto me.* The prisoner now at the bar had nothing to answer, unto what was thus witnessed against him, that was worth considering. Only he said, *Ruck, and his wife left a man with him, when they left him.* Which Ruck now affirmed to be false; and when the court asked G. B. *what the man's name was?* his countenance was much altered; nor could he say, who 'twas. But the court began to think, that he then stepped aside, only that by the assistance of the black man, he might put on his invisibility, and in that fascinating mist, gratify his own jealous humor, to hear what they said of him. Which trick of rendering themselves invisible, our witches do in their confessions pretend that they sometimes are masters of; and it is the more credible, because there is demonstration that they often render many other things utterly invisible.

VIII. Faltering, faulty, unconstant, and contrary answers upon judicial and deliberate examination, are counted some unlucky symptoms of guilt, in all crimes; especially in witchcrafts. Now there never was a prisoner more eminent for them, than G. B. both at his examination and on his trial. His tergiversations, contradictions, and falsehoods, were very sensible: he had little to say, but that he had heard some things that he could not prove, reflecting upon the reputation of some of the witnesses. Only he gave in a paper, to the jury; wherein, although he had many times before, granted, not only that there are witches, but also that the present sufferings of the country are the effect of horrible witchcrafts, yet he now goes to, evince it, that there neither are, nor ever were, witches that having made a compact with the devil, can send a devil to torment other people at a distance. This paper was transcribed out of Ady;[5] which the court presently knew, as soon as they heard it. But he said, he had taken none of it out of any book; for which his evasion afterwards was, that a gentleman gave him the discourse, in a manuscript, from whence he transcribed it.

IX. The jury brought him in guilty; but when he came to die, he utterly denied the fact, whereof he had been thus convicted.

II. The trial of Bridget Bishop: alias, Oliver, at the Court of Oyer and Terminer held at Salem, June 2, 1692.

I. She[6] was indicted for bewitching of several persons in the neighborhood, the indictment being drawn up, according to the form in such cases usual. And pleading, not guilty, there were brought in several persons, who had long undergone many kinds of miseries, which were preternaturally inflicted, and generally ascribed unto a horrible witchcraft. There was little occasion to prove the witchcraft; it being evident and notorious to all beholders. Now to fix the witchcraft on the prisoner at the bar, the first thing used was, the testimony of the bewitched; whereof, several testified, that the shape of the prisoner did oftentimes very grievously pinch them, choke them, bite them, and afflict them; urging them to write their names in a book, which the said specter called, ours. One of them did further testify, that it was the shape of this prisoner, with another, which one day took her from her wheel, and carrying her to the riverside, threatened there to drown her, if she did not sign to the book mentioned: which yet she refused. Others of them did also testify, that the said shape, did in her threats, brag to them, that she had been the death of sundry persons, then by her named; that she had ridden a man, then likewise named. Another testified, the apparition of ghosts unto the specter of Bishop, crying out, you murdered us! About the truth whereof, there was in the matter of fact, but too much suspicion.

II. It was testified, that at the examination of the prisoner, before the magistrates, the bewitched were extremely tortured. If she did but cast her eyes on them, they were presently struck down; and this in such a manner as there could be no collusion in the business. But upon the touch of her hand upon them, when they lay in their swoons, they would immediately revive; and not upon the touch of anyone's else. Moreover, upon some special actions of her body, as the shaking of her head, or the turning of her eyes, they presently and painfully fell into the like postures. And many of the like accidents now fell out, while she was at the bar. One at the same time testifying, that she said, she could not be troubled to see the afflicted thus tormented.

III. There was testimony likewise brought in, that a man striking once at the place, where a bewitched person said, the shape of this Bishop stood, the bewitched cried out, that he had tore her coat, in the place then particularly specified; and the woman's coat, was found to be torn in that very place.

IV. One Deliverance Hobbs,[7] who had confessed her being a witch, was now tormented by the specters, for her confession. And she now testified, that this Bishop, tempted her to sign the book again, and to deny what she had confessed. She affirmed, that it was the shape of this prisoner, which whipped her with iron rods, to compel her there-unto. And she affirmed, that this Bishop was at a general meeting of the witches, in a field at Salem Village and there partook of a diabolical sacrament, in bread and wine then administered!

V. To render it further unquestionable, that the prisoner at the bar, was the person truly charged in *this* witchcraft, there were produced many evidences of *other* witchcrafts, by her perpetrated. For instance, John Cook testified, that about five or six years ago, one morning, about sunrise, he was in his chamber, assaulted by the shape of this prisoner: which looked on him, grinned at him, and very much hurt him, with a blow on the side of the head: and that on the same day, about noon, the same shape walked in the room where he was, and an apple strangely flew out of his hand, into the lap of his mother, six or eight foot from him.

VI. Samuel Gray, testified, that about fourteen years ago, he waked on a night, and saw the room where he lay, full of light; and that he then saw plainly a woman between the cradle, and the bedside, which looked upon him. He rose, and it vanished; though he found the doors all fast. Looking out at the entry door, he saw the same woman, in the same garb again; and said, *In God's name, what do you come for?* He went to bed, and had the same woman again assaulting him. The child in the cradle gave a great screech, and the woman disappeared. It was long before the child could be quieted; and though it were a very likely thriving child, yet from this time it pined away, and after divers months died in a sad condition. He knew not Bishop, nor her name;

but when he saw her after this, he knew by her countenance, and apparel, and all circumstances, that it was the apparition of this Bishop, which had thus troubled him.

VII. John Bly and his wife, testified, that he bought a sow of Edward Bishop, the husband of the prisoner; and was to pay the price agreed, unto another person. This prisoner being angry that she was thus hindered from fingering the money, quarrelled with Bly. Soon after which the sow, was taken with strange fits; jumping, leaping, and knocking her head against the fence, she seemed blind and deaf, and would neither eat nor be sucked. Whereupon a neighbor said, she believed the creature was over-looked; and sundry other circumstances concurred, which made the deponents believe that Bishop had bewitched it.

VIII. Richard Coman testified, that eight years ago, as he lay awake in his bed, with a light burning in the room, he was annoyed with the apparition of this Bishop, and of two more that were strangers to him; who came and oppressed him so that he could neither stir himself, nor wake anyone else: and that he was the night after, molested again in the like manner; the said Bishop taking him by the throat, and pulling him almost out of the bed. His kinsman offered for this cause to lodge with him; and that night, as they were awake discoursing together: this Coman was once more visited, by the guests which had formerly been so troublesome; his kinsman being at the same time struck speechless and unable to move hand or foot. He had laid his sword by him; which these unhappy specters, did strive much to wrest from him; only he held too fast for them. He then grew able to call the people of his house; but although they heard him, yet they had not power to speak or stir, until at last, one of the people crying out, *what's the matter!* the specters all vanished.

IX. Samuel Shattuck testified, that in the year 1680, this Bridget Bishop, often came to his house upon such frivolous and foolish errands, that they suspected she came indeed with a purpose of mischief. Presently whereupon his eldest child, which was of as promising health and sense, as any child of its age, began to droop exceedingly; and the oftener that Bishop came to the house, the worse grew the child. As the child would be standing at the door, he would be thrown and bruised against the stones, by an invisible hand, and in like sort knock his face against the sides of the house, and bruise it after a miserable manner. Afterwards this Bishop would bring him things to dye, whereof he could not imagine any use; and when she paid him a piece of money, the purse and money were unaccountably conveyed out of a locked box, and never seen more. The child was immediately hereupon taken with terrible fits, whereof his friends thought he would have died: indeed he did almost nothing but cry and sleep for several months together: and at length his understanding was utterly taken away. Among other symptoms of an enchantment upon him, one was, that there was a board in the garden, whereon he would walk; and all the invitations in the world could never fetch him off. About seventeen or eighteen years after, there came a stranger to Shattuck's house, who seeing the child, said, *This poor child is bewitched; and you have a neighbor living not far off, who is a witch.* He added, *Your neighbor has had a falling out with your wife; and she said in her heart, your wife is a proud woman, and she would bring down her pride in this child:* He then remembered, that Bishop had parted from his wife in muttering and menacing terms, a little before the child was taken ill. The abovesaid stranger would needs carry the bewitched boy with him, to Bishop's house, on pretence of buying a pot of cider.[8] The woman entertained him in furious manner; and flew also upon the boy, scratching his face till the blood came, and saying, *Thou rogue, what? dost thou bring this fellow here to plague me?* Now it seems the man had said before he went, that he would fetch blood of her. Ever after the boy was followed with grievous fits, which the doctors themselves generally ascribed unto witchcraft; and wherein he would be thrown still into the fire or the water, if he were not constantly looked after; and it was verily believed that Bishop was the cause of it.

X. John Louder testified, that upon some little controversy with Bishop about her fowls, going well to bed, he did awake in the night by moonlight, and did see clearly the likeness of this woman grievously oppressing him; in which miserable condition she held him unable to help himself, till near day. He told Bishop of this; but she denied it, and threatened him, very much. Quickly after this, being at home on a Lord's day, with the doors shut about him, he saw a black pig approach him; at which he going to kick, it vanished away. Immediately after, sitting down, he saw a black thing jump in at the window, and come and stand before him. The body, was like that of a monkey, the feet like a cock's, but the face much like a man's. He being so extremely affrighted, that he could not speak; this monster spoke to him and said, *I am a messenger sent unto you, for I understand that you are in some trouble of mind, and if you will be ruled by me, you shall want for nothing in this world.* Whereupon he endeavored to clap his hands upon it; but he could feel no substance, and it jumped out of the window again; but immediately came in by the porch, though the doors were shut, and said, *You had better take my counsel!*

He then struck at it with a stick, but struck only the groundsel, and broke the stick. The arm with which he struck was presently disenabled, and it vanished away. He presently went out at the back door, and spied, this Bishop, in her orchard, going toward her house; but he had not power to set one foot forward unto her. Whereupon returning into the house, he was immediately accosted by the monster he had seen before; which goblin was now going to fly at him: whereat he cried out, *The whole armor of God, be between me and you!* So it sprang back, and flew over the apple tree; shaking many apples off the tree, in its flying over. At its leap, it flung dirt with its feet, against the stomach of the man; whereon he was then struck dumb, and so continued for three days together. Upon the producing of this testimony, Bishop denied that she knew this deponent: yet their two orchards joined, and they had often had their little quarrels for some years together.

XI. William Stacy testified, that receiving money of this Bishop, for work done by him, he was gone but a matter of three rods from her, and looking for his money, found it unaccountably gone from him. Some time after, Bishop asked him whether his father would grind her grist for her? He demanded why? She replied, *Because folks count me a witch.* He answered, *No question, but he will grind it for you.* Being then gone about six rods from her, with a small load in his cart, suddenly the off-wheel slumped and sunk down into a hole upon plain ground, so that the deponent, was forced to get help for the recovering of the wheel. But stepping back to look for the hole which might give him this disaster, there was none at all to be found. Some time after, he was waked in the night; but it seemed as light as day, and he perfectly saw the shape of this Bishop, in the room, troubling of him; but upon her going out, all was dark again. He charged Bishop afterwards with it: and she denied it not; but was very angry. Quickly after, this deponent having been threatened by Bishop, as he was in a dark night going to the barn, he was very suddenly taken or lifted from the ground, and thrown against a stone wall; after that, he was again hoisted up and thrown down a bank, at the end of his house. After this again, passing by this Bishop, his horse with a small load, striving to draw, all his gears flew to pieces, and the cart fell down; and this deponent going then to lift a bag of corn, of about two bushels; could not budge it, with all his might.

Many other pranks, of this Bishop's, this deponent was ready to testify. He also testified, that he verily believed, the said Bishop, was the instrument of his daughter, Priscilla's death; of which suspicion, pregnant reasons were assigned.

XII. To crown all, John Bly, and William Bly, testified, that being employed by Bridget Bishop, to help take down the cellar wall, of the old house, wherein she formerly lived, they did in holes of the said old wall, find several poppets, made up of rags, and hog's bristles, with headless pins in them, the points being outward. Whereof she could now give no account unto the court, that was reasonable or tolerable.

XIII. One thing that made against the prisoner was, her being evidently convicted of gross lying, in the court, several times, while she was making her plea. But besides this, a jury of women, found a preternatural teat upon her body; but upon a second search, within three or four hours, there was no such thing to be seen. There was also an account of other people whom this woman had afflicted. And there might have been many more, if they had been, inquired for. But there was no need of them.

XIV. There was one very strange thing more, with which the court was newly entertained. As this woman was under a guard, passing by the great and spacious meetinghouse of Salem, she gave a look towards the house. And immediately a demon invisibly entering the meetinghouse, tore down a part of it; so that though there were no person to be seen there, yet the people at the noise running in, found a board, which was strongly fastened with several nails, transported unto another quarter of the house.

III. The trial of Susanna Martin, at the Court of Oyer and Terminer: held by adjournment at Salem, June 29, 1692.

I. Susanna Martin,[9] pleading, not guilty to the indictment of witchcrafts brought in against her, there were produced the evidences of many persons very sensibly and grievously bewitched; who all complained of the prisoner at the bar, as the person whom they believed the cause of their miseries. And now, as well as in the other trials, there was an extraordinary endeavor by witchcrafts, with cruel and frequent fits, to hinder the poor sufferers, from giving in their complaints; which the court was forced with much patience to obtain, by much waiting and watching for it.

II. There was now also an account given, of what passed at her first examination before the magistrates. The cast of her eye, then striking the afflicted people to the ground, whether they saw that cast or no; there were these among other passages, between the magistrates, and the examinate.

Magistrate. Pray, what ails these people?

Martin. I don't know.

Magistrate. But, what do you think ails them?

Martin. I don't desire to spend my judgment upon it.

Magistrate. Don't you think they are bewitched?

Martin. No, I do not think they are.

Magistrate. Tell us your thoughts about them then.

Martin. No, my thoughts are my own when they are in, but when they are out, they are another's. Their master—

Magistrate. Their master? who do you think, is their master?

Martin. If they be dealing in the black art, you may know as well as I.

Magistrate. Well, what have you done towards this?

Martin. Nothing at all.

Magistrate. Why, 'tis you or your appearance.

Martin. I cannot help it.

Magistrate. Is it not *your master?* How comes your appearance to hurt these?

Martin. How do I know? He that appeared in the shape of Samuel, a glorified saint, may appear in anyone's shape.[10]

It was then also noted in her, as in others like her, that if the afflicted went to approach her, they were flung down to the ground. And, when she was asked the reason of it, she said, *I cannot tell; it may be, the devil bears me more malice than another.*

III. The court accounted themselves alarmed by these things, to inquire further into the conversation of the prisoner; and see what there might occur, to render these accusations further credible. Whereupon, John Allen, of Salisbury, testified, that he refusing, because of the weakness of his oxen, to cart some staves, at the request of this Martin, she was displeased at it, and said, *It had been as good that he had; for his oxen should never do him much more service.* Whereupon, this deponent said, *Dost thou threaten me, thou old witch? I'll throw thee into the brook:* Which to avoid, she flew over the bridge, and escaped. But, as he was going home one of his oxen tired, so that he was forced to unyoke him, that he might get him home. He then put his oxen, with many more, upon Salisbury Beach, where cattle did use to get flesh. In a few days, all the oxen upon the beach were found by their tracks, to have run unto the mouth of Merrimack River, and not returned; but the next day they were found come ashore upon Plum Island. They that sought them, used all imaginable gentleness, but they would still run away with a violence that seemed wholly diabolical, till they came near the mouth of Merrimack River; when they ran right into the sea, swimming as far as they could be seen. One of them then swam back again, with a swiftness, amazing to the beholders, who stood ready to receive him, and help up his tired carcass: but the beast ran furiously up into the island, and from thence, through the marshes, up into Newbury Town, and so up into the woods; and there after a while found near Amesbury. So that, of fourteen good oxen, there was only this saved: the rest were all cast up, some in one place, and some in another, drowned.

IV. John Atkinson testified, that he exchanged a cow, with a son of Susanna Martin's, whereat she muttered, and was unwilling he should have it. Going to receive this cow, though he hamstringed her, and haltered her, she of a tame creature grew so mad, that they could scarce get her along. She broke all the ropes that were fastened unto her, and though she were tied fast unto a tree, yet she made her escape, and gave them such further trouble, as they could ascribe to no cause but witchcraft.

V. Bernard Peach testified, that being in bed, on a Lord's-day night, he heard a scrabbling at the window, whereat he then saw, Susanna Martin come in, and jump down upon the floor. She took hold of this deponent's feet, and drawing his body up into a heap, she lay upon him, near two hours; in all which time he could neither speak nor stir. At length, when he could begin to move, he laid hold on her hand, and pulling it up to his mouth, he bit three of her fingers, as he judged, unto the bone. Whereupon she went from the chamber, down the stairs, out at the door. This deponent thereupon called unto the people of the house, to advise them, of what passed; and he himself did follow her. The people saw her not; but there being a bucket at the left hand of the door, there was a drop of blood found on it; and several more drops of blood upon the snow newly fallen abroad. There was likewise the print of her two feet just without the threshold; but no more sign of any footing further off.

At another time this deponent was desired by the prisoner, to come unto a husking of corn, at her house; and she said, *If he did not come, it were better that he did!* He went not; but the night following, Susanna Martin, as he judged, and another came towards him. One of them said, *Here he is!* but he having a quarter-staff, made a blow at them. The roof of the barn, broke his blow; but following them to the window, he made another blow at them, and struck them down; yet they got up, and got out, and he saw no more of them.

About this time, there was a rumor about the town, that Martin had a broken head; but the deponent could say nothing to that.

The said Peach also testified, the bewitching of cattle to death, upon Martin's discontents.

VI. Robert Downer testified, that this prisoner being some years ago prosecuted at court for a witch, he then said unto her, *He believed she was a witch.* Whereat she being dissatisfied, said, *That some she-devil would shortly fetch him away!* Which words were heard by others, as well as himself. The night following, as he lay in his bed, there came in at the window, the likeness of a cat, which flew upon him, took fast hold of his throat, lay on him a considerable while, and almost killed him. At length he remembered, what Susanna Martin, had threatened the day before; and with much striving he cried out, *Avoid, thou she-devil! In the name of God the Father, the Son, and the Holy Ghost, avoid!* whereupon it left him, leaped on the floor, and flew out at the window.

And there also came in several testimonies, that before ever Downer spoke a word of this accident, Susanna Martin and her family, had related, how this Downer had been handled!

VII. John Kimball, testified, that Susanna Martin, upon a causeless disgust, had threatened him, about a certain cow of his, that *She should never do him any more good:* and it came to pass accordingly. For soon after the cow was found stark dead on the dry ground; without any distemper to be discerned upon her. Upon which he was followed with a strange death upon more of his cattle, whereof he lost in one spring to the value of thirty pounds. But the said John Kimball had a further testimony to give in against the prisoner which was truly admirable.

Being desirous to furnish himself with a dog, he applied himself to buy one of this Martin, who had a bitch with whelps in her house. But she not letting him have his choice, he said, he would supply himself then at one Blaisdell's. Having marked a puppy, which he liked at Blaisdell's, he met George Martin, the husband of the prisoner, going by, who asked him, *Whether he would not have one of his wife's puppies;* and he answered, *No.* The same day, one Edmund Eliot, being at Martin's house, heard George Martin relate, where this Kimball had been, and what he had said. Whereupon Susanna Martin replied, *If I live, I'll give him puppies enough!* Within a few days after, this Kimball coming out of the woods, there arose a little black cloud, in the N.W. and Kimball immediately felt a force upon him, which made him not able to avoid running upon the stumps of trees, that were before him, albeit, he had a broad, plain cart way, before him; but though he had his axe also on his shoulder to endanger him in his falls, he could not forbear going out of his way to tumble over them. When he came below the meetinghouse, there appeared unto him, a little thing like a puppy, of a darkish color; and it shot backwards and forwards between his legs. He had the courage to use all possible endeavors of cutting it, with his axe; but he could not hit it; the puppy gave a jump from him, and went, as to him, it seemed, into the ground. Going a little further, there appeared unto him a black puppy, somewhat bigger than the first; but as black as a coal. Its motions were quicker than those of his axe; it flew at his belly and away; then at his throat; so, over his shoulder one way, and then over his shoulder another way. His heart now began to fail him, and he thought the dog would have tore his throat out. But he recovered himself, and called upon God in his distress; and naming the name of Jesus Christ, it vanished away at once. The deponent spoke not one word of these accidents, for fear of affrighting his wife. But the next morning, Edmond Eliot, going into Martin's house, this woman asked him where Kimball was? He replied, *At home, a bed, for ought he knew.* She returned, *They say, he was frighted last night.* Eliot asked *With what?* She answered, *With puppies.* Eliot asked, *Where she heard of it, for he had heard nothing of it!* She rejoined, *About the town.* Although, Kimball had mentioned the matter to no creature living.

VIII. William Brown testified, that heaven having blessed him with a most pious and prudent wife, this wife of his, one day met with Susanna Martin; but when she approached just unto her Martin, vanished out of sight, and left her extremely affrighted. After which time, the said Martin often appeared unto her, giving her no little trouble; and when she did come, she was visited with birds that sorely pecked and pricked her; and sometimes, a bunch, like a pullet's egg would rise in her throat, ready to choke her, till she cried out, *Witch, you shan't choke me!* While this good woman was in this extremity, the church appointed a day of prayer, on her behalf; whereupon her trouble ceased; she saw not Martin as formerly; and the church, instead of their fast, gave thanks for her deliverance. But a considerable while after, she being summoned to give in some evidence at the court, against this Martin, quickly thereupon, this Martin came behind her, while she was milking her cow, and said unto her, *For thy defaming me at court, I'll make thee the miserablest creature in the world.* Soon after which, she fell into a strange kind of distemper, and became horribly frantic, and uncapable of any reasonable action; the physicians declaring, that her distemper was preternatural, and that some devil had certainly bewitched her; and in that condition she now remained.

IX. Sarah Atkinson testified, that Susanna Martin came from Amesbury, to their house at Newbury, in an extraordinary season, when it was not fit for anyone to travel. She came (as she said, unto Atkinson) all that long way on foot. She bragged, and showed how dry she was; nor could it be perceived that so much as the soles of her shoes were wet. Atkinson was amazed at it; and professed, that she should herself have been wet up to the knees, if she had then came so far; but Martin replied, *She scorned to be drabbled!* It was noted, that this testimony upon her trial, cast her into a very singular confusion.

X. John Pressey testified, that being one evening very unaccountably bewildered, near a field of Martin's, and several times, as one under an enchantment, returning to the place he had left, at length he saw a marvellous light, about the bigness of a half bushel, near two rod, out of the way. He went, and struck at it with a stick, and laid it on with all his might. He gave it near forty blows; and felt it a palpable substance. But going from it, his heels were struck up, and he was laid with his back on the ground: sliding, as he thought, into a pit; from whence he recovered, by taking hold on the bush; although afterwards he could find no such pit in the place. Having after his recovery, gone five or six rod, he saw Susanna Martin standing on his left hand, as the light had done before; but they changed no words with one another. He could scarce find his house in his return; but at length he got home, extremely affrighted. The next day, it was upon inquiry understood, that Martin was in a miserable condition by pains and hurts that were upon her.

It was further testified by this deponent, that after he had given in some evidence against Susanna Martin, many years ago, she gave him foul words about it; and said, *He should never prosper more;* particularly, *That he should never have more than two cows; that though he were never so likely to have more, yet he should never have them.* And that from that very day to this; namely for twenty years together, he could never exceed that number; but some strange thing or other still prevented his having of any more.

XI. Jarvis Ring, testified, that about seven years ago, he was oftentimes and grievously oppressed in the night; but saw not who troubled him, until at last he lying perfectly awake, plainly saw Susanna Martin approach him. She came to him, and forcibly bit him by the finger; so that the print of the bite is now so long after to be seen upon him.

XII. But besides all of these evidences, there was a most wonderful account of one Joseph Ring, produced on this occasion.

This man has been strangely carried about by demons, from one witch-meeting to another, for near two years together; and for one quarter of this time, they have made him, and kept him dumb, though he is now again able to speak. There was one T. H. who having as 'tis judged, a design of engaging this Joseph Ring, in a snare of devilism, contrived a wile, to bring this Ring two shillings in debt unto him.

Afterwards, this poor man would be visited with unknown shapes, and this T. H. sometimes among them; which would force him away with them, unto unknown places, where he saw meetings, feastings, dancings; and after his return, wherein they hurried him along through the air, he gave demonstrations to the neighbors, that he had indeed been so transported. When he was brought unto these hellish meetings, one of the first things they still did unto him, was to give him a knock on the back, whereupon he was ever as if bound with chains, uncapable of stirring out of the place, till they should release him. He related, that there often came to him a man, who presented him a book, whereto he would have him set his hand; promising to him, that he should then have even what he would; and presenting him with all the delectable things, persons, and places, that he could imagine. But he refusing to subscribe, the business would end with dreadful shapes, noises and screeches, which almost scared him out of his wits. Once with the book, there was a pen offered him, and an inkhorn, with liquor in it, that seemed like blood: but he never touched it.

This man did now affirm, that he saw the prisoner, at several of those hellish rendezvous.

Note, this woman was one of the most impudent, scurrilous, wicked creatures in the world; and she did now throughout her whole trial, discover herself to be such a one. Yet when she was asked what she had to say for her self, her chief plea was, that she had led a most virtuous and holy life!

IV. The trial of Elizabeth How, at the Court of Oyer and Terminer, held by adjournment at Salem, June 30, 1692.

I. Elizabeth How,[11] pleading, not guilty, to the indictment of witch-crafts, then charged upon her; the court, according to the usual pro-ceeding of the courts in England, in such cases, began with hearing the depositions of several afflicted people, who were grievously tor-tured by sensible and evident witchcrafts, and all complained of the prisoner, as the cause of their trouble. It was also found that the suf-ferers were not able to bear her look, as likewise, that in their greatest swoons, they distinguished her touch from other people's, being thereby raised out of them.

And there was other testimony of people to whom the shape of this How, gave trouble nine or ten years ago.

II. It has been a most usual thing for the bewitched persons, at the same time that the specters representing the witches troubled them, to be visited with apparitions of ghosts, pretending to have been mur-dered by the witches then represented. And sometimes the confes-sions of the witches afterwards acknowledged those very murders, which these apparitions charged upon them; although they had never heard what information had been given by the sufferers.

There were such apparitions of ghosts testified by some of the present sufferers, and the ghosts affirmed that this How had murdered them: which things were feared but not proved.

III. This How, had made some attempts of joining to the church, at Ipswich, several years ago; but she was denied an admission into that holy society, partly, through a suspicion of witchcraft, then urged against her. And there now came in testimony, of preternatural mischiefs, presently befalling some that had been instrumental to debar her from the communion, whereupon she was intruding.

IV. There was a particular deposition of Joseph Safford, that his wife had conceived an extreme aversion to this How, on the reports of her witchcrafts: but How, one day taking her by the hand, and saying, *I believe you are not ignorant of the great scandal, that I lie under, by an evil report raised upon me,* she immediately, unreasonably, and unpersuadably, even like one enchanted, began to take this woman's part. How being soon after propounded, as desiring an admission to the table of the Lord, some of the pious brethren were unsatisfied about her. The elders appointed, a meeting to hear matters objected against her; and no arguments in the world could hinder this Goodwife Safford, from going to the lecture. She did indeed promise with much ado, that she would not go to the church meeting, yet she could not refrain going thither also. How's affairs there were so canvassed, that she came off rather guilty, than cleared; nevertheless Goodwife Safford could not forbear taking her by the hand, and saying, *Though you are condemned before men, you are justified before God.* She was quickly taken in a very strange manner; frantic, raving, raging, and crying out, *Goody How must come into the church; she is a precious saint, and though she be condemned before men, she is justified before God.* So she continued for the space of two or three hours; and then fell into a trance. But coming to herself, she cried out, *Ha! I was mistaken,* and afterwards again repeated, *Ha! I was mistaken!* Being asked by a standerby, *Wherein?* She replied, *I thought Goody How, had been a precious saint of God, but now I see she is a witch. She has bewitched me, and my child, and we shall never be well, till there be testimony for her, that she may be taken into the church.* And How said afterwards, that she was very sorry to see Safford at the church meeting mentioned. Safford after this, declared herself to be afflicted by the shape, of How; and from that shape she endured many miseries.

V. John How brother to the husband of the prisoner testified, that he refusing to accompany the prisoner unto her examination as was by her desired, immediately some of his cattle, were bewitched to death. Leaping three or four foot high, turning about, squeaking, falling, and dying, at once; and going to cut off an ear, for a use that might as well perhaps have been omitted, the hand wherein he held his knife, was taken very numb; and so it remained, and full of pain for several days; being not well at this very time. And he suspected this prisoner, for the author of it.

VI. Nehemiah Abbott testified, that unusual and mischievous accidents would befall his cattle, whenever he had any difference with this prisoner. Once, particularly, she wished his ox choked; and within a little while, that ox was choked with a turnip in his throat. At another time, refusing to lend his horse, at the request of her daughter, the horse was in a preternatural manner abused. And several other odd things, of that kind were testified.

VII. There came in testimony, that one Goodwife Sherwin, upon some difference with How, was bewitched, and that she died, charging this How of having a hand in her death. And that other people, had their barrels of drink unaccountably mischiefed, spoilt, and spilt, upon their displeasing of her.

The things in themselves, were trivial; but there being such a course of them, it made them the more to be considered. Among others, Martha Wood gave her testimony, that a little after, her father had been employed in gathering an account of this How's conversation, they once and again lost great quantities of drink, out of their vessels in such a manner, as they could ascribe to nothing but witchcraft. As also, that How giving her some apples, when she had eaten of them, she was taken with a very strange kind of a maze, insomuch that she knew not what she said or did.

VIII. There was likewise a cluster of depositions, that one Isaac Cummings, refusing to lend his mare, unto the husband of this How, the mare was within a day or two, taken in a strange condition. The beast seemed much abused; being bruised, as if she had been running over the rocks, and marked where the bridle went, as if burnt with a red hot bridle. Moreover, one using a pipe of tobacco for the cure of the beast, a blue flame issued out of her, took hold of her hair, and not only spread and burnt on her, but it also flew upwards towards the roof of the barn, and had like to have set the barn on fire. And the mare died very suddenly.

IX. Timothy Perley and his wife, testified, not only that unaccountable mischiefs, befell their cattle, upon their having of differences, with this prisoner: but also, that they had a daughter destroyed by witchcrafts; which daughter still charged How, as the cause of her affliction: and it was noted, that she would be struck down, whenever How were spoken of. She was often endeavored to be thrown into the fire, and into the water, in her strange fits; though her father had corrected her, for charging How with bewitching her, yet (as was testified by others also) she said, she was sure of it, and must die standing to it. Accordingly she charged How to the very death; and said, *Though How could afflict and torment her body, yet she could not hurt her soul: and, that the truth of this matter would appear, when she should be dead and gone.*

X. Francis Lane, testified, that being hired by the husband of this How, to get him a parcel of posts and rails, this Lane hired John Perley to assist him. This prisoner then told Lane, that she believed the posts and rails would not do, because John Perley helped him; but that if he had got them alone, without John Perley's help, they might have done well enough. When James How came to receive his posts and rails of Lane, How taking them up by the ends, they, though good and sound, yet unaccountably broke off, so that Lane was forced to get thirty or forty more. And this prisoner being informed of it, she said, she told him so before; because Perley helped about them.

XI. Afterwards, there came in the confessions of several other (penitent) witches, which affirmed this How, to be one of those, who with them had been baptized by the devil, in the river, at Newbury-falls: before which, he made them there kneel down by the brink of the river, and worship him.

V. The trial of Martha Carrier, at the Court of Oyer and Terminer, held by adjournment at, Salem, August 2, 1692.

I. Martha Carrier[12] was indicted for the bewitching of certain persons, according to the form usual in such cases. Pleading not guilty, to her indictment, there were first brought in a considerable number of the bewitched persons; who not only made the court sensible of a horrid witchcraft committed upon them, but also deposed, that it was Martha Carrier, or her shape, that grievously tormented them, by biting, pricking, pinching, and choking of them. It was further deposed, that while this Carrier was on her examination, before the magistrates, the poor people were so tortured that every one expected their death upon the very spot; but that upon the binding of Carrier, they were eased. Moreover the look of Carrier, then laid the afflicted people for dead; and her touch, if her eye at the same time were off them, raised them again. Which things were also now seen upon her trial. And it was testified, that upon the mention of some having their necks twisted almost round, by the shape of this Carrier, she replied, *It's no matter, though their necks had been twisted quite off.*

II. Before the trial of this prisoner, several of her own children, had frankly and fully confessed, not only that they were witches themselves, but that this their mother had made them so. This confession they made with great shows of repentance, and with much demonstration of truth. They related place, time, occasion; they gave an account of journeys, meetings, and mischiefs by them performed; and were very credible in what they said. Nevertheless, this evidence was not produced against the prisoner at the bar, inasmuch as there was other evidence enough to proceed upon.

III. Benjamin Abbott, gave in his testimony, that last March was a twelve month, this Carrier was very angry with him, upon laying out some land, near her husband's: her expressions in this anger, were, *that she would stick as close to Abbott, as the bark stuck to the tree, and that he should repent of it, afore seven years came to an end, so as Doctor Prescott should never cure him.* These words were heard by others, besides Abbott himself; who also heard her say, *She would hold his nose as close to the grindstone, as ever it was held since his name was Abbott.* Presently after this, he was taken with a swelling in his foot, and then with a pain in his side: and exceedingly tormented. It bred into a sore, which was lanced by Doctor Prescott, and several gallons of corruption ran out of it. For six weeks it continued very bad; and then another sore bred in his groin, which was also lanced by Doctor Prescott. Another sore then bred in his groin, which was likewise cut, and put him to very great misery. He was brought unto death's door, and so remained until Carrier was taken, and carried away by the constable; from which very day, he began to mend, and so grew better every day, and is well ever since.

Sarah Abbott also his wife testified, that her husband was not only all this while afflicted in his body, but also that strange, extraordinary and unaccountable calamities befell his cattle; their death being such as they could guess at no natural reason for.

IV. Allen Toothaker testified, that Richard, the son of Martha Carrier, having some difference with him, pulled him down by the hair of the head. When he rose again, he was going to strike at Richard Carrier; but fell down flat on his back to the ground, and had not power to stir hand or foot, until he told Carrier he yielded; and then he saw the shape of Martha Carrier, go off his breast.

This Toothaker, had received a wound in the wars; and he now testified, that Martha Carrier told him, *He should never be cured.* Just afore the apprehending of Carrier, he could thrust a knitting needle into his wound, four inches deep; but presently after her being seized, he was thoroughly healed.

He further testified, that when Carrier and he sometimes were at variance, she would clap her hands at him, and say, *He should get nothing by it;* whereupon he several times lost his cattle, by strange deaths, whereof no natural causes could be given.

V. John Roger also testified, that upon the threatening words of this malicious Carrier, his cattle would be strangely bewitched; as was more particularly then described.

VI. Samuel Preston testified, that about two years ago, having some difference with Martha Carrier, he lost a cow in a strange preternatural unusual manner; and about a month after this, the said Carrier, having again some difference with him, she told him; *He had lately lost a cow, and it should not be long before he lost another!* which accordingly came to pass; for he had a thriving and well-kept cow, which without any known cause quickly fell down and died.

VII. Phoebe Chandler testified, that about a fortnight before the apprehension of Martha Carrier, on a Lord's day, while the psalm was singing, in the church, this Carrier then took her by the shoulder and shaking her, asked her, *where she lived?* She made her no answer, although as Carrier, who lived next door to her father's house, could not in reason but know who she was. Quickly after this, as she was at several times crossing the fields, she heard a voice, that she took to be Martha Carrier's, and it seemed as if it was over her head. The voice told her, *she should within two or three days be poisoned.* Accordingly, within such a little time, one half of her right hand, became greatly swollen, and very painful; as also part of her face; whereof she can give no account how it came. It continued very bad for some days; and several times since, she has had a great pain in her breast; and been so seized on her legs, that she has hardly been able to go. She added, that lately, going well to the house of God, Richard, the son of Martha Carrier, looked very earnestly upon her, and immediately her hand, which had formerly been poisoned, as is abovesaid, began to pain her greatly, and she had a strange burning at her stomach; but was then struck deaf, so that she could not hear any of the prayer, or singing, till the two or three last words of the psalm.

VIII. One Foster,[13] who confessed her own share in the witchcraft for which the prisoner stood indicted, affirmed, that she had seen the prisoner at some of their witch-meetings, and that it was this Carrier, who persuaded her to be a witch. She confessed, that the devil carried them on a pole, to a witch-meeting; but the pole broke, and she hanging about Carrier's neck, they both fell down, and she then received a hurt by the fall, whereof she was not at this very time recovered.

IX. One Lacey,[14] who likewise confessed her share in this witch-craft, now testified, that she and the prisoner were once bodily present at a witch-meeting in Salem Village; and that she knew the prisoner to be a witch, and to have been at a diabolical sacrament, and that the prisoner was the undoing of her, and her children, by enticing them into the snare of the devil.

X. Another Lacey,[15] who also confessed her share in this witchcraft, now testified, that the prisoner was at the witch-meeting, in Salem Village, where they had bread and wine administered unto them.

XI. In the time of this prisoner's trial, one Susanna Shelden, in open court had her hands unaccountably tied together with a wheel-band, so fast that without cutting, it could not be loosed: it was done by a specter; and the sufferer affirmed, it was the prisoner's.

Memorandum. This rampant hag, Martha Carrier, was the person, of whom the confessions of the witches, and of her own children among the rest, agreed, that the devil had promised her, she should be queen of hell.

1. George Burroughs graduated from Harvard College in 1670. He preached in Casco, Maine (now Portland), in the 1670s until the town was destroyed in an Indian raid. He was hired to preach in Salem Village in November 1680 but had left by early 1683, in part because some of the villagers were refusing to pay their share of his salary. While trying to arrange for these payments, he was arrested for a debt he owed John Putnam. Thereafter Burroughs returned to Maine. He seems not to have baptized one of his children, and other ecclesiastical irregularities told against him in 1692.
2. John Gaule, English author of *Select Cases of Conscience touching Witchcrafts* (1646).
3. Probably a misprint for "considered," which is how the London (1693) printing of *Wonders* reads.
4. The Lancashire witches: an outbreak of presumed witchcraft in Lancashire, England, in 1612 that was widely publicized at the time.
5. Thomas Ady, an Englishman who criticized witch-hunting in *A Candle in the Dark* (1656); Burroughs apparently borrowed his argument to this effect.
6. Bridget Oliver of Salem married Edward Bishop of Salem in 1685. She was probably middle-aged at the time, for Edward was her third husband. Bridget was a member of Beverly church, as was her husband. According to testimony (not part of Mather's summary) at her trial in 1692, she "did entertain people in her house at unseasonable hours," which suggests that she ran an unlicensed tavern where young people congregated. She had been accused but not convicted of witchcraft in 1679–80; Samuel Shattuck referred to that situation in his testimony. In other testimony witnesses told of finding "poppets" at her house. This evidence, together with certain statements made by Mrs. Bishop, has persuaded one student of New England witchcraft that she was a practicing witch. *Essex Ct. Recs.*, 7, pp. 329–30; Chadwick Hansen, *Witchcraft at Salem* (New York, 1969; Signet edition, 1970), pp. 94–102; Upham, *Salem Witchcraft.*
7. Deliverance Hobbs, a middle-aged woman, was the first of the many "confessing

witches" whose testimony confirmed the existence of a grand conspiracy. She had initially been among the "afflicted" persons.

8. The "pretence" probably had to do with countermagic, as did the "stranger's" proposal to "fetch blood" of Mrs. Bishop. Cf. Hansen, *Witchcraft at Salem*, pp. 96–97.

9. Susanna Martin of Amesbury, Massachusetts; an older woman, she had been accused but not convicted of witchcraft in 1669. In 1692 she resisted all attempts to make her confess.

10. The reference is to Saul's consulting the witch of Endor (1 Samuel 28:7–14).

11. Elizabeth How (or Howe) of Ipswich; a quarrel that began in 1682 between her family and the Perleys of Topsfield lay behind Timothy Perley's charge that his daughter died from Elizabeth's witchcraft. Other neighbors (not quoted by Mather) testified that she was "Christianlike in her conversation."

12. Martha Carrier, the wife of Thomas Carrier, a Welshman; the Carriers, who had four children and seem to have been impoverished, were residing in Andover at the time of the witch-hunt. Her children as well as a sister and brother-in-law were charged with witchcraft; all of them confessed to being witches. The testimony of her eight-year-old daughter, Sarah, who said her mother induced her to compact with the devil, is a striking example of collective fantasies. Karlsen sketches the family's history in *Devil in the Shape of a Woman*, pp. 98–101.

13. Ann Foster, a confessing witch.

14. Mary Lacey, a confessing witch and Ann Foster's daughter.

15. Mary Lacey, daughter of the above, and granddaughter of Ann Foster.

Source: Cotton Mather, *Wonders of the Invisible World* (Boston: Printed, and sold by Benjamin Harris, [1692] 1693), pp. 94–138.

Appendix:
Statutes Relating to Witchcraft in New England

▲

Massachusetts Bay Colony

1641: If any man or woman be a witch (that is hath or consulteth with a familiar spirit), they shall be put to death. Exodus 22:18 Leviticus 20:27 Deuteronomy 18:10.

1648: If any man or woman be a WITCH, that is, hath or consulteth with a familiar spirit, they shall be put to death. Exodus 22:18 Leviticus 20:27 Deuteronomy 18:10–11.

Source: *The Laws and Liberties of Massachusetts, 1641–1691,* ed. John D. Cushing (1976), *3,* p. 701; *2,* p. 11.

Plymouth Colony

1671 and 1685: If any Christian (so called) be a witch, that is, hath, or consulteth with a familiar spirit; he or they shall be put to death.

Source: *The Laws of the Pilgrims . . . 1672 and 1685,* ed. John D. Cushing (1977), p. 4 of the 1671 laws, and p. 10 of the 1685 laws.

Rhode Island and Providence Plantations

1647: Witchcraft is forbidden by this present Assembly to be used in this colony; and the penalty imposed by the authority that we are subjected to is felony of death. 1 Jac. 12 ch. 4.

Source: *Records of the Colony of Rhode Island and Providence Plantations in New England 1636–1663*, ed. John R. Bartlett (1856), *1*, p. 166.

New Haven Colony

1656: If any person be a witch, he or she shall be put to death, according to Exodus 22:18 Leviticus 20:27 Deuteronomy 18:10–11.

Source: *The Earliest Laws of the New Haven and Connecticut Colonies 1639–1673*, ed. John D. Cushing (1977), p. 18.

Connecticut

1672: If any man or woman be a witch, that is, hath or consulteth with a familiar spirit, they shall be put to death, Exodus 22:18 Leviticus 20:27 Deuteronomy 18:10–11.

Source: Ibid., p. 83.

New Hampshire

1679/80 (Cutt Code): If any Christian, so-called, be a witch, that is, hath or consulteth with a familiar spirit, he or they shall be put to death.

Source: *Acts and Laws of New Hampshire 1680–1726*, ed. John D. Cushing (1978), p. 205.

A Selective Bibliography

▲

Historiography and Bibliography

Black, George F. "List of Works relating to Witchcraft in the United States." *Bulletin of the New York Public Library 12* (1908), pp. 658–75.

Hall, David D. "Witchcraft and the Limits of Interpretation." *New England Quarterly 58* (1985), pp. 253–81.

Larner, Christina. *Enemies of God: The Witch-hunt in Scotland* (London, 1981), chap. 2.

Midelfort, H. C. Erik. "Witchcraft, Magic, and the Occult." In *Reformation Europe: A Guide to Research*, ed. S. Ozment (St. Louis, 1982), pp. 183–209.

Monter, E. William. "The Historiography of European Witchcraft: Progress and Prospects." *Journal of Interdisciplinary History 2* (1972), pp. 435–51.

Witchcraft and Witch-hunting in Europe: Historical Studies

(*See also* Larner, above)

Cohn, Norman. *Europe's Inner Demons: An Enquiry Inspired by the Great Witch-Hunt* (New York, 1975).

Ginzburg, Carlo. *The Night Battles: Witchcraft and Agrarian Cults in the 16th and 17th Centuries* (1966; repr. Baltimore, 1983).

Kittredge, George Lyman. *Witchcraft in Old and New England* (Cambridge, Mass., 1929).

Macfarlane, Alan. *Witchcraft in Tudor and Stuart England* (New York, 1970).
Midelfort, H. C. Erik. *Witchhunting in Southwestern Germany* (Stanford, Cal., 1972).
Monter, E. William. *Witchcraft in France and Switzerland: The Borderland during the Reformation* (Ithaca, 1976).
Thomas, Keith. *Religion and the Decline of Magic* (New York, 1971).

Popular Culture, Mentality, and Religion

(*See also* Thomas, above.)

Anglo, Sydney, ed. *The Damned Art: Essays in the Literature of Witchcraft* (London, 1977).
Baroja, Julio Caro. *The World of the Witches* (Chicago, 1965).
Clark, Stuart. "Inversion, Misrule and the Meaning of Witchcraft." *Past and Present 87* (1980), pp. 98–127.
Godbeer, Richard. "The Devil's Dominion: Magic and Religion in Early New England" (Ph.D. thesis, Brandeis University, 1989).
Hall, David D. *Worlds of Wonder, Days of Judgment: Popular Religious Belief in Early New England* (New York, 1989).
Kieckhefer, Richard. *European Witch Trials: Their Foundations in Popular and Learned Culture, 1300–1500* (Berkeley, Cal., 1976).
MacDonald, Michael. *Mystical Bedlam: Madness, Anxiety, and Healing in Seventeenth-Century England* (Cambridge, 1981).
Muchembled, Robert. "Sorcellerie, culture populaire, et christianisme au xvie siècle, principalement en Flandre et Artois." *Annales: ESC 28* (1973), pp. 271–84.
Swan, Marshall. "The Bedevilment of Cape Ann, 1692." *Essex Institute Historical Collections 117* (1981), pp. 153–77.
Walker, D. P. *Unclean Spirits: Possession and Exorcism in France and England in the Late Sixteenth and Early Seventeenth Centuries* (Philadelphia, 1981).
Weisman, Richard. *Witchcraft, Magic, and Religion in Seventeenth-Century Massachusetts* (Amherst, Mass., 1984).

Witchcraft and Witch-hunting in New England

Burr, George Lincoln. "New England's Place in the History of Witchcraft." *American Antiquarian Society Proceedings, n.s. 21* (1911), pp. 185–217.

Demos, John P. *Entertaining Satan: Witchcraft and the Culture of Early New England* (New York, 1982).

— — —. "Underlying Themes in the Witchcraft of Seventeenth-Century New England." *American Historical Review 75* (1970), pp. 1311–26.

Drake, Frederick S. "Witchcraft in the American Colonies, 1647–1662." *American Quarterly 20* (1968), pp. 694–725.

Fox, Sanford J. *Science and Justice: The Massachusetts Witchcraft Trials* (Baltimore, 1968).

Heyrman, Christine L. "Spectres of Subversion, Societies of Friends: Dissent and the Devil in Provincial Essex County, Massachusetts." In *Saints and Revolutionaries: Essays on Early American History,* ed. David D. Hall et al. (New York, 1984), pp. 33–74.

Kences, James E. "Some Unexplored Relationships of Essex County Witchcraft to the Indian Wars of 1675 and 1689." *Essex Institute Historical Collections 120* (1984), pp. 179–212.

Kibbey, Anne. "Mutations of the Supernatural: Witchcraft, Remarkable Providences, and the Powers of Puritan Men." *American Quarterly 34* (1982), pp. 125–48.

Konig, David Thomas, *Law and Society in Puritan Massachusetts: Essex County, 1629–1692* (Chapel Hill, N.C., 1979).

Middlekauff, Robert. *The Mathers: Three Generations of Puritan Intellectuals* (New York, 1971).

Poole, William F. "The Witchcraft Delusion of 1692." *New England Historical and Genealogical Register 24* (1870), pp. 381–414.

Taylor, John M. *The Witchcraft Delusion in Colonial Connecticut 1647–1697* (New York, 1908).

Tomlinson, R. G. *Witchcraft Trials of Connecticut* ([Hartford, Conn.], 1978).

Gender

Garrett, Clarke. "Women and Witches: Patterns of Analysis." *Signs 3* (1977), pp. 461–70.

Horsley, Richard. "Who Were the Witches? The Social Roles of the Accused in the European Witch Trials." *Journal of Interdisciplinary History 9* (1979), pp. 689–715.

Karlsen, Carol. *The Devil in the Shape of a Woman: Witchcraft in Colonial New England* (New York, 1987).

Koehler, Lyle. *A Search for Power: The "Weaker Sex" in Seventeenth-Century New England* (Urbana, Ill., 1980).

Anthropological, Psychological, and Sociological Perspectives

(*See also* Demos, Thomas, and Macfarlane, above.)

Erikson, Kai T. *Wayward Puritans: A Study in the Sociology of Deviance* (New York, 1966).

Mair, Lucy. *Witchcraft* (New York, 1969).

Spanos, Nicholas. "Witchcraft in Histories of Psychiatry: A Critical Analysis and an Alternative Conceptualization." *Psychological Bulletin 85* (1978), pp. 417–39.

Thomas, Keith. "The Relevance of Social Anthropology in the Historical Study of English Witchcraft." In *Witchcraft Confessions and Accusations*, ed. Mary Douglas (London, 1970), pp. 47–79.

The Salem Witch-hunt

Boyer, Paul, and Stephen Nissenbaum. *Salem Possessed: The Social Origins of Witchcraft* (Cambridge, Mass., 1974).

Hansen, Chadwick. "Andover Witchcraft and the Causes of the Salem Witchcraft Trials." In *The Occult in America: New Historical Perspectives*, ed. Howard Kerr and Charles L. Crow (Urbana, Ill., 1983), pp. 38–57.

– – –. *Witchcraft at Salem* (New York, 1969).

Holmes, Thomas J. *Cotton Mather: A Bibliography of His Works*, 3 vols. (Cambridge, Mass., 1940). See especially the discussions of *Memorable Providences* (2, pp. 649–63) and *Wonders of the Invisible World* (3, pp. 1234–66).

– – –. "Cotton Mather and His Writings on Witchcraft." *Papers of the Bibliographical Society of America*, 18 (1924), pp. 31–59.

– – –. *Increase Mather: A Bibliography of His Works*, 2 vols. (Cambridge, Mass., 1931). See especially the discussion of *Cases of Conscience* (1, pp. 108–33).

Starkey, Marion. *The Devil in Massachusetts* (New York, 1949).

Upham, Charles W. *Salem Witchcraft: With an Account of Salem Village* (1867).

Index

▲